ROOM FOR MANEUVER

ROSS CHAMBERS

ROOM FOR MANEUVER

Reading (the) Oppositional (in) Narrative

The University of Chicago Press
Chicago and London

Ross Chambers is the Marvin Felheim Distinguished University Professor of French and Comparative Literature at the University of Michigan, Ann Arbor.

The University of Chicago Press, Chicago 60637
The University of Chicago Press, Ltd., London
© 1991 by The University of Chicago
All rights reserved. Published 1991
Printed in the United States of America
00 99 98 97 96 95 94 93 92 91   5 4 3 2 1

Library of Congress Cataloging-in-Publication Data

Chambers, Ross.
    Room for maneuver : reading (the) oppositional (in) narrative /
Ross Chambers.
       p.   cm.
    Includes bibliographical references and index.
    ISBN 0-226-10075-8. — ISBN 0-226-10076-6 (pbk.)
    1. Literature and society.   2. Social change in literature.
3. Opposition (Political science) in literature.   I. Title.
PN51.C45   1991
809'.93358—dc20   90-21630

⊗ The paper used in this publication meets
the minimum requirements of the American National
Standard for Information Sciences—Permanence of
Paper for Printed Library Materials, ANSI Z39.48-1984.

Contents

Qui est le meilleur, le plus fort et le plus rusé, du renard ou du loup? . . . Je les crois bien équivalents, et je crois que cela dépend. Tantôt c'est Achille, tantôt c'est Ulysse, tantôt penche la balance dans ce sens, tantôt elle change ses poids, vire au guindeau dans l'autre sens. Ce jeu est une machine qui va et vient, comme une pesette oscillante. Et c'est notre fléau.

— Michel Serres, *Le Parasite*

[Of the fox and the wolf, which is the better, the stronger, the smarter? . . . I think they are really equivalent, and I think it all depends. Now Achilles, now Ulysses, the pendulum sometimes swings this way, sometimes changes its weights, sometimes veers in the other direction. The game is that of a machine that comes and goes, like the balance-beam of an assaying scale. And it is our scourge.]

Là où il y a pouvoir, il y a résistance et . . . pourtant, ou plutôt par là même, celle-ci n'est jamais en position d'extériorité par rapport au pouvoir.

— Michel Foucault, *La volonté de savoir*

[Wherever there is power there is resistance, and . . . yet, or rather for that very reason, resistance is never in a position of exteriority with respect to power.]

A Note on Translations

One of the minor irritations of reading a book such as this derives from the hopelessly distended sentences that result when an embedded quotation in a foreign language is followed by its translation into English. I have attempted to mitigate this problem by substituting a flexible practice for formal consistency. Verse quotations and longer stretches of narrative prose are regularly given both in the original and in translation. But a shorter quotation in the body of the text may appear—where I judge it helpful—both in the original and in translation, or in translation only (if this seems relatively unproblematic), or sometimes (if a translation or paraphrase is in the vicinity, or the context is clear) in the original language only. Parentheses around a number after a quotation indicate the page number of the edition in the language quoted and where parentheses and square brackets co-occur after a translated quotation, the former refer to the original language edition I have used, the latter to the published translation. Unless otherwise indicated, all translations from La Fontaine, Nerval, and Aquin are my own; and in them I have sought accuracy rather than elegance. Translations from Spanish-language texts are taken, however, from published English versions, as indicated in the appropriate place. I have occasionally modified them silently.

Preface

The "events" of May 1968 in France, like other similar occurrences elsewhere in the world, demonstrated both the fragility of the structures of authority in Western societies and their extraordinary resilience and powers of recuperation. *Room for Maneuver* is not in any specific sense a reflection on the "lessons" of '68, but it seeks to understand some possible implications of the propositions, taken jointly, that there are no hegemonies so absolute or systems of control so strict that they are not vulnerable to disturbance, and that, conversely, the disturbance in such systems cannot be so radical as to break with them. In this, the book attempts to make a contribution, however minor, to the extensive thinking that has been going on, especially since 1968, and especially in France, about the politics of oppositionality, and hence about the possibilities for social change in a world where the violence of revolutionary reversals is less and less felt to be justified while modern apparatuses of social control are increasingly experienced as alienating and intolerable.

Many groups of people are concerned, these days, with this problem of bringing about desirable social change without violence. Members of post-colonial societies and those engaged (mainly in Western societies) in the struggles of women and Blacks or of sexual minorities or marginalized ethnicities are faced with the following political situation: (1) they are not "in power" (although they are to various degrees and in various ways empowered); (2) their "identity" has been constructed by dominant power structures and in the interests of those structures; and (3) it is necessary to change the reality that has been constructed in this way, but starting—because there is no alternative—from the way things are now, that is, from within the "given" situation of power. Theirs must be a politics of oppositionality, if by that is understood the form of resistance available to the relatively disempowered.

As its title suggests, this book proposes that between the possibility of disturbance in the system and the system's power to recuperate that disturbance there is "room for maneuver," and that it is in that space of "play" or "leeway" in the system that oppositionality arises and change can occur. But not radical, universal, or immediate change; only changes local and scattered that might one day take collective shape and work socially significant transformations. My model for such change is the phenomenon that occurs when one reads a book—whether a work of fiction or not—and is "influenced," that is changed, by it; and I will suggest that such "influence" is best accounted for as that which brings about a change in *desire*—the further implication being that to change what people desire is, in the long run, the way to change without violence the way things are.

The issue of how to change the world is obviously at a rather remote horizon of the question I focus on: "what happens when we read?" But I would not have undertaken this study if I had not thought the one was relevant to the other. My concern is not with what literature *is*, but with what it can *do*, and beyond that with the conditions of possibility that constrain what it can do. What it can do, I suggest, is to change desire; "reading" is the name of the practice that has the power of producing shifts in desire; and desire does not produce just "fantasy" but reality itself. That is why a rather technical study of reading as an oppositional practice can hope to have something to say about changing the world.

May '68, to the extent that it was an alternative way of doing politics, was already a symptom of the disenchantment with revolution that its failure—to the extent that it partook of a certain revolutionary tradition in which the Paris Commune of 1871 was its chief predecessor—also fueled. For our contemporary disillusionment with revolutionary politics arises partly from the history of revolutionary failures in the West, combined however with the increasingly inescapable evidence that revolutions, wherever they occur, add to the load of social misery rather than mitigating it, through the phenomenon of state violence (from the guillotine to the gulag). More fundamentally still, however, it is a certain fading of confidence in the Great Narratives of history, to which Jean-François Lyotard drew attention in *La Condition postmoderne* (1979),[1] that underlies the increasing unwillingness, among people on the left, to commit to a politics that dirties one's hands and spills blood without its being evident that there are, in a properly "teleological" sense, ends that might justify unsavory means. Meanwhile, so-called "conservative revolutions" in Great Britain and the United States, not to mention the continued flourishing of repressive dictatorships and juntas in many parts of the world, especially Latin America and Africa, maintain the desire for change and a sense of its urgency.

Under these circumstances, oppositionality appears as a way of thinking a politics of change without destructive social confrontations that reverse power relations rather than modify them, and independently of the end-directed narratives that seem to legitimate violence. Hence its attractiveness to a number of post-1968 thinkers whose work frames my own, not—to be honest—in the sense that I initially saw the importance of their concepts and drew conclusions from them, but in the sense that now that I have worked my own way through certain problems, I am able to grasp the nature of the sustenance I had more or less unconsciously drawn from them. Paul Valéry liked to say, in a predatory metaphor that was intended to justify the fact that even the greatest geniuses (such as Valéry) undergo influences, that "lions are made of assimilated sheep." *Room for Maneuver*—a book that proposes a nonpredatory view of influence—is a sheep that had the luck to be able to assimilate, without quite knowing it, a number of intellectual lions.

A consciously assimilated lion, however, was Michel de Certeau, who published in 1980 his *Arts de faire*, of which a long extract was translated by Fredric Jameson and Carl Lovitt the same year, pending a full translation in 1984 under the title *The Practices of Everyday Life*.[2] Here I found the concept of oppositionality, as well as the key element of its definition as an appropriative practice, demonstrating that the discourses of power are not simply open to disturbance, as communication is subject to "noise," but that the disturbance introduces change. It does so, moreover, without challenging the system, since it consists of making use of dominant structures for "other" purposes and in "other" interests, those of the people—all of us—whom power alienates or oppresses. I shall return to de Certeau's definitions and analyses in the Introduction. But a few years earlier, Jean-François Lyotard had already begun to show what a specifically discursive analysis of oppositional appropriation might look like in a brilliant essay entitled "Sur la force des faibles," of which there is a somewhat different English version, apparently derived from a lecture, under the title "On The Strength of the Weak."[3]

Lyotard shows why it is impossible for the discourse of power, of which the philosophical discourse of "Truth" exemplified by Plato and Socrates is emblematic, ever to have the "last word." For the discourse of Truth necessarily employs a metadiscourse incorporating the "law" by virtue of which "Truth" is defined. As a result, and as the Sophists knew, that law can always be invoked against any particular application of it for the production of a given truth. If the law of truth is verisimilitude, one can always find a counterverisimilitude—or if it is slavery, even slavery can always be used against slavery. Diogenes, sold as a slave by pirates, was asked: "What can you do?" "I give orders," he said, "sell me to that fellow over there. He looks as if he needs a master." The Sophists knew, in other words, that there can be no "last word" because, as Lyotard puts it, "il y a toujours moyen de moyenner."[4] One might translate this in word-for-word fashion as: "There's always a way to mediate," or "There's always a way to find a way." But I will propose a tactical translation: "There's always a way to make (a) shift," because my concern is precisely with finding the Northwest Passage (the mediation) between discourse as an appropriative practice, making shift in the sense of making use of the means available (the discourse of power), and the shifts in desire that produce change.

What Lyotard shows is that "Truth" is never directly represented but always depends on a mediation (it is always produced in terms of some "law"), which the discourse of Truth has no interest in foregrounding but which oppositionality can seize on and make use of. The fact of mediation is the key to oppositionality, which is therefore necessarily situated *within* the (mediated) structure of the discourse of power itself. In the English version, Lyotard makes it clear that he was not thinking exclusively of the conflict—what he was later to call a "différend"[5]—between the Sophists and those he calls the "friends of wisdom," but that he was engaging in a contemporary polemic, one of whose objects was the "schizo-culture" of the seventies, most prominently represented by Gilles Deleuze and Felix Guattari's *L'Anti-Oedipe* of 1973.[6] Lyotard's point is that the recourse to schizophrenic desire is a misguided attempt to situate the possibility of opposition outside the discourse of power by claiming for it some sort of privileged "exteriority: spontaneity, libido, drive, energy, savagery, madness and perhaps schizo" (206). It is worth attending to the implication here. Lyotard is suggesting that it is deluded to seek to ground resistance to power in anything external to power because power has no "exteriority": in the manner of Derrida's famous announcement that "il n'y a pas de hors-texte" ["there is no outside of text"], he is saying that *il n'y a pas de hors-pouvoir*, there is no outside of power.

But the classic statement of the ubiquity of power was, of course in Michel Foucault's work of the seventies, notably *Surveiller et punir* (1975) and the first volume, entitled *La Volonté de Savoir*, of his *Histoire de la Sexualité*.[7] There Foucault insists that in the modern social formation, power is diffuse—not localized, but available in different situations and in different degrees to different people—and that it is not "repressive" so much as it is enabling. He thus makes it possible and necessary to think oppositionality as similarly diffuse, a matter of local resistances, "*des* résistances qui sont des cas d'espèce" ["a plurality of resistances, each a special case"], but also as inevitably produced by the (uneven) distribution of power while being itself grounded in power. For oppositionality presupposes the power to oppose at the same time that its essential tactic—consisting, as Lyotard showed, in using power against itself—makes it dependent on the power it opposes. Foucault does not, of course, deny the realities of hegemony and of revolution, but sees both social control and its violent disruption as outgrowths of the more dispersed relations of power and opposition that now—contrasting to an important degree with the ancien régime—traverse the social fabric.

> Just as the network of power relations ends by forming a dense web that passes through apparatuses and institutions, without being exactly localized in them, so too the swarm of points of resistance traverses social stratifications and individual unities. And it is doubtless the strategic codifications of these points of resistance that makes a revolution possible, somewhat similar to the way in which the state relies on the institutional integration of power relationships. (127) [97]

I will make a distinction later in this book between "opposition," which works within the structure of power, and "resistance," which challenges the legitimacy of a given power-system and, perceiving it therefore not as "power" but as *force*, seeks to overturn it by a counterforce. Revolution would be a case of resistance in this sense. But the distinction is a dubious one if it is taken to mean that "resistance" relies on a force that is independent of the power system; rather it is responding to power in the very terms that are established by the exercise of power. Thus it is a common perception in Latin American novels, including two that I discuss in this book (Alejo Carpentier's *El siglo de las luces* and Miguel Angel Asturias's *El Señor Presidente*), that revolution and dictatorship are part of the same system of power: they may reverse the respective positions within the structure of power, but without changing that structure itself—it is all "el recurso del método." This does not mean, of course, that there are not occasions when one might choose to "resist" power rather than "oppose" it (one rarely *chooses* to oppose, in any case); but it does mean that where power is (perceived as) illegitimate, and hence as violent, there are no options in response that are not tinged by the nature of that power. Oppositionality, as I will be showing, can only be complicitous, but violence repeats the methods of power in overcoming it.

Be that as it may, and accurate as Lyotard's criticism is—"schizo-culture" does presuppose an exteriority of power—Deleuze and Guattari made an important contribution to the understanding of oppositionality in their own right. They did so by introducing into the pack of conceptual cards the "joker" that is desire, and more particularly by defining desire not, in traditionally Freudian terms, as that which is repressed by reality, but as that which produces the real. Desire, for Deleuze and Guattari, is repressed, not by reality, but by the structures of power, which themselves correspond to a certain restricted and restricting form of desire: the desire to control desire, that is, the desire for power. *L'Anti-Oedipe* is an extended, lyrical, and delirious affirmation of the power of desire to elude the structures of power so as to release, instead, a "schizophrenic" desire. For the schizophrenic can free us of the restraints of a power-constructed identity, the *ego*—"not that desire is asocial; on the contrary. But it is explosive; there is no desiring-machine capable of being assembled without demolishing entire social sectors" (xxiii).

The quotation gives an idea of the book's immoderate rhetoric and of the desire to release desire that animates it. But the idea for us to hold on to is the idea that desire can change, and that changes in desire affect the social formation, that is, the real. It will then suffice to reinscribe the possibility of a change in desire *within* the overall system of power, and not as something fueled by an "exteriority," for it to become possible to construct an alliance between Lyotard's demonstration of the potential for oppositionality inherent in the discourse of power and Deleuze and Guattari's urgent affirmation of the need to change desire. But much of the work of Lacan was addressed, precisely, to demonstrating that desire is a phenomenon of mediation;[8] and if we assume as we must that it is mediated in the first instance by the discourse of power—that what we desire and the ways in which we desire are produced for us in the interests of the maintenance of power—and if further we accept that mediated phenomena are, by virtue of the fact of mediation, vulnerable to oppositional "disturbance" in the system, then we can look for that which mediates shifts in desire. My attempt in this book is to define oppositional discourse, the product of a (mis-)reading of the discourse of power, as that which mediates the deflections of desire that can change the real. "Reading," then, as the practice that activates the mediated quality of all discourse, is the "moyen de moyenner" that produces oppositionality and realizes it as change.

Lyotard makes the assertion that the example of the Sophists can suggest strategies that work *with*, and *within*, the discourse of power and "tap the strength of power to neutralize it" (207). This, too, is slightly immoderate: power cannot be "neutralized" by means that themselves depend on power and acknowledge the "law" that makes power possible. It is rather that oppositionality taps the strength of power in ways that produce deflections in desire, and hence a certain mode of change. It constitutes a politics, as Lyotard puts it, "whose aim would not be to convince [i.e., it would make no appeal to Truth] but which would seek discontinuous local effects" (214)—the effects I now specify as deflections of desire. So in order to understand how oppositionality works, one must be ready to conceive discourse, not as a representation whose power depends on its adequacy to a (preexisting) real, but as a mediating practice with the power to produce the real. Within the framework of that conception, I will describe the discursive strategies—more precisely the tactics—of oppositionality under the general head of "irony," that is, as the production through reading of a meaning that is not said, a (mis-)reading that thereby appropriates the discourse of power—working the irony of that (mis-)appropriation—and makes it available to mediate "other" effects than those of power, the "discontinuous local effects" I describe as deflections of desire. The irony of reading causes the irony of (mis-)appropriation which enacts the ironical character of power, which is that the system of power produces change. And my definition of reading will consequently be as a "space" where there is room for oppositional maneuver in that the discursive practice of irony works seductively to shift desire. So the question becomes: how does an irony work (as) a seduction?

Maybe those pirates who had captured Diogenes smiled at his ironic sally and let him go. Maybe they didn't. But if they did, one can propose that it was less because they were convinced by his "demonstration" (in the mode of

Truth) that the master is a kind of slave (a slave to giving orders) and the slave, in consequence, a kind of master, than because their desire had been changed, as a result of an oppositional discursive act, from a desire to enslave to a desire to liberate. Producing only "discontinuous local effects" and having no opportunity to effect change in the sense implied by Great Narratives, oppositionality does nevertheless seek forms of change that go in the general direction suggested by this anecdote, and by Deleuze and Guattari's understanding of the repression of desire by the desire for power. Oppositionality seeks, that is, to shift desire from forms that enslave to forms that liberate, that is from the modes of desire that are produced by and in the interest of the structures of power to forms that represent a degree of release from that repression, which is simultaneously a political oppression. If reading is indeed the "way to make (a) shift" that works in this way, then that is perhaps a good enough reason to justify its teaching in schools and colleges.

But the fact that reading, as an oppositional practice productive of change, needs to be *taught* draws attention once more to an important fact, and simultaneously poses a problem. We cannot think of reading, or of oppositionality, as an innocent or spontaneous practice, appearing within the system of power but with its roots in what Lyotard or Foucault might call an "exteriority." It is, to the contrary, produced by the system as part of the system. One must therefore ask what advantage there is to the system of control that reading should exist, with its potential for disturbance and change. Because it is counterrepressive, I will describe reading, in the final stages of this book, as a matter of self-education, one for which the oppositional text provides the necessary occasion. But such an understanding makes reading an example of what Michel Foucault might call a "technology of the self," and, as such, a form of *discipline* whose raison d'être must axiomatically be the production of power.[9] It is, to be sure, an *odd* technology of the self, since it functions to generate oppositionality and the reading subject is produced as the site of a shift in desire that in fact implies a critique of the very notion of "self." But it necessarily poses the question I will briefly address in the Conclusion, of the benefits to power of the phenomenon of reading that seems to exist in order to undermine the structures of power from within.

At every stage, then, one encounters the law of oppositionality, which is that change of an oppositional kind is generated *within* a system of power even as it works against it. Discursive irony invokes the "law" that produces power (Truth) against the discourse of power. It thereby mediates a shift in the desire that is itself mediated by the discourse of power in the interests of power. And this is the outcome of a practice of reading, a technology of the self, that in turn forms part of the apparatus of power. This "fatal" involvement of oppositionality in the system of power means that one should not look to it for dramatic ruptures, absolute disjunctures, "revolutionary" changes. The changes it produces being themselves systemic cannot be discontinuous with the system.

It is not easy to grasp the idea that the role of power, while it is inescapable and limiting, is also—as Foucault taught—enabling. The condition of there being change is also the condition that constrains the nature of change. This book is the record of my grappling with that idea, and with some of its consequences. For rather than thinking of "power"—as a strong "liberal" tradition encourages us to do—as that against which "freedom" asserts itself (i.e., from a position grounded outside of power), we can attempt to see how it can be the same system that generates both power (as the "effect of power") and the changes in which we recognize our liberty. And in that effort the role of discourse theory can be to produce models of the functioning of a system in which the production of power simultaneously implies the production of that which opposes power.

In *Story and Situation*[10] I wrote of the production of narrative "authority" (although the word "power" surfaces in the subtitle); and the shift in my vocabulary toward the idea of "power" signals a shift in interest toward the study of narrative effects as a means of approach to the theory of social formations. But the point of *Room for Maneuver* is precisely that the "authority" that permits literary narrative to function oppositionally through the phenomenon of reading is not different in kind, because it is a manifestation of the same discursive system, than the effects of power that reading "opposes." It is just that power has an interest in keeping the functioning of its authority unexamined, whereas literary discourse—as a "technology of self," a discipline that must be taught and learned—*foregrounds* the practice of reading that produces authority, and on which the whole system depends. That is why literature can provide such fertile ground for speculation on the nature of the system itself.

This book, which draws so much on the thinking of the seventies, took me almost the whole decade of the eighties to write. One consequence of this long period of gestation is that what I just referred to as its "argument" might be charitably described as a matter of palimpsestic "layering" rather than linear exposition. There have been three main "levels," each corresponding to a somewhat different conception of the book's "project." While finishing *Story and Situation* in 1982, I had already begun to think of a sequel, and the earliest work in the present volume (on Nerval in chapter 3, and the whole of chapter 2, on La Fontaine) dates from the period 1981–83, while the Introduction and chapter 1 were largely drafted in 1983. The reading of Hubert Aquin's *Prochain Épisode* that occupies much of chapter 3 was not written, however, until the summer of 1986; and at that time I took time out to work on a related project, published in French as *Mélancolie et Opposition*.[11] Here I sought to read the melancholic writing of Second Empire France in terms of a theory of reading as oppositional practice but also in a way more specifically historicized than has been possible in *Room for Maneuver*. It was then only after a further long gap that I completed chapter 4 (on three Latin American novels), the Conclusion and this Preface, during the spring and summer of 1989. The evolution of my thinking over this relatively long period means that the reader will not fail to become aware of significant differences of tone and conception between, broadly speaking, the Introduction, chapter 1 and chapter 2, taken as a unit, the work on "suicidal" writing in chapter 3, and then, finally, the discussion of writing "under dictation" in chapter 4 together with the framing of the book provided in the Conclusion and this Preface.

One reason for this discontinuity has been the pressure of professional obligations, which seem increasingly to prevent university literary critics from doing the work the existence of the profession is supposed to make possible. But I was slowed, also, by a more profound reason, which was my continuing uncertainty about the propriety of doing theoretical analyses of the practice of opposition. My early anxiety about "blowing" oppositionality's "cover" was quickly allayed when I realized how little chance I had of getting far into its secrets—but as a result that anxiety yielded to a new anxiety about the oppressive effect of theory itself, in its tendency as a discourse of knowledge to produce as "enigma" that which resists the theoretical "look" and holds it at bay, an anxiety that surfaces, without being resolved, in the final paragraphs of chapter 4. After toying with the idea of presenting the book as a collection of essays—a currently popular way of dealing with these kinds of problems—I decided however to retain the discontinuity of a "palimpsestic" argument, so as not to efface from the finished text the traces of its conditions of production that are, precisely, its unresolved problems and its looseness of structure. For it is, after all (if I am half-way right in my views), the readability of these difficulties in the text that provides it with such oppositional potential as it may itself have. My reader is invited, in other words, to make use of the book as the occasion for a self-education in attempting to construct an account of what my work may "mean" that it does not (cannot) say with respect to the social context in which it is embedded and against which it oppositionally struggles.

Although it has been relatively easy to acknowledge the major intellectual appropriations that occurred in the writing of *Room for Maneuver*, it is a more difficult matter to specify the help that I have received over such a long period of time from students, colleagues, and friends. But, for the stimulus of their own thinking (whether expressed in conversation or through published work or, as often, by sharing work in progress) and/or the encouraging reactions, helpful comments, friendly criticism and searching questions they provided in response to my own work (at various stages and in various drafts), I can at least record my deep gratitude to a number of people, including Rolena Adorno, Ali Behdad, Alina Clej, Christopher Davis, John Erickson, Anne Freadman, John Frow, Jean Joseph, Marie Maclean, Walter Mignolo, Meaghan Morris, Stephen Muecke, Michael-Patrick O'Connor, Jim Porter, Ian Reid, Michael Taussig, and Richard Terdiman. Invitations to speak on aspects of this project at the University of Wisconsin, Madison in 1985 and Vassar College in 1989 provided opportunities for valuable intellectual exchange, as did similar invitations on my own campus from the Critical Theory Colloquium and the Anthropology Seminar. Colleagues in both the Department of Romance Languages and the Program in Comparative Literature generously shouldered extra burdens when I took leave from the University of Michigan in 1986–87 and again in 1989. For the granting of these leaves, without which the book would certainly not have been completed, I am grateful to the university authorities, and especially to Dean Peter Steiner. For help with bibliography and typing, I thank Paul Erb; and for their able and indispensable help on the computer, Kathe Johnson and Barbara Wexall.

Finally, I thank the respective journals and publishers for permission to reprint the following material, usually in modified form: "'Narrative' and 'Textual' Practices, with an Example from La Fontaine," in James Phelan, ed. *Reading Narrative: Form, Ethics, Ideology* (Columbus: Ohio State University Press, 1989),29–36; "The Uses of Narrative: La Fontaine on the Power of Fables," *Paragraph* 2 (December 1983), 24–41; "Histoire d'Oeuf: Secrets and Secrecy in a La Fontaine Fable," *SubStance* 32 (1981), 65–74; "Narrative in Opposition: Reflexions on a La Fontaine Fable," *French Forum* 8, 3 (September 1983), 216–31; "Opposition by Appropriation: Manuel Puig's *Kiss of the Spider Woman, AUMLA* 74 (special number on "Narrative Issues," forthcoming in 1991). I am particularly grateful for permission to reprint Paddy Roe, "Mirdinan" from *gularabulu*, ed. Stephen Muecke (Fremantle: Fremantle Arts Centre Press, 1983), 3–17 and notes.

Introduction

> If the enemy concentrates he loses terrain,
> if he spreads out he loses strength.
> —General Giap

1. Changing the World

The point, then, without doubt, is to change the world. But how? Marx thought revolution the only effective force; but we have seen revolutions harden into situations that themselves cry out for change. This book is about a means of change that is not radical or even forceful, and indeed mostly passes unnoticed, but that functions as a critical agency in liberal democracies as well as in situations revolutionary or totalitarian: the power of the oppositional, and more specifically of (the) oppositional (in) narrative. (These irritating parentheses, I hope to suggest, correspond to something that conventional language tends to occlude: the fact that power is a relational, mediated phenomenon.)

Oppositional behavior consists of individual or group survival tactics that do not challenge the power in place, but make use of circumstances set up by that power for purposes the power may ignore or deny. It contrasts, then, with revolution, which is a mode of *resistance* to forms of power it regards as illegitimate, that is, as a force that needs to be opposed by a counterforce. But revolutionary materialism tends to undervalue the power of words, and in correctly diagnosing oppositional behavior as ultimately conservative (in that it helps the existing power structure to remain in place by making the system "livable"), it fails to see that in the universe of discourse, which is that of human "reality", oppositional behavior has a particular potential to change states of affairs, by changing people's "mentalities" (their ideas, attitudes, values, and feelings, which I take to be ultimately manifestations of *desire*), a potential that is not available to "other" forms of oppositional practice. This potential derives from the mysterious phenomenon of *authority*, whereby anyone, given the opportunity to speak, may so use words as to change situations. Although it derives its power initially from preexisting power relationships (the right to speak is itself such a derived power), and although it seems

1

never to challenge them openly, "oppositional authority," once gained, has the extremely tricky ability to erode, insidiously and almost invisibly, the very power from which it derives. It seems almost that power needs, or at least produces, oppositional discourse and so authorizes it, whereas the latter relies in its turn for its genuine oppositional effectiveness on the power it undermines. Much of this essay will be about these complex mutual entailments of power and opposition in the world of narrative discourse.

In an important book, *Discourse/Counter-Discourse*,[1] Richard Terdiman, in studying some oppositional modes of nineteenth-century French art, argues with great subtlety and nuance for what I take to be the standard claim, at least among Marxists and Marxians, that because "counter-discourse" depends on hegemonic (in this case, bourgeois) discourse, it becomes an instrument of the hegemony itself. Daumier's caricatures of the bourgeoisie depend, even materially, on the newspaper in which they are published, i.e., on a characteristic invention of entrepreneurial capitalism. Daumier—to put the argument crudely—sells papers even as he deploys a critique of bourgeois materialism and complacency. More generally, counter-discourse appears as the form taken in the nineteenth century by bourgeois art—an idea confirmed, for example, by Dolf Oehler's idea of the "anti-bourgeois esthetic" operating in such figures as Heine, Daumier, and Baudelaire, an esthetic that critiques the middle class for a middle class audience.[2] With this argument I have no quarrel; but it represents only half of the picture, as Oehler's analysis of these art forms as presupposing a readership that does not exist in their own contemporary (bourgeois) public itself begins to suggest.

For it is the ongoing *readability* of texts (and works of art), their ability to transcend the context of their production, that enables them to make all the necessary concessions and compromises with the prevailing power of the moment—to make use of the existing means of publication, for instance—but to do so, so to speak, as a tactic of "survival," so that their oppositional readability can become available, at a later date and in changed historical circumstances, to a readership that is the true object of their "address." In using this word, "address," I am exploiting a submerged etymological pun that is clearer in the French word *adresse: adroitness* (from Latin *directus*) defines an *address* (<pop. Latin *directiare*, formed on *directus*, from *dirigere*) that is *other than it seems*; and it is adroitness in the management of address that defines the oppositional text, as I propose to show in chapter 1.

As a consequence, the question that will arise in this book is that of the power of oppositional discourse, *in spite of* its counterhegemonic (and therefore ultimately hegemonic) status, to bring about change. Richard Terdiman establishes, in a few powerful pages, the inevitability for modern semiotic thought, of theorizing the fact that "a fundamental asymmetry is a primary fact in the world of discourse":

Engaged with the realities of power, human communities use words not in contemplation but in *competition*. Such struggles are never equal ones. The facts of domination, of control, are inserted in the signs available for use by all members of a social formation. (38)

These Bakhtinian and more particularly Gramscian formulations have the disadvantage, however, of suggesting that the inequality of social struggle, and the "facts of domination, of control," exclude the possibility of anything but *either* repression *or* cooption for counter- or oppositional discourse. But, without falling into idealism, it is possible, I believe, to argue that discourse—and notably the discourse called literary—has characteristics that enable it, in an important sense, to elude both repression and recuperation, or more accurately to "maneuver" within the "room" that opens up *between* the two. These are the characteristics of address that imply reading as a mode of reception inscribed *without closure* in time, and hence history.

Repression and cooption—so long as a text remains readable—are, in this way, never definitive. Terdiman writes that "the apparatus of dominant discourse, *unlike the text*, has no final sentence and never concludes" (60, my italics). Against this view that the discourse of power is unstoppable, I will wish to argue, after Derrida, that there is no stopping *texts*: in their readability lies their potential for oppositional resilience. For that reason I shall be distinguishing, in the coming pages, within the overall phenomenon of oppositional practice, between oppositional "behavior"—of a kind which, whatever its value, changes nothing essential—and oppositional "narrative" as a discursive practice which, I will argue, *is* capable of producing the kinds of change that derive, through reading, from the phenomenon of *acquired* authority—that is, authority acquired through local discursive means (as opposed to "preexisting" or "socially derived" authority), and capable of producing similarly local effects.

The fact remains, however, that such oppositional authority does derive in the first instance from preexisting power, and paradigmatically (as well as primarily) from the power of speech. There are those who are denied the right of speech and who, in etymological terms (Latin *in-fans*, not speaking), are infantilized; so that oppositional discourse can sometimes be seen to have an "on behalf of" function, using its own power of speech vicariously, so as to represent the voices of those who are condemned to silence. To this, oppositional *literature* is able to add in particular the ability to work on behalf of those who cannot achieve publication, an immense amplification of the power of speech. For deprivation of the power to speak is most usually not literal: if one excludes infants and animals, and those who are held incommunicado (such as certain prisoners and other victims of what Foucault termed *enfermement*, confinement), what is usually meant by the phrase is exclusion from the powerful discursive positions of "preexisting," socially derived authority (the media, including print; the professions, including in particular the profession of politics; and so forth). Such exclusion strikes and incapacitates all groups that are minoritized, marginalized, underprivileged, domesticated, privatized or more actively persecuted, repressed, or oppressed. In contemporary North America, where so many people belong to at least one such group (51 percent of the population, for instance, consisting of women) and where very significant numbers belong to two or more of the "silenced" categories, the practice of "piggybacking" is widespread and well recognized—I mean the (characteristically oppositional) tactic whereby membership of a relatively privileged group can be used as a discursive base to speak of and from the situation of underprivilege (the black Lesbian using, perhaps, hard-won middle-class status; the Hispanic teenager his status as a male, etc.). I want to suggest that "literature" is available as a piggyback for the silenced in general.

For the paradoxical position of literature is one of enjoying very considerable social privilege, as a high-cultural form largely used by the dominant class—Bourdieu's "inheritors"[3]—as symbolic capital, a marker and justification of privilege and a sign of distinction, while simultaneously being realizable as a "voice" of opposition. In the terms I will use in my conclusion (taking inspiration from David Malouf's *An Imaginary Life*), literature manages to be both the "Court Poet" and the "Wild Child" of society. These are both of course, images of marginalization; and it can be argued that, since the modern concept of "literature" (briefly, as an autonomous form of privileged discourse) has been current—that is, it seems, from some time in the eighteenth century—literature has been *constitutively* marginalized, albeit in these two different ways. The question is most often discussed in terms of either/or: literature is either minoritized as an "instrument" of the dominant class (so that even "counter-discourse" is subject to co-option), or it is seen as a potentially disruptive force (a means, as Rimbaud put it, to "changer la vie") but one that seems never quite to unleash the hoped-for revolution. Again, I will want to propose a both/and view, arguing that it is literature's marginalization as "Court Poet" at the behest of the mighty, and what might be called the "flattery"-role assigned to it, that *enables* it, more covertly, to act as an oppositional (but not revolutionary) "Wild Child"—the necessary disturbing force that the system cannot do without. It is this both/and situation that produces it, precisely, as a site where there is room for oppositional maneuver.

In view of the generalized "Wild Child" function I assign to literature itself, it has not seemed necessary to play the game of representing in my corpus the bewildering number of minoritized groups whose specific oppositional voices one or another of my readers may particularly wish to hear (or to hear discussed). All my authors are men; the so-called Third World is not un-equivocally represented; nor is Eastern and Central Europe, although it is a major producer of oppositional literature, from Gogol to Hasek and Kundera. I make no apology, either, for the preponderance of texts originally written in French (or Spanish); nor for the fact that my English-language texts are of marginal provenance, representing two branches of Australian literature, with respect to the prevailing canon.

These options have to do with oppositional preferences that have, at differ-ent times in my own life, gone into determining the choices from which such things as my professional specialty and cultural identity derive. The high cul-ture of continental Europe was once, for me, an important "oppositional" place of refuge from a rural and underprivileged English-speaking environment; Australianness has more recently become, in turn, an oppositional "gesture" with respect to the cultural hegemony exercized by Europe; and attention to Latin América and Québec functions, in the United States, as a necessary reminder that we live, not in America, but in *las Américas*. My reader may wish to consult his or her own literary preferences and to check my analyses against them.

But, that said, this is the place for me to enter an expression of dissent from the prevailing practice, in critical circles, of classifying literary productions in terms of the gender, national origins, socio-economic status, race, or sexual orientation of *authors*—a practice fully justified as part of a struggle against the historical exclusions that were posited on precisely such grounds, but which nevertheless argues for the specificity of texts on the basis of assump-tions that are theoretically no longer defensible (the oppositional, as I am about to explain, always necessarily fights on terrain it has not chosen). I hope it will be clear that my argument in this book is emphatically *not* an argument in favor of the so-called universality of literature—an idea I do not subscribe to—but one in favor of understanding textual specificity in terms more appro-priate than those that are assumed when authorial agency is privileged. In particular, I want to show that one must take account of the role of reading in the production of textual "meaning," and that consequently one must ac-knowledge and indeed assert the relational character of textual identity; but one must consider also the mediation of the reading-writing relation in what is referred to as the "context" of reading. Textual authority is not determined by the social characteristics of an author so much as it is produced in specific circumstances of reading, and the specificity of a given text will arise from the way the relation of text and reader is mediated, wherever and whenever the text is read. So I am not claiming that the "reader" produces the text (an error symmetrical with the claim that it is the author who produces it); but I want rather to support the implication in this book's subtitle (with its irritating parentheses), that "reading oppositional narrative" is rather a reading of the oppositional in narrative, a reading that both produces that oppositionality and is responsive to it, and does so in ways that are themselves situationally mediated. My claim, then, is that the category of "oppositional narrative" is coextensive with the category of texts that can, at any given historical moment, be oppositionally read, and in that sense only, coextensive with "literature."

2. Oppositional Practices

That prevailing structures are daily used for *other* purposes and are, so to speak, turned against themselves, is demonstrated by the ubiquity of what Michel de Certeau has identified as "oppositional practices."[4] These consist of transforming imposed structures, languages, codes, rules, etc., in ways that serve individual or group purposes other than those "intended." I am a non-driver who lives, perforce, in a city whose street-grid serves the needs of the automobile; I don't agitate for "pedestrian rights," but I do construct itineraries through the city that are *mine*, adopting in particular a widespread student practice—students, too, are largely pedestrians in this college town—called "cutting through" (i.e., using buildings and allotments as thoroughfares). Or I am perhaps a waiter, at the beck and call of a demanding general public that forces me to smile (through gritted teeth, sometimes) for the tips I demeaningly live on—but I can give myself the mild satisfaction of punishing my more obnoxious customers by selective application of the house rules, blandly denying them a second dinner roll or their first choice of salad dressing. Or again I am a student, attempting to achieve an education in the face of academic rules and a computerized bureaucracy; but I can use nice old Dr. X in the clinic to get a certificate that will oblige Professor Y to give me the extension I need on my term paper so that I can study for Professor Z's final. . . .

A paradigmatic case of oppositional behavior is the practice of "ripping off," called *la perruque* in French factories, and described by de Certeau as follows: "workers who 'rip off' subtract time from the factory (rather than goods, for only scraps are used) with a view to work that is free, creative and precisely without profit. In the very places where reigns the machinery they must serve, they inveigle for the pleasure of inventing gratuitous products intended solely to signify their own know-how by their work and to respond to the fellowship of workers with a gift."[5] The picture has perhaps been somewhat idealized here and the translation is unidiomatic, but the point is clear: against the alienating assembly line and within the capitalist profit economy, work satisfaction and a gift-giving economy are reinvented. A memorable novelistic account of oppositional practices in the more rebellious context of Australian industry is David Ireland's *The Unknown Industrial Prisoner*; while many of the North Americans interviewed in Studs Terkel's *Working*—notably the waitress who imagines herself a ballerina on stage—refer to the oppositional practices that help them survive on the job. More gently, humorously, and ironically, Italo Calvino studies in *Marcovaldo* the strategies of an urban survivor; while, as its title indicates, Maya Angelou's *I Know Why the Caged Bird Sings*, constitutes a wonderfully matter-of-fact catalogue of Black oppositional responses to the oppression of segregation. These are random examples, chosen among many others. But all such practices avoid overt challenges to the prevailing situation and concentrate instead on personal or, at least, nonsystemic transformations of its features into something more congenial to individual or group needs and purposes. One can surmise that, in the modern world, there is no one who does not indulge in practices of this kind, and that they supply one answer to the question that crosses the mind when one reads sophisticated analyses of the alienations of urban and industrial life and indeed of modernity generally. Why are we not all driven completely crazy? Oppositional practices help us to maintain *some* sense of dignity and personhood.

What this means, however, is that oppositional practices do not really work against prevailing systems but, to the contrary, strengthen them by making them livable. They are in one sense what Michel Serres would call the "noise" that seems to disturb the system but without which it would not work; they are in this sense needed by the system, and an integral part of it. Thus every rule produces its loophole, every authority can be countered by appeal to another authority, every front-stage social role one plays has a backstage where we are freer to do, say, or think as we will. The *diffuseness of power*, in short, both makes "opposition" possible and supports the structures of power that are in place. In this respect, however, it is worth noticing that there are societies whose power structure is relatively "loose" and those where, to the contrary, it is relatively "tight," and in the latter the degree of tolerance towards oppositional behavior that characterizes "loose" societies is replaced by an effort to stamp it out. In particular, in societies in which the dream of a concentrated power, centralized in a single person or office, presupposes absolute control of the population, the effort is to penetrate the "backstage" areas of the personal, the private, the informal (by "thought-police"), to prevent the use of authority against authority (by making them all accountable to a central power), and to cut out loopholes (sometimes by abolishing rules themselves and substituting the reign of the arbitrary).

These are societies in which "opposition" is perceived as an enemy, perhaps indeed *the* enemy—i.e., a form of *resistance*—and relentlessly pursued (such, we shall see, is a major insight of Miguel Angel Asturias's *El Señor Presidente*). But it is in these societies, of course, that it thrives in its most inventive and ingenious—if invisible—forms. The law of repression is that the repressed must return in transformed guise, and social repression produces opposition in proportion to the degree and intensity of the repression, or—to put it in even plainer terms—the more regimented a society, the greater the need that is felt within it for oppositional satisfactions. If the North American campus is an example of a relatively "loose" society, the prison can exemplify a "tight" society (and prison memoirs, from Silvio Pellico's *Le mie prigioni* [*My Prisons*] to Jacobo Timerman's *Preso sin nombre, celda sin número* [*Prisoner without a Name, Cell without a Number*], are repertories of oppositional practice.) And where liberal democracies turn a blind eye to *most* oppositional practices (but not all: teenagers are persecuted in high schools for symbolic opposition in dress or behavior, the "drug culture" is perceived as a threat to our "way of life"), it is totalitarian societies—the modern dictatorships, whether of the Left or the Right—that most treat "opposition" as a form of effective resistance (which, in those cases, it is). These are in effect prison societies, and it is perhaps not accidental that both my examples of prison memoirs were written by political prisoners, nor that the theme of *enfermement* and political imprisonment will haunt the later chapters of this book.

Oppositional behavior, then, may vary considerably in degree of overtness, depending on the looseness or tightness of the social context; but no oppositional behavior can be *fully* acknowledged, in any society, under pain of being perceived as resistance, that is, as a challenge to the structures of power that are in place. (That is the problem with teenage fashions and the drug culture: they are too visibly and obviously oppositional.) Invisibility, then, as de Certeau points out, is a rule of the oppositional: its *modus operandi* is disguise. So invisible may the oppositional be that its practitioners themselves are frequently unaware of it: who, on my campus, thinks of "cutting through" a building or "taking an incomplete" as anything more than normal behavior, "what people do around here?" Opposition is most generally an involuntary and unexamined response to structures that, although alienating, are not themselves perceived, in "loose" societies, to be other than normal. For that reason, the general category of oppositional practices itself tends to go unrecognized; and people are surprised when it is pointed out to them how much of their own and other people's daily behavior consists of the creative adaptation of dominating systems to uses for which they were not "intended."

On the other hand, some oppositional behavior is both intentional and self-aware; and such tends to be the case, obviously, in the tighter systems that are *perceived* as repressive or restrictive, so that even for the oppositional "subjects," opposition tends in that case more towards the status of covert resistance and can become a form of behavior that, although it should still be regarded as an *involuntary* survival response to dehumanizing conditions of existence, is consciously planned. But such behavior, I would say, remains merely "oppositional" unless and until it is perceived by the power structure itself, in which case it is classified as illicit or even criminal resistance (and so represents a failed form of "opposition"): just so, in Milan Kundera's *The Joke*, for instance, an "innocent" wisecrack draws upon itself the weight of state repression. If cheating on exams is an example of fairly conscious student oppositional behavior, the cheater who is *caught* changes category and is now defined, by the power structure, as a delinquent. Opposition, in short, has the structure of "hypocrisy"—or, to modernize the concept, of the "presentation of self in everyday life": although it works in "disguise," the disguise can be worn completely unconsciously (it can be second nature) or quite consciously, or with all the degrees of partial awareness that lie in between. Duplicity is its essential characteristic.

What distinguishes oppositional behavior of even the most conscious and intentional kind from what I have been calling and will continue to call resistance is, however, its attitude to power. The power that is in place can be perceived as illegitimate, in which case it becomes not "power" but a *force*, to be opposed by a counterforce. Thus, bourgeois capitalism, perceived as a system that exploits the proletariat and alienates all members of society, calls for revolution in order to change the structures of society; or, in the invaded European countries of the World War II period, the German occupation forces and the puppet régimes they sustained were perceived by the resistance movements as illegitimate presences to be fought against and if possible expelled. "Freedom fighters" the world over are in overt resistance to régimes they wish to see overthrown so that the social system may change.

Oppositional behavior, on the other hand, does not *seek* change, although it may produce it, because it does not perceive the power it is opposing to be illegitimate (even though it is experienced as alienating). Rather than challenging the power that is in place, oppositional practices seek to solve an immediate problem—how to survive another day on the assembly line; how to wangle the extension of time one needs from a boss/professor/journal/administrative agency/debt-collector—or to survive a local situation (one has been pulled over by a traffic cop or has been "called on" in class and is unprepared to answer). No critique of industrial alienation, no challenge to the bureaucracy, no protest against the automobile culture, no stand against authoritarian pedagogy is implied; just a need to escape their effects. Even the most conscious of oppositional practices do not qualify as resistance, then, so long as, failing to challenge the power structure, they retain their "disguise" as submission to the prevailing state of affairs. (In "tight" societies, it is when they are perceived as challenging power that they are stigmatized and punished as political crimes.)

So it follows that opposition is always on the weaker side of any given power relationship, and consequently that it tends to be improvisational and tactical rather than strategic, planned or calculated. It cannot rely on preformulated rules or preexisting positions of strength: it is always a matter of skill, adroitness, flair, of seizing the inspiration of the moment, of exploiting the specifics of a given here-and-now. It is not a *savoir* but a *savoir faire*, a "knack"; indeed, it cannot be fully theorized or formalized, and become a (teachable) *savoir*, without losing its oppositional quality (and tending in the direction of a preplanned line of resistance). It is, in short, an "art," a *techné*, for which there are at best only rules of thumb; if it becomes coded, regulated or theorized (as I am attempting *not* to do, or not to do too much in this book), it has to reinvent itself, by discovering other devices, maneuvers and techniques, in order to remain oppositional. De Certeau (p. 21) [p. xix] makes a useful distinction between *strategy*, which is the behavior of those in control of a given situation, and *tactics* as the art of existing in territory that is occupied by an other (what Deleuze and Guattari might call a "deterritorialized" situation); in those terms, oppositional behavior is a perpetual recourse to tactics, and it cannot become strategic without simultaneously losing its oppositional quality. It is that which eludes definition, the residue of all attempts at pinning it down.

However, there *is* a rule that defines oppositional behavior, which is the rule of using the characteristics of power *against* the power and *for* one's own purposes. This is the wrestler's tactic, or the flatterer's, or that of guerilla warfare, as brilliantly formulated by General Giap in his observation that his enemy (the U.S. and South Vietnamese forces) could not concentrate their overpowering military strength without losing control of the countryside, and could not occupy the countryside without dispersing their strength. To be in power, in this view of things, is to be vulnerable; and it is on the vulnerability of power that oppositional behavior—the employee who butters up the boss, the student who sets the examiners quarreling among themselves— characteristically relies.

To turn the power of the narratee in the interests of the narrator is also what defines the "art" of the storyteller, which Michel de Certeau has briefly described as oppositional, and whose oppositional structure, as an art of seduction, I attempted to explore in the volume *Story and Situation*, to which the present book is a successor.[6] A narrator must always have the know-how to take advantage of a preexisting situation that gives the narratee the power to decide on the interest of a given story; without a narratee, the story has no point, so that the narrator's skill consists of making the "narrator's story" interesting to the narratee. This, in short, is a matter of recruiting the power of the narratee in such a way as to produce what is called "authority" for the narrator; it is a seduction of the preexisting desire for narration in favor of the desire to narrate. The power of the other is not thereby challenged, but used; and the improvisational and adaptational character of what is, in essence, a feedback situation, is most evident in the case of oral narrative.

What written, and especially printed narrative, makes most evident, however, is a peculiarity of discursive "authority" that I analysed in *Story and Situation* as a function of textual redundancy, which substitutes in this case for oral feedback. This is a feature of authority whereby, once it is achieved—once the hearer's interest has been recruited, once a reader has "gotten into" a book—it retains a certain effectiveness beyond the storytelling moment, an effectiveness most clearly exemplified by the phenomenon of "readability" (as the ongoing interpretability of a text). Such authority does not, as in other forms of oppositional behavior, only solve an immediate problem or relate to a local circumstance; it produces an effect on the hearer or reader that outlasts the original situation; and in the case of "readability," a narrative text achieves—in addition to this memorable quality of all narrative authority—a power similarly to affect a theoretically infinite series of *new* readers.

It is worth making some distinctions here. The "ripper off" in the factory makes an object and gives it away—but the assembly line rolls on; the student wangles yet another "incomplete"—but professors go on giving grades; nothing that is essential has been changed by oppositional behavior of this type. Oppositional narrative is a form of "behavior," and like other forms of oppositional behavior, cannot—and does not attempt to—change the structure of power in which it operates (that situation in which the narratee has greater power than the narrator); it merely exploits that structure of power for purposes of its own. But oppositional narrative, in exploiting the narrative situation, discovers a power, not to change the essential structure of narrative situations, but to *change its other* (the "narratee" if one will), through the achievement and maintenance of authority, in ways that are potentially radical. The local and immediate oppositional success of a storyteller *also* makes possible another form of success, one that transcends the moment and makes it necessary to discuss narrative in terms that go beyond the ad hoc savoir faire and artistry deployed by oppositional subjects in general. Hearers can be changed by successful storytelling; narrative texts have the potential to achieve ongoing readability; and therein lies a form of effectiveness that is unknown to other, nonverbal, forms of oppositional behavior.

The important distinctions that must be made in order to bring the subject matter of this book into focus are, therefore, first that between resistance and "oppositional practice," and second that between oppositional "behavior" that does not have change as its outcome, and discursive, or "narrative" opposition[7] which has as its distinguishing feature the power of "authority" to affect people, mentally and emotionally, and by that means to change states of affairs in general. Finally, a third important distinction is that between narrative that realizes in this way the potential of its authority and narrative that remains close to oppositional "behavior," in that, although an immediate and local success is achieved (a story is successfully told), the longer-term effects of authority, achievable through memorability and/or readability, are scarcely felt. From the narratee's point of view, such a story is one that "goes in one ear and out the other" (or in the case of a reader, "in one eye and out the other"); it is heard/read and quickly forgotten. From the narrator's point of view, no lasting seduction of the narratee's point of view has been achieved. This book will concentrate on narratives that, in addition to the first kind of success, also realize the potential inherent in all narrative authority of bringing about change. Its subject is not the oppositional character of narrative in general, but the particular success of narrative in influencing the desires and views of readers; and a not inconsiderable part of my intention is to propose that it is a quality (although not an exclusive one) of narratives that achieve the status of the "literary" to exercise oppositional authority in this way. They do it most particularly through the mutually implicated and implicating phenomena of textuality and readability, at which I will look more closely in chapter 1.

It scarcely needs to be stressed that all these distinctions are heuristic and of considerable fragility. That there is a very large gray area straddling the categories of resistance and opposition is demonstrated, for example, by guerilla warfare à la Giap—a mode of resistance that relies on oppositional tactics—but also by the way oppositional behavior shades towards resistance as it becomes more self-conscious and/or in "tight" contexts where (à la Kundera's joke) it is *regarded* as a form of resistance. The distinction between oppositional "behavior" and narrative opposition breaks down, not only in the many cases of narrative success that do not transcend immediate and local contingencies, but also when one realizes that there is *no* behavior that does not have the potential for bringing about some sort of important change, just as discourse does. "Behavior," in short, is *readable* too; it cannot be excluded from the world of *discourse* any more than narrative can be excluded from the arena of *action*. Finally, there can be a difference of degree, but not of kind, between forms of authority that succeed for the duration of a storytelling act and those that succeed in a more amplified way. If authority is the seduction of the other's interests and desires in favor of those of the narrative, then it must, by definition, produce some change in its hearer; and what has once changed, however minimally, cannot be unchanged—the change has happened. Texts such as those I will be examining in later pages—those of La Fontaine, narratives such as those of Gérard de Nerval and Hubert Aquin that exploit the "suicide tactic," and a group of Latin American novels of "dictation"— advertize their oppositional status, in part through self-reflexivity, in ways that make them designated objects for an investigation into the oppositional working of narrative authority. But there is no way of drawing a clear boundary between the historically specific narrative situation to which these and many other texts owe their special oppositional status and the more general conditions that make narrative itself an oppositional phenomenon, and oppositional narrative—that is, the oppositional in narrative—is not different in essence from other forms of oppositionality.

But, if there is narrative "in opposition," there is also, of course, narrative that realizes the potential of its authority in ways that can be called "authoritarian." This distinction—my final one—is a tricky one, and cannot be mapped onto that between the oppositional "good guys" on the political Left and the authoritarian "bad guys" on the political Right, since authoritarian discourse occurs as much in support of radical change as it does in favor of the conservative status quo. In terminology I will elaborate in chapter 1, authoritarian discourse is describable technically as that in which a "narrative function" having ideological affinity with autonomized subjects and centralized power is foregrounded and tends to position the reader so as to encourage maximum identification with the (textually produced) narratee. It is a limitation of "readerly" freedom. But as Susan Suleiman has shown in a striking chapter of her study *Authoritarian Fictions*,[8] even in the *roman à thèse* this "narrative function" is subject to erosion and subversion by a less controlled and controlling "textual" function. I will be proposing, quite symmetrically, that oppositional narrative similarly combines a "narrative" and a "textual" function, but in a reversed hierarchical relationship: in oppositional narrative, a "narrative function" that respects the power structure serves as a form of disguise for a "textual function" whose operation is more covert, but ultimately more significant, and serves as an appeal to the "readerly" activity of interpretation, thereby subverting notions such as those of the autonomous subject or the discursive "transmission" of information that the "narrative function" enacts.

Such symmetry suggests, of course, that in this case also the terms of the distinction should not be regarded as discrete entities and reified into water-tight categories. Rather they can be seen as polarities, opposed tendencies that define a literary continuum along which a whole range of differing degrees of relationship may prevail between the "narrative" and the "textual" functions of discourse, according as that relationship is situationally mediated through reading. But this is a point that must await further amplification. Suffice it for the present to say that, if literature is simultaneously "Court Poet" and "Wild Child," it has at its disposal *joint* modes of seduction that can flatter the powerful and (or) empower the excluded. So any either/or, here, is very much a function of a both/and: the "Court Poet" implies (and implicates) the "Wild Child"; while the "Wild Child," in turn, cannot do without the "Court Poet."

3. Literature as Oppositional Discourse

Story and Situation is a largely formal study of the modes of situational self-figuration in some nineteenth-century "art"-tales, and its methodological assumptions lie in the background, also, of the present volume. But its conclusion—that such stories produce as their relevant communicational context one that identifies the relation of text to reader in terms of seduction—raises a number of questions that demand considerable further reflection. Among them are these:

Why does literature (in general? or nineteenth-century literature in particular?) self-contextualize as seduction?

Does textual self-contextualization as seduction describe in any sense *what actually happens between text and empirical reader* when a real act of reading occurs?

If so, *how* does this form of seduction work? How to explain the seductive impact of texts on readers, and their power, therefore, to produce change?

I want here, if not actually to answer such vast questions, at least to circle a little closer to an understanding of some of their implications.

It is more than a little embarrassing to reread the formulation in *Story and Situation* that rather grandly foreshadowed the present project as an exploration of the proposition that narrative seduction, "producing authority where there is no power, is a means of converting (historical) weakness into (discursive) strength" (212). *"No power,"* in particular, is an overstatement, so too, perhaps, is "(discursive) *strength*" ("influence" might have been a better word); and the dichotomization of "historical" and "discursive" is a dubious one. I spoke, too, even more dramatically (8), of examining "more specifically the relationship between narrative and history, taking as my focus the problematics of storytelling in circumstances of social violence." My reader will measure without difficulty the shortfall of the present book with respect to these rash promises. But I do want to do here two more modest but still important things that relate to the project so boldly described. One is to examine the act of reading as the mode of contact between a text and a subject, and to attempt to throw some light on the nature of this interface, understood as the necessary mediation by which the impact of narrative discourse on history can make itself felt and change occur. Chapter 1 is devoted to this task.

The remainder of the book, except for the Conclusion, consists of extended readings of a small number of texts: these are intended as exemplifications of the readability that makes the texts instances of discursive opposition. This readability, it will be seen, is once again a function of textual self-contextualization, but now in oppositional terms. For texts do not only *produce* change through the mediation of their readership; they *are produced* also in historical circumstances whose features the text necessarily takes into account—most notably, in my view, in its figuration of the communicational circumstances that give it point. And it is this figuration, when it is oppositional, that becomes the object of an oppositional reading that is itself generated in a specific historical context, and hence the means whereby the text achieves authority.

Because oppositional reading is a reading of the oppositional situation produced in texts, my readings will sketch, in very broad terms, something like a historical account of the changing circumstances of power that the texts (as read) produce as the relevant context of their reading. Certain fables of La Fontaine—"Le loup et l'agneau," which I will read in chapter 1, being a significant exception—produce kingship as such a context, and their readability consists in the functioning of a certain irony by which the text's "narrative" address to the kingly site of power becomes readable as a vehicle for other, "textual" meanings and claims. But in the modern world—and I will take the French Revolution as the watershed here—power is not so easily located; and the writing of Nerval in mid-nineteenth century France and of the Québec novelist Hubert Aquin in the politically turbulent 1960s wrestles, still ironically but also melancholically now, with the consequences of an alienation that results from awareness that subjects do not enjoy self-identity but are produced as a function of otherness, the "I" being only that which is not "not-I," and the diffuseness of identity mirroring the new diffuseness of power. This is an awareness that shifts the responsibility for the production of the text's oppositional identity even more heavily than in classical irony onto the act of reading for (and to) which the text "appeals."

However, the crisis of legitimacy that accompanied the abolition of kingship at the Revolution can be seen also as responsible for the formation of modern dictatorships, a political phenomenon of "tight" control in which oppositionality is both fostered and severely punished by state violence. My readings of novels by Alejo Carpentier, Miguel Angel Asturias, and Manuel Puig tend to show that, in such circumstances, discursive opposition is tempted to adopt a witnessing stance, a response that is however deeply flawed by its inability to dissociate witnessing, as a discursive act that seeks to deny the phenomenon of mediation, from the forms of discursive control that characterize societies "under dictation." Puig's novel, *El beso de la mujer araña* [*Kiss of the Spider Woman*], demonstrates in this context the benefits of, precisely, an alliance with mediation, which permits the appropriation of the discourse of power in ways that *seduce* the reader—as his hero Molina seduces his cellmate Valentín—from the desire for power to a more liberating form of love.

But I want this historical outline to function simultaneously as a kind of theoretical parable, in which a shift from the "ironic" to the "seductive" model of textual oppositionality is mediated by the "melancholic." My conclusion will attempt its own reading of this parable, but I can foreshadow it now by saying that I seek to bring together and find the interface of—or the "room for maneuver" between—two models of reading, the "ironic" and the "seductive." Reading is the production of oppositional irony with respect to the textual "address" to power; reading responds to a textual "appeal" by shifting from the position of addressee (in the discourse of power) to an "other" position—no longer a "position"—that represents an "other" form of identity and an "other" mode of desire. Both cases hinge on a certain textual duplicity, in that the discourse of power (what I will call the "narrative function") reveals, through reading, an "other" meaning (its irony), or its address coincides with an "other" appeal, again realized in reading; and it is what I will call the "textual function," understood in these two ways—the "other" meaning and the "other" appeal—that constitutes textual identity as *split*.

The argument I will make at greater length in the Conclusion is that between reading as the ironic production of (another) meaning and reading as the production within the reading subject of a shift—a deflection of desire—that responds to the seduction of textual "appeal," the split text mediates the possibility of a movement, such that the one can shift into the other. In this way, oppositional reading, as the production of the oppositional in texts, can become an agency of change, since it changes in the first instance something in the economy of the reader's desire. In other words, the "influence" that texts can exert on the "minds" of their readers needs to be analyzed, on the one hand, as a function of the duplicity of literary discourse, its constitutively split identity implying an appeal to be read otherwise, but also, on the other hand, in terms of the vulnerability of our desires—produced as they largely are by the mediations of the system of power—to seduction.

"Seduction" is a term that implies a certain violence, and it was a fault of *Story and Situation* that I did not take that connotation of violence into account. It had to be pointed out to me by an angry feminist that—because in the patriarchal tradition subjects are thought of as male and objects as female—we tend to gender the seducer as masculine and the seducee as feminine. As a consequence, we picture seduction as a mode of exploitation that takes advantage of the relatively disempowered. An argument can be made, and I attempted to see what it would look like soon after writing *Story and Situation*,[9] that narrative exerts a "violence" of this seductive kind. But there is seduction and seduction; and my argument here is about seduction, not as an exploitive effect of power but as an oppositional response to alienation, that is, as a way—the only nonviolent way, perhaps—of turning the alienating other from attitudes that are oppressive (including self-oppressive) to a more sympathetic "understanding."

In the case of textual seduction, this "turning" of the reader takes the form of seducing the reading subject away from the subject position produced in the text as that of the narratee—the position of power—towards that of *interpretive subject*, a position that manifests the dependency of identity on otherness. For the text becomes "text" only through interpretive reading—it cannot of itself produce its meaning as the "other" of its discourse—but in the same process the reader becomes the site of a shift that manifests an otherness within the reading subject, an otherness necessarily mediated by the (split) discourse that is "text" just as the textual otherness is itself produced by the (split) reading subject. It is in this way that oppositional reading, *because* it is the production of an "ironic" *other* meaning in the text that relativizes its address to the position of power, has as its corollary an oppositional shift in readerly identity, from that of addressee-subject of the discourse of power toward an "other self" whose identity is produced only as a function of *its* other, the text.

So seduction in this sense is something like a joint recourse, on the part of the text and on the part of the reader, to a mediated production of otherness. The text cannot mean "otherwise" without the intervention of reading, but the reader cannot shift from narratee to interpretive subject without the mediating intervention of text. The change in the reader that occurs as a result of oppositional reading thus necessarily has the character of a conversion from "autonomous" identity (the addressee as a "you" defined, in a dual relationship, as not the addressing "I") to a sense of self that depends on a triangular system of otherness, in which dualities are mediated by a third which prevents any of the terms from claiming an autonomous identity or a "positive" status. The text's "difference" from its own discourse is mediated by reading, the reader's "difference" from self is mediated by text; the relation of text to reader—another relation of "difference" or mutual otherness—is mediated by discourse itself, as that which guarantees the production of such differences because it necessarily entails them. For if the system of communication was an unmediated one, all meanings would be literal and—there would be no system. It is because discourse is systemic that it produces "room for maneuver," and reading is the name of that maneuvering, out of which change can result.

If reading, then, is the mediation by which narrative discourse makes its impact in history—my first point—this impact depends on the fact—my second point—that reading is itself a realization of the implications—for identity, for authority, for desire—of the phenomenon of mediation itself. Discourses of power seek to downplay their (inevitably) mediated character; but literature as oppositional discourse, dependent as it is on readability, is a realization of the characteristics of mediated discourse, some of which will be explored in the chapters to come under headings such as irony (the mediated production of meaning as the "other" of discourse), melancholy (the production of textual identity as a phenomenon of mediation), and seduction (the mediated production of shifts in desire). More particularly, though, literature can be described as *the discourse of power made readable*, that is, realized as the mediated phenomenon that it is, and so as subject to reading. And it is because it is subject to reading that it can be relativized through irony, or it can have its authority eroded through the melancholic "fading" of autonomous identity into otherness, or finally it can be appropriated and turned to "other" purposes, which are those of seduction as the deflection of desire.

To read, then, is to understand the discourse of power in the text, not as a natural phenomenon, but as a *simulated* discourse, and thus to be *distanced* from it (distanced from the position of reception it produces for itself in the "addressee" slot). This difference between a simulation and the distance it produces is exactly the difference between what I am about to describe as the "narrative" and the "textual" functions of (especially) literary discourse. And it is in the *possibility* of this distance (which can arise in any discursive situation), and in the potential for change that it opens up, that the opportunity for discursive oppositionality resides.

1   Reading (the) Oppositional (in) Narrative

1. Power in the Belly

The place is *gularabulu*: the coast where the sun goes down—a section of the north-western coast of Australia running in both directions from the town of Broome. The storyteller is Paddy Roe, a man of great maturity, experience, wisdom, and prominence in the Aboriginal community, a fully initiated Nyigina who knows the stories and holds the ceremonies, and who acts on occasion as spokesperson and ombudsman for the Aboriginal people of the region (Garadjeri, Yaour, Nyul-nyul and Djaber-djaber as well as Nyigina). The listener is Stephen Muecke, a young white Australian linguist. They are friends, but the power relationship is clear. Paddy has the advantage of all authoritative narrators, that his knowledge is desired by the other—but Stephen, as narratee, has the power of defining what in Paddy's knowledge is desirable (worth hearing) by extending or withholding his interest and approval. And if Paddy is a representative of his people, so too is Stephen—young and ignorant of Aboriginal knowledge as he is—by virtue of his whiteness and Western education, the symbolic representative of a historically dominant, not to say oppressive, society, that of white Australia. If Paddy, taking advantage of Stephen's initial desire to know, can make him "enjoy" the story, his seductive narrative art will also have social consequences: Stephen's interest in a story that is public property in Paddy's group ("oh everybody know this story you know") will be a minor victory for people who are unaccustomed to any interest in their culture on the part of white Australia. Stephen, as it turns out, will be so interested in Paddy's oral narrative that he will want to transcribe and publish it, with others of Paddy Roe's stories, in the volume where I am able to read it.[1]

The language in use is Aboriginal English, which has the characteristics of a *lingua franca* in this region.

Aboriginal English is a vital communicative link between Aboriginal speakers of different language backgrounds. It also links blacks and whites in Australia, so, as it is used in these stories, it could be said to represent the language of "bridging" between the vastly different European and Aboriginal cultures. It is therefore in this language that aspects of a new Aboriginality could be said to be emerging.[2]

Paddy Roe is conscious, in his storytelling, of reaching out, through Stephen Muecke, to white Australia in general, that is of performing a mediating function. But the very bridging language he uses, for me as a white Australian, has the effect of *staging* him as an Aboriginal: its difficulty and difference from my own dialect are a manifestation of the social and political gulf he is trying to cross. Indeed, its more prominent grammatical and phonetic features, experienced by me as *lacks* with respect to my own English ("dropped" consonants, "missing" gender-distinction [he/she] in third-person pronouns . . .) enact this speech as a language of deprivation—I am already responding to mediation by a corresponding act of interpretation. And, as it happens, nourishment—the food Mirdinan is given by white police and "converts" into oppositional behavior—is a theme of the story, which thereby situates the oppositional as an appropriative response to an imposed deprivation.

For (see Appendix) it is the story of Mirdinan, a *maban*, or doctor, who—as we will eventually learn—was a countryman of Paddy's parents:

> he had power in his —
> in him you know -
> in his belly -

(Dashes and hyphens indicate longer and shorter pauses in the storyteller's delivery.) Paddy, we will be led to think, has certainly inherited from his "uncle" some of this "power in the belly," which he puts to narrative use, as the ability to use power against itself. Mirdinan catches his wife in adultery, and according to custom kills her—but white justice sends the police to arrest him. Mirdinan has no sense of guilt:

> "All right: he said "you bin kill your missus?" -
> "Yes" he tell-im -
> "Aha" —

On the way back to Broome, the group camps overnight, leaving Mirdinan in chains at the foot of a tree. In the morning, he has vanished, leaving only the empty fetters. The "police boy" (i.e., an Aboriginal) senses the truth of the matter:

> "Ooooh" the p'lice boy say "Might be tha's -
> that man must be *maban* man -
> he very clever man" -

Twice more Mirdinan will be arrested, his location revealed to the police by his dead wife's relatives; twice more he escapes. The first time, he is put in the lockup in Broome, and walks out through the door in the guise of a cat, shooed on his way by the Police Sergeant himself. The next time, the situation has escalated: Mirdinan is taken as far as Fremantle (in the more densely white-settled South, and the site of a major jail), tried, and sentenced to be hanged. As the trapdoor drops, he transforms himself into an eaglehawk and flies to safety:

Each time the man is taken further away (Cockle Well, Broome, Fremantle), each time the escape is more difficult (chains, lock-up room, gaol in the city) and each time the transformation becomes more dramatic in a climactic progression. First he disappears without leaving a trace, then he changes into a 'pussycat', which is an animal introduced into Australia, then finally into an eaglehawk, an animal of mythological significance. It might well have been the totem animal for Mirdinan since as this bird he flies back to his 'country', the place representing his spiritual home.[3]

It is only on the occasion of his third recapture that Mirdinan is finally defeated. Betrayed yet again by his people into the hands of the police, he is given liquor this time and made drunk; it is then an easy matter to shut him up in a box and drop him into a "deep hole" in the middle of the ocean:

> they had to make-im drunk (Laughs) -
> and the poor bloke -
> they bin make-im drunk eh (Nangan: Yeah) -
> yeah, an' he lose himself -
> but he coulda come out of that box too if they didn' -
> give-im drink -

In retelling the story of Mirdinan, I have deliberately emphasized its character as a narrative of cultural clash. Guilty by the laws of white Australia, Mirdinan is unaware of having committed a crime (this is a not unfamiliar situation when Aboriginals are tried in Australian courts of law). But he has nevertheless acquired enemies: his late wife's relatives, who set the power of white justice on him, at first for purposes of revenge, and later because they "didn't want to get trouble—/ from the police, they had to give-im to the police -" (so they too are victims of white society and are attempting to defend themselves from it). Mirdinan uses his power as a *maban*—"he was a very clever man"—in oppositional ways: he does not fight back or attack the police, he always "goes quietly" when arrested (i.e., he does not *resist*), *but* he has the skill of making himself invisible (the disappearing act), that of disguise (he becomes what—an Aboriginal in white society—he metaphorically *is*: a tame pussycat), that of converting his hanging (the supreme expression of the other's material power over him) into flight (the supreme expression of his freedom and identity—a spiritual triumph).

they didn't know me he say I gonta fly -
gonta (Laughs) turn into eaglehawk -
that's when he kept that inside here -
in his, *maban* in his belly you know -

It is only when the whites attack him *spiritually* with their liquor (the emblem in the story, and in Australian society, of the European sway over Aboriginal people as it is achieved, maintained and enforced through moral and social degradation) that Mirdinan suffers loss of self ("yeah, an' he lose himself") and, concomitantly, loss of his means.

However, as I have suggested, the power in Mirdinan's belly has been transmitted to his descendant, and has become the power in the belly of Paddy Roe, storyteller. The storytelling situation continues and extends the story beyond Mirdinan's defeat, and Paddy's narrative repeats Mirdinan's oppositional acts. As narrator, he "disappears" into his story (he is a master of narrative *showing*, impersonating the characters—including the cat—and allowing the story to build its own momentum, with few evaluative comments beyond the recurrent "he was a very clever man"). He also adopts narrative "disguise," making acknowledged concessions to Stephen's presence in the circle; for example,

Fisherman Bend in Broome, *karnun* -
we call-im *karnun* -

and using to the full his knowledge of police practice and lingo ("they went out for him pick-im-up", "oh they got a few statement off him"), not to mention the mechanics of hanging; using also devices of suspense and cumulative effect—the countdown at the hanging, the buildup of Mirdinan's increasingly spectacular escapology—which are characteristic of Western-style narrative rather than Aboriginal storytelling.[4] Finally, he identifies fully with Mirdinan at the point of the latter's triumph, when the *maban's* song (composed to celebrate his victory in transforming into an eaglehawk) is gleefully sung, *in Nyigina*, by Paddy and his friend Nangan, then no less gleefully glossed for Stephen's benefit, before the crucial family-identification is made.

. . . and that man name is -
(Stephen: I got 'im—Mirdinan) ahh Mirdinan (Stephen: Yeah Mirdinan)
     Mirdinan yeah -
huncle too —
my uncle I call-im uncle . . .
this one call him *djambardu*, grandfather (Nangan: Mm *djambardu*) *djambardu*
     yeah grandfather -
call-im huncle —
(Stephen: That story's in your family!) (Laughs) yeah yeah-

oh yes he's a family -
he belong to this country too . . .
he mix with (Nangan: Aaaall what Nyigina) -
Nyigina Yaour Garadjeri everything he's -
we all one —
so he's one of our people too that fella -

Not coincidentally, this song introduces an important variant of the story of the hanging, one in which the knowledge of white ways nourishes something approaching satire, or at least a strong sense of absurdity (in the comic vision of the judge in his "red clothes" and the frantic telephoning: "everybody bin ringin' up to hang this man"—in short, the full-scale mobilization of white society's repressive equipment, which Mirdinan is about to foil). And the satire co-occurs with praise of Mirdinan's exploit as a manifestation of the power in his belly:

mudjaring ngalea he bin run away *mudjari* - . . .
ngalea means that's his -
he had power in his -
in him you know -
in his belly -
maban maban . . .

This is the moment, then, where Paddy's narrative—as the power to make white society look ridiculous—most nearly identifies itself with Mirdinan's own oppositional practice, as the power to make white society look small.

But where the storytelling departs from this identification of its own power, its own ruses, with those of Mirdinan, is in the narrative of the latter's defeat, which in the telling acquires an almost triumphal tone.[5]

that's the only way they can beat-im the some other ways they couldn' beat-im -
he was a very clever man -
this fella -
oh everybody know this story you know

"Everybody," that is, except Stephen and the readers of Stephen's transcription to whom it is addressed. . . . The story is here celebrating its own skill, in having made *us* learn something that, from the Aboriginal perspective, "everybody know"; for its seductiveness, as narrative, has worked to give us some sense of what it is to belong to a defeated culture like Mirdinan's. We have seen our own repressive culture (the police, the judge, the telephones, the ritual of hanging) *from the other side*, and we have seen it partly as an instrument used by Aborigines for Aboriginal motives (the wife's relatives' denunciation of Mirdinan), partly as excessive and grotesque in its overkill (the chains, lockups, instruments of execution—all powerless against Mirdinan's spiritual being), partly as repulsive in its deployment of means of spiritual warfare, such as alcohol. This is technically an effect of "defamiliarization," but it has been produced by the recruitment of our perspective to that of Mirdinan (and Paddy). In this respect, the narrative of Mirdinan's *defeat* is a major instrument of the story's oppositional *success*, since we are thereby led to empathize with a defeated character whom our own culture is destroying. So the triumphant tone at the end is well justified: such an outcome is the sign of the storyteller's having been able to deploy a very considerable "power in the belly" indeed, demonstrating on one hand that defeat is not final or complete ("some other ways they couldn' beat him"), and on the other the ability of narrative to shift something decisively in its hearer.

It is not simply, then, that the story is seductive, although seductive it is. (It is not accidental that Stephen Muecke, as editor, has placed "Mirdinan" first in Paddy Roe's book, and that I have followed suit by placing it first in mine: the *captatio benevolentiae* is a powerful one.) But the real sign of the narrative's success is that something has been changed by the seduction. It is no longer possible for me to think in abstract terms about Aboriginal-White relations in Australia, once my vision of them has been turned out of the ways of (seduced from) my white perception (with all the power implied by the ability to think of them "in abstract terms"), and I have had a glimpse of them from the point of view of the defeated, where they are experienced very concretely indeed. In a sense, I have come to acknowledge what I already "knew." It is this power to *change the hearer* that gives narrative "power in the belly" its ultimate superiority over the type of "cleverness" displayed by Mirdinan, whose "power in the belly" was real but could change nothing, and whose spirit, in the end, was overpowered. *Room for Maneuver* can be thought of in part as an exploration of such narrative power as a form of historical revenge, and in particular of narrative's ability oppositionally to achieve such compensatory effects by changing the way people think and feel, that is by changing their desires.

But Paddy's oral story (told to Stephen) has become for me, through transcription and publication, a narrative *text*: one in which "Paddy" and "Stephen" are not real people communicating but names given to *textual roles*, that of "narrator" and "narratee." The communicational relationship between text and myself, as *reader*, is of a different kind, and positions me in such a way that I coincide fully neither with "Paddy" nor with "Stephen" but find myself in a triangulated relationship in which the third position (mine) is, with respect to the textual relationships, both that of *tiers exclu*—the excluded third party—and that of *tertius gaudens*, the third who enjoys or profits. Deferring, however, a fuller discussion of the implications of textuality and readability until the following sections, I will simply state for now that the "power in the belly" displayed by Paddy (as real storyteller in an empirical situation) is amplified in a number of ways through the readability it acquires as text. To achieve publication, for any oppositional story, is in itself a highly significant amplification of its effectiveness (it has seduced Stephen into desiring to edit and publish it).

But the constitutive practice of reading text as self-reflexive also makes it possible to see the story, once it has become available through publication, as thematizing the extraordinary accounting of profit and loss that makes oppositional behavior possible—a phenomenon I shall be making abundant use of in what follows. Thus, for example, I have already suggested that, in "Mirdinan," food—the three-fold serving of supper to the police captive—symbolizes the oppositional hero's ability to appropriate the power of the other to his own uses, taking from his captors, in this case, the power to disappear, to disguise himself, and to fly away. Mirdinan's power in the *belly* is directly nourished by the white society it opposes.[6] Liquidity, on the other hand—that of strong drink and of the sea—is the instrument of his downfall, it "drowns" the power in his belly—and it is notable, on the one hand, that the initial villain, the seducer of Mirdinan's wife, is a Malay fisherman (and thus doubly associated with the sea), whereas the narrative itself associates itself with the between-world of *gularabulu*, the marshy coast and the "seaside" people who live there, and whose "country" it tells of.[7] Is narrative itself such a between-world, a *gulurabulu* of contending forces, of power and opposition?

For the most significant aspect of narrative textuality is its *staging* of the roles of "narrator" and "narratee," which makes visible a structure of relations in which, as I hope to show, the "narratee" is always put into *the position of greater power*. Thus, "Stephen"'s whiteness, in spite of his relative youth and his desire for the knowledge possessed by "Paddy," is the marker of the power that requires the story to be seductive. And a narrative text can always use the respect for the position of power inscribed in its narrator-narratee relationship as a form of "disguise"—of that disguise without which no oppositional act can occur; that is, it can "pass" as an act of submission to, or at least acknowledgement of, the power ascribed to the "narratee" with whom an unsuspecting empirical reader (especially a powerful one) can readily identify.

On the other hand, as a reader of textuality, I do not occupy exclusively that position of power. It is true that the seductiveness of a story such as "Mirdinan" reaches me (as another white Australian male) through "Stephen," but at the same time I can be a *witness* of the act of seduction itself, as well as its *object*. As such, I can simultaneously perceive and empathize with the moves that are being made by the narrator ("Paddy") from his position of relative powerlessness, and can be led to ask what they *mean*. The visibility of the narrator-narratee relationship in the text functions here, not as disguise, but as a sign requiring interpretation, that is requiring "reading." For my role as reader of a text is not so much to receive a story (identifying with the narratee position) as to collaborate with the text in the production of meaning, a task that redistributes—perhaps equalizes—the power relationship, and certainly dissolves the simplistic distinctions of self and other, sender and receiver that are inherent in the concepts of narrator and narratee.

The distinction between *sujet de l'énoncé* and *sujet de l'énonciation* is relevant here: the former is a grammatical category, identified with its predication(s)—and such is the "narrator," presupposing the "narratee" as another definable and defined ("predicated") subject. The *sujet de l'énonciation*, or "textual" subject, however, is always already and can only ever be produced as the object of interpretation: it is hypothesized as the originless source of an act, unknowable because split and plural, traversed by the symbolic codes (linguistic, social, cultural . . .) that constitute it, and energized by psychic and other "drives."[8]

The "power in the belly" with which this book is concerned can be thought of, then, as the availability to oppositional interpretation of the *textual* "subject" of narration, and consequently as the power to produce in the reader an identity shift, from identification with the "narratee" ("Stephen") to that of interpreting subject. In such an understanding, the responsibility for the oppositional quality attributed to "text" is a *joint* one: it is a quality of *text subject to interpretation*, of text in the context of its reading. In light of this understanding, it becomes urgent to ask questions both about the act of reading (specifically, what is the nature of the empirical reader's involvement with text and how does this involvement produce a shift in the reading subject?) and about the nature of text (most particularly, for present purposes, about the relation of narrative *énoncé*, as constituted by the narrator-narratee relation, to narrative *énonciation* as a manifestation of textuality).

2. *Tiers exclu/Tertius gaudens*: No One, in particular

From the *One Thousand and One Nights* through *La Princesse de Clèves* to *A la Recherche du Temps Perdu*, there runs a curious thematic thread: that of eavesdropping and voyeurism ("snooping" could be the general term). Narrative art, when it deals (as is so often the case) with the secrets of intimacy, seems sometimes to respond to a need to figure the means (the "snooping") whereby it comes by such private knowledge; but it simultaneously figures the act of reading as similarly a form of "snooping." The narrator, in producing himself as eavesdropper/voyeur and sharing his knowledge of others' business with the narratee, simultaneously implicates the latter in this invasive act, and a kind of gossiping relationship is formed.[9] In interesting themselves in other folks' affairs, narrator and narratee are simultaneously making them their own business; they are, if one will, on the one hand excluded third parties, but on the other quite passionately involved. My suggestion is that this narrator-narratee relationship, characterizing the participants as "outside" the narrative event while simultaneously drawing them into the group of those whom it concerns, is interpretable as casting metaphorical light on the text-reader relation as well, of which it is precisely a self-reflexive figure.

Over a wall, the sultan witnesses the sexual orgy of his brother's wife with her slaves. This seems to set him off, mimetically, on an orgy of his own (making love each night with a new wife, who is executed in the morning), for which Scheherazade substitutes in due course a nightly orgy of storytelling (the sultan having shifted successively from passive voyeur to active orgiast to again passive hearer). At Coulommiers, the Duc de Nemours overhears Mme de Clèves telling her husband of her lover's dangerous ardor, and thereby confessing the strength of her love for him (the reader knows this lover to be none other than Nemours). The Duke is thus outside of the (narrative and sexual) relationship of M. and Mme de Clèves, in which at the same time he figures as the intrusive object of a profound love that he passionately returns. This structure will be confirmed, after the Prince's death, when a second act of voyeurism at the same site permits Nemours, rapturously, to see Mme de Clèves (who will, however, remain faithful to conjugality) gazing adoringly at a battle-painting in which Nemours is prominently represented. (She had earlier watched him stealing a representation of herself, a portrait in miniature, so this second situation symmetrically reverses the first.) This motif of representation will be taken up by Proust, for instance in the scene at Montjouvain when the narrator witnesses Mlle de Vinteuil's desecration of her father's image; but the most notable episode of snooping in the *Recherche* is on the occasion when "Marcel," from behind a stairway, first watches the courtship dance of Charlus and the tailor Jupien, then overhears what the reader deduces is their lovemaking and their ensuing dialogue.

I proposed in *Story and Situation* that the narrative relationship (narrator-narratee) is regularly figured in texts as an erotic one and the act of narration as the metaphoric equivalent of an act of seduction. If one grant this point, the relevance of the thematics of eavesdropping/voyeurism to the act of reading becomes apparent: this act is thereby figured as the triangulation of the narrative relationship through the introduction of a third party who "witnesses" the art of narrative seduction over the wall, through the window, or from behind the stair of text. These barriers between the fictional observer and what is observed (or overheard) signify the reader's position outside of the textual concerns; the motif of portraiture signifies the reader's interest in represented figures ("narrator" and "narratee" are of course fictive personages no less than Charlus or the Princesse de Clèves, or Scheherazade and Shahryar); but the mimetic substitutions point, not simply to a certain interchangeability of roles among the triangulated figures but to the *mode of desire* whereby an initially excluded reader can become "involved" in the textual concerns.

It is notable, in particular, that the thematics of "snooping" in these texts does not confine the reader to possible identification with the narratee (as object of the narrative act of seduction); as already mentioned, the narrative transmission of knowledge acquired through voyeurism and eavesdropping allies the reader equally with the narrator. This reader, so to speak, is a party to *both* of the instances (subject and object) engaged in the act of seduction, which is what makes readerly involvement a *third* position in the system (and not simply a repetition of one of the others). Particularly suggestive in this respect is the homosexual theme in Proust, in which the similarity of gender—all three participants in the encounter (Charlus, Jupien, and the watching Marcel) are men—suggests a similarity of *kind*, and hence involvement in the *same* system, between narrator, narratee, and reader, who, in commonsense terms, as two represented figures and an empirical person, are different. Since, manifestly, narrator and narratee cannot easily be considered "real" in the sense that a reader is real, it seems to be entailed that the reader must be considered, like Charlus and Jupien—but also, most tellingly, like "Marcel"—a fictive figure, the product of purely discursive operations. If so, this underlying similarity of structure would be the secret of the reader's ability to identify from "outside" the text—but now is the moment to recall Derrida's dictum that *il n'y a pas de hors-texte*—with the purely textual figures of narrator and narratee in erotic relationship. It is highly significant, too, that in Proust there is no (nor can there be any) specific designation of seducer(narrator)-seducee(narratee) roles: engaged in a *mutual* courtship dance, Charlus and Jupien are each, simultaneously, courter and courted, seducer and seducee (gay people will recognize the role equality associated with what is now called "cruising"). That this role equality has implications for the *text*(narrator-narratee)-*reader* relationship as well is a conclusion that Proust's text is inhibited from making explicit (it would entail acknowledgement that Marcel too is the site of homosexual desire) but it is implied by Marcel's evident excitement and his alert interest as "reader" of the scene before his eyes.[10] And Julio Cortázar has a famous, two-page short story, "Continuidad de los parques" ["Continuity of Parks"], that allegorizes precisely, not only the ontological "continuity" between text and readership, but also the "continuity" of desire and readerly "involvement" that is its manifestation. His reader-figure, at first relatively uninterested, is soon a fascinated "witness" to the lovers' plotting, before becoming their actual victim: the victim, that is, in a

triangulated affair of mimetic desire and jealousy, a male struggle for possession of the woman that figures control of textual meaning.

The reader, for the text, is No One (Charlus and Jupien do not know that
Marcel is present; Cortázar's lovers are unaware of the third party who "fue
testigo del último encontro en la cabaña del monte" ["was witness to the
meeting in the mountain cabin"]).[11] But such a reader is "No One, in particular"—a No One to whom the particularities of the text are somehow of compelling interest (Cortázar's reader is so caught up in the suspense that he
becomes a textual victim; Marcel is specifically *addressed* by—concerned and
implicated in—the Charlus-Jupien encounter, and is indeed finding out something about *himself* on this occasion as well as about his friend Charlus). "No
One, in particular" is a formula of Kafka's ("I address No One, in particular")
of which Vincent Kaufmann makes telling use in an important article, "Le
tiers-lecteur," in which the reader is seen as fictively addressed by, but actually
excluded from, the (self-reflexive) text.[12] The article's focus on modern and
postmodern writing (Mallarmé is its other hero) leads it perhaps to overstress
the aspect of readerly exclusion; but it does give appropriate weight to readerly
inclusion in a text that "positions him [or her] as a third party" in the concession I emphasize in the following quotation (202, my translation):

Deploying against a background of nothing all its interlocutory pretenses, the text
includes the reader only as the voyeur or witness of a process whose conclusion
. . . escapes him, and condemns him to silence . . . .

Kaufmann's starting point has been one of Mallarmé's little versified "addresses" from *Les loisirs de la poste*, which interests him because it is self-
address (a "self-addressed envelope"):

> Monsieur Mallarmé. Le pervers
> A nous fuir pour les bois s'acharne
> Ma lettre, suis sa trace vers
> Valvins, par Avon, Seine-et-Marne.[13]

> [Monsieur Mallarmé. Wrong-headedly
> He insists on fleeing us for the woods
> My letter, follow his tracks toward
> Valvins, via Avon, Seine-et-Marne.]

But the poem is readable also as a piece of playful coquetry, a seductive invitation to pursue the elusive "Monsieur Mallarmé" into the thickets where,
like some "wild child" escaping civilization, the textual *sujet de l'énonciation,*
perversely, has fled, and whose location is further despecified by the vague
prepositions ("*vers* / Valvins, *par* Avon") of the address. To whom is this
invitation addressed? Not to a reader, it seems, but to "Ma lettre". . . . Yet,

the careful distinction that is being made here between the grammatical *sujet de l'énoncé* (the "je" who says "ma lettre") and the elusive *sujet de l'énonciation* of whom there are only traces (cf. the third person of "*sa* trace") is mapped onto the *destinateur-destinataire* [addresser-addressee] distinction of post offices (and communication theory), in such a way as to imply the intervention of a third party, acting as the *agency* whereby the "letter" is to reach its destination. In short, the unmentioned "facteur" (letter carrier) is the *factor* the text simultaneously fails to acknowledge (it is "no one" for the text) yet relies on (its "implied address," beyond the explicit address to "Ma lettre," is "in particular" to the anonymous postman who can ensure that the letter reaches "Monsieur Mallarmé"). "Les bois" having a deservedly erotic reputation, both in Mallarmé's time and in our own, it is not difficult to imagine what will happen in the (hypothetical) event of the letter's catching up with its (perhaps unreachable and certainly fugitive) addressee. In that event, the *facteur*-agent-reader will be there to watch; for the role of the reader as *tiers exclu* is also that of *tertius gaudens . . . .*

The term *tiers exclu*—the excluded third party—figures prominently in the thinking of Michel Serres, where it stands for the necessary exclusions on which all communicational contracts repose, those that make dialogue (including debates and quarrels) possible. As the English translation of a key essay has it, "To hold a dialogue is to suppose a third man [*un tiers*] and seek to exclude him"[14]—for the basic level of *agreement* (say, the convention of speaking English) that is indispensable for even the most hostile communicational exchange to become feasible always presupposes innumerable exclusions (for instance, of non-English speakers). Applied to the phenomenon of reading, this notion is the measure, then, of the remoteness and distance of *any* empirical reader from the concerns of *any* given text. I would not bother to read at all if I did not suppose I would *learn* from the text, i.e., experience something *new* in reading it. But what's Hecuba to me? What have I in common with the affairs of the court of Henri II (*La Princesse de Clèves*)? With the narrator-narratee relationship in the *Odyssey* or Mallarmé's little poem? I am "No One" to all these texts. . . .

Serres insists, however, that since such exclusions are a necessary element in the functioning of the system, the excluded third is an essential component *in* the system, in which it figures (to which it "returns," as the repressed) in the form of "noise." The agreement to speak English *fails to exclude* all the failures of communication, *les ratés du système*, that are due, for example, to dialect variations, differences in degrees of literacy, stuttering, stammering, or other deficiencies that are not so much accidents as *characterizations of speech* (they are an integral part of it). "Noise" (Fr. *le parasite*) ought then—since it is the indexical sign of the excluded mediator—to be a welcome element in all dialogues and exchanges, just as the social parasite is often a welcome guest, one whose business it is to "make the party go."[15] Like the letter carrier, "excluded" from Mallarmé's poem, the mediating "factor" is the necessary agency without which the system cannot work. Readerly involvement in a text then, does not so much intrude as constitute the indispensable "noise" that disturbs the perfection of "purely" textual relationships, but without which they cannot function. Such readerly involvement goes by a number of names: phenomenologists call it "actualization," "concretization," or "realization" of the text; hermeneuticists call it "interpretation," as I will mainly do in what follows; structuralists and poststructuralists refer to "analysis" or (its synonym) "deconstruction". . . . But without this noise in the system, there would be no system.

If, however, the text includes the reader as excluded third, we are entitled to ask also, from the point of view of the empirical reader, what it is that prompts readerly "interest" in a text. What is the mode of *desire* that accounts for readerly involvement? I rephrase the question thus because the most convenient model, here, is the concept of "mimetic desire" developed by René Girard.[16] One desires the desirable, and the desirable is identifiable as that which is seen or known to be already desired by another; hence, the structure of desire is always triangular because it is always mediated. Consequently, in reading a text in which I "see" (voyeuristically) or "overhear" a seducer-seducee relationship between the represented narrator and the represented narratee (or other represented figures, of course), I identify as desirable the object of the seduction, and am thus led to involve myself in the relationship, both by desiring in my turn the seducee and (as a consequence of this desire) by identifying mimetically with the seducer-figure. But equally, one does not only desire to love, but also to be loved; and this is the principle of readerly identification with the seducee/narratee. Again, mimetic activity is involved, for—as I put it in my earlier volume (15)—"when we are seduced, are we not always seduced into conforming ourselves with an image: the simulacrum of one whom we believe can be loved?" The reader is simultaneously a rival of the narrator (as seducer), sharing with this figure a desire for the narratee, and of the narratee (as seducee), with whom is shared the desire to be desirable—but, as Girard has taught us, rivalry is a principle, not so much of hostility and dissimilarity, as of identification, involvement with the other, and assimilation.

The functioning of the two principles I have canvassed—reading as exclusion from the text, reading as inclusion through mimetic desire—obviously produces the phenomenon of reading as a matter of rather delicate balance. Unchecked, mimetic desire will produce a situation without a difference, the stasis of absolute similarity which, as René Girard insists, is a form of chaos:

reading, in this case, becomes pure identification. Absolute exclusion of the empirical reader from the textual concerns (the case of the book that falls from my hands because I "cannot work up an interest" in it) produces another sterile situation, the incommunicability inherent in absolute difference. Like spectatorhood at the theater, productive "reading" falls then between the extremes of absolute identification and absolute uninvolvement, falling somewhere *between* these two poles and, as a consequence, entailing differently proportioned "doses" of involvement and distance—that is, the necessary "mix" of similarity and difference that makes the system "go." What, to me (Ross), are the concerns of "Paddy" and "Stephen?" I am "No One" to them, but inasmuch as I become "interested" in them, I begin to share in those concerns and to become "No One" in a more particular way, a way defined by the textual concerns. I note that "Paddy" has an interest in seducing "Stephen" through his narrative, and that is the principle of my identification both with "Paddy" (with whom I now have in common a shared object of desire) and with "Stephen" (whose desirability I am likewise moved to share). But I am still Ross, and must remain Ross—the noise in the "Paddy"-"Stephen" system, the difference that makes sense of their relationship—under pain of ceasing, through over-identification, to be the *reader* of their joint text.

Acts of seduction *in* the text thus become, for the reader, a seductive action *of* the text. And, if narrative texts have the power to change their readers, it is because one cannot unbecome what one has once become, unthink, unfeel, or undesire what one has once thought, or felt, or desired. To be seduced by a text—to identify with textual relations that exclude one as, by definition different—must logically, therefore, produce *change*, change being understood as *becoming less different* from the textual concerns than one once was. In this sense, reading can be defined as the movement whereby the *tiers exclu* tends to be realized as a *tertius gaudens.*

But it will be apparent from the foregoing that, although a reader tends to identify with both the narrator and with the narratee, and with both simultaneously, the *degree* of readerly identification with each can easily vary: one can, as empirical reader, assimilate more closely with the narratee (as object of desire) or with the narrator (as desiring subject), the *norm*—of unsophisticated or perhaps simply cursory reading—being perhaps that of maximal identification with the narratee, a norm that corresponds to a maximal repression of the reader's function as mediating *tiers.* The reader, here, simply "slips into the slot" furnished—often as a vacancy—in the text as that of the narratee, and becomes the object of the narrator's seduction. The reason for this is evident if one reflects that the position of narratee is the position of greater power. To be desirable is to be more powerful than to desire; to exert control over the narrative situation *by virtue of position* is a state of greater strength than to be obliged to acquire, and maintain, the more fragile control that arises from the rhetorical maneuverings and tactics of narrative seduction. It is almost shamefully *easy* for me, as a normally unreflective reader (but also given my own power-laden status as a white Australian male), to read the story of "Mirdinan" in *major* identification with the position of "Stephen"—i.e., as the object to whom "Paddy"'s narrative act of seduction is addressed.

The alternative to reading in this way "with" the narratee is not, however, reading "with" the narrator, a feat as *difficult* in its way (and for symmetrical reasons) as the former is easy. The alternative consists of reading, if one will, "with" the (unknowable) *sujet de l'énonciation*, that is, it consists of "textual" reading, in which, as a consequence, the reader's mediating role is maximally realized as that of (involved) *tertius gaudens*. In narrative terms, such a reading, as I have suggested, is identificatory, but it entails identification with both narrator and narratee and hence awareness of (voyeuristic involvement in) the relation between the two. I read, not with "Stephen" nor yet with "Paddy"; but in reading with "Paddy" *and* "Stephen," I am led to become the locus in which is negotiated the contractual relationship between "Paddy" and "Stephen"—the relationship on which the narrative act depends and which it is my function as mediator to realize, but which, to the extent that, as reader, I am excluded from it, I am simultaneously in a position to analyse, interpret, concretize, empathize with, and attempt to understand through my reading, remaining always to some degree distanced from it.

My model, of course, brutally simplifies a complex phenomenon, as will be demonstrated in the course of this book. But it is on such a model of reading that oppositional narrative texts rely. For such texts tend in the first instance to position their reader "with" the narratee, in the position of greatest power; but this is their mode of "disguise," for the reader who yields to that positioning becomes an object of the narrator's seduction, and to that extent cannot *witness* it (as voyeur or eavesdropper); such a reader functions as *tiers exclu* but not as *tertius gaudens*. A shift of the reading position away from the position of power to one of collaboration with the *text* in its production of meaning will suffice, however, for the text to become visible as the site in which narrative is staged as an oppositional act, i.e., the narrator's seductive maneuvers now become readable as signs of a specific effort to recruit the power of the "narratee" in the interests of the "narrator." The difference is that between an essentially dual reading situation (narrator-narratee/reader) and a more triangular one, which produces the reader as *tiers exclu/tertius gaudens*, involved in *because* excluded from the oppositional act. It is in this sense that reading oppositional narratives is synonymous with reading the oppositional in narrative texts, i.e., situating oneself in the reading position where the oppositional character of the narrative act becomes visible. And it is in this sense, also, that the reading of oppositional narratives *involves* the reader as "moyen de moyenner," making a shift between *tiers exclu* and *tertius gaudens* without fully abandoning or fully coinciding with either position.

Such an analysis depends crucially on a distinction between what I will call the "narrative function" and the "textual function" of narrative discourse. The narrative function is an address to the narratee, and implies a narrator as *sujet de l'énoncé*; the textual function, however, addresses the reader as "No One, in particular" and implies the *sujet de l'énonciation* as originless origin, and as unidentifiable object of reading, another "No One, in particular," like "Monsieur Mallarmé." It is with the coexistence in fiction of "narrative function" and "textual function" and hence, of the two modes of reading they make possible, that the following section will essentially be concerned.

For the sake of clarity, however, let me first specify some points that emerge from the preceding analysis and whose significance should become clearer as the book develops:

(a) The reading subject is defined as a site of desire, and in particular of the complex form of desire figured in certain texts as voyeuristic;

(b) For a double seduction is involved: if the narratee is the object of a "narrative" seduction with which the reader can identify, a seduction that in oppositional terms might be thought of as a form of flattery (since it identifies the narratee-position as the position of power), there is also a "textual" seduction producing the text-reader relation as one of "No Ones, in particular" and making possible a *distanced* interpretive attitude to the narrator-narratee relation that is simultaneously one of textual involvement.

(c) This distance between the narrator-narratee relation and the text-reader relation makes it possible on the one hand to understand oppositional narrative as discourse that relativizes, in its "textual" manifestation, the relation to power that it enacts in its "narrative" manifestation; and on the other hand to understand oppositional reading as entailing a shift between two addressee positions (and two constructions of subjectivity)—the position of (identification with) the narratee (a virtual exclusion of the reader as mediating *tiers*), and that of interpretive or reading subject (the inclusion of the reader as *gaudens*).

(d) Finally, therefore, the "split" introduced into narrative discourse by this distance and the triangulation of the situation of narrative communication that ensues, producing reading as the "noise" in the system without which there would be no system, enacts the system as an inevitably *mediated* one ("noise" being the necessary accompaniment, and so the indexical sign of mediation). The very possibility of discursive oppositionality can thus be seen to be dependent on the phenomenon of mediation as its necessary condition; and it is because without reading (i.e., mediation) there would be no system and so no possibility of opposition, that what I refer to sometimes in short-hand as "oppositional narrative" must *always* be understood as the reading of the oppositional in narrative.

3. Functions of Discourse

Literary discourse is sometimes described as a "pretended" speech-act; or a speech-act is said to be "mimed" in (or by) the text; my own metaphor, derived from the thematics of voyeurism and eavesdropping, has been that of "staging"—the narrative act (narrator-narratee in relationship) is said to be readable because staged textually.[17] There is, in short, a prevailing sense of a distinction to be made, within a text, between the mode of communication it *represents* and the mode of communication it *enacts* (partly by means of that representation) as text. Barbara Herrnstein Smith, as always, puts the case clearly: "As a general class, literary artworks may be conceived of as depictions or representations, rather than instances, of natural discourse."[18] Her distinction between natural and represented discourse is, as she well knows, vulnerable; but it is the other distinction she implies, between the represented discourse and the textual enactment, that will mainly concern me here; and this is in spite of the fact that, most frequently, the two are (in purely formal terms) coextensive. Indeed, it is because an identical stretch of text can be read in two ways, in the mode of identification with the narratee of the (represented) speech-act, and in the more triangulated mode I have called textual reading, that it is necessary to distinguish them and to contemplate some of the implications of each mode of reading.

In speaking of a "narrative function" and a "textual function," I am anxious to respect as closely as possible this frequent situation of coextension.[19] For the represented discourse is not, strictly speaking, "pretended," "mimed" or "staged" any more than is the represented "world" in a text (fictional or otherwise). It is rather that it conforms to a representational mode (and hence determines a mode of reading) that differs, on the one hand, from the mode of *reference* (by which discourse "refers" to or reminds us of what is given as a preexisting "real" or possible world), and on the other from the self-referential or self-representational mode—more accurately still, the mode of self-figuration—that is thought to be characteristic of the text in its writerliness, as *écriture*. I will argue that this mode of representation that is neither reference nor metareference (self-representation) can be described as productive of a simulacrum of communication. It should be clear, then, that I am describing (literary) discourse, not as a representational phenomenon in the naïve sense (presupposing an existential universe that preexists it and that it designates or names) but as a signifying system that makes use of a complex representational apparatus not to name the preexisting but to produce a set of *contexts* and thus to make meaning.

Text, then, performs in all *three* signifying "functions"—the "referential," the "narrative" and the "textual"—to which correspond three modes of production of context—by reference, that is production of a "world" given as preexisting, by simulacrum, the mode of production of the narrative relationship, and finally by self-figuration, the mode of production of a reading context. These functions are simultaneous in the sense that there is normally no discrete segment of text that can be perceived as exercizing, specifically or uniquely, any one given function.

My use of the word "function," it will be perceived, derives from the influential paper entitled "Linguistics and Poetics"[20] in which Roman Jakobson identified the six "functions" of discourse. These I need now, very briefly, to rehearse in order to show their relevance to the three modes of representation (or production of context) that I am positing. Jakobson's "emotive/expressive" and "conative" functions (relating to the I-you of discourse), if taken together, define the relationship of narrator and narratee that constitutes what I wish to call the "narrative" function, i.e., the mode of address that "expresses" the self while taking note of, and exerting impact on, the other. The remaining Jakobsonian functions may similarly be paired, and indeed *need* to be paired if one is to understand how discourse works as representation, or the production of context(s): my implication is that each of the three representational functions combines two Jakobsonian functions in a way that ultimately makes the distinction between the two unnecessary. Thus, Jakobson's "referential" function, in conjunction with the structuring of discourse he calls the "poetic" function, accounts for the ability of language *not* to refer to a supposedly nonlinguistic context (the world in which we live) but to produce that context as meaningful because structured by language (structured like a language): the "world of the text" is a referential object produced by discourse. Similarly, the "metalinguistic" and the "phatic" function (relating respectively to the code and the channel of communication) need to be taken together because, as is demonstrable,[21] literary self-representation or figural self-reflexivity works, not to determine an allegedly autotelic text, as is sometimes asserted, but to indicate the understandings about communicability that are appropriate, in the text's self-conception, for it to be readable as a meaningful phenomenon.

In reordering in this way the Jakobsonian categories, it is clear that I am disturbing their original philosophical underpinnings. I am responding in particular to two related trends of thought that have been influential in the past quarter century and that permit us, now, to see the inevitable portion of "blindness" Jakobson's insights entailed. One such blindness is in his idea of "dominance," for example of the "poetic" function, as a marker of a given type of discourse, an idea that has become difficult to sustain in the light of demonstrations (most memorably by Jonathan Culler and Barbara Herrnstein Smith[22]) that "types" of discourse shade imperceptibly into one another and are determined less by objective structural features than by the ways we choose (or are led) to frame them: "poetry" is what we take to be poetry, "fiction" is what we take to be fiction (I am aware that these formulations beg as many questions as they solve, but I cannot pursue them here). As a consequence, Jakobson's view of the "poetic" message's focus on itself as a sign of its autotelic character is belied, in part by his own demonstration that the "poetic function" as a structuring of discourse serves rather to produce meanings (and hence to construct worlds), and in part by the observation that autotelism is itself a product, less of specific textual features in themselves, than of autotelic readings. In my view, then, a text may produce itself as "autotelic," just as it may produce itself as "referential," but this will be a *prescription for reading* resulting from the self-referential apparatus of the "textual function;" and it is possible for a self-figuring (or self-reflexive) text not to produce itself as autotelic but to require another reading situation altogether. Nor, in my view, is self-figuration itself necessarily a textual "dominant," although I clearly accord it hierarchical superiority over the other two functions.

Jakobson's functions inherited also a positivist view of communication that situated its essential components in human subjects, considered as the active agents (addresser-addressee) of an act of communication understood as an interaction between autonomous "selves," and in a referential "world" whose extra-linguistic reality and self-identity were taken for granted. The six functions derive from a preexisting three-part model of speaker, hearer, and world. The brilliance of Jakobson's move was to introduce into the picture those elements of the communicational situation previously bracketed out and assumed to be "transparent": the "code," the "channel," and the "message," i.e., those elements that refer to the phenomenon of mediation and so introduce opacity, obliqueness, duplicity, accident, and "noise" into the system. But the structuralist revolution his paper in part initiated has had the effect of toppling from their position of autonomy, with respect to language, those elements of the communicational model which, in Jakobson, still occupy the *strong* positions: the addresser, the addressee, and the context of reference, all of which are now increasingly perceived, in our poststructuralist era, to be *traversed by language*, and indeed—more accurately—to be *produced by discourse*, rather than existing as entities independent of language-in-use. They are, in short, not the givens whose purposes language serves or whose nature language attempts to reproduce; but they must be thought of as products of the functioning of language itself (as code, channel, and message), that is, of language as a signifying practice.

In reverting to a tripartite scheme, then, I am simultaneously reversing the positivist hierarchization so as to put in the strong position language itself, but language as a signifying practice, the products of this practice (the illocutionary partners, and the world of which they speak) now appearing as discursively produced constructions rather than as prior givens. The significance of the "textual function" is, indeed, that its self-figuration necessarily describes (or rather produces) discourse as a signifying system. Without being a discursive "dominant," it can therefore be seen to have a logical and hierarchical importance that derives from its power to define (Jakobson's) "illocutionary" or (my) "narrative" representation as well as "referential" representation as being themselves products of discourse as a signifying (not reflecting or reproducing) system. That these two latter modes of representation themselves work in ways that are significantly different—the referential "world" being produced as a preexisting context, the illocutionary partners, however (to reintroduce the theatrical metaphor), as "roles" that represent the conditions of possibility of a narrative relationship—does not in itself affect the primary perception that both the illocutionary partners and the referential world are part of the discourse's representational apparatus and cannot be apprehended independently of it.

I mean the system I am sketching to be particularly appropriate to the analysis of fictional discourse (i.e., the discourse we take to be fictional), whether "narrative" or "lyric" in genre. (The lyric can be seen, as Herrnstein Smith shows, to be producing the lyric I-thou figures in the way that narrative fiction produces the narrator-narratee relationship; the theater, as a "density of signs" [Barthes], requires a more complex analysis than I can give here.) But even though the proposition may be more counterintuitive (less commonsensical), I have no doubt that, philosophically, the same structure of functions—"referential," "narrative," and "textual"—also governs (what we take to be) "natural" or "everyday" discourse, the discourse we frame as "nonfictional." That such discourse has "textual" features (i.e., in my sense, it is "metalinguistic" *and* "phatic"—self-reflexively concerned with establishing or confirming its communicational situation in terms of "code" and "channel") is something that Jakobson's article itself draws attention to. That it has a "referential" function (producing the world as a meaningful context of speech) is a proposition likely to be commonly, if not universally, accepted. The greatest likely stumbling block is the implication that in everyday discourse as in fiction the addresser-addressee (narrator-narratee) positions are produced as grammatical "roles" necessitated by a "narrative function" of discourse—"roles" that *produce* real people as "subjects" rather than the reverse.

That is why the distinction between the way the referential context is represented in discourse and the way the narrative participants (the narrative context) are produced is crucial. For the former is represented as preexisting discourse and as forming its contextual "world" (i.e., as a referent in the strictest sense, that to which language performs the gesture of referring), whereas the human subjects who are represented as preexisting conditions of possibility for the discourse itself are produced in the discourse as *simulacra*, that is as "models without an original," identified absolutely with the sign-world that produces them, and capable of representation but not of reference. Quite similarly, a "shifter" such as the pronoun "I" has no content other than the grammatical predication that constitutes a sentence; but the sentence produces "I" as communicational subject, a "role" that can be assumed in turn by real people—now me, now Susan, now Johnny—who are thus produced (represented in discourse) as the "subjects" who are the discourse's own condition of possibility. But some illustration may be helpful at this point.

In "Mirdinan," for example, a world exists with its places (Cockle Well, Broome, Fremantle, the "deep hole" in the sea where the steamer passage is) and its population (Mirdinan, his wife, a Malay fisherman, relatives, police, etc.); the interaction of people and people and people and places is the object of a referential gesture (this is what the narrative is "about") even as it is clear that this world is being structured by the discourse in ways that make it meaningful. Thus, the respective positions of Cockle Well, Broome, and Fremantle matter, as do such oppositions as Mirdinan and his wife's relatives or his wife's relatives and the police, or again the distinct connotations of eating and drinking, or drowning and flying, or again of sea and coast. This is not "the world," although we may recognize it as such: it is a "possible" world produced in its shape, texture, and meaning by the discourse, but produced as preexisting the narrative. The characteristic Aboriginal linkage of narrative to its "country"— the narrative is about a specific "country" which it produces in its meaningfulness—might be thought to be emblematic in this respect.

Similarly, the Mallarmé quatrain gestures to a known universe, with its woods, the administrative grid imposed on its geography (Seine-et-Marne), the postal services that make use of the grid, the named communities (Valvins, Avon) and individuals (Monsieur Mallarmé) the postal service connects. But at the same time, and indissolubly, this universe is structured discursively in ways that are, here, playful and poetic: hence, it matters that "fuir" and "suis" are in a relation of phonetic and semantic equivalence; that a collectivity ("nous") is produced from which an individual ("Monsieur Mallarmé") is said, delinquently, to have fled; that m's figure prominently at the opening and closing of the text while a sudden flurry of v's links "pervers" with "vers / Valvins, par Avon" and coincides with a provocative enjambment to suggest a pun: *verse* ("vers"), like the letter, goes *toward* ("vers") M. Mallarmé, but verse also (<Lat. *versus*) is an affair of twists and turns, and so "per-

verse". . . . Other puns, too, then become noticeable: a "seine" or trawler's net is useful, like the postal grid, in tracking down a perverse individual who has made for the woods, while "marne" (English "marl") is a somewhat indeterminate mixture of clay and chalk; "Avon" in a language known to M. Mallarmé (who taught it) is not a village but a river, like the Seine and the Marne, and one associated with the poet Shakespeare, an author whose name stands for a largely unknown individual, etc. In other words, the "world" of the poem is being produced, here, as both gridded (by language)—a structure emblematized by the geographical and administrative gridding of France that enables letters to be addressed—and (also as a result of the characteristics of language) indeterminate, a place of "words" for which language serves, at best, as a "trace."

"Paddy" and "Stephen," however—as the conditions of possibility of the narrative occurrence called "Mirdinan"—are names given to grammatical subjects whom we can know only as they are predicated in the discourse that produces them as its subjects. These are figures who *coincide with their discursive function*, as narrator and narratee respectively, of the story. A "possible world," such as those constructed in "Mirdinan" or the Mallarmé quatrain, is only recognized as possible on the condition of its intersecting, at some point and in some way, with the world we conceive of as "real" and hence as preexisting the textual world. What preexists "Paddy" and "Stephen," however, is *only* the general notion of human subject—the type of which they are produced as tokens—and, as represented subjects, they are more like a computer projection (of, let us say, a bridge that has not been built and may never be built) than they are like a landscape depicting Salisbury Cathedral or a portrait of Mallarmé. Like the represented bridge in the computer projection (itself a token of the type "bridge"), they are produced as an assemblage of signs, and have no independent existence except as that assemblage of signs might lead us to imagine it. If, for example, I know that each is a representative of a cultural community, it is because their discourse gives them that "role": "Paddy" asks "Stephen" for confirmation of his information about Fremantle and the procedures of a hanging (which establishes "Stephen" as Westerner and "Paddy" as non-Westerner); but "Paddy" also says "oh everybody know this story you know," where the two uses of the verb *to know* effectively cast "Stephen" as belonging to a different cultural community than ("Paddy"'s) "everybody," and "Paddy" as spokesperson for that "everybody."

The theatrical metaphor ("staging," "casting," "roles") is perhaps useful here in clarifying the relation of "real" people to the narrative "roles" they may be assigned through discourse. There is in Broome a person named Paddy Roe who is planning a third book, and in Sydney a person named Stephen Muecke who teaches at the University of Technology. But these *persons* (one might think here of the etymological metaphor: *persona* = mask) are not knowable except as they may be constructed from the discourse they emit, much as one may imagine as real the bridge (never constructed) that is produced by the computer-projection of a bridge. . . . The difference, however, is important: the bridge is not produced by the computer-projection as the origin of its own representation, whereas "Paddy" and "Stephen," as speaking subjects, are precisely produced as the originating source—the condition of possibility—of the discourse that produces them.

Hence the nice equivocation in "Monsieur Mallarmé," whom the text produces as a figure in the real world, produced by the "grid" and to whom it is possible to address letters, while simultaneously showing "him" to be elusive, an *être de fuite*, whose "traces" can only be "followed"—"Monsieur Mallarmé" is simultaneously a simulacrum, and a figure of the more elusive *sujet de l'énonciation*, who slips through the linguistic grid. In this latter respect, "Monsieur Mallarmé" is an indicator of "textual" function, for the actualized "narrative" function in the quatrain arises as the relationship of an "I" who speaks and addresses "ma lettre." But who are these entities? We know them only as they are predicated in the text: "I" is a member of a certain collectivity ("nous"), and knows "Monsieur Mallarmé" as a "twisted" creature who has fled; simultaneously "I" is the subject of a conative use of language (the imperative "suis sa trace") of which "ma lettre" is the addressee—"ma lettre," of which we know perhaps two things only. One is that, written by "I," it has no content inasmuch as it coincides with an inscription on an envelope, that is, an address to Monsieur Mallarmé ("ma lettre" is thus coextensive with the discourse we are reading). The other is that this letter does not coincide with "Monsieur Mallarmé," whose "trace" precisely it is enjoined to follow. Rather it coincides with "je"—a figure entirely shadowy except as the predicated subject of this act of address (i.e., the act of address that is the quatrain, and the act of address the quatrain enacts, as "Ma lettre, suis sa trace"). Rather tellingly, the addresser-narrator ("I") coincides here with the addressee-narratee ("ma lettre") because both coincide with the same piece of discourse that produces them.

"Monsieur Mallarmé," then—as object of pursuit—is the name given by the text to its "textual function"; it is its textual self-representation as an object of reading, producing in this way the third type of context—after the "referential" and the "narrative" contexts, the context of reading as an "interpretive" context—that needs to be briefly illustrated and described. "Monsieur Mallarmé," as simultaneously defined by the grid and elusive object of pursuit, enacts the identity of—and yet the absolutely crucial distinction between— the self-same discourse in its "narrative" and in its "textual" functions; so, too, do the poetic equivalences between *suivre* (the action enjoined on "ma lettre" in the hands of the letter-carrier/reader) and *fuir* (what "Monsieur Mallarmé" has done), and between "ma lettre" (producing "I" as the subject who has produced the letter) and "sa trace" (left behind by "Monsieur Mallarmé"). The discourse produced narratively by "I" as "ma lettre" is simultaneously none other than—because it is simultaneously readable by the reader in pursuit of "Monsieur Mallarmé" as—"sa trace."

In "Mirdinan," the most prominent indicator of "textual function" is also, not coincidentally, in the final line, which we have already read as an enactment of the "narrative function": "oh everybody know this story you know." The repetition of the verb "to know" functions on the one hand to "cast" the different cultural roles of narrator and narratee, but on the other as an invitation to a double reading of the story, *both* from the viewpoint of "Paddy" as representative of his people, for whom the story of "Mirdinan" (the story of oppression and opposition) is nothing new, *and* from the viewpoint of "Stephen," as representative of his people, who precisely has had to learn, not only this story that "everybody know," but also (otherwise this last line has no real point) the fact that "everybody know" it.

The mode of representation operative in the "textual" function is very puzzling, and I am not at all sure, in spite of having devoted a book (*Story and Situation*) to it, that I fully understand it. It depends, however, on textual self-representation as a matter of figuration—it is in figuring itself self-reflexively that text produces itself as figural (that is, readable) discourse. For the "figural" is the other of the literal: we take to be "figural" any discourse that requires interpretation, and conversely, any discourse that we interpret necessarily signifies in the mode of figurality. Textual self-representation is certainly a form of mimesis, in the strict sense of that term (in which only words can "imitate" words); but the representation and the represented are here more intimately identified (and interchangeable) than in any other form of representation. Instead of speaking of signifier and signified, we are rather in the position of speaking of discourse as simultaneously "signifying itself" and "signified by itself," the split within the discourse that is the split between "signifying" and "being signified" being produced, precisely, by the intervention of an act of reading. And the fact that such a cleavage can be introduced at all into the otherwise seamless web of text is therefore a sign of the intrusive but necessary reader as a manifestation of mediation, that is of the indispensable agency by means of which signs come to yield meaning.

In producing a portion of text as a "figure" for the whole, then, the reader is enacting the very procedure—the production of the discourse as figural— by which textual discourse is itself produced as meaningful (that is, as other than literal: as readable or interpretable). When we say that a text figures "itself," therefore, we must necessarily understand "itself" to mean itself-as-an-object-of-reading, itself-as-figural-discourse; and that is why, as I tried to show in *Story and Situation*, textual self-figuration is always situational. What is figured does not produce the text as an "autotelic" object, as is still sometimes claimed, so much as it incorporates a model of the relational apparatus, the context of reading, that will produce the text as meaningful. But conversely, the understanding of reading that is implied by textual self-figuration will necessarily be that of reading as a signifying practice—a relation of interpretation—not as a mode of "communication" between defined and definable, autonomous subjects (the kind of communication that is simulated in the "narrative function"). The figuring of the text as readable implies, in short, that reading be the interpretation of figures. Thus, in moving from the "referential" through the "narrative" to the "textual" function, we have moved simultaneously through contextualizations that with increasing clarity propose discourse itself—that is, language but language in use—as the sole agency, productive of the referential world (but as a preexisting reality), productive of the illocutionary or "narrative" roles as models without an original (but as models of an autonomous source of the narrative act), and productive finally of its own "textuality," split by the act of reading into a subject and an object of interpretation of whom, or of which, the text is only a "trace."

Story and Situation was, in essence, a study of some modes of textual self-situation through (self-)figuration. The "textual function" in certain examples of nineteenth century literary art is described in that book as their figural self-representation as "readerly" objects dependent on forms of seduction to elicit reading and interpretation. I will make use in *Room for Maneuver* of similar techniques of reading, including the presupposition of situational self-figuration (referred to in the earlier book as self-reference or self-reflexivity). I do so in order to show that literature can designate itself, in its "textual function," as a site of discursive oppositionality; that is, that it produces, as the context that makes it meaningful, a context of oppositional relations to power. But such oppositionality, I further suggest, takes the form, precisely, of a split between the "narrative" and the "textual" functions of discourse such that the "narrative function," as the site of an address to the narratee in the position of power, comes to be relativized—or, more technically, *ironized*—by a "textual function" that distances the reader from the narratee position and requires the "narrative function" to become part of the text *as an object of interpretation.* Everything thus depends on the intervention of a reader capable of manifesting the discourse as a mediated phenomenon by producing the crucial split between "narrative" and "textual" functions. Discourse that is not, in this sense, read cannot be oppositional.

Now, I have already mentioned that, logically, the "textual" function—since discourse is always mediated—occupies a hierarchically superior position in that, as indicator of the appropriate understandings that constitute a reading context, it necessarily indicates among other things the degree of importance and the kind of significance that should—as far as textual assumptions go— be accorded any given text's "referential" and "narrative" functions. The point matters, among other reasons, because it is the *relation* of "textual function" to "narrative function" that crucially defines narrative oppositionality, which always depends on the production of difference between the two. One can imagine a narrative whose "textual function" would be exhausted by the in- struction to the reader to heed only the "narrative function," that is to occupy the position of absolute identification with the narratee (the text, in turn, co- inciding absolutely with its narration and having no subject other than the narrator, as *sujet de l'énoncé*—except of course, for the source, in reading, of the initial instruction!). Such a case would be that of a discourse of absolute power: if it could exist at all, which I doubt, it would be an extreme and exceptional instance, and it would inhibit any potential for oppositional read- ing, as what I will later (in chapter 4) call "dictation" seeks to do, by excluding the role of reading in the realization of textual meaning as a mediated phe- nomenon—that is, by excluding mediation itself.

Much more common, and perhaps characteristic of classical and neo-clas- sical literature, is a very large preponderance accorded—textually—to the "narrative function." Thus the *textual* concern in the Gospels, for instance, with the nature of authority and its maintenance (figured in particular as a "charismatic" understanding of Christ) translates into an instruction to the reader to understand the *narrator's* (evangelist's) voice as similarly authorita- tive and to accord it belief, as deriving from the demonstrated authority of Jesus, whose voice is that of God. But here one begins to discern the possibility of an oppositional reading that would reside in making an ironic distinction between the authority thus *claimed* for the narrator and the textual *means* by which that authority is produced, means which function as a denial of the "charismatic" because they constitute a rhetorical "device." And it is the pos- sibility of such an ironic reading, inherent in the split between the "narrative" and the "textual" functions, that defines the oppositionality of narrative dis- course generally. It is in such terms that I will study La Fontaine, in the following chapter, as a neo-classical ironist.

However, at a period that can best be situated in the latter part of the nineteenth century in Europe (1857, the year of *Madame Bovary* and *Les Fleurs du Mal*, can be more or less pinpointed in French literature, but in English one must await the late Victorians and Edwardians), something begins to change. The characteristic of literary "modernism," concomitantly with the rise of "writerly" style and a new foregrounding of self-reflexivity, is that of a discourse in which the "textual function" tends to submerge or devalue, instead of putting forward and supporting, the "narrative function."[23] This is not the place to rehearse the history of modernism, but to note that this recession of the "narrative function" in favor of an ever more prominently (self-)advertised "textual function" has not been without consequences for oppositional writing (or the oppositional in writing). It amounts to a certain abandonment of ironic disguise, a gradual emergence from "cover"; and it allows me to propose an important difference between ancien régime oppositional narrative and nouveau régime oppositional writing, as that between covert "textual" opposition readable in overt "narrative" acknowledgement of seats of power—a practice of irony then—and the reverse, i.e., more overtly oppositional "writing" that contains, rather more covertly, in its vestigial "narrative function," the acknowledgment of power that constitutes the oppositional act *as* oppositional (by contrast, for example, with actual resistance). I will identify this writing (in chapter 3) as "melancholic," and point to the "appeal" it makes for reading as both the sign of its assumption of melancholic identity (as nonautonomous because necessarily produced by the other) and that of its concomitantly *emergent* oppositionality.

Part of the story of this book, which produces the ironic La Fontaine (in chapter 2) as its token neo-classical oppositional figure and—in this respect— the Québec writer Hubert Aquin as its token modern, or "writerly" figure of opposition, will be the story of that "emergence" of the textual. We will see in particular that what entails the partial eclipse of the "narrative function" is its unspoken solidarity with ideological assumptions concerning the "autonomous" subject and concomitant political positions of centralized power. In the modern world, where power has itself become diffuse and the dividedness, multiplicity, and "otherness" of the subject a phenomenon difficult to evade, in spite of various strategies of authority and closure, textuality as the site of a Mallarméan "omission of the self" both becomes more visible and simultaneously exerts a more difficult and problematic mode of oppositionality (since what it is "opposing," now that power is no longer visible, central, and autonomous, is a world *like itself*). I will treat such texts in chapter 3 as enacting a melancholic "suicide tactic" of opposition.

At the same time, however, the emergence of melancholic oppositionality and the new prominence of the "textual" as an appeal for reading should not be taken to imply an eclipse of irony, but rather a transformation in the mode of its functioning. Because it implies reading as the production of difference between the "narrative" and "textual" functions, irony is *always* fundamental to discursive oppositionality. But where the prominence of the "narrative function" as a flatteringly seductive address to power tends, in La Fontaine for instance, to produce the ironic "textual function" as that which *negates* the address to power, the decreased centrality and visibility of power in the modern era, and the "fading" of the "narrative" function into the "textual" that accompanies it in melancholic texts, tend rather to produce the ironic relation of the "textual" to the "narrative" as a matter of *appropriation*, in which textual seduction of the reader is seen to be making use of its "narrative" apparatus less as a matter of real disguise—although in Nerval it still provides an alibi, as my discussion in chapter 3 will show—and more as a "hook" without which that seduction, as a departure precisely from the discourse of power and the forms of desire it produces, could not proceed.

It is this appropriative form of oppositional irony, as the turning of the discourse of power to the purposes of oppositional (textual) seduction, that predominates—as I shall stress in chapter 4—in a modern, and indeed postmodern, text such as Manuel Puig's *El beso de la mujer araña* [*Kiss of the Spider Woman*], the suggestion being that appropriative irony is particularly relevant to the situations of social violence that—in contradistinction to the acknowledged authority of La Fontainean kingship—characterize modern dictatorships as "prison" societies. For where the oppositionality of "witnessing" is in such circumstances always open to appropriation by the discursive apparatus of power, as my discussion of two other Hispano-American novels—Alejo Carpentier's *El siglo de las luces* [*Explosion in a Cathedral*] and Miguel Angel Asturias's *El Señor Presidente*—will attempt to show, it is nicely and ironically appropriate that an oppositionality of ironic appropriation should displace the ironic appropriability of the oppositionality of witness. . . .

But if, from one angle, oppositional reading is involvement in a situation of seduction productive of shifts in the reading subject as a site of desire—the topic, broadly speaking, of section 2 of this chapter—while on the other the split in discourse (between "narrative" and "textual" functions) that reading produces appears, as I have just attempted to suggest, as the principle of oppositional irony, then the *question of reading*, which I now leave suspended until the final pages of this book, becomes that of the relation between reading as the production of irony (whether negative or appropriative) and reading as "involvement" in a seductive relationship. For it seems that it is at the interface of these two aspects of reading that there exists the "room for maneuver" out of which oppositional change can arise.

I turn back now, however, to consider more extensively the question of irony; and as I do so it is necessary to acknowledge immediately that, like all the other heuristic distinctions I find myself making in this book in an attempt to say something worthwhile about oppositionality, the distinction between the irony of negation and the irony of appropriation is an easily deconstructed one, if only because one cannot negate without appropriating what one negates, just as one cannot appropriate without to some degree negating—by turning to another use—what one appropriates. In token of which, I now read a fable of La Fontaine's in which the "referential function," producing a world of violence that is like ours in that it is a world without kingship, goes with a relation of "textual" to "narrative" functions in which the former stands as a negation of the latter while simultaneously appropriating it as the indispensable vehicle for (or mediation of) its own enactment of the powers, but also the conditions, of oppositional discourse.

4. Wolfishness, Lambishness, and Running Streams

The world of La Fontaine's well-known fable, "Le loup et l'agneau" (I, x—see any standard edition of the *Fables*), in which relationships must be negotiated in the absence of privileged sources of authority, is, then—by contrast with others of his fables—a recognizably modern one. We live in a wolfish world,[24] the fable indicates, one that makes us as vulnerable as the innocent lamb; *homo lupus homini* is the ancient wisdom that furnishes what Michael Riffaterre would call the "hypogram" of the text (the discourse to which, intertextually, it refers).[25] In such a world, wolves themselves feel as much victims as lambs, and La Fontaine's Wolf does indeed display resentment against the alliance of humans, dogs, and lambs he sees as his enemies: *agnus homo lupi is his* motto. Thus, a vendetta chain is put in place, in which humans attack wolves because wolves attack lambs because, in turn, they are victimized by "vous, vos bergers, et vos chiens," and universal wolfishness is the outcome.

Such a structure of violence is unleashed here because there is no recognized power figure—no king, wise hermit, or jurisprudential Raminagrobis—capable of breaking the chain of dispute, even (as often in La Fontaine) by superior predation: "His Majesty" is here a courtesy title (usurped from the Lion?) that the Wolf owes to his terrifying strength, like those flattering titles bestowed on modern dictators, although it is not clear whether the Lamb is being characteristically ingenuous in mistaking the Wolf for a king, or whether he is being uncharacteristically guileful in bestowing the inappropriate title. With no recourse to civil authority ("sans autre forme de procès," as the fable says), brute strength is what determines disputes, which is why the Lamb is silly not only to try to argue with the Wolf, but also to have strayed so far from its protectors (mother, sheepdogs, and shepherds). The question, however, is whether in such a world a third mode of behavior that would be neither wolfish brutality nor lambish silliness might not nevertheless be available.

Such a possibility is what the narrative apparatus indicates, by deploying a foregrounded "narrative function" that is subverted by a more covert "textual function" so as to produce irony. For irony, dependent as it is on a split between "narrative" and "textual" functions, is—as has already been pointed out—a function of *reading* (and in classrooms and elsewhere one still meets innocent readers who take this fable at face value, i.e., read in the position of narratee and exhaust the text in its "narrative function," so that the possibility of irony has to be pointed out to them). But, because it has a citational structure,[26] irony functions also to produce an unnamable, unlocatable, and invisible *sujet de l'énonciation* as undecidable "subject" of the act of citation. The invisible quotation marks around ironic discourse imply (but do not reveal) a "quoter" whose only manifestation is in the text itself, i.e., in the textual enactment of a reading situation. So it is the ironic reading of the narrative that here manifests the "textual function," or the "textual function" that enacts an ironic reading of the text.

LE LOUP ET L'AGNEAU

La raison du plus fort est toujours la meilleure:
    Nous l'allons montrer tout à l'heure.
    Un Agneau se désaltérait
    Dans le courant d'une onde pure.
Un Loup survient à jeun qui cherchait aventure,
    Et que la faim en ces lieux attirait.
Qui te rend si hardi de troubler mon breuvage?
    Dit cet animal plein de rage:
Tu seras châtié de ta témérité.
    —Sire, répond l'Agneau, que votre Majesté
    Ne se mette pas en colère;
    Mais plutôt qu'elle considère
    Que je me vas désaltérant
        Dans le courant,
    Plus de vingt pas au-dessous d'Elle,
    Et que par conséquent, en aucune façon,
    Je ne puis troubler sa boisson.
    —Tu la troubles, reprit cette bête cruelle,
Et je sais que de moi tu médis l'an passé.
    —Comment l'aurais-je fait si je n'étais pas né?
    Reprit l'Agneau, je tette encor ma mère.
        —Si ce n'est toi, c'est donc ton frère.
    —Je n'en ai point.—C'est donc quelqu'un des tiens:
    Car vous ne m'épargnez guère,
    Vous, vos bergers, et vos chiens.
On me l'a dit: il faut que je me venge.
    Là-dessus, au fond des forêts
    Le Loup l'emporte, et puis le mange,
    Sans autre forme de procès.

[THE WOLF AND THE LAMB

The reason of the stronger is always the best. We will show this straightaway. A Lamb was quenching his thirst in the current of a pure stream. A fasting Wolf arrives, in quest of adventure, and drawn to this spot by hunger. "What makes you so bold as to muddy my drink?" said this animal, full of rage: "You will be punished for your temerity." Sire, answers the Lamb, "may it please Your Majesty not to become angry; but rather let Him consider that I am quenching my thirst in the stream more than twenty paces below Him; and that as a result in no way can I muddy his drink." "You are muddying it," responded this cruel beast; "and I know you slandered me last year." "How could I have done so, if I wasn't yet born?" responded the Lamb, "I am not yet weaned." "If it wasn't you, then it was your brother." "I have no brother." "Then it was one of your clan: for you hardly let up on me, you, your Shepherds, and your Dogs. I was told about it; I must avenge myself." Thereupon deep into the woods the Wolf carries him off, and then eats him without standing any further on ceremony.][27]

The narrative "voice" of the fable clearly associates itself, from the first two lines, with the Wolf. Its assignment of ethical value to the position, not of power, but of strength (it is not that the reasoning of the strongest always prevails, but that it is "always *best*"), and its imperturbably dominant tone, its assumption of pedagogic authority, identify the narrative as on the side of strength. The "nous" of "nous l'allons montrer" is the usurped "royal" plural of pedagogical authority, whose function is more accurately "rhetorical": it mendaciously associates the addressee with what is planned in fact (and announced) as a demonstration, for which, properly speaking, only the "I" should take responsibility. (Cf. "as we will see later," and similar remarks in critical discourse.) So the resemblance with the Wolf does not arise solely from the narrator's strong assumption of authority, but also from a certain cynicism in the way the authority is exercised. It is not just that the Wolf's own cynicism (he is hungry but "cherchant aventure," as if he were a knight errant, rather than seeking prey—and he will suddenly become thirsty instead when a tasty Lamb is discovered drinking at the stream) is presented by the narrative without comment or judgment, and apparently even without so much as noticing it; the narrative voice has a cynicism of its own, which is readable initially in the equivocations of the opening lines. Does "la raison," in l. 1, mean *reasoning*, or does it mean "reasons" in the sense of *motivation*? The narrative is careful not to specify, although the difference is crucial. Does "montrer," in l. 2, mean *demonstrate* (which would imply a logical exposition) or is it closer to the idea of *indicate* (i.e., *tell* what is the case)? In each instance, what seems to be being said (the *reasoning* of the strongest is always best, as I am about, rationally, to *demonstrate*) is not what turns out to happen (for the narrator in fact *indicates*, merely by producing an example, that wolfish *motivations*—the needs of the strong—will not be denied). Clearly, one single case does not "demonstrate" that a proposition is universally ("toujours") true. In exactly similar fashion, the Wolf pretends to *demonstrate*, by *reasoning*, why the Lamb must be eaten—but his pretended demonstration is rather an *indication* of his *motivation*, the "reason" that impels him to eat the Lamb being nothing other than hunger.

So we ("we?") must ask, too, what motivation underlies the narrator's pretence of reasoning. The answer will derive from the observation that his discourse implies a *double* addressee or narratee, which can be called the "apparent" and the "actual" addressee (in other words, the discourse is mendacious in this respect as well) of the text's "narrative function." The apparent addressee is defined by the pedagogical tone: some innocent, young, inexperienced, lamb-like hearer is being educated as to the facts of real life. But what are the implications of this? The lambish addressee is not being taught how to become less vulnerable to the attacks of a wolfish world, but is only being told what does not work. It is no good arguing with the strong (as the Lamb so disastrously does), for in a wolfish world the reasons of the strong are "better" than those of the weak (it is better to be wolfish than lambish). Better to run away, perhaps (to be eaten another day)? . . . This doctrine, of course, is exactly what the wolves of the world most want lambs to hear; and the narrative's bland assumption of the Wolf's distorted logic, its espousal of a wolfish "ethics" suggest that what is being performed here is in actuality an *act of flattery* whose "actual" addressee is no innocent child but a Wolf—one of those whose "reasons" are always strongest, i.e., "best." Behind the lambish addressee, an approving wolfish addressee who "overhears" the address to the lamb, is implied, and the position of "strength" the narrator assumes with respect to the apparent narratee belies the *actual* position of weakness implied by the narrative's respect for the wolfish "actual" narratee, whom the address to the lambish narratee is intended to please. (There are unflattering implications here, of course, for educators in general: what we teach the young is acceptance of a wolfish world, and we do it by teaching wolfishly, because we need to "flatter" the world's wolves. . . .)

The narrator, in other words, is adopting a survival tactic, but one that is diametrically opposed to the Lamb's. Where the latter relies rather pathetically on genuinely logical demonstrations, and attempts to refute the Wolf's (pseudo-)reasonings, the former adopts discourse that flatters wolfishness, at once by its acceptance of wolfish cynicism, by its imitation of that cynicism in its own duplicity, and finally by producing (confirming) the lambish addressee in its role as prey. The "narrative function" reproduces a discourse of power. But behind the narrator's mendaciousness, then, we must read a *motivation* and one that turns out however to be diametrically opposed to that of the Wolf. Not "hunger," but "thirst"—the thirst to survive—animates the narrator, a motive that obviously associates this figure less with the Wolf whose mode of discourse he imitates, than with the Lamb whose motivation (and status as weakling) he shares, even though his survival tactics are more subtle and, one must assume, more successful. For any real reader who opts for the narratee position in reading this fable will thereby opt for the position of wolf and become the object of narrative flattery, hearing approvingly *only* what the wolfish want to hear (i.e., that in a wolfish world it is only normal, and therefore "good," for the strong to eat the weak), and failing to perceive that what this is, is flattery.

Read *otherwise*, however, the didactic narrator's shared motivation with the Lamb and the position of weakness from which he speaks is quite visible. It is visible not only in the successful mendaciousness and flattery of his discourse, but in certain "weaknesses" the flattery itself obliges him to display, or rather the vulnerability it forces him into. To make his point about the superiority of strength over logic, he is obliged to show his own knowledge of the basis in fact and logic of the Lamb's argument, and thus to betray a certain order of solidarity with the Lamb. In order to show the Wolf's cynicism (so as to endorse it), he is obliged to acknowledge, again, without apparently "noticing" them, a whole series of facts that are damaging indeed to the wolfish argument, and hence an impediment to the flatterer's project: the fact that the water is clear ("une onde pure") as the Lamb claims and the Wolf denies; the fact that the Lamb is downstream from the Wolf and so cannot be muddying the latter's drinking water; the fact that, being a spring lamb ("je tette encor ma mère"), it cannot have slandered the Wolf "l'an passé". . . . All these claims are never refuted by the Wolf (if he were to do so, he would cease to be wolfish and the dispute would become precisely a "forme de procès")—and as a result they stand as the acknowledged facts of the matter. In order to show that rights and wrongs are immaterial, the narrator must acknowledge the wrongness of the Wolf's stance, which leads him into contradiction of the wolfish ethics ("toujours la meilleure") he is supposedly recommending. It is in a lambish moral perspective that the Wolf can be described—as the narrator coolly does—as "plein de rage" (where the word has some of its etymological sense [>*rabies*] of raving, ravening, furor) and "bête cruelle," characterizations that scarcely accord with the flattering act we ("we"!) attributed a moment ago to the narrator.

Does this mean that the narrative "voice" is somehow inconsistent with itself? Not at all. It can only achieve its end (a flattering endorsement of cynicism) by acknowledging the logic that makes the cynicism cynical. But a reader is being invoked here by means of these contradictions, a reader who, unlike the reader who simply identifies as narratee-object of flattery, is able to perceive the narrator's difficult situation, obliged as he is by his own survival tactic to acknowledge his master's cruelty and rage in the very discourse that seeks to placate him through flattery. In short, the narrative *ironizes itself*; but the irony requires it to be read, not now *in* a position that would be identical with either of the narrative roles (narrator or narratee), but *from* a position that takes in the narrator-narratee relationship as a *relationship* and hence sees some of its implications.

No one, be it noted, is being asked (or if one will, "No One" is *not* being asked) to identify with lambishness: the stance of the Lamb is shown in the fable to be unrealistic and self-destructive, and the lambish addressee of the pedagogical narrative figures, again, only as an innocent pawn in (or victim of) a power game being played out between narrator and "actual" narratee. The Lamb is not a model of oppositional behavior, but of a predestined sacrificial victim. But, although the narrator offers a more successful oppositional model than the Lamb, his position is shown to be uncomfortably close to that of being a pawn of wolfishness, too. His survival technique, as flatterer and pedagogue, puts him too close to the wolfishness of the strong—as is demonstrated in particular by *his* sacrifice of the Lamb, as "apparent" addressee, to the interests of his own survival, which happen to be also the interests of the wolfish—to be a model of effective opposition. In particular, nothing in the power relationship of the wolfish and the lambish is *changed* by the narrator's successful survival tactic, which therefore qualifies as oppositional "behavior," but not as exercising the genuine educational effect—the potential for change—that characterizes effective textual opposition. In short, it is neither through the Lamb's (failed) standpoint and behavior, nor through the narrator's (successful) survival techniques that the text demonstrates effective oppositional values, but rather through its own textual enactment, in ironizing its own "narrative function" and showing its *reasons* for duplicity to be, albeit directly opposed to the Wolf's reasons for cynicism, productive of wolfish results and able to realize only wolfish objectives. It is in this sense that it both appropriates and negates the discourse of power represented in its own "narrative function."

I want to show that, in leading the reader to understand this, the text itself performs an oppositional act that is different in kind from that of the narrator, since it does not entail mendaciousness, cynicism, or flattery, although it certainly does proceed under cover of disguise and profits from a certain wolfish opacity of discourse (by contrast with lambish limpidity). Its educational force, unlike the narrator's pedagogy, resides in its textual enactment of a certain art of disguise, which serves as a demonstration having as its *actual* addressee the lambish, who can learn here an art of opposition less lupine than the narrator's out-and-out flattery. The name of this oppositional art is, of course, not flattery but irony.

If one takes the stream as a figure of "textual function," the fable itself requires us to ask a question: is the text stream limpid or muddy? The repeated collocation of the word "courant" with the verb *se désaltérer* (ll. 3–4 and 13–14) would suggest that if "thirst" is the sign of a need to oppose wolfish hunger, the textual stream may offer more oppositional satisfaction (or slaking of thirst) than the Lamb (who gets eaten instead of slaking his thirst) can achieve. It also suggests, not coincidentally, that textual opposition has something to do with *running* (Fr. *courir*)—but not running away (Fr. *se sauver*), and hence, perhaps, with a prominent characteristic of what is not coincidentally called "dis-course." In direct contrast to the silly Lamb's misguided attempt to stand and argue with the Wolf, the stream offers a model of perpetual running—of a constantly moving and elusive target—whose *current* makes it possible for water to be either clear or muddy and simultaneously introduces the upstream-downstream positions that raise the whole question of clarity or muddiness in the first place. Thus the stream figures a relationship between positions of power, on the one hand, and, on the other, the question of discursive readability. Of the stream, it is the Lamb who asserts that it is clear, a fact that the narrative has already acknowledged ("une onde pure"); and there is a sense, of course, in which the text too is transparent, i.e., to those readers who, taken in by its disguise, innocently adopt the narratee position. But such readers, wonderfully, are wolfish ones (who thereby demonstrate lamb-like innocence when it comes to reading texts). On the other hand, it is the Wolf in the fable who declares the stream to be muddy ("Tu la troubles"), and so the conclusion with respect to text must be that it is because of the strength of wolfishness that discourse, if it is to survive, had best *obey the decree*, and *be* muddy (that is opaque, difficult to read through, having "raisons" that are as duplicitously concealed as are the Wolf's own motivations). Note that the Wolf's assertion takes the form of throwing responsibility for muddiness onto the Lamb. Irony, in this reading, would be a muddying of textual appearances such that it corresponds symmetrically— and responds—to the "muddying" of discourse practised by the wolves of this world. Wolfish meretriciousness produces narrative mendaciousness, but it also *commands* textual irony, as the art of being limpid to some but muddy to others.

The muddiness of irony is clearly unlike the Lamb's reliance on the clarity and limpidity of logic, for although it makes use of that logic in achieving its own purposes, it has murkier depths. It is also unlike the duplicities deployed, wolfishly, both by the Wolf, as predator, and by the narrator, as survivalist, for oppositional irony *uses transparency as its disguise*, where they use opacity. Both the Wolf and the narrator imply an addressee or a narratee who *cannot see through* the murk of their discourse; but irony implies a reader who, precisely, *can* see beyond the apparent transparency to muddier "depths." Such a reader, unlike the wolfish reader who identifies with the narratee position, but also unlike the Lamb who stands and argues, is a reader capable of learning from the text an art of "running" that is not synonymous with flight. Since, precisely, the reasons of the strongest are—if not "toujours" the best—"toujours" operative, an art of running that is an art of *always* being running, as is the stream—an art of permanent elusiveness—is obviously preferable to running *away* (to be eaten another day). This, of course, is the art of irony, itself a function of textual readability.

That the need for oppositional muddiness is a response to the discursive world produced by wolfishness is—if the term is appropriate—clear from the Wolf's peremptory response to the Lamb's carefully logical demonstration that the water is pure.

> —Tu la troubles, reprit cette bête cruelle,
> Et je sais que de moi tu médis l'an passé.

Plain-speaking (genuine as opposed to deceptive limpidity) such as the Lamb's only opens one up to accusations of *médisance*, or slander, on the part of the wolfish, and so amounts to an act of suicide, since the wolfish can always make an accusation stick (their "reasons" being always "best"). In this case, guilt by association is the chosen method, a form of "justice" that perverts the justice of due process ("procès") exactly as wolfish reasoning perverts rationality. But it is to the many other duplicities at work at this point in the Wolf's discourse that I wish to point, since it is here, in the accusation of *médisance* that finally justifies the Wolf's eating of the Lamb, that his discourse becomes so genuinely muddy that one cannot tell whether his resentful accusation is cynical or genuinely meant (albeit mistaken). Is he lying when he says: "On me l'a dit?" His previous cynicism suggests it. On the other hand, he does have a *plausible* grievance (as opposed to his previous, quite implausible accusations) when he alleges that dogs, lambs, and shepherds are allied in order to "n'épargner guère" wolves, so his resentment, at least, is quite possibly genuine. And it is equally possible that he *has* been told that some lamb or other has spoken ill of him (and it would be not unlikely for a lamb to have mentioned to another lamb that wolves are dangerous). In that case, given his generalized resentment and perhaps the "racist" difficulty, for a wolf, of distinguishing one lamb from another (or indeed from shepherds and dogs), it would not particularly matter to the Wolf *which* lamb was the guilty individual. What is most characteristically wolfish, here, is of course the innocent reading that has led him to believe what he was (possibly) told—it has not occurred to him, obviously, that it is perhaps the *Lamb* who has been slandered in this report, which he has taken at face value (that is, without suspecting that it might have been a piece of "flattery"—telling him what he wanted to hear—on the part of someone trying to make up to the Wolf, or even save his/her own skin . . .).

Wolfish textual behavior, then, consists of reading flattering discourse as if it were transparent even though one's own discourse, to the contrary, is impenetrably muddied. For, whereas I have just rehearsed the reasons for thinking him genuine here, it is entirely possible, as initially noted, that he is only pretending to have received the report about the Lamb's *médisance*; or if he *has* received such a report, he may well be only pretending to have believed it, since after all that is what he needs to do in order to have an excuse (in his view, a "reason") to eat the Lamb. . . . This impenetrability in the Wolf's discourse, the impossibility it produces for a reader to pin down a definable, discursive subject, combined with the necessity to *read*—to attempt to penetrate the murky discourse—is, of course, the (counter)model, in the text, for its own deployment of the impenetrability of irony, which similarly produces a "subject" but produces the subject as elusive, indefinable, always "on the run" and impossible to pin down. Ironic "muddiness" is the way to elude the accusations of *médisance* that plain speaking inevitably draws and the consequences that follow when the lambs of this world oppose the wolves.

Taking its cue, then, from the discourse of the wolfish, the fable thus defines itself as following the only possible oppositional tactic, one that imitates neither the naive and self-destructive resistance of the misguided lamb, nor the ultimately wolfish duplicity of the narrator, but derives its power as opposition from the very *refusal to be pinned down* that characterizes the wolfish (the Wolf is a master at *shifting his ground*). The real moral of the fable is: do not *argue* with the wolfish, out-wolf them. For, instead of argument, or flattery (which either vainly resists or else ultimately serves the purpose of the wolfish) one can always turn the strength of the wolfish, that is, the duplicity they have produced in language, against them. All the discursive tricks of wolfishness are available, also, to lambs, provided only they are given the chance to speak. Whether oppositional irony be negative or appropriative with respect to the discourse of power—and it is clearly both—this fable teaches us to understand it as being made not only necessary but also possible by a duplicity that is, in the first instance, the mark of the discourse of power. Oppositionality exploits, for "other" purposes, the readability of discourse on which power itself rests.

2 Power and the Power to Oppose: Irony and its Ironies

In "Le loup et l'agneau," power is primarily a matter of force, or strength; and legitimizing institutions—or "formes de procès"—are mentioned only as something that is missing (or present as a perverted and cynical practice, such as the Wolf's "trial" of the Lamb). The fable foreshadows in this way worlds not of absolute, but of arbitrary power, such as we shall rediscover in the Hispano-American "dictator" novel. But La Fontaine's world is more characteristically a world of kingship, and it is the relationship of mutual dependency between the exercise of legitimate and acknowledged power and the practice of opposition that his fables tend largely to explore.

Power in this sense—the legitimization of force—depends on a stock-in-trade of laws, rules, and codes, of conventions and customs (in short, of institutions) that in turn produce all sorts of possibilities for oppositional maneuver. There are no laws without loopholes and special cases, no institutions without the possibility of deploying the power of one against the authority of another; and so prisons breed jailhouse lawyers, using the law against the processes of justice, students may sue a professor over a bad grade, workers can negotiate a medical certificate for a few days "off" from the assembly line. In short, power is necessarily a mediated phenomenon; and so it produces in the *means* of its legitimization the very instruments that can be used against it oppositionally—which means that, conversely, the practice of opposition is itself a function of power. Thus, under capitalism, as Paul Willis and Phillip Corrigan point out,[1] it is possible for the working class "to see formal discourses of control as sites of contestation," but equally for such proletarian cultural forms "to bring about the fundamental conditions for the reproduction and continuation of capitalism." The first law of oppositional behavior is, then, that the power to oppose derives from the power that it contests. As a result, one can easily think of the practice of opposition as one of the institutions of power itself. Outside of working class culture, it is clear for example that in modern societies the university functions as an authorized site of opposition; and literature is another socially legitimated institution that has opposition as (part of) its function.

In the France of Louis XIV, when all power was understood to have its source in and to be guaranteed by the central presence of the King, literature figured very clearly as one of the institutions of kingship; and royal "protection" was extended, not only to artists like Racine—whose work was seen as contributing to the "glory" of the court and the age and who was rewarded ultimately by the position of *historiographe* (i.e., eulogist) *du Roi*—but also to dissidents, or near dissidents, such as Molière. But where Molière's oppositional role was relatively overt and his status as the (necessary) "noise" in the system sometimes embarrassingly clear, it was La Fontaine's privilege to discern and to fulfil a more characteristically oppositional literary role, one that was, and is, discreet, disguised, and elusive—difficult to see and difficult to grasp when seen. The *Fables* can easily pass for entertaining "light" verse, infused perhaps with a disabused acceptance of the ways of the world. But read more suspiciously, as I propose to show, they begin to display oppositional values; and indeed a fable such as "Le milan, le roi et le chasseur" is readable as a disguised reflection on, and simultaneously an enactment of, exactly the institutionalized status of literary opposition and its dependency on kingship under the ancien régime.

For what this phenomenon of the institutionalization of opposition itself demonstrates, and the fable of "Le milan, le roi et le chasseur" confirms, is that, whereas the *establishment* of power may be a relatively straightforward matter of legitimizing and institutionalizing practices, the *practice* of power—its maintenance—is no simple matter at all. It involves some quite tricky manipulations and maneuverings, involving subtle and flexible judgments, together with some tolerance of paradox and the ability to compromise. Thus, power needs opposition, as one of the means by which it maintains itself; but it cannot allow opposition to evolve too far in the direction of resistance, becoming overly conscious of itself and hence tending to delegitimize the power structure. There are limits that have to be judged and set.

This was precisely the problem posed, in the France of Louis XIV, by Molière and his relatively overt challenging of power structures, in contradistinction to La Fontaine's more acceptable, because ironic and duplicitous, practice of oppositional discourse. La Fontaine's most prominent fascination seems rather to be with the *analysis of power*—the relationship of power to force, its means of legitimization, and the ruses and strategies to which it has recourse to maintain itself—so that his *Fables* appear in the first instance as a manual for those who would wield power, not oppose it. That has certainly been a dominant reading of them over the centuries.[2] But it happens that to know the strategies of power serves also the needs of opposition, whose tactics are entirely and exclusively determined by the nature of power and its practices, as the jailhouse lawyer demonstrates; so that La Fontaine's revelation of the workings of power turns out simultaneously, if less obviously, to have ironic relevance as an education in oppositional behavior. My reading of "Les femmes et le secret" will show how, in analyzing the workings of power, La Fontaine is simultaneously carrying out an oppositional programme—but a covert one only, not an act of open resistance or revolution, since the very conditions of its possibility lie in the power it is opposing.

That the power to oppose derives directly from the power that is being opposed will therefore be the keynote of this chapter, since it is the central feature of the theory of opposition that can be derived from La Fontaine's texts. But since, as we have already seen, their own oppositional status derives from their practice of irony, it follows that irony has ironies of its own; it is not as divorced from the structures of power as one might like to think. In the specific terms of oppositional narrative, the power to oppose is dependent, as I have already mentioned, on the power to narrate, a power far from evenly distributed in a society such as that of Louis XIV's France, in which the right of speech was itself the privilege of a few. But in addition to the power to narrate there is the power that derives from the act of narration itself; so that the *social* theory of oppositional authority is incomplete without the adjunction of a *rhetorical* theory that shows in what way and for what reason discourse is itself available as an agency of oppositional practice. The next fable I shall discuss, "Le pouvoir des fables" has been read, understandably and accurately enough, in terms of the relationship of rhetoric to the exercise of power; but it requires also a complementary reading that demonstrates the availability of discursive duplicity for the practice of opposition. Here, too, however, as in "Le loup et l'agneau," power and the power to oppose prove to share common ground; and in this fable specifically focussed on discourse it becomes inescapably apparent (a) that it is the very *means* whereby power is exercized that offer an opportunity and an agency for oppositional intervention so that (b) the oppositional must acknowledge in turn its own ironical dependency on the means of power.

The better to make its point about the nature of "pure" rhetoricity, "Le pouvoir des fables" presents a poet-figure—an inhabitant of Parnassus— whose relation to the social power structure is artificially, or disingenuously, occluded, as if Parnassus was not a fiefdom of Olympus. Similarly, in "Les femmes et le secret," the fact that the narrative's oppositional thrust derives from the privileges and power of men is implicit, albeit readable, in the fable. Only "Le milan, le roi et le chasseur," as a fable in praise of kingship, explicitly identifies the enabling conditions of opposition in the seat of power itself. Consequently, I shall order my discussion of these fables in a sequence that brings out increasingly the insight that the power to oppose is a function of power *tout court*.

1. The Power of Fable, or the Uses of Narrative

Louis Marin is surely right to describe narrative as a matter of setting traps, and right also to point by way of exemplification to La Fontaine's fable (VIII, iv) on the power of fables.[3] As his discussion shows, the story of an ancient Orator (it seems to be an anecdote about Demosthenes) who uses a fable to trap an indifferent crowd into giving him their attention forms part of the text's own attention-getting apparatus in its appeal to M. de Barrillon, Louis XIV's ambassador to London, to work for European peace. What I want to suggest, however, is that there are traps and traps, and that these two demonstrations of—to retranslate the title—the power of fable (the Orator's and the fabulist's) are not quite the same. In fact the fable suggests that it is worth distinguishing between two ways in which narrative power is available (between two kinds of narrative "traps," if one will, or better still between narrative "traps" and what I shall call oppositional "seduction"), depending on the situation with respect to power—by which I now mean "extra-narrative" power, historical, social, and political—of the storyteller.

LE POUVOIR DES FABLES
A M. De Barrillon

La qualité d'Ambassadeur
Peut-elle s'abaisser à des contes vulgaires?
Vous puis-je offrir mes vers et leurs grâces légères?
S'ils osent quelquefois prendre un air de grandeur,
Seront-ils point traités par vous de téméraires?
Vous avez bien d'autres affaires
A démêler que les débats
Du Lapin et de la Belette:
Lisez-les, ne les lisez pas;
Mais empêchez qu'on ne nous mette
Toute l'Europe sur les bras
Que de mille endroits de la terre
Il nous vienne des ennemis,
J'y consens; mais que l'Angleterre
Veuille que nos deux Rois se lassent d'être amis,
J'ai peine à digérer la chose.
N'est-il point encor temps que Louis se repose?
Quel autre Hercule enfin ne se trouverait las
De combattre cette Hydre? et faut-il qu'elle oppose
Une nouvelle tête aux efforts de son bras?
Si votre esprit plein de souplesse,
Par éloquence, et par adresse,
Peut adoucir les coeurs, et détourner ce coup,

Je vous sacrifierai cent moutons; c'est beaucoup
    Pour un habitant du Parnasse.
    Cependant faites-moi la grâce
    De prendre en don ce peu d'encens.
    Prenez en gré mes voeux ardents,
Et le récit en vers qu'ici je vous dédie.
    Son sujet vous convient; je n'en dirai pas plus:
    Sur les Éloges que l'envie
    Doit avouer qui vous sont dus,
    Vous ne voulez pas qu'on appuie.

Dans Athène autrefois peuple vain et léger
Un Orateur voyant sa patrie en danger,
Courut à la Tribune; et d'un art tyrannique,
Voulant forcer les coeurs dans une république,
Il parla fortement sur le commun salut.
On ne l'écoutait pas: l'Orateur recourut
    A ces figures violentes,
Qui savent exciter les âmes les plus lentes,
Il fit parler les morts; tonna, dit ce qu'il put,
Le vent emporta tout; personne ne s'émut.
    L'animal aux têtes frivoles,
Étant fait à ces traits, ne daignait l'écouter.
Tous regardaient ailleurs: il en vit s'arrêter
A des combats d'enfants, et point à ses paroles.
Que fit le harangueur? Il prit un autre tour.
«Cérès, commença-t-il, faisait voyage un jour
    Avec l'Anguille et l'Hirondelle.
Un fleuve les arrête; et l'Anguille en nageant,
    Comme l'Hirondelle en volant,
Le traversa bientôt.» L'assemblée à l'instant
Cria tout d'une voix: «Cérès, que fit-elle?
    —Ce qu'elle fit? un prompt courroux
    L'anima d'abord contre vous.
Quoi, de contes d'enfants son peuple s'embarrasse!
    Et du péril qui le menace
Lui seul entre les Grecs il néglige l'effet?
Que ne demandez-vous ce que Philippe fait?»
    A ce reproche l'assemblée,
    Par l'apologue réveillée,
    Se donne entière à l'Orateur:
    Un trait de Fable en eut l'honneur.
Nous sommes tous d'Athène en ce point; et moi-même,
Au moment que je fais cette moralité,
    Si peau d'âne m'était conté,
    J'y prendrais un plaisir extrême;

Le monde est vieux, dit on; je le crois, cependant
Il le faut amuser encore comme un enfant.

[THE POWER OF FABLE
To M. de Barrillon

Can Ambassadorial status stoop to hear common storytelling? Am I permitted
to offer you my verses with their light-hearted graces? If now and then they dare
take on an air of grandeur, will they not be dismissed by you as overweening? You
have many other matters to sort out than the debates of the Rabbit and the Weasel:
read them, don't read them; but do prevent the whole of Europe from being set
about our heels. That from a thousand places on earth enemies should come to us,
I can accept; but that England should wish our two Kings to weary of being friends,
is a thing I do find hard to digest. Is it not yet time for Louis to take some rest? Is
there another Hercules, after all, who would not weary from combatting this Hydra? And must it raise yet another head against the efforts of his arm? If by elo-
quence and skill your versatile wit can soften hearts and turn away this blow, I shall
sacrifice to you a hundred sheep; that's a lot for an inhabitant of Parnassus. But
please do graciously receive the gift of this small quantity of incense. Kindly accept
my ardent wishes, and the tale in verse I am hereby dedicating to you. Its subject
is an apposite one for you; that's all I shall say: you prefer people not to be heavy-
handed in the Praise that envy itself must admit is your due.

In Athens of yore, a frivolous and light-hearted people, an Orator seeing his
country in danger hastened to the Tribune; and with tyrannical art attempting to
force hearts in a republic, he spoke strongly on the common weal. They did not
listen: the Orator had recourse to the kind of violent figures of speech that are
capable of arousing the slowest souls, he had the dead speak, he thundered, said
what he could, but his words were wafted away on the wind; no one was stirred by
them. The animal with the many empty heads, being accustomed to these devices,
did not deign to listen. They were all looking somewhere else: the attention of
some, he saw, was fixed on some street-urchins fighting, and not on his words.
What did the tub-thumper do? He tried another tack. "Ceres," he began, "was
travelling one day with the Eel and the Swallow. A river stops them; and the Eel
soon swam, the Swallow soon flew across." Immediately the gathering cried out in
a single voice: "And what did *Ceres* do?"—"What did she do? Her quick anger
straightway arouses her ire against you. What, her people bother themselves with
children's stories! And they alone of all the Greeks neglect the consequences of the
peril that threatens them! Why not ask what Philip is doing?" At this reproach the
gathering, brought to its senses by the Fable, now gives itself over completely to
the Orator: the honor of this was due to a piece of Fiction. We're all Athenians on
that score; and I myself as I write this moral, were I to be told the tale of Donkey
Skin, would take extreme pleasure in it; it's an old, old world, they say; and so I
believe, but it still has to be amused like a child.]⁴

As Louis Marin noticed, trapsetting is certainly being posed here as a model
of storytelling. But the prime model, I think, is not so much the Athenian

orator as the unmentioned winner of the story of "les débats / Du Lapin et de la Belette," itself mentioned in a disarmingly offhand way by the fabulist in his dedication to M. de Barrillon ("Gageons," says Marin, "que Son Excellence relit la fable ici nommée" ["Let us wager that His Excellency will reread the fable so mentioned"]). Raminagrobis, in the fable of "Le chat, la belette, et le petit lapin" (VII, 15), uses a rhetorical device (a lie) to get his listeners' close attention:

> "Mes enfants, approchez,
> Approchez, je suis sourd, les ans en sont la cause."

["Come closer, my children, come closer, I am deaf, the years are the cause of it."]

—he feints, then, makes a show of weakness—then pounces, and proceeds to gobble them up. The Athenian narrator, too, after having tried coercive rhetoric ("art tyrannique . . . figures violentes"), resorts to "un autre tour"—another device from his bag of tricks—and feigns a weaker approach, via storytelling. But as soon as *his* hearers are caught (caught up in the tale), as they reveal by the question: "Et Cérès, que fit-elle?", he too suddenly pounces with his reproach and berates the crowd: it has been overmastered ("l'assemblée . . . se donne entière"), conquered by "un trait de Fable." Before they know it, one realizes, the indifferent Athenians will be at war with Philip of Macedon, as the Orator (not they) wanted. Raminagrobis strikes again.

But what of Louis XIV, suing for peace with the European alliance? If these models refer to him, their clear implication is that he is Raminagrobis III, speaking softly (for the moment [1677]) with a view to beguiling not only England, but Holland, Spain, and the Empire as well—but doing so the better to defeat them in the end (doubtless with a sudden pounce at an unexpected moment). As the King's *porte-parole*, the ambassador is a personification of the royal discourse in its current soft-spoken mode; but he is being used as a device in a strategic move. A political trap is indeed being set, or so at least the fable seems to imply.

Louis Marin shows in very convincing detail how the narrator of the fable similarly "traps" his *dédicataire*, M. de Barrillon, into giving attention to his message, the principal device employed being the promise of pleasure in the form of praise, if only the Ambassador will attend to the anecdote. In this reading, the dedication (occupying fully one-half of the text) sets the trap, and the fable proper springs it. The parallel between the narrator and the other trapsetters in the piece is more than plausible, as far as it goes. In particular the initial situations are similar: like the Cat facing the Rabbit and the Weasel, like the Orator facing the multi-headed crowd, "l'animal aux têtes frivoles," like Louis dealing with the Hydra of Europe, the fabulist's major problem is the number of his "adversaries," the weighty concerns that occupy the Ambassador's mind:

> Vous avez bien d'autres affaires
> A démêler que les débats
> Du Lapin et de la Belette.

The tactics he resorts to, notably his self-denigration ("La qualité d'Ambassadeur / Peut-elle s'abaisser aux contes vulgaires?"), his assertion of weakness concealing, as one realizes, an intention to wield the full "power of fable" when once the adversary has been duly trapped, present clear similarities with the tricks of the Cat, the Orator, and (doubtless) the King. *But* there are at least two major differences between the fabulist and the other trapsetters in the text.

Raminagrobis, the Orator, Louis, and M. de Barrillon himself are all figures who are in possession of a form of power independent of their tale-telling prowess. A magistrate combined with a priest ("saint homme de chat . . . arbitre expert"), the Cat has behind him the strength of two powerful institutions (it is this prestige that draws the two victims to him in the first place). The Athenian's power is that of the *official* orator, whose education in the devices of persuasion actually sets him at odds with the democratic principles of Athens ("voulant forcer les coeurs dans une république"). Louis's power is that of Hercules himself, the power of military might (I shall return to the implications of the mythic reference). M. de Barrillon's power, as the mere *porte-parole* of another and an incarnation of "souplesse . . . éloquence . . . adresse," is the least evident, but that is why the fable insists on his magnificence. And it does so, in a way highly significant for our purposes, by stressing the gulf between the ambassador's greatness and the truly lowly status of the fabulist. All these figures, then, are unlike the narrator in their possession of extra-narrative power: he, by contrast, has only his "contes vulgaires," his "vers et leurs grâces légères" (contrasting clearly with the Orator's "art tyrannique") on which to rely. Indeed, he has no status or identity independent of these—he is just, as he says, "un habitant du Parnasse," a shepherd whose "sheep" (l. 23) are metaphorically equivalent to his verses (l. 3).

The power figures, though, at the moment they have recourse to rhetorical traps, are in positions of *relative* weakness, it is true. The Cat faced with the two litigants, the Orator unable to make headway against the crowd's "frivolity," Louis and his Ambassador faced with the prospect of having "toute l'Europe . . . sur nos bras," all have more to deal with than their sheer strength alone can quite manage. "Quel Hercule enfin ne se trouverait las / De combattre cette Hydre?" asks the fabulist of Louis. But they *all* resemble Hercules in his fight with the proliferating heads of the Hydra of Lerna, for

the myth tells us that it was in such circumstances that the hero was obliged
to accept the aid of his humble charioteer (who cauterized the wounds as the
heads were struck off, preventing the growth of new ones). So it seems that
the trap is being proposed as the model of narrative rhetoric for those who
are strong, but whose strength needs temporary and supplementary reinforcement when faced with a difficult and multifarious adversary. This imagery puts rhetorical strategies in the position of a mere subservient auxiliary
(something like a charioteer or a royal ambassador, in fact) with respect to
the exercise of those forms of power that are associated with (extra-narrative) authority. The "habitant du Parnasse," on the other hand, has no other
power whatsoever except that which derives from his (narrative) powers of
persuasion.

The second difference between him and the more powerful trapsetters concerns intentions and outcomes. Raminagrobis sets his trap, then pounces and
settles the difference between the litigants "en croquant l'un et l'autre" ["by
crunching them both up"]. The Orator too lays his trap, then pounces and
leads the Athenians into war. Louis and M. de Barrillon may be strongly
suspected of having similar intentions, suing for peace as a move in the power
politics of Europe. But the fabulist genuinely wants peace, and he wants it as
an end in itself. For it is peace, not war, that makes life secure for a shepherd
on the slopes of Parnassus, and—excluded as he is from the politics of
power—he can have absolutely nothing to gain by duplicity about his motives
in this. The appeal to M. de Barrillon to bring about peace—

> Si votre esprit plein de souplesse,
> Par éloquence et par adresse,
> Peut adoucir les coeurs, et détourner ce coup,
> Je vous sacrifierai cent moutons . . .

—is not in itself a device or trick; there is no reason to suspect its sincerity.

The fabulist's motives then, can be described as "oppositional," if by oppositional one understands the preference of an individual for self-preservation
and self-interest in circumstances where these are put at risk by the power
ploys of the great; he needs peace, they want war. In this respect, he has
something in common with the Athenian crowd, a "peuple vain et léger" (cf.
the fabulist's self-identification with "grâces légères") uninterested in politics
and war and more concerned with entertaining themselves with children's
fights and what the Orator scornfully calls "contes d'enfants" than they are
with the matters of high concern he has to trick them into attending to. But,
unlike the Athenians and the other victims of rhetorical trapsetters, the fabulist is not just a passive victim; he has means at his disposal for achieving his
own ends, in spite of those whose goals he does not share.

What he does share, or seems to share, with the powerful is precisely these means, a certain duplicitous control of discourse. Louis Marin is correct; the fabulist lays a trap. But he lays his trap in the interests of peace, and the trap does not work in quite the same way as the other rhetorical traps we have looked at. Indeed, it cannot, for the fabulist has no other power to which to have recourse than the "power of fable." So, unlike the Orator, he does not interrupt his discourse in order to pounce; on the contrary *he pursues his story to its end*. He is not in the business of deceiving rhetorically so as to win on another terrain altogether; he wishes to gain his own (oppositional) ends, certainly, but he does it, not by arousing hopes and desires that are to be cruelly dashed, but through the *satisfaction* of narrative desires. So pleasure is his byword, for it is pleasure which, for him, equates with the power of fable:

> Au moment que je fais cette moralité,
> Si peau d'âne m'était conté,
> J'y prendrais un plaisir extrême.

And he rightly points out that "nous sommes tous d'Athène en ce point," for it is the Ambassador's interest in receiving pleasure from a narrative, just as the Athenians do, that he is exploiting in his own storytelling. However, this pleasure (the Ambassador's) is not the pure, unmixed pleasure the reference at the end of the fable to fairy stories and children would seem to suggest; for—even though narrative-for-pleasure contrasts with narrative-as-trap-setting—the fabulist's storytelling is entirely manipulative and it remains closely and intimately bound up with political aims, motivations, and actions. It is just that the politics are now oppositional.

Oppositional practices, in Michel de Certeau's formulation,[5] are a matter of tactics as opposed to strategies. Strategy, as we have noted, is the privilege of those who are masters of the terrain of action; tactics the resource of those who must take advantage of momentary circumstances and chance opportunities to further their ends. The ground rules are defined by those who have power; the less powerful and the powerless must work within the situation thus defined and develop an art which is the art of inhabiting a space possessed by the other. Thus, the La Fontaine fable works by promising M. de Barrillon pleasure and by delivering that pleasure; and it is in this satisfaction of its own promise that it distinguishes itself from the traps of the powerful, which may promise, but deliver something radically different from what they seemed to promise. And the pleasure the narrative delivers is of a kind determined exclusively by the needs and desires of the great: it is the pleasure of praise ("éloge") which, in the figurative system of the text, constitutes the incense burned by the "habitant du Parnasse" in exchange for peace—an incense furnished by the sacrifice of one hundred sheep which themselves, as we have said, serve as metaphors for "mes vers." All the subtlety consists of hinting in the dedication that the subject of the story will be a form of praise, so that the Ambassador, his desire for incense aroused, will go ahead and read the tale.

For this tale, unlike the Athenian orator's, is *complete*, and it yields a *meaning*. Louis Marin shows in detail why the interrupted Athenian fable is uninterpretable; but the French fable about the interruption of the Athenian tale is readily interpreted, and its message tells M. de Barrillon that rhetorical "souplesse . . . éloquence . . . adresse" such as he is called upon to display at the English court is part of the exercise of noble (power) politics and consequently counts as an *honorable* activity. (The word "honneur" associated with "un trait de Fable" at the end of the anecdote is symmetrical with the word "qualité" associated with "Ambassadeur" at the beginning of the dedication.) The flattery (for that is the name for self-interested praise giving) takes the form of reassurance to an individual whose status, in terms of power, is actually quite dubious (he is playing the charioteer to Louis's Hercules) and whose prestige, in terms of honor (he is called upon to exercise trickery, not heroism) is equally questionable. His "pleasure" in reading of the precedent furnished by the Athenian can readily be imagined. Like the wolfish "actual narratee" I identified in "Le loup et l'agneau," he is being told exactly what he wishes to hear.

The other way in which the fabulist demonstrates the opportunism of oppositional politics is this, that the "lesson" so wrapped up in flattery is a lesson in the (power) politics of traps. As such, it appeals to M. de Barrillon as the agent of Louis XIV's military strategies—but it is offered with a view to bringing about the genuine peace the "habitant du Parnasse" craves. In this, as in the previous case, the trick consists of identifying the desire of the *other* (on the one hand, M. de Barrillon's need for reassurance as to the honorability of his function, and on the other his need for encouragement as a practitioner of rhetorical trap setting), and of satisfying this desire while simultaneously harnessing it to the accomplishment of one's own personal ends. Such a practice is certainly no less duplicitous, no less politically impure, than the trap setting in which power figures indulge—but it is an ironic skill and its name is not trap setting but seduction. Its most prominent feature is that it is through the satisfaction of the other's desire that one simultaneously achieves one's own ends. Like the skilled wrestler, the oppositional narrator *turns* the opponent's strength in his own favor. The situation is one in which the desire of the narratee is satisfied through the selfsame discourse that meets the textual subject's own needs. This, then, is the form of narrative "trap" which is at the disposal of those who do not enjoy extranarrative power; and it can be seen, of course, as a model of *all* storytelling (i.e., all storytelling is oppositional) to the extent that storytelling situations can be described in purely narrative terms. For the desire to narrate must always succeed in accommodating itself, as its prime enabling condition, to the listener's desire to hear.

Louis Marin imagines M. de Barrillon rereading "Le chat, la belette et le petit lapin." One must wonder why he does not, symmetrically, suppose him to go off and reread "Peau d'Ane," a story which after all is recommended in unmistakably more enthusiastic terms than the fable. The oversight in Marin's analysis betrays, I think, an unexamined but accurate intuition: Raminagrobis, the sleek hypocrite ("un chat faisant la chatemitte"), is the Ambassador's rhetorical model, not poor little powerless Donkey Skin, who on the contrary is that of the fabulist himself. It is for the "general reader" of the fable, as opposed to its *dédicataire*, to read and reflect on the fairy story—for the recipient of a dedication is not the sole reader of a published text and should not be mistaken for a figure of textual address. Such a figure functions somewhat like the addressee of what is called an "open letter," whose name and known status "key" the reading of the text by the general public for whom it is intended. Rather than reading this fable as if in M. de Barrillon's shoes, the reader must, on the contrary, view its address to M. de Barrillon, not as the communicational act it is *performing*, but as the communicational act it is *representing* and inviting us to understand.[6] Such a reader cannot fail to ask the question: what, then, does the narrator's recommendation of the Donkey Skin story, at the moment of formulating his general conclusion in a *moralité*, have to tell *us*?

An answer is made difficult by the fact that there are so many widely differing versions, both popular and literary, of the tale. Of the literary versions, Perrault's (the most celebrated today) was unpublished in 1677 (which does not mean it was necessarily unavailable to La Fontaine and his contemporary readership); but the version then attributed to Bonaventure Des Périers was widely known.[7] I will hazard a speculation that the lower-case typography of the words "peau d'âne" in the fable signals a generalized reference to a generic figure, and interpret this, in turn, as a way of stressing the pure, "childish" pleasure of storytelling, a pleasure presented here, so to speak, as the raw material of all narrative traps. But the fable as a whole is about the *uses* of narrative pleasure; and what the "Donkey Skin" stories seem to have in common, across wide differences in their affabulation, is a pervading theme which is that of "opposition" to authority, and more specifically a form of opposition which consists of getting one's own way through apparent submission to the (desire of the) other.

A victim of the incestuous desires of her royal father, Perrault's princess-become-slave finally marries her prince; opposed by her mother, Des Périers's Pernette finally marries the gentleman's son she loves. The submissiveness of this oppositional character typically takes the form of accepting oppressive conditions and turning them to advantage. Perrault's heroine plays along with her father for a time (but must finally flee), Des Périers's, told by her mother she can marry her beloved only if she uses her tongue to pick up, grain by grain, a bushel of spilled barley—told, that is, that she cannot marry him—proceeds to fulfill the conditions (with the aid of some friendly ants) and to turn the interdiction into the means of her success. In the context of La Fontaine's fable, these performances, and especially that of Pernette (to whom it seems most specifically to refer—those ants are very La Fontainean!) function as metaphors of the no less paradoxical achievements of oppositional narrative, condemned as it is to getting its way through the satisfaction of desires that are actually oppressive to it. Such success, one might think, cannot be achieved without fairy assistance, the narrative equivalent of Perrault's fairy godmother or of those helpful little insects in Des Périers. But what, then, is the "pure" and irresistible pleasure provided by narrative, its appeal to the "child" in everyone, great or small, if it is not this element of unhoped for, miraculous assistance made available to the relatively powerless of the earth in their struggle against the depredations of the powerful?

To a modern reader, dissatisfied perhaps with the idealism or obscurantism of this solution and tempted to look for less "magical" accounts of the conditions of success of oppositional narrative, the idea of an inherent doubleness—due to mediation as the twofold "input" from emitter and receiver—in communicational situations, and of a consequent duplicity of narrative discourse itself, may be helpful. As previously mentioned, the etymology of the Romance verbs for *to speak* is interesting, because it suggests that historically there has been in the linguistic consciousness the sense of a link between speech and figurality or fictiveness, each of which implies (in a "logocentric" framework) a duality between what is said and what is intended. *Hablar* derives from *fabulare*, itself a derivative of *fari*, to speak: *parler* (and *parlare*) come from *parabolare*, ultimately from Greek *parabole*, a comparison (lit. a throwing beside). The descendants of *fabulare* and *parabolare*, at certain times and in certain regions of the Romance domain, must have been close neighbors and in close competition; and the semantic affinity of the "fable" and the "parable"—each teaches a lesson by means of an arrant fiction—is striking to this day (La Fontaine's text throws in another synonym with the word "apologue" in l. 62, which etymologically means "away from the word"). All this suggests that there is some fissure (sometimes imperceptible, sometimes gaping), not exactly between what is said (for the other) and what is meant or intended (for oneself)—for who shall determine "what is said" and "what is meant?"—but resulting from the necessarily dual understanding of human discourse that derives from its status as an agent of mediation. Such a split or fissure is in other words, *constitutive* of communication situations in general.

One is tempted, therefore, to adapt to the *fable* the suggestive account of the biblical *parable* proposed by René Girard, anxious as he is to account for the troubling fact that Christ, in his parables, speaks a language of collective violence (e.g., the casting out of devils), even though—as the supreme scapegoat himself—his intended message, according to Girard, is an oppositional one that demystifies this "mythic" reliance on exclusionary violence:

Open your Greek dictionary at *paraballo* [sic]. . . . *Paraballo* means to throw a sop to the crowd to appease its appetite for violence, preferably a victim, a man condemned to death; that is the way to extract oneself from a thorny situation, obviously. The reason the orator resorts to parable, that is to say metaphor, is to prevent the mob from turning against him. There is no discourse that is not parabolic. . . . (My translation.)[8]

Girard goes on to add (271) that "it would be inaccurate to conclude from this that parable does not have as its goal the conversion of its audience." His conception, then, is of an "oppositional" discourse designed to protect the speaker by adopting the language of the oppressor while nevertheless converting its hearers to a nonviolent cause. The argument is at best schematic and it takes the form of unsupported affirmations, but it does seem to confirm what has emerged for us from La Fontaine's fable. La Fontaine, I think, is not suggesting the possibility of any true "conversion" of the powerful, and his ambitions are something less than Christ-like; but his text proposes that a fable may speak the language of traps and of power in order to *turn* the strength of its hearers to the advantage of those, such as the poet, who are weaker.

Girard also enables us to see what may be the common function of rhetorical duplicity—the adoption of the language of the other for purposes of one's own—in the discursive practices of both the nonpowerful and (when they are at some disadvantage) the powerful. For Girard's analysis of Christ's "oppositional" situation and of his use of the parable as a sop to Cerberus is strikingly superimposable on the situation of La Fontaine's powerful Athenian, faced with a crowd whose lack of sympathy for his political message is evident in its indifference, and whose language (the language of entertainment and frivolity) he adopts in order, first to save himself from the threat of (rhetorical) extinction, and then to promote his own political aims.

It follows from this that the "power of fables," deriving from the constitutive duplicity of speech, is available to all who enjoy the right to speak. Whether such duplicity functions as a "trap" or as a "seduction" will depend on situational, i.e., extranarrative, circumstances, the situation of the speaker with respect to power and consequently the social, historical, and political motivation that prompts the narrative act. But conversely, whether or not a given narrative is traplike or seductive in its function—an instrument of power or an agent of opposition—should be readable in the narrative itself, as a function precisely of the degree of *respect* it accords its hearer (this function being understood here as one that can be construed from the narrative discourse as it accommodates itself to the hearer's supposed desires and "pleasure").

Thus, the elaborate precautions with which the fabulist addresses his *dédicataire*, M. de Barrillon, contrast markedly with the Athenian's contempt for his audience, readable in the totally meaningless tale he embarks on as well as in his willingness to interrupt it once his aim of getting attention has been achieved. The oppositional narrative (this is a law) is one that is always aware of the possibility of its own failure because, in the first instance, it must address a more powerful other whose attention or inattention, like M. de Barrillon's, means life or death for the narrative, and who must consequently be accorded full respect. Its rule is to spin out the pleasure (of the other), because that is the condition of its own existence, and the only means available to it of achieving its own purposes. By contrast, the "powerful" narrative can be interrupted *at the pleasure of its narrator*, as the Athenian demonstrates, because it does not depend on satisfying the desires of the other, but only on arousing them.[9]

We can now appreciate the ambiguity, and indeed the irony, in La Fontaine's concluding couplet, which has a message for the powerful but an oppositional implication as well:

> Le monde est vieux, dit-on; je le crois, cependant
> Il le faut amuser encore comme un enfant.

The "infant" is, in a sense, the only appropriate audience for "fables" because the child (*in-fans*, again from *fari*) does not have the power of speech. Successful narration, in exercising its power of fabulation, always reduces its other to silence, and hence to powerlessness, to the extent that it exerts its own "sway" by appealing to the desire of the other. But much depends on whether, here, one lays stress on the verb "amuser" or on the adverbial phrase "comme un enfant." "Comme un enfant" (picking up the Athenian's scorn for the audience he accuses of being childlike) encapsulates the fable's message to the powerful: treat your adversaries like powerless children, trick them with stories (then pounce). But "amuser"—that is what the fabulist does, and what the reader sees him doing, to M. de Barrillon.

For there is a trivial sense in which "amuser" means to occupy someone with trifles (and indeed the Ambassador is assumed to take an interest, in spite of his pressing affairs, in the fabulist's "contes vulgaires," his "vers et leurs grâces légères"). But more appositely, the verb has—and had very prominently in the seventeenth century—a sense implying duplicity. "Amuser" in this sense involves diversionary tactics and the raising of false hopes with a view to achieving some other end; and this sense hints strongly, not only at the duplicities of power, but also at the essence of oppositional practice, as the *turning* of power, the recruitment of the other's desire. For a final, rather submerged, sense of the verb is its etymological one of "faire muser," where *muser* ("rester le museau en l'air," cf. "rester bouche bée") implies loss of (self-)control, loss of power (in this case to the narrator of the story): musing, in this sense—like the pensiveness of certain characters at the end of Balzac's stories—is a symptom of the duplicitous narrative's ability to convert its hearer to concerns of its own. But, in whatever sense, to amuse a child is an interpersonal act, involving some respect for (and understanding of) a child's taste and interests. Similarly, the great can be *amused* like children—but only on condition they are accorded a full measure of respect and their desires satisfied. Such, spelled out very artificially, is the oppositional message of the final lines.

The ambiguous readability of the moral is, of course, a function of the fable's own duplicity, or what I referred to earlier (see the Introduction) as the skill it employs (its *adresse*) in the manipulation of "address." Through its *dédicataire*, M. de Barrillon, it addresses an audience of the powerful; but through its positioning of the *dédicataire* as the object of its own tactics of amusement, it proposes a message readable, as an enactment of oppositional rhetoric, by the less-than-powerful to whom, by publication, it is available. One of the functions of the lengthy dedication is to serve as a screen for this oppositional function; by defining so blatantly an audience of the powerful, the fable preserves its oppositional status from the eyes of all but a scrupulously alert—and sympathetic—readership.

If this is the case, then Louis Marin, in reading the fable as an exemplification of trap setting while failing to perceive its oppositional relevance, can be counted as one of the victims of the text's duplicity. Oppositional practice, as we know, tends to work in disguise and to enjoy a paradoxical invisibility; and critics who would perceive and understand the oppositional force of narrative must of necessity begin by dissociating themselves from the position of power—in this case, the identification with M. de Barrillon as narratee and object of seduction—into which the text so actively seeks to lead them. A more patient apprenticeship and more sensitive attention are necessary if one wishes to catch some slight glimpse of what the fable works so hard to obscure.

One's reward is then an insight into the significance of this obfuscation itself. Where "Le loup et l'agneau" shows the murkiness of textual irony to derive, as a necessary response, from the duplicitous discourse of the powerful, it is the seductive manipulations of storytelling that become readable here no less ironically as both deriving from and opposing the trap setting of the mighty. That it is necessary to "amuser [le monde] (. . .) comme un enfant" is a lesson useful to the powerful, but usable also *against* them, by those who feel the need to protect themselves from unscrupulous exploiters of *le pouvoir des fables*. This second understanding is available, however, only to those who are unwilling to be tricked, seduced, into paying exclusive attention to the first, and able as a consequence to penetrate beyond the "narrative function" to a readable "textual function."

Something quite similar, we shall see, is at work in "Les femmes et le secret" (VIII, vi), an "histoire gauloise" that turns out, in its "textual function," to be readable as enacting an uncovering of the oppressive and sexist ideology that underlies the tradition of "broad" humor that is called *gauloiserie*. But where irony, in "Le loup et l'agneau," appears as a response to the duplicities of wolfish discourse; and where narrative seduction, in "Le pouvoir des fables," is ironically revealed as an oppositional counterploy to the trap setting of the powerful, this new fable will permit us to achieve a higher degree of generalization. For it identifies *secrecy* as the fundamental instrument of power and no less fundamentally determines, as its oppositional counterpart, the various forms of "disguise"—textual obscurity, irony, narrative seduction, readability, etc.—we have begun to explore. Power consists not only of using the means of power, but also of concealing power's reliance on means; and oppositionality therefore demonstrates its knowledge of power's secret in its symmetrical recourse to those means—the duplicities of discourse as a mediated phenomenon—for its own purposes. To be oppositional is also to be *in the secret* of power.

Consequently, we will see that "Les femmes et le secret," by its "on-behalf-of" status with respect to the women *for whom* it speaks, betrays very tellingly its own ambiguous position with respect to the discourse of (male) power, which it ironizes, but from which women are excluded. For to be in the secret of that power, if only to the extent of learning from it the *modus operandi* of power so that those modes can be used to oppose power, and even if for the very purposes of revealing the power of secrecy and the secrecy of power, is to demonstrate that opposition itself has its complicities with power, and so is itself an exercise of power. "Les femmes et le secret" would not, could not, exist as an oppositional text, contesting chauvinist ideology, if it were not itself *in the secret* of patriarchal power, as a "trick" played on women. So it is not just that oppositional discourse, as a practice of irony, is dependent on the powerful discourse it mimes and which serves as its "disguise." There is also the irony of such irony, which is that of its condition of possibility: it necessarily participates in the power structure that it can oppose only because it is, precisely, initiated into that structure, and so part of its functioning.

2. The Story of an Egg

LES FEMMES ET LE SECRET

Rien ne pèse tant qu'un secret;
Le porter loin est difficile aux Dames:
Et je sais même sur ce fait
Bon nombre d'hommes qui sont femmes.

Pour éprouver la sienne un mari s'écria
La nuit étant près d'elle: "O dieux! qu'est-ce cela?
  Je n'en puis plus; on me déchire;
Quoi! j'accouche d'un oeuf!—D'un oeuf!—Oui, le voilà
Frais et nouveau pondu: gardez bien de le dire:
On m'appellerait poule. Enfin n'en parlez pas."
    La femme neuve sur ce cas,
    Ainsi que sur mainte autre affaire,
Crut la chose, et promit ses grands dieux de se taire.
    Mais ce serment s'évanouit
    Avec les ombres de la nuit.
    L'épouse indiscrète et peu fine,
Sort du lit quand le jour fut à peine levé:
    Et de courir chez sa voisine.
"Ma commère, dit-elle, un cas est arrivé:
N'en dites rien surtout, car vous me feriez battre.
Mon mari vient de pondre un oeuf gros comme quatre.
    Au nom de Dieu gardez-vous bien
    D'aller publier ce mystère.
—Vous moquez-vous? dit l'autre. Ah, vous ne savez guère
    Quelle je suis. Allez, ne craignez rien."
La femme du pondeur s'en retourne chez elle.
L'autre grille déjà de conter la nouvelle:
Elle va la répandre en plus de dix endroits.
    Au lieu d'un oeuf elle en dit trois.
Ce n'est pas encor tout, car un autre commère
En dit quatre, et raconte à l'oreille le fait.
    Précaution peu nécessaire,
    Car ce n'était plus un secret.
Comme le nombre d'oeufs, grâce à la renommée,
    De bouche en bouche allait croissant,
    Avant la fin de la journée
    Ils se montaient à plus d'un cent.

[WOMEN AND SECRECY

Nothing weighs so heavy as a secret; to carry one far is a difficult feat for Ladies; and indeed in this connection I know quite a few men who are women.

To test his wife a husband cried out one night, lying at her side: "Ye Gods! What is this? I cannot endure it; I am being torn apart; What! I am giving birth to an egg!"—"An egg?"—"Yes, here it is, fresh and new laid; take care not to talk of it: I would be called a hen. In short, not a word." The wife, new to this kind of thing, as to many another affair, believed it, and swore to the gods to keep silence. But her oath vanished with the shades of night. The indiscreet and none too bright spouse left her bed when day had scarce dawned: and off she ran to a neighbor's house. "Gossip dear," says she, "a strange thing has happened: whatever you do say nothing about it, or you would get me beaten. My husband has just laid an egg as big as four eggs put together. In God's name take care not to go publishing this mystery."—"Are you joking?" says the other. "Ah, you have not much of an idea of the kind of person I am. Go, and fear not." The egg-layer's wife returned home. The other was already burning to tell the news: she spreads it in more than ten places. Instead of one egg she said three. And that is not all, for another gossip said four, whispering the tale in people's ears, an unnecessary precaution, for by now it was no secret. As the number of eggs, through the operation of fame, got increasingly larger from mouth to mouth, by the end of the day the total had reached five score and more.]

If one imagines a secret to be that which is *not known*, then there are no real secrets but only secrecy, for it is divulgence—that is, discursive realization—that makes a secret. Obviously, the secret need not be *actually* divulged; but I cannot say "I have a secret, I won't tell it to anyone," unless I have previously thought "I *could* tell it to someone." It is only the shared secret, however, that achieves full reality and performs the true function of secrecy, which is not private and personal, but public and social. I mean that the sharing of a secret defines social groups by the simple criterion of inclusion or exclusion: there are those who are "in" the secret and those who aren't, or to complexify, those who know the secret, those who know there is a secret but are not permitted to share it, and those who are ignorant both of the existence of the secret and of its content. In this way, secrecy has obvious links with the distribution of power, since those who are *in possession* (of the secret, and of power) are in a position to use for their own purposes the desire to know (in those who know they are excluded from the secret) or else (in the case of the ignorant) to perpetrate all kinds of mystifications.

But the secret of secrets, the secret which it is most vital to know, is therefore that there are no secrets but only secrecy. In initiation rites, the candidates frequently discover the triviality of the alleged mysteries they are being inducted into, and sometimes they learn that the mysteries are more accurately a mystification, the point being to *exclude* women and children by secrecy, and hence define the "men," rather than to make available information of a transcendent or even indispensable kind.[10] But initiation is only a special case. Generally speaking, there are no secrets because a secret exists only as discourse, and the discourse which "realizes" the secret is that which destroys it as a "secret" (as something unspoken). In this sense I spoke of secrecy as a language which constitutes and defines, by inclusion, the "in" group while identifying by exclusion those "others" who do not belong. This means that, being a public phenomenon, a secret is the opposite of what one imagines. It is not a blank or a zero (zero information, zero communication) unavailable for investigation; it is an *egg*, a palpable object which can be examined and studied. But it follows, as in La Fontaine's fable, that there are those who are in the secret about secrecy and who know that there are no secrets that are not eggs, and others for whom the egg is a deceptive object, since they see it as a true secret.

But—still according to La Fontaine—the secret is an egg also because, as speech, it contains within itself a certain power of growth: since it exists only through being communicated to others, it is capable of initiating an infinitely expanding discursive process, and thus of giving rise to a whole community of sharers of the secret, grouped around a nucleus (the "secret") which, as such, has no existence whatsoever. Word spreads "de bouche en bouche" (l. 35) and, independently of truth or falsity, the original egg becomes "plus d'un cent" (l. 37). But falsity, as we know, is of the essence, both for those who, being aware of the nature of secrecy, know that a secret is not a secret but an egg (the opposite of itself), and (more especially) for those who mistake the egg for the true secret. This fact—that falsity is consequently a characteristic of all exchanges of "secret" information—is what the fable indicates by the process of exaggeration which accompanies the spread of the story: the original egg is soon "gros comme quatre" (l. 21), then it is three (l. 29), then four eggs (l. 31) before becoming "plus d'un cent." In short, the multiplication of the number of people who are in on the secret produces a corresponding degree of falsity in the information involved, so that the people are less and less the sharers of the "same" secret; and the egg thus comes to figure the galloping fictionality of all language.

For this reason there is a close kinship between secrecy on the one hand and, on the other, that discursive and social phenomenon *par excellence*, that feast of fictionality which is called gossip. I am not sure that the functionality of gossip, as a means of testing circuits of communication and maintaining group structures, has been fully recognized. Its informational unreliability being commonly acknowledged, it serves of course as a scapegoating mechanism (the object of gossip being by definition excluded from the discourse group, and such an object of scandal being necessary, as René Girard has abundantly demonstrated, to the health of social groups),[11] but it serves also to activate and employ—*à vide*, so to speak, or at least in a nontragic way— the channels of circulation which ensure the cohesion and identity of a given group. Through gossip, the scapegoat is expelled, not only in an eminently symbolic way but in a way which is frequently recognized as such; however the unity of the group is nevertheless confirmed and strengthened. Is there a social group in which gossip does not occur, and in which the practice is not at the same time condemned? This universality suggests the usefulness of the phenomenon, but our uneasiness over the uncontrolled propagation of false information is a sign that we are vaguely aware of the symbolic function it performs. Why would one promise to keep a supposed scandal to oneself, unless one was aware that in spreading it one was committing an injustice? But why should one spread it, then, unless it be that such an act of injustice is required by some social necessity? In La Fontaine's village, it is clear in any case that the group of "commères" is formed, not simply around the shared secret of the egg, but also, per medium of gossip, around the scandalous object that is the husband as monster, half man and half hen, excluded as the referent of female speech from their community.

At this point, however, it becomes necessary to ask who is the real victim of the practice of gossip. Reading the fable as an exemplification of the shared secret as discourse, we entered the text via its conclusion (informational falsity as the means whereby gossip constitutes a community through inclusion and exclusion). If one enters via the beginning, as the hen-man invites us to (as a manifestation of the theme stated in the moral of "hommes qui sont femmes," l. 4), then it is not so much the secret as discourse which engages our attention as the performative aspects of secrecy as a social "pact." A secret is a performative in the sense that only the act of telling it turns the content of the words into a "mystère" (l. 24), and this by virtue of a set of shared conventions between teller and tellee which produce a relationship of complicity. La Fontaine's narrative twice shifts into the mode of the "scene" so as to show the characters specifying the conventions of secrecy:

> ". . . Enfin n'en parlez pas."
>   La femme . . .
> Crut la chose, et promit ses grands dieux de se taire;

and

> "N'en dites rien surtout, car vous me feriez battre.
>   . . .
> —Vous moquez-vous? dit l'autre. Ah! vous ne savez guère
>   Quelle je suis. Allez, ne craignez rien."

However, what gives point to these exchanges is one's contextual knowledge that the vows of silence *will* be broken: these people are women, and the rules of gossip determine their treatment of secrets. This implies that although a promise is made to keep the secret, it is nevertheless understood that the secret is unlikely to be kept. In short there is second-degree complicity resulting from the fact that in addition to the promise to keep the secret there is a convention concerning the probability of its being divulged. This rule is known to the husband, who otherwise would have no reason to test ("éprouver," l. 5) his wife; and it is formulated at the outset by the fabulist:

> Rien ne pèse tant qu'un secret;
> Le porter loin est difficile aux Dames.

As for the women, who do not acknowledge the rule explicitly in their speech, they put it into practice by their actions.

However, there is a third and final convention which the fable does not formulate as a moral (like the second) or illustrate in specific dialogue (like the first); one just sees the women applying it automatically. This convention, which brings us to the deepest level of convention (since it goes completely unspoken), is embodied in the rule that, whereas a secret may well be repeated, it is not repeated indiscriminately. The news of the egg travels "de bouche en bouche," each woman as she hears it "grille déjà" (l. 27) to spread it; but the story travels only from woman to woman, "commère" to "commère," and no woman repeats it, for example, to her son or her husband. Among the conventions governing secrecy as a performative, there is a rule of repeatability, then (necessary, as stated, for the social functioning of the secret), but also a rule limiting this repeatability to appropriate hearers. This is of course an exclusion rule, defining *a contrario* the group which is positively defined by application of the repeatability rule. But this observation does not exhaust the social consequences of the discretion rule.

For, although in the fable men are excluded from the women's secret, the secret in question is a harmless one, and indeed it is a pure mystification invented by a man to test out ("éprouver"), or verify, a social phenomenon. And the moral makes it clear that in general terms discretion with respect to secrets is not a quality of women but an aspect of male superiority. For women, it is "difficult" to carry a secret far without divulging it (that is, there is no woman who does not experience this difficulty, even though some women are able to surmount it), whereas

> . . . je sais même sur ce fait
> Bon nombre d'hommes qui sont femmes

(some men, a majority perhaps, have no trouble in keeping secrets, even though exceptions exist in the shape of men-who-are-women). The text is ironic, of course, and the euphemistic humor functions to imply that, in fact, telling secrets is a universal phenomenon—which, as we have seen, is the prime lesson of the fable. But a further implication is that, within the context of universal divulgence, the concept of "keeping a secret" does not lose its meaning—it is synonymous with the practice of a certain discretion. In short, there are no secrets but there *is* secrecy—and it is in the art of discretion (of knowing when to speak and when not to speak) that "les Dames" are said to be deficient.

This means that the fact that the women in the fable do not tell the secret of the egg to their husbands or children does not count as discretion on their part, even though for us it may illustrate the rule limiting the repeatability of secrets. Their treatment of the story of the egg is accountable for in other terms and by virtue of another phenomenon: I mean the fact that in society dominated groups may well have, and keep, certain secrets—but secrets which are of derisory significance, since they have no impact on the distribution of power. The women are the victims of a mystification perpetrated by a man who *does* know how to keep a secret (the secret of the mystification)—or who, at least, keeps it for a time (since it is evident that at some point he must have gotten around to telling it to someone—but to whom?). This suggests clearly that the question of discretion, of discernment in the divulging of secrets, has to do with the larger question of the way power is exercised in society; and it requires us to take a closer look at the curious tripartite division—indiscreet women versus "hommes qui sont femmes" versus men capable of exercising discretion—indicated in the moral. For, following the logic of our analysis, male discretion in the end can only consist of that form of discernment which involves identifying those dangerous men who are women so as not to entrust secrets to them, thus ensuring that these secrets are not improperly divulged. And the fault attributed to women is not that they only tell secrets among themselves, but that they tell one another their secrets without restraint.

But the fable implies that the alleged character weakness of women, who cannot "carry far" a secret, is in fact the consequence of ignorance and the sign of their dominated position within society. For the wife of the fable is not just naïve,

> . . . neuve sur ce cas,
> Ainsi que sur mainte autre affaire,

she is kept in a state of naïveté by a husband who, far from wishing to enlighten her, is more concerned to *test* his "épouse indiscrète et peu fine" (l. 16), that is, to confirm her simplemindedness and thus guarantee his own superiority. To this end, he stoops to a quite grotesque deception. The text stresses the spontaneity of women's behavior: the wife

> . . . promit ses grands dieux de se taire.
> Mais ce serment s'évanouit
> Avec les ombres de la nuit;

and:

> L'autre grille déjà de raconter la nouvelle:
> Elle va la répandre en plus de dix endroits.
> Au lieu d'un oeuf elle en dit trois.

The unmotivated way these women run about telling secrets contrasts with the husband whose behavior is directed by precise intentions ("pour éprouver la sienne"). Perhaps this proves that it is difficult for them to carry a secret far without telling it; but it also suggests that if they were better informed they would be more cautious in their actions. For the secret which is carefully kept from them is precisely this, that secrecy, in the sense of being able to "keep a secret," is closely bound up with the maintenance of power.

What then of the husband? Is he a man or a man-woman? His abrupt, peremptory style of speech in addressing his wife (ll. 8–10) suggests a man who is not in the habit of communicating with his spouse other than by assertions and orders (and one might conclude that it is because the wife is not encouraged to communicate with her husband that she is so ready to hasten, when she has something to share, "chez la voisine," l. 18). The strange experiment he mounts does not simply reveal his contempt for the spouse whom he so coldly deceives; it reposes on the telling of a false secret, to be sure, but also on the maintenance of a true secret—the secret of the falsity of the first secret. In all this, it is easy to recognize the reserved behavior of a man concerned to maintain his position of mastery. And yet, to do this, he runs the risk of being thought a "poule" (l. 10), a "pondeur" (l. 26); and this is precisely the reputation ("renommée," l. 34) he does finally acquire. Reputation, however, does not make him *genuinely* a man-woman; rather what one sees here is the importance of the stakes, and the extent of the husband's cleverness. Ready as he is to risk his manly reputation and become a man-woman in public repute so as to confirm and maintain his conjugal superiority, he does not hesitate, as a means to that end, to play the role of an egg-layer ("pondeur") by indiscriminately revealing his male secret to his wife, who will proceed (as he knows and intends) to spread it throughout the village. In this sense, the content of his secret (the laying of an egg) is redundant with its performative effect.

However, let us not lose track of the vital point: the secret is false, the egg laying a simulation, and this falsity and simulation is the object of the husband's genuine secrecy. He can run the risk of acquiring the reputation of a man-woman among the women because (1) they are only women; (2) he himself knows the "renommée" to be false; and (3) he can always, if need be, tell the true secret to those who will appreciate it, that is, the men of the village. Indeed it seems that this latter course is actually the one he has taken since *we* know the secret from reading the fable: like the story of the egg, it can be said of the secret of the mystification that "ce n['est] plus un secret" (l. 33). And of course it *was* necessary for this secret to come to light, not only to protect the husband's reputation but also so that the naïveté of the women, their lack of discretion, their inability to carry a secret far, in short all the female faults that the mystification was supposed to confirm, could be brought to general notice. As an "histoire gauloise," the fable has a clear function: to tell the husband's male secret so as to enhance the prestige of men by confirming the poor reputation of women and exposing them to mockery.

But storytelling, as Louis Marin points out,[12] sometimes sets traps into which the trapsetters themselves fall. It seems that in this case, by pretending to be a hen-man, the husband has set off a mechanism of divulgence which, as its end result, turns him retrospectively into a real man-woman. "De bouche en bouche," the story told with a view to preserving male prestige (by countering the reputation of hen-man the husband has acquired among women) appears to have reached the ear, then the mouth (or pen) of a storyteller—the author of the fable—who spreads it *indiscriminately*, in violation of the rules of male discretion. "Publishing the mystery" (cf. l. 23) so that it now reaches an unrestricted audience, the fable makes its information available, not only to "appropriate" hearers, but also to those men and women who have the greatest stake in knowing it, the victims of male discretion. For there is no way to tell the story of "Les femmes et le secret" without laying bare the inner workings of the trick played on the wife, that is, the true secret which ought to have remained the property of men alone; and when these inner workings are revealed to those who ought not to be "in the secret," then the "histoire gauloise" ceases to play its traditional role and becomes something else again, let us say a "fable"—a form of discourse from which a lesson can be learned. In terms of our earlier analysis of oppositional duplicity, the "histoire gauloise," embodying the discourse of the powerful, thus comes to serve as narrative disguise for the "fable"'s oppositional function as an ironic text.

Storytelling is indeed traditionally conceived as a means of communicating knowledge, and the etymology of the word "narrator" (one who knows) links it to the family of the verb *cognoscere*. If a secret is necessarily a secret divulged, then narrative is the reverse of the coin, the necessary corollary of the notion of "secret." Hence the great interest displayed by La Fontaine's text in the act of narration, which it twice displays in a narrative "scene," and each time in paradigmatic form. The husband relates to his wife his fictional misadventure as it is supposed to be occurring, and he gives it the canonical tripartite structure recognized by narrative grammar: (1) "O dieux! qu'est-ce cela?" (2) "Quoi! J'accouche d'un oeuf!" (3) "D'un oeuf?—Oui, le voilà / Frais et nouveau pondu. . . ." The wife in turn uses the phrase now standard for describing narrative as a performative:[13] "Ma commère, dit-elle, un cas est arrivé. . . ." And twice more narration becomes the object of the narrative in the fable: one woman "grille déjà de raconter la nouvelle: / Elle va la répandre en plus de dix endroits" (ll. 28–29); and another "raconte à l'oreille le fait,"

> Précaution peu nécessaire,
> Car ce n'était plus un secret.

In all these cases, the act of narration constituted by the fable itself is being mirrored (or embedded, *mis en abyme*) within the narration: and one notes that the fact of storytelling itself is *common* to both the man and the women characters, independently of the different value attached to male and female divulgence of secrets. In Lucien Dällenbach's terms, "Les femmes et le secret" is a quite spectacularly "specular" text.[14]

If so, then the fact that its subject matter concerns the manner in which a secret comes to be "no longer a secret" (cf. l. 33) is significant. The subject matter reproduces the process of transformation, from secrecy to nonsecrecy, by which the text itself has come into being, since it repeats the characters' secrets and divulges their knowledge, but in such a way as to radically alter the rules. For whereas the repeatability of male secrets is determined by the rule of discretion, and that of female secrets conforms to the conventions of gossip, narrative is subject to a quite different repeatability rule. The addressee of a story is neither committed to repeat a story nor not to repeat it, since it is understood that a narrative not governed by the rules of secrecy is repeatable at will. But one does not repeat just any story to just any person; what determines the "tellability" of a story, and hence its repeatability, is the "interest" it has in the illocutionary circumstance of the moment, an interest which is determined by the relationship between teller and tellee in their own particular historical context. William Labov has pointed out that every narrator takes great care to establish the interest of what is being recounted, the reason behind the narration—in short, its "point."[15] As a literary text, the fable must presuppose this type of repeatability (as a function of interest), and that is why it can be said that, although it repeats secrets, it is no longer subject to the rules of secrecy.

This means, of course, that the narrator of "Les femmes et le secret," judged from the male point of view, is behaving like a woman, that is without discretion—but the secret he is divulging is *not* a female secret (which would have little importance); it is, quite to the contrary, the major male secret, the secret of secrecy itself. This is what makes him the true man-woman, or egg-layer of the fable. The husband is only apparently a man-woman, as a result of his lie; and he becomes a real man-woman more or less accidentally, having been sufficiently indiscreet as to reveal his secret to an informer who passed it on to the narrator. But the narrator, who is in on the male secret yet feels free to tell it like a woman, in such a way that it ceases to be a secret, is the genuine man-woman. The egg he lays, in the form of the fable, shares with the husband's egg its fictionality; but the difference lies in the fact that whereas the husband's egg is a mystification, the narrator's egg laying is a *demystifying*—and hence, oppositional—act.

For the great male secret, the secret of secrets which ought not to have been divulged, is a double secret. It is first of all the secret of the mystification perpetrated by men on women; but it is also the secret of the reasons behind this mystification. Men exercise power, in mediated fashion, and by means of deception, because their power has no natural basis: men are not a separate, radically different species, and the power they claim is consequently obtained only by virtue of a deception concerning this very fact, a deception calculated to prove, and perpetuate, women's "difference." But what the fabulist does is to tear aside the veil and reveal the essential secret, the secret which in fact comprises all the "knowledge" he lays claim to as narrator:

> Et *je sais* même sur ce fait
> Bon nombre d'hommes qui sont femmes. (My emphasis.)

If "quite a number" of men are women, the social division on which male power reposes is a false division, which is maintained only through the operation of male secrecy. And to declare, as the fabulist does, that there are "men who are women" is *automatically* to claim for oneself the status of man-woman, a status that, by definition, demystifies the male means of government, and makes the man-woman, also by definition, the ally of women.

So the "interest" of the fable—its point—is of an educational kind; but its pedagogy is liberationist. The text addresses itself to all those whose interest it is to learn what is being kept from them (what the fabulist "knows" and communicates). "To lay an egg," in English, suggests error and miscalculation; and in this English sense the true "pondeur" is the husband. For the fable makes no error and displays no deficiency in discernment (but only in male "discretion"). And the egg it lays is a truly fertile one, since the secret brought to light so long ago is still being learned and its consequences realized today: one of the functions of my critical discourse is to spread it.

But here is the final point: in the terms of the text, *only a man can become a man-woman*. To the extent that only a man is in a position to know the secrets of power and to reveal them like a woman, the power to lay the oppositional egg of the fable is restricted to a male fabulist, one who is both *in the know* and empowered to *publish*, reaching an audience at large through the practice of literature. In these two ways, he is distinguished from women, who are not in the know and whose power to speak is limited to the restricted coterie of gossips (other women). The fabulist's performance, then, is finally uncomfortably reminiscent of the husband's in that it is an example of what the anthropological literature refers to as *couvade*, the appropriation by males of the female mysteries of birth.[16] Consequently it reposes on the very structure of power that ostensibly it is opposing, so that its oppositional value (great as it may be) is relativized by the circumstance that it is, simultaneously, a manifestation of power. Such an oppositional act is not available to women; it can only be performed on their behalf; and this "on-behalf-of" gesture is one that exactly captures the ambivalence of oppositional narrative, manifesting power while it opposes it. That is the irony of its irony.[17]

3. The Wild Man and the Buffoon

What, then, are the conditions of the oppositional? What are the circumstances in which one may get away with clawing a King's nose? This is the question to which La Fontaine addresses himself in "Le milan, le roi, et le chasseur" (XII, xii); and in the world of Louis XIV's France, it is perhaps the very fact of raising such a question almost explicitly that makes the fable itself an act of opposition, for where most of the "Fables" are enactments of oppositionality, this one goes close to theorizing it as well. There is really no *content* here that might be judged subversive, no "critique" of royalty, for instance; just (it seems) an edifying and amusing story told on the occasion of a princely wedding. The characters—the Huntsman and his Kite—certainly behave indecorously, not to say scandalously, with respect to the King; but they are not oppositional figures, since the one is entirely well meaning and the other an innocent wild thing. Yet the tale—so I want to suggest—does act as the narrative equivalent of a tweak on the royal nose to the extent that it dares to inquire into the *conditions of possibility* of behavior that demeans royalty and even to hint, in its moral, that if kings were to display more clemency their noses would be in more danger.

LE MILAN, LE ROI, ET LE CHASSEUR
A Son Altesse Sérénissime Monseigneur le Prince de Conti

Comme les Dieux sont bons, ils veulent que les Rois
Le soient aussi: c'est l'indulgence
Qui fait le plus beau de leurs droits,
Non les douceurs de la vengeance:
Prince c'est votre avis. On sait que le courroux
S'éteint en votre coeur sitôt qu'on l'y voit naître.
Achille qui du sien ne put se rendre maître
Fut par là moins Héros que vous.
Ce titre n'appartient qu'à ceux d'entre les hommes
Qui comme en l'âge d'or font cent biens ici-bas.
Peu de Grands sont nés tels en cet âge où nous sommes.
L'Univers leur sait gré du mal qu'ils ne font pas.
Loin que vous suiviez ces exemples,
Mille actes généreux vous promettent des Temples.
Apollon Citoyen de ces augustes lieux
Prétend y célébrer votre nom sur sa Lyre.
Je sais qu'on vous attend dans le Palais des Dieux:

Un siècle de séjour doit ici vous suffire,
Hymen veut séjourner tout un siècle chez vous.
    Puissent ses plaisirs les plus doux
    Vous composer des destinées
    Par ce temps à peine bornées!
Et la Princesse et vous n'en méritez pas moins;
    J'en prends ses charmes pour témoins:
    Pour témoins j'en prends les merveilles
Par qui le Ciel pour vous prodigue en ses présents,
De qualités qui n'ont qu'en vous seuls leurs pareilles,
    Voulut orner vos jeunes ans.
Bourbon de son esprit ces grâces assaisonne.
    Le Ciel joignit, en sa personne,
    Ce qui sait se faire estimer
    A ce qui sait se faire aimer.
Il ne m'appartient pas d'étaler votre joie.
    Je me tais donc, et vais rimer
    Ce que fit un Oiseau de proie.

Un Milan, de son nid antique possesseur,
    Étant pris vif par un Chasseur,
D'en faire au Prince un don cet homme se propose.
La rareté du fait donnait prix à la chose.
L'Oiseau, par le Chasseur humblement présenté,
    Si ce conte n'est apocryphe,
    Va tout droit imprimer sa griffe
    Sur le nez de sa Majesté.
—Quoi! sur le nez du Roi?—Du Roi même en personne.
—Il n'avait donc alors ni Sceptre ni Couronne?
—Quand il en aurait eu, ç'aurait été tout un.
Le nez royal fut pris comme un nez du commun.
Dire des Courtisans les clameurs et la peine
Serait se consumer en efforts impuissants.
Le Roi n'éclata point; les cris sont indécents
    A la Majesté Souveraine.
L'Oiseau garda son poste. On ne put seulement
    Hâter son départ d'un moment.
Son Maître le rappelle, et crie, et se tourmente,
Lui présente le leurre, et le poing; mais en vain.
    On crut que jusqu'au lendemain
Le maudit animal à la serre insolente
    Nicherait là malgré le bruit,
Et sur le nez sacré voudrait passer la nuit.
Tâcher de l'en tirer irritait son caprice.
Il quitte enfin le Roi, qui dit: «Laissez aller

Ce Milan, et celui qui m'a cru régaler.
Ils se sont acquittés tous deux de leur office,
L'un en Milan, et l'autre en Citoyen des bois.
Pour moi, qui sais comment doivent agir les Rois,
         Je les affranchis du supplice.»
Et la Cour d'admirer. Les Courtisans ravis
Élèvent de tels faits, par eux si mal suivis:
Bien peu, même des Rois, prendraient un tel modèle;
Et le Veneur l'échappa belle,
Coupable seulement, tant lui que l'animal,
D'ignorer le danger d'approcher trop du Maître.
Ils n'avaient appris à connaître
Que les hôtes des bois: était-ce un si grand mal?

Pilpay fait près du Gange arriver l'Aventure.
         Là nulle humaine Créature
Ne touche aux Animaux pour leur sang épancher.
Le roi même ferait scrupule d'y toucher.
«Savons-nous, disent-ils, si cet Oiseau de proie
         N'était point au siège de Troie?
Peut-être y tint-il lieu d'un Prince ou d'un Héros
         Des plus huppés et des plus hauts.
Ce qu'il fut autrefois il pourra l'être encore.
         Nous croyons après Pythagore,
Qu'avec les Animaux de forme nous changeons,
         Tantôt Milans, tantôt Pigeons,
         Tantôt Humains, puis Volatilles
         Ayant dans les airs leurs familles.»

         Comme l'on conte en deux façons
L'accident du Chasseur, voici l'autre manière.
Un certain Fauconnier, ayant pris, ce dit-on,
A la Chasse un Milan (ce qui n'arrive guère),
         En voulut au Roi faire un don,
         Comme de chose singulière.
Ce cas n'arrive pas quelquefois en cent ans.
C'est le *Non plus ultra* de la Fauconnerie.
Ce Chasseur perce donc un gros de Courtisans,
Plein de zèle, échauffé, s'il le fut de sa vie.
         Par ce parangon des présents
         Il croyait sa fortune faite,
         Quand l'Animal porte-sonnette,
         Sauvage encore et tout grossier,
         Avec ses ongles tout d'acier
Prend le nez du Chasseur, happe le pauvre sire:
         Lui de crier, chacun de rire,

Monarque et Courtisans. Qui n'eût ri? Quant à moi,
Je n'en eusse quitté ma part pour un empire.
        Qu'un Pape rie, en bonne foi,
Je ne l'ose assurer; mais je tiendrais un Roi
        Bien malheureux s'il n'osait rire.
C'est le plaisir des Dieux. Malgré son noir sourci,
Jupiter, et le Peuple Immortel rit aussi.
Il en fit des éclats, à ce qui dit l'Histoire
Quand Vulcain clopinant lui vint donner à boire.
Que le Peuple Immortel se montrât sage ou non,
J'ai changé mon sujet avec juste raison;
        Car, puisqu'il s'agit de morale,
Que nous eût du Chasseur l'aventure fatale
Enseigné de nouveau? l'on a vu de tout temps
Plus de sots Fauconniers que de Rois indulgents.

[THE KITE, THE KING, AND THE HUNTSMAN
To His Most Serene Highness, Mylord the Prince of Conti

As the Gods are kind, they wish Kings to be kind also: indulgence, not the
sweetness of revenge, is the fairest of their rights: Prince, such is your opinion.
Anger, we know, is extinguished in your heart as soon as it arises there. Achilles,
who was unable to master his own anger, was in that respect less a Hero than you.
Such a title belongs only to those among men who as in the golden age perform a
hundredfold goodness here below. Few of the Great in our present age are by
nature so. The Universe is grateful to them for the harm they do not do. Far from
your following their example, a thousand noble acts promise you Temples. Apollo,
a Citizen of those august places, lays claim to celebrating your name on his lyre. I
know you are awaited in the palace of the Gods: a century of living here must
suffice you. Hymen wishes to sojourn one whole century with you. May his
sweetest pleasures compose destinies for you that are scarcely limited by the time-
span! Both the Princess and you merit nothing less: I appeal, as evidence, to her
charms, I appeal to the wonders by which Heaven, showering its presents on you
both, wished to adorn your young years with qualities that have an equal in your
own selves alone. Bourbon seasons these graces with wit. Heaven joined in her
person that which merits esteem with that which requires to be loved. It is not for
me to make a show of your joy. I shall be silent, then, and will rhyme what a Bird
of prey did.

A Kite, the ancient possessor of his nest, having been taken alive by a Huntsman, this fellow proposes to make a gift of it to the Prince. The rarity of the
happening gave the object its price. The Bird, humbly presented by the Huntsman,
unless this tale is apocryphal, goes straight and plants its claws on his Majesty's
nose.—What, on the nose of the King?—The King himself in person.—Then he
was without Scepter or Crown at that moment?—Had he had them, it were all one.
The royal nose was clasped like any commoner's. To tell how the Courtiers clamored

and lamented would be to waste oneself in impotent efforts. The King did not exclaim; cries do not befit Sovereign Majesty. The Bird stuck to its post. It was impossible even to hasten its departure by a moment. Its Master calls to it, and shouts, and fusses, offers it the lure and holds out his wrist; all to no avail. They thought the accursed animal with its insolent talons would perch there until the next day, despite the noise, and would wish to spend the night on the sacred nose. To attempt to remove it only stirred up its capriciousness. Finally, it leaves the King, who says: "Let the Kite and him who thought to make me a present go. They have both acquitted their appointed role, the one as a Kite, and the other as a Citizen of the woods. For my part, I who know how Kings must act, I exempt them from punishment." The Court falls to admiring. The delighted Courtiers sing the praises of such deeds, so little imitated by them: very few, even among Kings, would adopt such a model; and the Hunter had a narrow escape, guilty as he was, he and his animal too, only of ignorance of the dangers of approaching too closely the Master. Their only acquaintance was with the denizens of the woods: was that so very culpable?

Pilpay has the adventure occur near the Ganges. There no human creature touches Animals to spill their blood. The King himself would scruple to do so. "Can we tell," they say, "whether this Bird of prey was not at the seige of Troy? Perhaps he was there in the stead of some Prince or Hero among the most crested and the most elevated? What he once was he can become again. We believe, after Pythagoras, that we exchange forms with Animals, being now Kites, now Pigeons, now Humans and again Fowls, having their families in the air."

As the Huntsman's accident is told in two manners, here is the other way. A certain Falconer, having taken, as they say, a Kite in the hunt (an unusual occurrence), wished to make a gift of it to the King, as a singular thing. Sometimes such a thing does not happen in one hundred years. It is the *Non plus ultra* of falconry. So this Huntsman pushes through a throng of Courtiers, full of zeal and excited if ever he was in his life. He thought his fortune made by the paragon of presents, when the bell-carrying Animal, still wild and quite untamed, takes the Huntsman's nose in its steely claw, and grabs the poor wretch: *he* sets to shouting, and everyone else to laughing, the Monarch and the Courtiers both. Who would not have laughed? For my part I would not have foregone my own share for an empire. That a Pope should laugh is something that in good faith I do not affirm; but I should consider a King most unfortunate if he did not dare to laugh. It is the pleasure of the Gods. Despite his dark troubles, Jupiter and the population of Immortals laughed also. They laughed uproariously, as History tells, when Vulcan came limping to serve their wine. Whether or not the Immortals were correct in their behavior, I have changed my subject with excellent reason; for, since it's time for a moral, what would the Huntsman's fatal adventure have taught us that we did not know? At all times there have been more stupid Falconers than indulgent Kings.]

How, then, is the fable like, yet unlike, the Huntsman and his Kite? How does it convert the story of their gaucherie into an oppositional narrative? And how does it hope to get away, as they do, with its own *lèse-majesté*? My way of demonstrating that the fable *is* an oppositional act will be to suggest answers to these questions. In light of what the narrative shows to be the conditions of possibility of an act that challenges royal dignity—conditions relevant to and valid for the France of Louis XIV—I want to examine its own exploitation of such conditions, the rhetorical defenses and strategems it deploys as oppositional discourse. As it happens, the first of these, if my hunch is right, has been identified already: it is, of course, disguise. Presenting a piece of nose tweaking as an epithalamium, stating one thing (that royal clemency is desired by the Gods) while implying another (that royal clemency would be good for humans), the fable presents to a would-be censorious audience a certain appearance of bland innocence, which is reinforced by the absence of critical "content." Once more, the oppositionality of narrative, thanks to rhetorical duplicity, is "invisible."

Not the least subtle, and certainly the most important manifestation of this oppositional "invisibility" is the textual exploration of the conditions of oppositional success through the narrative deployment of figures and actions—the story of the Kite and the Huntsman—that can scarcely be suspected of having oppositional significance. If the Kite attacks the monarch's nose, it is because wild animals behave wildly; if the Huntsman makes an inappropriate gift to the King in offering the Kite, it is because he is an untutored man of the woods who means well but knows no better. But, precisely—as Michel de Certeau pointed out—the "oppositional practices of daily life" share with the behavior of the Kite and the Huntsman their spontaneity and naïveté: unpremeditated, unself-conscious, untheorized, oppositional behavior quite characteristically is unaware of itself as oppositional. It is "just behavior." If it opposes the power structure, it is not from having made any political analysis, but because opportunities arise for behavior that is unknowingly contestatory. Oppositional behavior, as we know, is behavior that does not challenge the way things are, and indeed strengthens the status quo by its acknowledgment of the structures that are in place—and we may note already that, quite similarly, the unintended attack on the King's dignity by the Kite and the Huntsman proves to be an occasion for monarchical power to reaffirm and strengthen itself, an occasion for a display of magnanimity and "indulgence."

But oppositional as the behavior of the Huntsman and the Kite may be in its *effect* (the attack on the King's dignity and its upshot of reinforcement of royal power), there is clearly a crucial, if elusive, nuance that distinguishes the pair's at best "accidental" opposition from what might be thought to be more thoughtful and even self-conscious oppositional action. It is on this nuance that the text depends in using them, on the one hand, as "cover" and, on the other, as a "model" for its own oppositional behavior. But a second distinction is relevant here as well: that between supposedly nonverbal oppositional "behavior," with the unexamined spontaneity described by Michel de Certeau (and its consequent failure to produce change), and oppositional discourse, which—as I am attempting to suggest—deploys the textual characteristic of "readability." If the wild pair *can* be shown to be a "model" for textual oppositional practice in the fable, then the characteristic of readability will be seen to derive precisely from the recursivity characteristic of the "textual function"—the "fold" by which the text differs from itself and that enables it to produce its characters and events as *mise en abyme* of its own situation with respect to power.

And to the extent that such recursivity constitutes something like self-theorization on the text's part, it will then be seen as the crucial difference that distinguishes *textual* practice from the naïve *behavior* of its "models," constituting the former as in some sense "self-conscious" or "self-aware" and, hence, unable to claim quite the same innocence, spontaneity, and wildness that disculpates the Huntsman and his Kite. My task, then, in what follows, will be to show that the rhetorical gestures of the text "imitate" the behavior of its protagonists, but on the understanding that, precisely because it is "imitation," such discursive behavior belongs in a different category—the category of the oppositional and of the ironically "knowing"—than the "wild" and spontaneous behavior the text describes.

The fable's understanding of the category of wildness is consequently of central importance. The wildness of nature, represented by the bird; the "wildness" of the man of the woods, who nevertheless belongs sufficiently to society that he can decide to offer the Kite to the King; the *sauvagerie* that I propose to demonstrate characterizes the textual performance—these differing degrees and kinds of wildness correspond to increasing proportions of social responsibility and self-consciousness. The question posed by the fable is *at what point the oppositional begins to appear*, given that all these forms of wildness, including the "natural" category itself, are subject to royal authority. It is Cocteau's memorable question of *jusqu'où on peut aller trop loin*: how far one can take "going too far" and still "get away with it." The fable is discreet: the closest it comes to an oppositional *proposition* is in the moral's implied wish that there be more royal clemency (since that is the condition of possibility for oppositional behavior). But it can be seen to enact something like a theorization of the oppositional act, not through any criticism of royalty, but by demonstrating an "art" that is the art of getting away with it—an art that takes for its model the completely unself-conscious behavior of the Huntsman and the Kite but that should not be confused with this behavior. And my contention, then, is that it is here that a decisive threshold is crossed, and that it is on this discursive and textual level that the oppositional begins.

The claim for me to support, then, is that the fable is readable, simultaneously, as a self-described oppositional act and as an exploration of the problematics of the oppositional with respect to power, the problematics, that is, of the authority that permits it to be oppositional, of the power to oppose in its relation to the power that is "in power." And since authority is the key to the success of narrative, whether oppositional or not, it will be useful to look at this text in the light of the simple(-seeming) questions one might ask about any narrative. What claim to authority does the text make? By what appeal to its addressee (by what seductive strategies) does it seek to maintain its authority? And finally, what sense does it display of its ultimate dependence on a power that may or may not respond favorably to the seductive devices that characterize its mode or modes of address? These questions are simply an expansion of my initial question (how does the oppositional narrative "get away with" its nose tweaking?), which in fact asks not only what devices the text employs but also what limitations it sets on their success.

Perhaps one should attach special importance to this latter point because acknowledgment of the possibility of failure is central to the text's (self-described) oppositional status. Since the possibility of failing is what guarantees a narrative act's oppositional status (those that have "power" behind them do not need to worry about failing), the acknowledgment of such a possibility is a vital means, for a text, of identifying itself as oppositional. So, in "Le milan, le roi, et le chasseur," all the rhetorical devices I am about to explore are framed by the textual appeal to royal "indulgence" (or is it *for* royal indulgence?). For it is of the nature of clemency to be arbitrary, or at least unpredictable; and the praise of "indulgence" thus constitutes a recognition that the royal power to punish surpasses any countervailing authority the text may attempt to set up for itself.

By a piece of good fortune, a manuscript version of the fable has survived which contains some explicit commentary on its own rhetorical moves. In the printed version this commentary is gone, although the moves are essentially unchanged—*except*, of course, for this crucial suppression of self-commentary itself. As far as scholarship knows, the story of the fable was invented by La Fontaine, a fact which the MS goes close to admitting openly:

> Je change un peu la chose. Un peu? J'y change tout.
>
> [I'm changing things a bit. A bit? I'm changing everything.]

The fabulist's responsibility for his fiction is thereby laid bare. And, what is more, this freedom to fictionalize is explicitly related, in the MS, to the privilege whereby the fabulist is permitted to correct kings:

> . . . c'est à cette licence
> Que je dois l'acte de clémence
> Par qui je donne aux rois des leçons de bonté.

[. . . to this licence I owe the clemency that permits me to give lessons in goodness to kings.]

Thus, the text freely acknowledges that "clemency," as the authorization to perform oppositional acts ("donner aux rois des leçons") is obtainable by rhetorical means—for, although changing the fable is in fact *not* what the narrator has done (he has invented it), it *is* exactly what he will do when he gives two versions of the "same" story.

A little later, there is a similar giveaway of the devices of authority. The published version has an ascription to Pilpay of a version of the story; but the MS admits that such an ascription would only be a cover for the narrator's own responsibility:

> Si je craignais quelque censure
> Je citerais Pilpay touchant cette aventure.
> Ses récits en ont l'air: il me serait aisé
> De la tirer d'un lieu par le Gange arrosé.

[Were I afraid of censure I would cite Pilpay with respect to this adventure. His stories are like it: it would be an easy matter for me to derive it from a spot watered by the Ganges.]

In light of this, we may be sensitive to the stance adopted by the narrator of the published version, who in a number of ways disclaims personal responsibility and appeals for authority to a narrative tradition. For now, not only is there suddenly a Pilpay version which he describes (without narrating it), but also, with respect to the two versions he does give, he is content, as he says, to "rhyme" (l. 34) a narrative that "l'on conte en deux façons" (l. 89). This looks like a defensive tactic, by contrast with the self-assurance of the MS narrator who denies his fear of "censure" by so ostensibly disdaining to bring Pilpay into it and who does not hesitate to give away the (rhetorical) secret of his success in obtaining indulgence. This is a "successful" narrator, secure in the knowledge that he is supported by power, and who does not doubt his own authority—whereas, in the published version, we see a narrator looking for support to a narrative tradition (which we happen to know is entirely fictional) and attempting to derive authority from that.

But there *are* a number of rhetorical advantages in this latter stance. First, the "existence" of narrative predecessors supports the fabulist's claim to the authority of truth, i.e., the supreme authority claim (stronger even than the claim to royal favor). Unlike the MS narrator, who admits to changing things around, "je . . . vais rimer," says he (tactically limiting his intervention), "ce que fit un Oiseau de proie" (as if there was no question of the event's factual character). And the same limiting of personal responsibility permits him to adopt the scholarly pose of one who merely sorts out the different versions of what is later referred to, no less comfortably, as "l'accident du Chasseur," commenting on them objectively ("Pilpay fait près du Gange arriver l'aventure") and transmitting them, indiscriminately, as being all equally interesting.

On the other hand, narrative rhetoric (Louis Marin's point again) is a tricky business. Does not the self-assured narrator of the MS betray a certain *nervousness* in admitting his reliance on rhetoric and his awareness of the possibility of "censure?" And similarly, in the published version, does not the fabulist finally undercut his own effect of authority and end up—like the MS narrator, but involuntarily, it seems—revealing rather than concealing his narrative ploys? The claim to know from tradition "ce que fit un Oiseau de proie" is subverted by the very profusion of versions he produces in evidence. *Did* it happen "près du Gange," or where? Did the Kite attack the *King*? Or did it attack the *Huntsman*? "Ce que fit un Oiseau de proie" is in point of fact what the narrative does not permit us to know with any certainty; the most we learn is that, somewhere, sometime, a Huntsman suffered an "accident" in presenting a Kite to a King, and survived. . . . In similar fashion, the very deployment of authorizing references (I have not even discussed the roles of Pythagoras and Homer) functions to defeat its own purpose—it does not *support* the fabulist's authority, but rather *shows up his strategy* for producing it. In deleting the rhetorical self-commentary, the narrator of the published version has both strengthened his rhetorical hand (by not admitting to the tricks of the trade) and weakened it (by the attempt to conceal tricks which are nonetheless readable, i.e., discoverable). His authority ploy is also a way of courting failure.

There is another instance of an authorizing ploy that proves self-defeating in the dedication to the Prince de Conti, which functions as "cover," but in a way rather different from the dedication to M. de Barrillon of "Le pouvoir des fables." On the face of it, the evocation of Conti is an attempt to strengthen the fabulist's authority by associating him with a powerful personage under whose protection the text is placed. Thus the Prince's opinion of royal indulgence is adduced in support of the fable's own, and his practice of self-control and generosity is cited as a model, in an age when "peu de Grands sont nés tels." These are, of course precisely those virtues in the great on which the fable depends to bring off its oppositional act. Similarly, in the occasion of the Prince's marriage, the text seems to see a particularly opportune moment (it is, in a sense, "carnival time") in which to overstep the bounds of decorum. It offers itself, not so much *as* an epithalamium, as *in lieu of* the traditional hymn—a gesture which manages to place it under the traditional umbrella of "indulgence" associated with weddings while accomplishing the very kind of action (an overstepping of the bounds of decorum) that needs to benefit from such indulgence.

> Il ne m'appartient pas d'étaler votre joie.
> Je me tais donc, et vais rimer
> Ce que fit un Oiseau de proie.

Indeed, in offering the story of the Kite and the Huntsman instead of the conventional poem of praise and joy, the fable is doing to the Prince what the Huntsman did to the King: it is making a displaced and inappropriate gift, quite out of keeping with the rules that prevail in princely palaces and royal Courts. And the "outsider" status the fabulist claims in disclaiming the right to produce court poetry ("Il ne m'appartient pas . . .") quite naturally associates him with the Huntsman whose gift was so dangerously likely to be a self-defeating one.

But that is not all. One might think that the fable is using the princely power, in the "political" realm, as a source of authorization comparable to that which it attempts to derive, in the "discursive" sphere, from its alleged narrative sources. But the Prince is himself one who derives power from the power and protection—and indeed the "indulgence"—of the monarch. The MS balances (or tops) its appeal to the Prince with an even more hyperbolic piece of flattery addressed to the King:

> Louis seul est incomparable.
> Je ne lui donne point quelque éloge affecté:
> L'on sait que j'ai toujours entremêlé la fable
> De quelque trait de vérité.

[Louis alone is incomparable, I do not bestow on him some affected encomium: it is well known that I have always mingled fable with some element of truth.]

In tandem with its openness about its own "rhetoricity," the MS's flattering truth-claim here functions, understandably enough, as part of its reliance on the backing of ultimate political power. By contrast, the published version—with its rhetorically self-defeating truth-claim about "ce que fit un Oiseau" and its suppression of this praise of the King—is putting itself in a much more exposed position, also, by relying on the power of the Prince. For contemporary readers of the fable could not fail to be aware of the well-deserved reputation the Prince de Conti enjoyed at Versailles for unruliness: he had indeed himself been the beneficiary of royal "indulgence" (if *de facto* exile from the Court be considered an indulgence) and eventually of a grudging pardon, for his "oppositional" behavior.[18] He was a figure, then, to whom "l'accident du Chasseur" was uncomfortably relevant and whose own praise of royal clemency—like that of the fabulist—must have seemed to have a self-serving tinge. Rather than being in a position to strengthen the fabulist's authority, he rather epitomizes the exposed situation of one who, having committed an oppositional "gaffe," is himself in need of indulgence. And to dedicate a fable to him is, of course to commit just such a "gaffe."

Self-defeating, then, in its double claim to authority (whether it be from narrative predecessors or from a princely protector), this text is either an extraordinarily incompetent rhetorical performance or an extraordinary performance of rhetorical incompetence. Where the MS makes explicit claims to rhetorical know-how, what the published version knows how to do is to commit rhetorical (and political) mistakes. Its truth-claim reveals itself as an authority ploy, and thus self-destructs; it offers itself to the Prince as an inappropriate substitute for an epithalamium; and it inappropriately offers itself to the Prince instead of to the King. In all this, it is uncannily similar to the Huntsman's clumsy and self-defeating gift to the King.

But the Huntsman, it will be recalled, *got away with* making his singularly inappropriate gift. This suggests to me that the fable is basing itself, rhetorically, on the proposition that the kind of rhetorical know-how advertised in the MS version is, ultimately, less oppositionally "successful"—that is, less likely to draw indulgence from its powerful audience—than is (a display of) narrative incompetence. The narrative's maladroit and ineffective claims to *authority* are, in this reading, the means, subtle and carefully calculated, by which it produces (or hopes to produce)—in the form of "indulgence"—the *authorization* that it needs. Incompetence gets away with things for which competence would rightly be punished: that is what can be learned from the example of the Huntsman and his "accident."

I pretended just now not to decide whether this text is rhetorically incompetent or whether it is giving a successful performance of rhetorical incompetence. There are, of course, good reasons for thinking the latter: a text which produces its own model, as this fable produces the Huntsman, is certainly not naïve; and its "self-consciousness" becomes evident in the clear parallel it produces between the fabulist's displaced gift to the Prince (of the story of the Huntsman) and the Huntsman's displaced gift to the King (of a Kite). But, strangely, the model the text produces, in the Huntsman, of its own rhetorical operation, is a *double* one; and "l'accident du chasseur," although in each case it represents a (momentary) threat to royal dignity, is not the same in version one (ll. 36–74)—where the Kite attacks the King—as in version two (ll. 91–114), where the Kite attacks the Huntsman. This model (these models) clearly demand(s) closer attention: it (they) will lead me to suggest that, as oppositional act, the fable is describing itself neither as involuntary incompetence nor as deliberate performance, but as a paradoxical combination of both. Involuntary performance? Deliberate incompetence? An involuntary performance of deliberate incompetence? We do not have a word for behavior that lies somewhere between an act and an "act," that is neither self-conscious skill nor brute deed, but a skilled doing—a demonstration of *savoir-faire*.[19]

The difference is not simply that there is damage to the royal person in version one and to his dignity alone in version two, for the fable's reassuring insistence that kings *may* laugh suggests strongly that a royal fit of laughter can be as demeaning to a monarch as a kite physically attached to the royal nose. The essential point of difference appears to be rather that the actual attack on the royal person is attributed to a Huntsman and his Kite who are assimilated to each other as inhabitants of the woods (they are figures, I want to suggest, of the "wild man"), while the fit of laughter is attributed to self-defeating behavior—the gift-kite's attack on the donor—which is related to the paradigm of the court entertainer. If, indeed, the identification of Kite and Huntsman as manifestations of "wildness" is carried over from version one to version two (where they *combine* to produce a kind of droll act that amuses the King), then the description of the Kite as "l'Animal porte-sonnettes" in that version implies an interpretation of the Huntsman as an (involuntary) buffoon, or "homme porte-grelots." The bells in each case can be taken to signify the taming of wild power, its domestication or enculturation into an agent of divertissement, *used* by the King and his Court in one case for the entertainment of hunting, in the other as a butt of laughter. This is not to deny that the Kite of the fable is described as "Sauvage encor et tout grossier" and that the Huntsman, arriving straight from his native woods, is at best an "accidental" buffoon, whose clowning is quite unrehearsed and unintended. The element of wildness is still there, but it produces, in the Kite's case, behavior which, in the Huntsman's case, turns his overly pretentious gift giving into a risible spectacle for the King and the Court.

The fable suggests, then, that native wildness is at the heart of buffoonery, which therefore has the characteristics, at Court, of inappropriate spontaneity. It suggests also, however, that buffoonery is always, in some sense and at the same time, a performance of buffoonery, an "act." For the model adduced to justify the King's laughter is the Homeric example of Zeus and the gods breaking into a fit of helpless laughter at sight of a limping "Vulcain," or Hephaestus, serving them their wine. Hephaestus, of course is better known as an opponent of Zeus and as the artificer of the gods than as the butt of their laughter; and in the passage referred to (at the end of Book I of the *Iliad*),[20]

Homer is careful to recall both of these aspects of the personage. Hephaestus's buffoonery is involuntary, like the Huntsman's, but it is the buffoonery of one to whom the gods owe their luxurious culture (Hephaestus built their houses "with skillful hands") and whose grotesque limp seems to be the sign of an oppositional stance still remembered although currently renounced. In the quarrel between Hera, the queen, and Zeus whose abatement the gods' laughter celebrates, Hephaestus, "in his anxiety to be of service to his mother," has advised—this time—humble submission and a request for pardon.

"The Olympian is a hard god to pit oneself against. Why, once before when I was trying hard to save you, he seized me by the foot and hurled me from the threshold of Heaven."

A possible inference is that, if the buffoon's role is played involuntarily by the Court's "artificer" and if it gives him a place, albeit in a humble way, in the Heaven of Court, such a role nevertheless bears the trace—the limp—of oppositional practice, and indeed that its submissiveness may be more tactical than genuine. The Hephaestus model has bearing on the Prince de Conti (the royal indulgence obtained, after exile, through submission and a humble request for pardon), on the Huntsman (who comes from "exile" in the woods to amuse the Court, as Hephaestus from Lemnos) and on the fabulist's own practice as the author of a clownish rhetorical performance (it "limps" like Hephaestus, and is self-defeating like the Huntsman's gift) which can now be interpreted as both involuntary and even naïve, and yet, like both the Huntsman's "act" and Hephaestus's own involuntary buffoonery, as something of a *spectacle*, a "performance" that is produced, as such, by the very existence of a royal audience, i.e., by the circumstances of power in which it occurs.[21]

I doubt that the metaphor of "loss of face" was available to La Fontaine (whose extra-European reference is Indian, not Chinese), but it is a convenient way of pointing up the difference between version two, where the King's loss of face is confined to the symbolic domain, and version one, where the Kite's grip on his nose bids fair to produce some real loss of "face." This, it seems, is in keeping with the presentation of the Kite and the Huntsman, here, not as buffoons, but as genuine savages; and it is notable that, despite the damage to the "nez sacré," royal indulgence seems to come more easily and to be less problematic, in this case, than in the case of laughter (which, curiously, constitutes at once the Huntsman's offense and the grounds of his pardon). In spite of the temerity of the "maudit animal" and the lengthy indignity suffered by the King, the latter's indulgence is spontaneous, for it seems that the culprits have acted according to the order of things.

> "Ils se sont acquittés tous deux de leur office,
> L'un en Milan, et l'autre en Citoyen des bois."

And this is a point the fable itself hastens to confirm:

> Ils n'avaient appris à connaître
> Que les hôtes des bois: était-ce un si grand mal?

So the model, here, is not that of the court buffoon (a "wild man" enculturated) but of the "wild man" himself, perceived on the one hand as more dangerous to the king's actual person, but on the other as more easily forgiven— or, more accurately, as performing an actual duty, acquitting a responsibility, or "office" (an appointed function), in thus attacking the visage of power.

As "wild men," the Kite and the Huntsman reverse the situation of Hephaestus (whose model consequently remains relevant), in that, where he was hurled from the court of the gods into exile for his insolence, they *come out of exile into the Court*, where their insolence is treated as functional. Not that it is not a dangerous form of behavior:

> Bien peu, même des Rois, prendraient un tel modèle;
> Et le Veneur l'échappa belle,

but it seems that their power to attack, and their chances of attracting indulgence, are proportional to the humbleness, and I would say the "naturalness" of their behavior. In version two, the Huntsman is full of his own importance ("Plein de zèle, échauffé, s'il le fut de sa vie"), whereas in the first he is a much more modest figure ("L'oiseau, par le chasseur humblement présenté"), as befits his station as representative of nature ("Citoyen des bois") transplanted—if that is the word—into the world of the Court. He represents that which, having been excluded from "culture," acquires *as a consequence*, both very considerable critical power and remarkable immunity from punishment. An immunity that he earns, however, at the price of an institutionalization of that selfsame critical power—it becomes an "office"—through which it is appropriated by the dominant power structure that thereby lays implicit claim to having actually produced it. Here, too, as in the case of the buffoon, then, oppositional wildness is tamed by the culture to which, even while it is opposing it, it belongs.[22]

These, then—the wild man, the buffoon—are the two models of its own oppositional practice that the text produces. They are simultaneously very similar (each is a "wildness" appropriated and tamed by the power that produced it in the first place), and yet somewhat different. The buffoon is culturally accepted, yet allowed only *symbolic* access to power (the royal "face"); whereas the wild man is excluded from culture, but, as a consequence, allowed *real* access to power (the royal visage). That is why exile from the court functions for the former as a punishment (the punishment of exclusion from culture) and for the other as disculpation (exclusion from culture is what grounds the royal clemency). In view of this difference, it is hard to see how—

logically—both of these models can function at once as models of the text's own practice.

Yet, the text attempts precisely to reconcile these two models and make them one in the passage concerning Pilpay that mediates between and joins the two versions of the Huntsman's "accident." If, in allowing my categories to slip between "power" and "opposition" on the one hand, and "culture" and "nature" on the other, I have committed some logical laxity, I do so in response to the text's own transformation of its categories ("wild man" and "buffoon") into the "animal" and the "human" in these crucial lines (75–88). Their thrust is that Pythagoreanism (the doctrine of metempsychosis), in treating animals and humans as interchangeable ("avec les Animaux de forme nous changeons")—a treatment, incidentally, that characterizes the fable as a genre—argues both for the cultural inclusion of animals (like the buffoon) and for their genuine access to power (like the wild man). The rhetorical trick lies, of course, in the lines that treat the category of "animal" as meaning "excluded from culture" but the category of "human" as meaning "belonging to the great of the earth":

> "Savons-nous, disent-ils, si cet Oiseau de proie
>   N'était point au siège de Troie?
> Peut-être y tint-il lieu d'un Prince ou d'un Héros
>   Des plus huppés et des plus hauts."

The puns in "huppés" and "hauts" nicely catch what birds and aristocrats have in common, and thus bring the animal onto the same plane as court society. But here's the rub. The argument in favor of combining cultural inclusion with access to power also turns out to deprive the King's clemency of its justification, which rests precisely, in version one, on the cultural exclusion of the Kite and the Huntsman, and, in version two, on their exclusion as buffoons from the domain of actual power. So this is a point of aporia where the text deconstructs itself: either the King is justified in his indulgence, or "Pilpay" is wrong—if "Pilpay" is right, then the King's clemency makes no sense. The text cannot argue, on the one hand, for the inclusion of literature (the fable as generic site of the identification of "animal" and "human") into culture combined with genuine access to power—for literature's "humanity"—and on the other for royal indulgence towards its wildness and oppositional stance—that is, its "animality."

Yet, that is what it does. For there *is*, paradoxically, an existing model of this impossible combination, and that is the Prince de Conti—a Prince or Hero "des plus huppés et des plus hauts." His exile functions, like that of Hephaestus, as a punishment for opposition, and so it is a sign of his social and cultural inclusion—his buffoon-like status—in the Court; yet it functions, too, as the condition of royal indulgence, and thus implies his continued access to the seat of power, the actual, physical access for which the "wild man" is forgiven. If the Prince can exist—and get away with it—so too can literature, as buffoon and wild man combined, be admitted into culture like the former and given access, simultaneously, to power, like the latter.

But the condition that makes this possible, both in the case of the Prince and in the case of literature, is the *absolute arbitrariness* of royal clemency or "indulgence." The attempt to *justify* such clemency forces literature into becoming either the buffoon (with power only in the symbolic domain) or the wild man (with real power, but culturally excluded). The two models can combine and demonstrate their compatibility, and indeed complementarity, only if the King, quite arbitrarily, permits it, just as he, quite arbitrarily, permits the Prince to exist as Hero and Kite combined. What the wild man and the buffoon have in common is, precisely, that they exemplify a power, on the part of society, to produce, and to control, its own opposition. And the text defines itself, logically, as an "impossible" combination of these two oppositional forces—both act and "act"—which becomes possible only because, and to the extent that, it is—groundlessly—permitted. The limitation of its power, which makes it always possible for it to fail, is exactly that which gives its oppositional thrust some chance of success.

It is not contradictory then that the fable I have been reading in terms of its theory of opposition presents itself more openly as a theory of kingship. The power of the monarch appears as the power to determine the social significance of behavior, a power he exercises in and through his own behavior. The King's response, indicating his decipherment of the behavior of the Huntsman and the Kite, determines what that behavior *is*. In one case, it is his formulations ("Citoyen des bois," etc.) that determine the Huntsman's status as "wild man"; in the other, his laughter turns the Kite's wild attack on the Huntsman's nose into a spectacle, a performance—an act which becomes an "act."

But in order to do this, he must combine in his person a pair of attributes no less mutually exclusive than, although symmetrical with, those of the oppositional figures. These last are at once human (included in culture) and subhuman (animal, identified with nature): the King is simultaneously superhuman and human. Superhuman in the heroic exercise of restraint by which, under the Kite's attack, he preserves his dignity and, in showing indulgence, displays his affinity with the gods (an affinity implied in the fable's opening lines), he has also the courage to be human, and to display it, in the case of the Kite's attack on the Huntsman, by laughing (a response which distinguishes him, it seems, from a Pope).[23]

It is power, then, as the combination of the superhuman and the human in kingship, that produces its opposition, necessarily, as a combination of humanity and wildness. But although I have been reading the Huntsman and his Kite (in response to the fable's pairing of them) as a couple one must also see that eventually the title's triplicity is significant, as is its syntactic distribution of the Kite and the King, on the one hand, against the Hunter on the other. Between the wild unpredictability of the contingent world of nature, and the no less unpredictable transcendence of royal clemency, as a figure of the divine, it is oppositionality as the human that defines itself in the Hunter as a "Citoyen des bois" admitted into Court where its dealings are with those whose own model is the world of the gods.

Thus La Fontaine. The harmoniousness and symmetry of this wonderfully ordered relationship is so appealing that, now that it has been lost—now that "power" and "opposition" describe only relations of mutuality between humans—it is perhaps not so surprising that a strong nostalgia for it remains. This can be seen very clearly in situations of extreme social violence, pogroms or torture, for instance, whose victims tend to perceive power as a *transcendency*, out of reach of ordinary intervention, and where, inversely, the perpetrators show a compulsion to transform their opponents into creatures *less than human*, a situation we shall see figured in Asturias's *El Señor Presidente* (chapter 4). But what has been evacuated here, precisely, is the human and with it the oppositional, and it is among humans that we have, in less extreme circumstances, to sort out the tangled forces of power and opposition to power.

The chastisement of kings, in Bossuet's view of things (see his *Politique tirée des propres paroles de l'Écriture Sainte*), was the sole privilege of divinity. It is a sure mark of La Fontaine's modernity that he perceived the oppositional possibility of a mere subject's giving kings "des leçons de bonté," while remaining aware that royal absolutism, by virtue of its divine right, was both the ultimate source of oppositional authority and the clear marker of its limits. But what happens when there is no more divine right of kings and the site of power is no longer so easy to identify? It is to the consequences for opposition of that loss of centrality and visibility in the site of power and of that loss of transcendent guarantee in its functioning that I shall now be turning.

But two important and intimately related conclusions are worth drawing from La Fontaine's practice and retaining as pertinent in what follows. The one has by now been abundantly demonstrated: the power to oppose derives from power—a maxim no less true, although its ramifications (as we shall see) are even more intricate, when power has become decentralized, relative, diffuse, shifting, and shared. The other is that, *as a consequence*, irony as an oppositional mode must always end up ironizing itself. Like the Huntsman's gift, it has a certain knack of backfiring, because its power to oppose always turns out to be a function of the power it opposes.

As I have attempted to show, the educational value of the *Fables*, as oppositional discourse, lies in the readability they derive from their ironic structure, in which their apparent address on the narrative plane to the positions of power—incorporated, for example, in dedications to the great or in conformity to the phallocentric conventions of *gauloiserie*—is textually subverted. That is important. But in each case, we have seen a further irony, a further self-distancing of the text, arise from the realization that such ironies can work only in the context of power they are ironizing: irony's own murky discourse has more than accidental kinship with the narrative trap setting, the mystifications of secrecy and other discursive duplicities of the powerful, and its oppositional "wildness" is not easily distinguishable from the buffoonery that amuses courts and kings.

So if irony turns the tables on the discourse of power, those tables can always be turned again and ironic distance shown to be in complicity with what it opposes; with the result that there is an *infinite regress of irony* (for which Roland Barthes, in another context, has given a suggestive analysis)[24]. Thus, in "Les femmes et le secret," the ironic revelation of male secrecy as the means by which women are oppressed turns out to be itself dependent on participation in male power. Oppositional narrative's ability to turn to its own account the power it is opposing is unremittingly balanced—but never cancelled out—by a concomitant awareness that it borrows its strength from, and so is used by, the power it cannot avoid subserving as it opposes it. *That* is the irony of the oppositional.

But we have yet to see the possibility of another turn of the tables. In spite of its subservience and in spite of the vicious circle of "discourse" and "counter-discourse" in which it is caught, the readability on which oppositional irony rests can still open up a certain "room for maneuver" out of which forms of change can emerge, thereby disturbing (in the long term) the structures of power. In short, if there is an irony of oppositionality (the irony of oppositional irony), there is also an irony of power, which for the moment, can be formulated as follows: its control of oppositionality does not extend, fully, to control of the effects of oppositionality. That is why I give greater emphasis, in what is to follow, to the pole of *reading* that is implied by the readability of ironically oppositional discourse that this chapter has demonstrated.

3 The Suicide Tactic: Writing in the Language of the Other

Hier, Lotte! Ich schaudere nicht, den kalten schrecklichen Kelch su fassen, aus dem ich den Taumel des Todes trinken soll! Du reichtest mir ihn und ich zage nicht.

—J. W. Goethe, *Die Leiden des jungen Werthers*

[Here, Lotte! I do not shudder to grasp the cold and terrible cup from which I am to drink the transport of death. You handed it to me, and I do not hesitate.]

Je l'appelle quelquefois Lolotte, et elle me trouve un peu de ressemblance avec Werther, moins les pistolets, qui ne sont plus de mode.

—G. de Nerval, "Sylvie"

[Sometimes I call her Lolotte, and she thinks I am a little like Werther, minus the pistols, which have gone out of style.]

January 21, 1793. The Europe-wide wave of suicide triggered by the publication of *Werther* (first version 1774, final version 1786) still raged and the literary influence of the text was just beginning at the date of Louis XVI's decapitation. In cultural history there are no clean breaks or absolute origins, but this is an excellent symbolic moment from which to date a shift in the conception (if not the nature) of power and so, one of the prime components of modernity. The absolute monarchy had clung, at least theoretically, to a hierarchically structured, pyramidal disposition of power, at the topmost point of which the monarch by divine right embodied and rendered visible the seat and source of authority. In this dispensation—La Fontaine's world—justice was administered at every level, from the lowest to the highest, and throughout the realm, in the name of the King.

The decision of the Assembly to carry out an act of justice on the person of the King himself consequently posed—especially to a group largely composed of jurists—a difficult problem: in the name of whom or of what might one legitimately execute the King? The answer was quickly found: in the name of the People. But this answer was at the source of a new set of questions: for who is, or are, the People? As a practical matter, the people can manifest its, or their, will only through representatives, and it is in the politics of representation that the modern experience of the diffuseness and invi-

sibility of power, which Michel Foucault has memorably described,[1] finds a
clear manifestation. For who represents the people? Again as a practical matter, representation comes to mean the possession of a majority of votes,
which—by dividing the people's will—not only exposes this concept (*the
people*) as a myth but also raises the question of the status of the minority, or
minorities.

More radically still, a small group may achieve majority status simply
by controlling a majority of votes; and indeed it quickly becomes evident
that "majorities" are potential minorities—*always* representative of specific
interests—which happen to be in a position to dominate, and hence to claim
to represent (a majority of) the people. This situation is familiar in parliamen-
tary democracies of all kinds; but it was the Terror in France, with its fierce
politics of group interest and its wild swings of power (I will save the cult of
personality for the following chapter), that first experimented with the terrifying politics of power in a world in which there could no longer be any
absolute legitimation of authority. The results were bloody. But Marie-Hélène
Huet has shown that, simultaneously, there were immediate cultural consequences of the guillotining of the King, notably in a repeated recourse to the
agonistics of the trial form as a means of deciding rights and wrongs in drama
obsessively devoted, not to the execution of Louis, of course, but to the *assas-
sination* of Marat (who was known as "le roi du peuple," the people's king).[2]

I want to look in this chapter at a different but related form of cultural
fallout from the symbolic decapitation of power by examining the poetics, and
hence the politics, of suicide in the new kingless world, taking suicide the suppression of the subject—as an oppositional response to the world produced by
the execution/assassination of centralized authority: the world of majorities
and minorities, that is, of *relativized* power. But I will be concerned with a
suicide that takes its inspiration less from Werther's *act* than from the *letter*
in which he simultaneously embraces death ("Ich schaudere nicht, den kalten
schrecklichen Kelch zu fassen") and makes it an act of love that is at the same
time an accusation, and an accusation of murder ("Du reichtest mir ihn, und
ich zage nicht"). I am talking, in other words, of a form of *writerly suicide* as
an oppositional act, the essence of which is well caught by the narrator of
Nerval's "Sylvie," when he mentions of his lost love that "elle me trouve un
peu de ressemblance avec Werther, moins les pistolets,"[3] thus establishing that
there can be something like a *social agreement* to cast some (a minority of
"misfits" like the narrator) in the role of Werther, and others (the majority of
"realists" like Sylvie) in that of Lotte, an agreement that makes suicide without
pistols a mode of symbolic death that is also a *modus vivendi*. I do not have
space to read "Sylvie" here; but I will want to suggest that writerly suicide is
what occurs in the text of *melancholy*, as an enactment of the metaphoric

"drowning"—this is Hubert Aquin's word—of the narrative subject; and that this drowning in words, the words of the other or the words of otherness, has the oppositional status of a suicide note.

How does this come about? In a world of diffuse, distributed, and shifting power relations, with its constant temptation to settle matters by violence, the oppositional becomes a much less secure matter and a more problematic category. It becomes, specifically, a function of minoritization, and so is identified with interests that either are not *in* the majority or else do not *have* (i.e., control) a majority, that is, do not have majority *status*. But majority and minority status are themselves not stable: it is not only that the minoritized may become a majority and vice versa, but indeed that any given individual may have varying degrees of power in respect of certain of his or her interests and in specific aspects of his or her life while being minoritized in other ways, to different degrees and in respect of other interests. Thus, in contemporary society, I for instance may be relatively powerful (in certain situations) as a professional person and a male, less powerful as, say, a gay male or a foreigner, relatively powerless when I visit "my" doctor or dentist or battle with City Hall. But I am also clearly more powerful, in general terms, as a white male, than most white, let alone black or Hispanic, female citizens and any "illegal alien" or unemployed person or applicant for welfare or black teenager or street-person, whether male or female, gay or straight. And the ways in which I enjoy power are available to me as a basis from which to combat the minoritization to which I am subject in other respects. When one discusses the minoritization of literature in the modern world and the oppositional status it derives from its minoritization, it is as well to remember that to achieve "literary" status in the first place, however minoritized, it is necessary for an author, as the agent of textuality, to have access to education, leisure, the material opportunity to write, mastery of a "standard" language, modes of printing and distribution of texts, etc. It is only by virtue of this access to power that a minoritized literature can function oppositionally; and at the risk of being repetitive, I do not want this point to be lost sight of.

For the essence of oppositionality in the modern world—of course, it was clearly the case in many circumstances also during the premodern period—lies in a recognition that (a) power is not absolute, deriving only from social practices; but also (b) that *I (too) am the other* whose power produces me. The last phrase does not only mean that I am an other to other people and hence exert power over them as they do over me. It means more fundamentally that my identity, whether as a majoritized and powerful individual or as a minoritized and relatively powerless one, is *not my own*, is not "proper" to me, does not depend on "me," my wishes, actions or desires, but is a function of *otherness*. That is why power is diffuse; for, whoever I am, I am the product of relations and forces that are social in kind, and for which "my" language—as the medium of the social other without which I am nothing—can be seen to stand. Without my "other," I am not; I am neither minoritized nor majoritized, I am not powerful, not oppositional, not powerless; yet what *I* am can still only be thought of in turn—here is the paradox—as *other* than those others that produce me.

The paradoxes of mutual otherness need no insistence, they are among the clichés of modernity. But in them lies the key to understanding the oppositionality of modern textual practices. For, just as there is no absolute power and no correspondingly absolute power to oppose, there is equally no autonomous subject of opposition: I am the other. But it is in that otherness of the self that lies the *virtuality of power* that makes oppositionality possible, implying as it does the reversibility of relations of identity. Thus, the literature of melancholy has oppositional impact because it is the site of the "suicidal" gesture by which are enacted the implications of a certain "truth": the truth that "I am the other," for if the "other" has power over me, I am not without power over that other, since I am the other's other, the condition being only that I accept, "suicidally," the otherness of my own identity. And so, as Nerval scribbled on a portrait of himself, engraved by Gervais for the frontispiece of one of his books, *Je suis l'autre.*

Putting it in discursive terms, the condition of the modern practice of oppositionality resides, then, in the knowledge that the *language* I speak is the language of the "other." That such is universally the case is the burden of contemporary psychoanalysis, linguistics, discourse theory, much of philosophy and of what is called "theory," literary or otherwise. But it is minoritized people—women in male-oriented society, colonized people working in the cultural circumstances of "conquest," or even graduate students learning the discursive formations characteristic of some body of knowledge (e.g., "lit.-crit.-speak") or of some profession (e.g., legalese)—who are most inescapably *aware* that they are constituted by the language of the other while knowing themselves to be other than the language that constitutes them. For such people, oppositionality can only take the form of an appropriation to their own purposes of the alienating language of power, or as Deleuze and Guattari might put it,[4] of a (re-)minoritization of the majority language: I mean (and that is why I say: *re*-minoritization) of a minority language—the language of a particular set of interests or a specific group—that happens to be in power. And no one has written more suggestively than have Deleuze and Guattari of what is entailed in the production of a *minor* literature from a *major* language. (We must only remember that, as far as language goes, even "native" languages can themselves be experienced as alienating by subjects who identify with a "majority" group.)

I propose, in this chapter, to study two characteristically modern oppositional textual productions, and to do so in the light of their (re-)minoritization
of the major language it is given to them to speak, which in both cases is
ultimately the language called "French," the *sole* language available to them
in which to write.[5] It is part of their achievement to show us that "French" is
the name of a minority language that is in power. To Gérard de Nerval, a
socially minoritized writer in mid-nineteenth-century France who was diagnosed as "mad" (a "cyclothyme" or manic-depressive), "French" is the alienating language specifically of the medical profession (that is, of "alienists") and
more generally of bourgeois ideology. To Hubert Aquin, a politically minoritized writer in the Québec of the 1960s, it is, more intricately, the language
spoken in English-dominated Québec, a language of power that is not *the*
language of power, "majestic"—as he says—"but in second place."
     I shall concentrate on the effort in these texts to make the "major" language
serve the purposes of a discourse of opposition; and in conformity with my
overall thesis in this book, I will try to suggest that this effort takes the form
of textualization (or readability) as a subversion of the "narrative function"
of discourse. In thus substituting the complexities of the reader-text relation
for the narrator-narratee relation characteristic of "normal" (subject-centered)
modes, as described in chapter 1, such texts as those of Nerval and Aquin
foreground their own situation of enunciation—or, more accurately, they foreground themselves as *constituted* by an enunciatory situation—and invite the
reader to interpret the relations of narrativity that they produce, or of which
they furnish a mimesis, as a function, precisely, of their oppositional status.
What I shall call the "melancholic" or "suicidal" text is thus a form of textuality in which a certain "loss" of narrative identity is enacted as a "gain" in
oppositional impact, subject to their "appeal" for reading encountering an appropriate response.
     Deleuze and Guattari describe three main features of "minor" literature.
"The three characteristics of minor literature are the deterritorialization of
language, the connection of the individual to political immediacy and the collective assemblage of enunciation."[6] Deterritorialization as the construction
within the major language of a minor discourse "appropriate"—as the authors
say—"for strange and minor uses" (17) is a description of what I call textuality, especially as a subversion of the "narrative function." The implication
that "everything," however particular or individual, "is political" (17) implies
the readability that is also characteristic of textuality (and more especially the
readability of the oppositional therein). The backgrounding of subject-centered
discourse in favor of an apparatus of "collective enunciation" describes the
"suicidal" substitution of a plural and divided *sujet de l'énonciation* for the
autonomous subject presupposed by the "narrative function" as the relation of

narrator and narratee. These are three ways, then, of describing minoritization of discourse as a textualization, a conversion from modes of explicit and direct "communication" to relationships of "readability" that imply the interpretation of the *unsaid*. Language, conceived as a more or less transparent *means to an end*, is thus transformed into a discourse that produces itself as a "parole intermédiaire," a *medium* that, to the contrary, cannot be ended ("reading" being the name we give to the impossibility of closure that characterizes text), precisely because it enacts the situation of communication as a mediated one.

I could say the same thing by referring to the *allegorization* of discourse. It comes simultaneously (a) to mean more than it can say and (b) to resolve the quest for meaning (for that "more") into a process of substitution, deferral, and indeed drift. Text both requires to be *read*, in the strong sense of the term, and requires of reading that it forego the closure of meaning.[7] This situation can be seen to be the direct consequence of the textual production of its own *situation of enunciation* (which implies production of itself as a scene of writing and of reading), and of the *subject* of enunciation as a plural, divided self—an "I" indistinguishable from the other(s) that constitute(s) it—and hence as not admitting of interpretive closure, in the way that the supposedly autonomous subject of a communicative "message" would. For nothing more clearly enacts the meaning of the formula: "I am the other," than the enunciatory situation of a text that defines itself as realizable only through the intervention of an agency of reading.

But the characteristic mood of allegorization, as Walter Benjamin influentially noticed,[8] is melancholy; and it is as writers of melancholy that Nerval and Aquin, oppositional users of the language of the other, will be paired in this chapter. The key characteristics of melancholy are those, perhaps, that Deleuze and Guattari metaphorize as "deterritorialization" and "nomadism," and these are the metaphors that Nerval and Aquin themselves obsessively thematize in their writing. The Valois region near Paris is produced in Nerval as the space of the (always already) absent mother as against the city of Paris where the law of the father prevails, history (as the economic and material "progress" of the bourgeoisie) is made, and alienists minoritize "madness" by producing it in the diagnostic language of the other. The deterritorialized space of a Québec "occupied" by the political other of the English-speaking victors of the Plains of Abraham is ceaselessly rewritten, in Aquin's novels, as the marshy labyrinth of the Slave Coast (in *Trou de Mémoire*), the jagged and vacant coast of Spitzbergen (in *Neige noire*) or—in *Prochain Épisode* and *L'Antiphonaire*—as the mountainous topography of the Valais, the "pays de Vaud," the region of Lake Geneva and Piedmont—all of them metaphors for writing (in the sense of *écriture*), as a description of Alpine scenery in *Prochain Épisode* specifies:

je contemplais l'incomparable écriture de ce chef d'oeuvre anonyme fait de débris, d'avalanches, de zébrures morainiques et des éclats mal taillés d'une genèse impitoyable. (P. 107)[9]

[I contemplated the incomparable writing of that anonymous masterpiece composed of débris, avalanches, the zigzag of moraines and the rough-hewn splinters of a ruthless genesis.]

Meanwhile, the wandering, episodic text that is the hallmark of these two consciously and provocatively nonclosural writers—Nerval indicates in "Angélique" that the words "Et puis . . . " ["And next . . . "] are the key to his writing; Aquin's title, *Prochain Épisode*, specifies the perpetual displacement that is the mode of existence of his writing—thematizes the elusiveness of its writing subject in the nomadism of protagonists whose unpredictable itineraries trace labyrinthine paths across the Valois, like the errant point of Corporal Trim's stick in *Tristram Shandy*, or crisscross the region of Lake Geneva and perform high-speed slaloms on twisting Alpine roads, a *dérapage* [skidding] that again metaphorizes "la course effusive des mots" ["the effusive flow/chase of words"] (110).

Both deterritorialization and nomadism figure the melancholic sense of an identity that makes "I" a function of the "other." If I am the other, "my" territory is not *mine*—there is no *there* there, as Gertrude Stein might say; and my search for myself—for a self that might *stand* in resistance to the other(s) that constitute(s) me—can only engage me in an endless wandering, and in an oppositionality of elusiveness. It becomes a directionless pursuit that takes me from point to point in seemingly aimless and endless fashion, from moment to moment and from mood to mood, across a landscape of identity that has no center.

This sense of dispossession from one's "own" space and this awareness of an unendingly drifting self are among the symptoms of melancholia to whose oppositional function Freud pointed when he noted in his justly famous essay that the "complaints" of melancholics are in reality "accusations": *ihre Klagen sind Anklagen.*[10] In so doing, he was reactivating the etymological connection (via Greek *kholé*) between melancholy and anger (choler) and pointing out that melancholy is a phenomenon that requires *reading*. Melancholy is, in short, an oppositional text: in Freudian terms, a psychoanalytic text, but one that is necessarily also a *social* text, if only because melancholy results from the sense that "I am the other" (indeed, it is in this sense *the* disease of the "individual" as a social being). As a social text, then, melancholy requires reading, not as the site of a personal unconscious, harboring individual "anger," but as the "place"—a deterritorialized place crisscrossed by a nomadic subject—where a political unconscious becomes readable, in and as the tension of the self and the self-constituting other(s). The readability of the melancholic text, so viewed, constitutes in other words, *the return of the political repressed*; and that is why, as Deleuze and Guattari put it tellingly, the "cramped space" of minor literature—its space of repression—"forces each immediate intrigue to connect immediately to politics" (17), while taking on, as they suggest throughout their work, the anti-Oedipal characteristics of a "revanche," the revenge of desire on the law. The repressed, when it returns, always does so, as we say, "with a vengeance."

Getting back at the world is what suicide is frequently all about; and biographically speaking, both Nerval and Aquin ended their own lives (as did Benjamin). Their deaths are speech-acts, rhetorical performatives speaking to us, still, of the social and political extremities to which, as individual humans, they found themselves reduced. The diagnosis of madness had deprived Nerval of his sole means of livelihood, as a writer; Aquin's death is inseparable from the collapsed aspirations of revolutionary Québec separatism under the political crackdown of the late 60s and early 70s, and more especially under the reformist weight of the "quiet revolution." Aquin's texts, which almost obsessively foreground their own enunciatory situation, frequently figure that situation in terms of discursive suicide—what in *Prochain Épisode* is called a "noyade écrite," a drowning in writing (22) (and the narrator of *L'Antiphon-aire* echoes: "j'écris comme si je me noyais" ["I write as if I was drowning"]). But suicide in Aquin is itself bound up with, and sometimes inextricably inseparable from murder, and murder is in turn obsessively associated with rape. It is as if, in his world, one must either rape or be raped; one must *kill the other*—this is the theme of *Prochain Épisode*, as we shall see—or submit to the social murder that is elimination of the self, a situation in which only the long-drawn-out suicide that is writing offers, as we shall also see, the possibility of an oppositional tactic.

By contrast with these violent figurations, suicide is only discreetly thematized as such in Nerval. But his writing enacts itself as a gesture of love, and simultaneously as something almost like a *mort heureuse* in that it is the place of the disappearance of the autonomous self into a would-be harmonious enunciatory collectivity. The political reference, here, is to the utopian and early-socialist enthusiasms that gripped the Parisian intelligentsia in the 1840s and were swept away—after having been celebrated in February—in the divisive bloodshed of June 1848. Nerval's reference to this political trauma is in his association of the Valois with the wars of religion and specifically the massacre of St. Bartholomew's Day; and it is also in the apocalyptic battles of good and evil forces that constitute some of the more frightening visions of "Aurélia." But it is to the reduction of conflict and the realization of harmony through the practice of writerly "dialogism" that his late (post-1850) work tends—

witness the somewhat optimistic hopes for an East-West and North-South reconciliation as the outcome of the Crimean War that are also written into "Aurélia."

But whether antagonistic and violent, as in Aquin, or harmonian and dialogic, as in Nerval, it is nevertheless in terms of a poetics/politics of suicide that the oppositionality of the melancholic text is best understood; and the distinction between oppositional behavior and discursive oppositionality— dubious as it is from a certain point of view—is powerfully demonstrated by the contrast between the sad finality of suicide as an *act* and the readability that *writing* as a long suicide or "noyade écrite" can achieve. My understanding of such writing is that it combines symbolic suicide with the oppositional potential of the suicide note, of which Werther's final letter is paradigmatic. The announcement of the subject's death survives as the enunciation of a disappeared subject (and the verb "disappear" here has at least *something* of the sad transitivity it acquired in the tragic circumstances of junta-controlled Argentina).

It is not my intention to claim, however, that melancholy is *the* form of oppositional textuality that corresponds to the diffuseness of power characteristic of modernity. The following chapter will show that, under political situations of "dictation," modernity produces situations of writing that require even trickier appeals to reading. But that melancholy is a major and symptomatic response to the conditions of modernity is evident when one reflects on how much of the tradition of modernism, from Nerval, Baudelaire, and Flaubert to Benjamin, Artaud, Beckett, Aquin, or Sartre (whose *La Nausée* was originally entitled *Mélancholia*) has been placed under the sign of the saturnine.[11] The *other* response—I mean the "other" of the tradition of melancholy—has been, of course, from Friedrich Schlegel through Nietzsche and Derrida, that of irony and *gai saber*; but it is not obvious whether modern melancholy and this new, often playful, irony constitute different traditions, or aspects of the same subversive sensibility.

For what irony and melancholy have in common is precisely their erosion of the ideology of the autonomous subject, their recognition and enactment of the fact—with all its oppositional potential—that I am the other. For that reason, it is not surprising to find writers whose melancholy is indistinguishable from their irony: Heine is such a one, Laforgue perhaps another. So it is too in the writing of Nerval, which is successively and sometimes simultaneously playful and ironic in its oppositionality, as well as melancholic and nostalgic. That is a reason why I have chosen to discuss two Nerval texts here, one predominantly playful ("Angélique") but more than tinged with melancholy, the other ("Aurélia") explicitly placed under the patronage of Dürer's Angel of Melancholy and the sign of the saturnine ("Sylvie" would perhaps be the text in which the balance of irony and melancholy is most evenly maintained).

That irony and melancholy are aspects of the same sensibility is perhaps what is understood when writing such as Nerval's is discussed in terms of "Romantic irony," a term suggestive of an appreciation of irony significantly different from the more classical irony we saw functioning in La Fontaine. The disappearance of figures of centralized power, such as the King; the consequent new diffuseness of authority and the concomitant understanding that *I am the other*—that identity is other-constructed and hence a mediated phenomenon—these produce the oppositional relation to the "language of the other" less now as a matter of ironic distancing and more as an *intimate* matter. This I will describe as an affair of appropriation, since it is from the other's language that the self, understood as a difference from the "subject" that is produced in and by the alienating discourse of power—understood, that is, as an "other" of the other's alienating discourse—must necessarily be produced. In this circumstance, the ironic production of an oppositional self becomes a matter of making *use* of the discourse of power for purposes that controvert it, as my reading of "Angélique" will show.

If "Aurélia" is more melancholic than ironic, however, it is because the later text is the site of a stronger awareness of the degree to which this ironic subversion through appropriation of the language of power is itself dependent on the text's (identity) being *so produced* by the "other" that is its reader, and so on an abdication of any controlling "self" of its own. Even more than "Angélique," "Aurélia" consequently is traversed by an appeal *to* the reader that is an appeal *for* sympathetic, and indeed complicitous reading; so that the text becomes the site of a complex rhetorical operation aimed at the conversion of the reader, who must cease to occupy the position of power represented by the alienating discourse of medical science, so as to cooperate in the textual production of its *sujet d'énonciation* as other than the subject who is medically diagnosed as "mad."

The implication here is that reading must be an acknowledgment of textual alterity just as writing becomes an appeal for the production of textual identity addressed to the reader: each identity—that of the writing, and that of the reading—must define itself as mediated by the other, that is as mutually other-produced, since in order to produce the necessary shift in the position of reading that produces its own identity, the text must itself incorporate in its own discourse an acknowledgment of the position (of power)—that of the alienating other productive of a false self—from which the reader is to shift. The reader produces the text's oppositional identity as a matter of self-differentiation within the text; but the condition of this is that the text itself produce a shift within the reader, corresponding to what I have described earlier as a shift from the narratee-position to that of reading subject. Aquin's writing is exemplary in this respect, since it very prominently situates the mutually dependent relation of text and reading as one of double "suicide."

In this understanding, textual "suicide"—as the enactment of an identity that can be produced only as other than the subject produced by the alienating discourse of power (and hence by the "disappearance" of that subject)—itself functions, as in certain suicide notes, as an appeal to and for "suicidal" reading, as a similar abdication on the reader's part of the subject-position produced in the discourse of power, in favor of one mediated by the alterity of the text—a suicidal reading, therefore, without which the textual suicide, as the enactment of the death of the narrative "I" in favor of the continued life of a textual *sujet d'énonciation*, cannot itself take place.

Because Aquin's novels group more homogeneously, as melancholic writing in this sense, than Nerval's texts, I will read only one: the first, best-known, and (with *Trou de Mémoire*) politically most explicit of them, *Prochain Épisode*.[12] My attempt will be to show that it incorporates, on the "writing" side, a form of suicide that functions—as in "Angélique"—as an appropriative irony, but that this suicidal discourse simultaneously constitutes—as in "Aurélia"—an appeal for an act of love on the "reading" side. This act of love will symmetrically consist of another suicide, in the reader's conversion from alienating other of the text—the subject of power—to an *other-produced identity* that corresponds (in ontological terms) and responds (in communicational terms) to the textual *sujet d'énonciation*. Ideally, then, for Aquin, each of these s(uic)ides is the same s(uic)ide.

1. Dialogism and Opposition

Nerval's nomadism, both biographical and writerly, has been extensively studied.[13] The question that has gone largely unasked, however, concerns the social context of the shift in mode that produced, in the period of 1849 through 1854, a series of autobiographical texts whose main characteristic is that they limit the horizons of their traveling to the Valois, a small region of Ile-de-France (around Chantilly, Ermenonville, and Senlis), geographically close to Paris but—in Nerval's descriptions, at least—still "patriarchal," that is relatively untouched by the economic and social developments of nineteenth-century "civilization" and still faithful to the traditions of its own rural past.[14] Germany and Italy had been more characteristic Nervalian destinations, and in 1850, when he published in serial [*feuilleton*] form the first of the Valois texts, his *Voyage en Orient*, which is an account of an ambitious if partly fictional swing through Austria, Greece, Egypt, Lebanon, and Turkey—a text broadly reflective of the optimistic mood of the 1840s—was still to appear in its definitive version as a volume.

"Les Faux-Saulniers," from which "Angélique" was drawn in 1854 for inclusion in a volume of short stories and poems, *Les Filles du Feu*, appeared intermittently in the newspaper *Le National* over the months of fall 1850, that is at a time when the Republic, born in socialist enthusiasm in February 1848, had become—after the decisive and bloody turning point of June—a bourgeois political machine, or "République honnête," governed by a Prince-President and defined already by the type of repressive social apparatus that was to characterize more specifically, after the coup d'état of December 1851, the Second Empire. In this context, Nerval's turn to the proximity of the Valois has the effect of producing his travel writing, especially by the implied contrast with the more expansive reach and more hopeful mood of the *Voyage en Orient*, as a melancholic genre.

This latter text has the characteristics of a quest: its narrator is in quest of the sun, in quest of initiation—his ambition in Egypt is to "lift a corner of the veil" of Isis[15]—in quest also of social harmony (the text clearly thinks of itself as an intervention in what was already the "Middle Eastern question"). It is true that these quests are only imperfectly successful, and it is equally true that Nerval was never to abandon the ambitions that give some of his narrators the characteristics of a solar hero. But in the Valois, a veil has been, not lifted, but drawn; and it is a veil of mourning. The (already deficient) sunshine of the East is replaced by the misty forests of a water-logged landscape of woods, ponds, and streams; in lieu of the ambition to penetrate the veil of things, the narrators pursue a ceaseless and erratic, because frustrated, exploration of surfaces that are informed by absence; and the social(ist) concerns—this of course refers to early or "Utopian" socialism—are at least apparently replaced by an inward turn that focuses on the moods and melancholies of a personal history.

Of course, the *Voyage en Orient,* relative to the stately voyages of Lamartine and Chateaubriand that form a large part of its intertext, is already oppositional and already the account of a failure; but it seems never quite to abandon the hope of there being some sort of continuity between the present and the ideal past of human "origins" that the narrator seeks to reach. By contrast, it is discontinuity that defines the Valois: as the sun is cut off by the veil of mists, the personal past is irretrievable, although tantalizingly close in a region where old customs, traditions, and folkways persist and jog the memory at every turn; so that the narrators of the Valois tales typically wander in search of an elusive spatial center that would correspond for them to an origin in time, aware all along of its tantalizing proximity combined with a frustrating elusiveness. As Parisians, writing for Parisians in the discourse of the journals and feuilletons of the capital, they are irrevocably strangers in a land that is uncannily familiar to them, condemned to be observers, analysts, and describers of what once they lived—or *might* have lived had they not always already been destined to become Parisians.

For the decisive break in continuity that constitutes the Valois as melancholic is that between Paris, the place of history and modernity, and the hamlets where traditional ways survive, as if untouched by industry and the economy of capitalism, the hamlets whose names are frequently recited as in a litany—much as Aquin's text recites the place names of the Ottawa valley or the valley of the Rhone—as if a recitation in the present could act as an evocation, magically restoring a lost and originary past that seems to be separated only by the thinness of text:

La voiture va passer à Orry, puis à La Chapelle. A gauche, il y a une route qui longe le bois d'Hallate. C'est par là qu'un soir . . . (etc.) Nous rattrapâmes le parc à Mont-l'Évêque, et quelques minutes plus tard nous nous arrêtions à la maison du garde, à l'ancienne abbaye de Châalis.—Châalis, encore un souvenir! ("Sylvie," p. 256)

[The coach is about to go through Orry, then La Chapelle. On the left, there is a road that runs alongside the woods of Hallate. Over there one evening . . . (etc.) We met the grounds again at Mont-l'Évêque, and a few minutes later were pulling up at the guard's house, in the former abbey of Châalis.—Châalis, another memory!]

The geographical proximity of Paris and the Valois stands in this way for the propinquity in consciousness between a wandering self in the temporality of the present and a nostalgically remembered, but unattainable, center of stability and selfhood: in short, it stands for the dividedness of a melancholic consciousness. The Valois is less than 40 km from the capital (at a pinch, the modern air traveler can make it to Charles de Gaulle airport at Roissy in a little more than half an hour); but for Nerval it takes many hours to get there—and especially to penetrate to its heartland (near Ermenonville)—because it is necessary to take indirect and tortuous routes, by carriage and on foot. For the railroad, that fast modern invention, has passed it by, and even describes a vast curve as if to avoid it—a curve, Nerval very plausibly hints, that is the result of capitalist speculation. Cut off in this way from history and modernity, with which it lies in close proximity but from which it is simultaneously separated by an unbridgeable gulf—but similarly cut off from any reassuring sense of centeredness and origin—the Valois becomes the privileged site for an exploration of what might be called the temporality of homelessness.

But this melancholic separation-yet-proximity of home-space from the city-space of affairs and history makes the Valois available, simultaneously, as a place of oppositionality. In this sense, it stands for a privatized space, that is, the area of the "personal" which, in the bourgeois worldview, coexists with, but escapes the reach of, society and its laws. The privatized is the area of what is not forbidden, that in which oppositional behavior and/or discourse is consequently tolerated, precisely because, the private being defined as untouched by the social, by history and "politics," it is conceived as unable in its turn to affect the world of affairs, of laws, of industry and commerce, of what was called "progress" (read the interests of the middle class). It will be Nerval's achievement in "Angélique"—the first of the two texts I plan to read in some detail—to make appropriative *use* of the privatized space of the "personal" for oppositional purposes, while simultaneously making *readable* the isolation of the personal as itself the product of political gestures. By these I mean the gestures of minoritization that, in the authoritarian world of the bourgeois Republic, affect on the one hand, a disaffected "territory" such as the Valois, on the other a suspect profession such as that of writing, and ultimately—here we will need to turn to "Aurélia"—the category that is controlled and contained under the name of "madness."

What this means is that out of political minoritization as an act of repression (exclusion, containment, etc.) emerges the possibility of an oppositional act of "minoritization" in the sense of Deleuze and Guattari, the minoritization of a "major" or dominant language through the discursive "assemblages" that constitute textuality; a minoritization that is, as I would prefer to say, a re-minoritization in that it points up the relativity of the discourse of power and dominance itself. We will see that the source of "Angélique"'s oppositionality as writing lies in its textual mimesis of melancholy as the "elocutionary disappearance" (Mallarmé's *disparition élocutoire*)[16] of the individual self, replaced by an errant, nomadic textual subject whose voice melds into the text as "collective enunciation," as his uncentered identity fuses with the wanderings of temporality. But this pluralized text maintains a "narrative function" in apparent deference to the requirements of authority, as the discourse of bourgeois hegemony—maintains it, that is, in such a way that it is relativized, or "re-minoritized," in the context of the textual plurality and drift, where its maintenance appears as a necessary feint, a requirement of textual survival, a mask of submissiveness placed at the point where its privatized oppositionality comes into contact with the world of laws and power.

For the occasion of the disappearing act that produces textuality is produced in the text itself as the passing of an authoritarian law, a law of press censorship, directed against the freedom of commentary, direct and indirect, that existed in the institution of the feuilleton. The so-called *amendement Riancey* was one of a series of laws, including laws against anonymous and pseudonymous writing, that enforced the legal responsibility of individual writers for their discourse; but the Riancey amendment was particularly duplicitous in that it insisted on historical accuracy and proscribed the fictionality of the *feuilleton-roman*, or serial novel (a genre that had been notably hospitable to historical romance and hence to indirect comment, by that means, on the political activities of the day). As is pointed out in "Angélique," a "broad interpretation" of such a law enabled it to be used selectively, against *any* piece of writing whatsoever, fictionality and historicality not being watertight categories and being very much subject to definition; and a by-product of this act intended to control the press was consequently that it threatened the livelihood of the considerable number of writers whose economic survival depended on the institution of the feuilleton. The witty response of "Les Faux-Saulniers" takes the form of overt, and indeed ostentatious, submissiveness to the law, a submissiveness embodied in the narrative voice of the text, but combined with oppositional evasion of the antifictional requirement by recourse to quotation and intertextuality—the narrator reports, with submissive "historical" accuracy, the most outrageously oppositional behavior and/or fantastic discourse. The upshot of this technique of citation and this intertextual writing practice is that they finally produce the text itself as no longer in the control of the narrator, but as a form of collective enunciation (in which the narrator's voice is one of many).

The narrator reports that, in order to conform to the new law, he has promised his editor a feuilleton based on the adventures of a historical figure, one Abbé de Bucquoy, about whom he had discovered an old volume in Frankfurt. Confident that the book would be available in Paris, he had not bought it—but alas, it cannot be traced either in the libraries of the capital or through the network of its antiquarian bookstores and bibliophiles. Finally it turns up in the catalog for an auction, the date of which is repeatedly deferred. So, instead of being an account of the life and times of the Abbé, the feuilleton actually supplied becomes the hilarious recital of the hunt for the elusive volume in the labyrinthine world of library-catalogs and librarians, bibliophiles and antiquarians (the kind of people whose amiable eccentricity is inadvertently caught by their French designation as *curieux*). When finally the auction is announced, the focus of the narrative shifts to the need to *fill in the time* until then with writing—that is, to continue to furnish copy of scrupulously "historical" accuracy for an ongoing feuilleton—so that the account becomes now the haphazard report of the narrator's thoughts, encounters, and movements (including his return to the Valois) as he waits to have *something to say*. The characteristic of feuilleton-writing (paid by the column) had always been padding: Nerval brilliantly adapts this style so that it enacts the problematics, on the one hand, of a melancholic existence in temporality and, on the other, of a writing that can only be "in place of" a discourse that would have the characteristics of authenticity and truth.

The missing book signifies the unavailability to writing of an absolute referent that might guarantee something like historical accuracy; but its loss—the fact that it was once glimpsed but now cannot be found—underpins the melancholic dimension of the theme of lost identity, an identity which once was but now can only be mourned. Meanwhile, however, the account of the search, and then the wait, for the book, which occupies the whole of "Angélique" (Nerval strategically transferred the study he finally gave of the Abbé's life to another volume, *Les Illuminés ou les précurseurs du socialisme*), this account, then, never ceases conforming to the requirement of the law, since the narrator claims to be able to document as true the whole "pointless" recital of his day-by-day activities as he waits to be able to write the piece that is required of him. It is just that *that* feuilleton seems to be endlessly deferred (the joke was kept up over a period of several weeks in the original publication), while *this* feuilleton manages to be a demonstration of how to write a "feuilleton-roman" when the "feuilleton-roman" is forbidden, without however its being *quite* a "feuilleton-roman" and while protesting that one is writing history instead. . . . The text thus situates itself oppositionally, in terms of a melancholic epistemology—an epistemology of loss, unavailability, episodicity, and deferment—that puts into question the whole notion of truth, while ironically presenting itself *as* the truth, and hence as conforming to the naïve ideology of representation that the law upholds or pretends to uphold (and at least imposes). It thus enacts an appropriation of the discourse of truth for oppositional purposes that profoundly questions the possibility of such a discourse.

This oppositionality is inscribed in the text by a technique of *mise en abyme* and intertextuality. Where the narrator is law-abiding, the missing hero, the Abbé, who was in and out of the jails of seventeenth-century France and led Louis XIV's police a merry chase, is a figure of evasion, while his nomadism—the difficulty of tracking him down that matches the difficulty of tracking down the book about him—makes him both an ancestor of the narrator himself (whose pursuit of the book from library to library and bookshop to bookshop resolves finally into a more aimless, or at least directionless, wandering through the Valois) and a double for the figure of Angélique, his great-aunt. For, having been led to the Valois in the course of his pursuit of the Abbé/book about the Abbé, the narrator discovers instead traces of another elusive and oppositional personality, the eponymous Angélique de Longueval. Angélique defied her aristocratic father, and the law of the father, under

Louis XIII, by refusing to marry according to her station in life and by running off instead with a soldier, La Corbinière, who maltreated her, but to whom she remained faithful—out of fidelity, perhaps, to her own rebellious nature?—throughout the wandering life of exile they lived together.

If Nerval's text has a "core," it is in the account of Angélique's life which it produces, *en abyme*, largely by reproducing the heroine's own account of it from the manuscript the narrator claims to have discovered. But whereas the title "Angélique" (in 1854) suggests that the story of Angélique is indeed the textual core, the structure of the narrative—which now returns to the pursuit of the book about the Abbé, the narrator's wanderings being only complicated by a desire to visit the ruins of the Longueval château—suggests in turn that the episode of Angélique has been rather something of a digression from, or indeed a substitute for, the "main" story. Each story, indeed, seems "digressive" and/or secondary with respect to the other, so that, as Kurt Schärer has pointed out,[17] one has an exemplary case of Friedrich Schlegel's account of irony as "permanent parabasis." But there is irony too in the fact that a narrative made up only of digressions is a story without a "story"—or, in French, *une histoire sans histoire*, that is a story without history (lacking, that is, in the requirement specified by the *amendement Riancey*).[18] And yet, as the narrator points out at the end, he has never stopped *talking of* the elusive Abbé to the point of running the risk of boring his audience. . . . The oppositionality of these discursive moves, resulting as they do in the putting together of a text—an *agencement*—is clearly readable, then, as a function of the similarity between the textual discourse and the oppositional attitudes and behavior of the Abbé and of Angélique; but it remains true that it must be *read*, and the narrator's alibi (his cover as a straight reporter of his own investigations and discoveries) remains irreproachable; it is never "blown." If he is guilty of oppositionality, it is by association only, since he too, like the rebellious Angélique and her escapologist grandnephew, is a native of the Valois, and the Valois, we are told, has always been a place where the oppositional spirit was strong.

This means that the oppositionality that is inscribed in the text by *mise en abyme* is realized textually, not in the narrator's own discourse but in the way the narrator's discourse, out of conformity to the law, ends up disappearing, or tending to disappear, into a textual enunciation that has a collective, not an individual subject, so that there is no one to be held "responsible" for the text. Having—in the absence of the vital book—nothing to say, but being forced to write (he has promised a feuilleton), the narrator has no choice, since he is forbidden to invent, but to reproduce the triviality of his own day-by-day life: a life from which "the book" is lacking, a story without history. What we get, then, is an episodic transcription of passing encounters, thoughts and moods, reminiscences and associations of ideas, caprices and obsessions. In all this, quite naturally—alongside of perfectly subjective impressions of scenes, people, and places (justified, however, because they "actually" occurred and are reported, so to speak, *wie es eigentlich war*)—quotation tends to occupy a large part, in the form of transcriptions of conversations the narrator has had, anecdotes he has been told, documents he has encountered in libraries, archives, and bookstores. The playful freedom of this method is itself an ironic comment on, and appropriation of, the dispositions of the law it pretends to be so respectful of.

But the *reportage* technique is simultaneously a device by which—still without breaking the *letter* of the Riancey amendment—the text is able to make itself the channel by means of which the most outrageous and fantastic fictions, the most dubious historical speculations, the most personal and subjective of impressions and thoughts reach the reader. If he wishes to tell a ghost story, the narrator has only to reproduce it as a "memory of a fantastic tale I was told a long time ago" (175): *he* is being historically accurate, but the *text* is eluding the law. And it is the multiplication of this citational device that quickly transforms the text from the "monologic" narrative required by authority into a site traversed *dialogically*[19] by a plurality of enunciations, each of them "other" both to the narrator's voice and to all the other voices in the text. The narrator channels a Babel of quoted discourses— reported anecdotes and dialogues, documents and texts reproduced under various pretexts, literary reminiscences, and allusions—that form an equivalent on the plane of discourse of the "library of Babel" he explores diegetically and which itself represents (along with the identification of the Abbé with the book-about-the-Abbé) the antilogocentric epistemological framework of his oppositional stance.

Out of all these reported conversations and stories, all these quoted documents, texts, and literary precedents, all these folksongs, representative of the "voice of the people," all these *échantillons de style* (police documents dating from the seventeenth century, a letter written by "a provincial swain of Louis XIII's time," the faded verses of René de Girardin, letters written in to the paper by readers of *Le National* . . .), the narrative shapes its text as a vast orchestration of social voices—a "symphonie pastorale" (220)—that not only relativizes the voice of the narrator as one among many, but more especially reduces it to the status of a component in a multiplicitous community having both contemporary and transhistoric dimensions. And it is the plurality and harmony of this community that is implicitly contrasted with the defensive authoritarianism that requires of writing that it be monologic so that someone can be held responsible for deviations from an imposed line. For whose voice, here, can be taken to account?

In Bakhtinian terms, the practice of dialogism produces, then, a text that is
carnivalesque in character, reversing the official hierarchy of order and disorder
and substituting a chorus of voices for the monologism of a narrative function
that nevertheless remains perceptible. In Bakhtin, however, dialogism tends to
be described in terms of social antagonisms, whereas what is striking about
Nerval's writerly practice is its enactment of relationships of harmony among
the many voices it reproduces. For, just as the members of the Bucquoy family
resemble each other, and resemble the narrator, there is a strong strain of
"family" resemblance among all the librarians, bibliophiles, and archivists
whose discourse we encounter, all the amiable inhabitants of the Valois the
narrator meets or recalls, and—in the dimension of intertextuality—all the
writers whose style he evokes and whose writing, as "precursors of socialism"
(like the Abbé) and/or practitioners of the episodic technique of narration,
forms a long and continous chain of intertextual literary tradition:

"Et puis . . ." (C'est ainsi que Diderot commençait un conte, me dira-t-on.)
—Allez toujours!
—Vous avez imité Diderot lui-même.
—Qui avait imité Sterne . . .
—Lequel avait imité Swift.
—Qui avait imité Rabelais.
(Etc. . . .) (P. 239)

["And then. . . ." (That's the way Diderot once began a tale, someone will say.)
—Go on anyway!
—You have imitated Diderot himself.
—Who imitated Sterne. . . .
—Who imitated Swift.
—Who imitated Rabelais.
(Etc. . . .)]

The list of mutually imitating and imitated provocative writers goes back
finally to Homer. But it is clear that the narrator has affinities, not only—as
an artist—with this group of writers, but also, as a former citizen of the Valois
and a bibliophile, with the other two major groups as well, so that the disappearance or weakening of his voice in the multiplicitous chorus tends to be
perceived as part of a general phenomenon of harmonious merging, less a loss
of individuality than it is part of the creation of a collective, shared identity
that is plural but nevertheless cohesive, enjoying as it does a oneness resulting
from an awareness of similarity and *belonging*.

That the reader is produced by the text as a participant in this selfsame
"harmonian" community (to use an adjective that recalls the roots in early
socialism of Nerval's collective ideal) is inferable from its dependence, for op-

positional success, on complicitous, because necessarily implicit, understanding of its discursive tactics: what in French is called understanding à demi-mot. It would be self-defeating for the text to spell out its oppositional practice; but this practice would be inoperative unless there was a reader to perceive its point, to appreciate its tactics and enjoy its wit. Just as the innkeeper of the village of Ver throws a log on the fire when she sees the narrator and his friend Sylvain approach, damp and bedraggled after having been lost in the forest, for she knows they will be hungry, so too the reader the text produces will be hospitable to its unspoken intentions and appreciative, without explicit tutoring, of its oppositional moves. Such a reader will be similar to the complicitous readers presupposed by the long chain of witty and disruptive writers, from Diderot back to Homer, whom the narrator cites as his predecessors and, in this "family" environment, ancestors. But the model for this harmonious reader lies also in all the scenes of friendship and implicit understanding between basically similar people that the text incorporates. The reader, in short, is presumed to be also a member of the vast family of similarly disposed people whose voices constitute the text as a plural but cohesive "collective enunciation," and the oppositional identity of the text is inseparable from its (implicit) appeal to such a reader to realise its ironic and subversive implications by joining the textual "family."

   This is all well and good. However, there are characters in the text—notably Angélique's father and various members of the police—whose integration into the oppositional chorus is more problematic, and who represent the discourse of the text's *other* in a more antagonistic sense. The text's *racial* thinking (another hangover from the speculations of the 1840s), its tendency to set group against group (the Celts against the Franks, French women against Germanic women, the people of the Valois against Parisians), suggests that some Manichaean division of the world is also operative here, one in which figures of power and authority (fathers, conquerors, representatives of progress) are seen as irreducibly opposed, because opposed *by their nature*, to those without authority: the amiable eccentrics, witty writers, and friendly people who speak (in) the text. And there are other Nerval texts that would authorize the construction of whole complex lineages of opposed "families," in which Jehovah, Solomon, the "race of Abel," etc., are ranged on the side of power and the law, while Christ, the Queen of Sheba, the "race of Cain"—a race that includes oppositional artists—form an oppressed (but not submissive) group: that of rebellious daughters, divine sons, and Satanic or Byronian free spirits. The political implications of this social dualism, in a France recently rent by the divisive class war of June 1848 and undergoing the repressive and authoritarian régime of the "forces of order," do not need to be specified: the Manichaeism of "good" and "evil," or order and disorder, of the civilized and the "barbarians," as Dolf Oehler has shown,[20] was part and parcel of political thinking as a discursive formation in the period. But it implies that, logically, a text such as "Angélique" cannot count exclusively on a readership that is empathetic and complicitous. It has to survive also in a world of others whose alterity is radical; a world that not only contains but also is controlled by—witness the *amendement Riancey*—the representatives of restrictive authority.

The relation of the text to officialdom as a censorious readership is enacted, precisely, in an episode whose self-reflexivity is explicit. "People who suddenly change their minds always appear suspect," as Sylvain points out (215) to his friend the narrator: that is, members of the melancholic, ironic, capricious, freedom-seeking family of the oppositional live *under surveillance*, even in their "native land," their *pays*, the Valois. Sylvain is recalling the occasion when the two friends, having imprudently displayed their beards (a sign of democratic socialist beliefs) in a village café frequented by the gendarmerie, were almost arrested the following day for lack of an ID. Their inability to produce "papers" is here specifically related to the writing project of "Angélique," since the narrator attempts to talk them out of the difficulty by claiming the identity of a historical writer—that is, the precise form of writerly identity required by the *amendement Riancey*.

"Eh bien! monsieur le commissaire, ajoutai-je, je suis tout bonnement un écrivain; je fais des recherches sur la famille des Bucquoy de Longueval, et je veux préciser la place, ou retrouver les ruines des châteaux qu'ils possédaient dans la province."

Le front du commissaire s'éclaircit tout à coup:

"Ah! vous vous occupez de littérature? Et moi aussi, Monsieur! J'ai fait des vers dans ma jeunesse . . . une tragédie."

Un péril succédait à un autre; le commissaire paraissait disposé à nous inviter à dîner pour nous lire sa tragédie. (Pp. 188–89)

["Well, monsieur le commissaire, I added, I'm quite simply a writer; I am doing research on the Bucquoy family of Longueval, and I am trying to pinpoint the site, or rediscover the ruins of the castles they possessed in the province."

The police-superintendant's brow cleared suddenly:

"Ah! you dabble in literature? So do I, Monsieur! I wrote verse in my youth . . . a tragedy."

It was one danger after another; the superintendant seemed set to invite us to dinner and read us his tragedy.]

The passage makes it clear that oppositional writing is suspect not only in the eyes of civil authority but also with respect to an *other* form of literature: official literature, a literature of (and for) gendarmes, of which (neoclassical) tragedy is the paradigmatic genre, and with which "unofficial," minoritized literature must contend, playing a game of ruses so as to pass for what it is not. "History" is its alibi with respect to the gendarme *and* with respect to the gendarme's tragedy, which are perils of a similar kind. And since the narrator's friendship with Sylvain is at issue (the resident of the Valois and his Parisian, literary friend, who has "come home," are about to be arrested together), the text can be seen to be producing a remarkably economical figuration of its historically complex discursive situation, allied as it is—self-defined as an alliance—with the socially excluded and the marginal (Sylvain's name suggests a man of the woods, if not exactly a "wild man"), against another alliance, social and literary, of forms of authority and officialdom that regard oppositional "alliance"—or "collective enunciation"—as a punishable crime: the crime of nonidentity.

As the country of personal melancholy—the melancholy of "I am the other"—but also of collective identity and complicitous oppositionality, the Valois stands, then, for the "deterritorialized" territory of a literature that can be *depersonalized* only at the expense of undergoing *privatization*. For it is only as a privatized phenomenon, that is as an enactment of bourgeois, individual identity, that that oppositionality—as the enactment of nonbourgeois, collective identity—is tolerated. The territory of the Valois, *cut off* as it is from the city where the affairs of bourgeois, capitalist society are conducted, yet simultaneously *under the surveillance* of the gendarmerie (and indeed, as "Sylvie" shows, gradually penetrated by bourgeois culture), is a figure for this privatization. It is not genuinely "private," as territory might be that would be controlled by its own citizenry and enabled to have a history of its own; but it is occupied by the authorities of the bourgeois Republic who insist on *outward* conformity to the dictates of individual identity (not appearing "capricious," for instance) as the price to be paid for their tolerance of *inward* enjoyment of an oppositional identity that is one of plurality, collectivity, and harmony. But that there is contradiction and tension between a literature of collective enunciation and the privatized status—a function of the ideology of individuality—that it must conform to in order to exist, is evident: it reproduces the constituent tension of all oppositionality, forced as it is to depend on the power that it opposes, and enacts that tension as an irony.

But it is also a form of alienation, and it is evident that in Nerval there is a structural homology between the privatized isolation of a Valois where the collective values of oppositional identity are celebrated, but under surveillance, and the social-medical practice of—to use Foucault's word—*enfermement*,[21] or enclosure, which is enforced by alienists on those they designate ("diagnose") as mad. The de-alienating discourse that Nerval will attempt in "Aurélia" as an account of the "dreams" (some nocturnal, others "visions" or hallucinations) of his madness, will be oppositional, then, in a new sense. Without betraying the oppositional values of collective identity, it will seek to extend those values and create a wider, all-encompassing harmony, not by protecting them behind a duplicitous submission to the dictates of society, but by recruiting for them the sympathetic understanding of readers identified with the alienating forces of authority itself, that is, by involving them in an experience of reading as an apprenticeship of collective enunciation and plural identity. Since these readers are represented by the medical profession and those who subscribe to its diagnostic assumptions and practices—the first of such assumptions being that identity is individual and autonomous, so that the experience of collective identity (of "I am the other") is either "megalomania" in its manic form or "melancholia" in its depressive moment, and in any case a disease of shifting moods called "cyclothymia"—the rhetorical task, which is that of converting the reader from a position of repressive power to one of oppositional sympathy will be one of some difficulty and complexity.

It is nevertheless the task undertaken in "Aurélia," where the "cure" of the individual diagnosed as mad is demonstrated by a narrative that undertakes to work in its turn a complementary form of social cure, bringing about a reconciliation of the two groups or families—those representative of authority and those who subscribe to oppositional values—whose enmity is elsewhere described as basic and seemingly irreducible. The protective duplicities practiced in "Angélique"—the submissive acceptance of privatization and the production of a conforming, individual narrator, as the condition of "collective enunciation"—are now irrelevant: it is in the public domain, where the official discourses of medicine, philosophy, and "common sense" prevail, that the enterprise of writing in the language of the other so as to bring the other to terms with the values it minoritizes must be effected; and it is the privatizing forces themselves—those which enclose the mad and send gendarmes to "occupy" the Valois in the name of individual and responsible identity—whose complicity in the discourse of collective enunciation must now be obtained. No diagnosed madman can expect to find for his tale an *already* complicitous reader; at best he may hope for a measure of patience, tolerance, interest, and curiosity, perhaps a certain desire to understand. But the readership he must target is the alienating reader, not the oppositional one—the "alienist" reader who produces as *aliéné* (alienated, or mad) the subject of an enunciation that cannot be faithful to itself unless it is collective. It is to the daunting complexities of such a rhetorical task, but also to its seductive underlying logic (for if identity is plural, then the error of those who subscribe to a notion of individual identity *can* be corrected), that the extraordinary discursive shifts of "Aurélia," the multiplication of its textual voices and its production of text as "parole intermédiaire"—a subjectless site where discourses meet and cross— must be attributed. Inspired by the melancholic understanding that identity is a matter of alterity, "Aurélia" will attempt, then, to enact its own reading as an exemplification and confirmation of that axiom.

"What happens when people talk, what is at stake when we talk?" is the opening question of François Flahault's *La parole intermédiaire*.[22] Roland Barthes' preface to the same book gives an elegant and untechnical account of the answer Flahault develops much more formally:

The *homo loquens* François Flahault describes is a subject dialectically free and constrained. On one hand he is free because he does not preexist language and constitutes himself as a subject in and as he speaks, listens and better still speaks the listening to his own speech that he imagines; in speaking, man does not express himself, he realizes or produces himself; his freedom comes not from God or Reason, but from the *play* (take the word in all its meanings)[23] afforded him by the symbolic order, without which he would not speak and would not be a human. On the other hand he is constrained because he can only be acknowledged [by others] in a certain place, and this positioning is part of an already constituted system, so that it is not within his power to situate himself on the basis of an essence, since he is only in proportion as he speaks, that is, inevitably, only as he takes up a position in relation to the image he believes the other to hold of him; this is the revolving door that gives something like a definition of the vertigo of being human. Man is literally only a tactics. . . . [24]

If this is the case, and I find the analysis strikingly plausible, any given narrative will need to be analyzed similarly, in terms of a dialectic of freedom and constraint determining it in its enunciatory aspect, that is as contextualized *and* self-contextualizing (situating itself with respect to the image it believes the other to have of its own "place"). Every narrator, in other words, is forced to justify the attention of the other by establishing the "interest" *for that other* of what the narrator proposes to tell: he must in this sense speak, or write, the other's language, if only to the extent that he situates his discourse with respect to the positioning of himself as subject that he believes the other to be performing.[25] *All* narratives are consequently best understood as "parole intermédiaire," dialogically inflected by the trace of the other (of the other as conceived by the subject) as this is inscribed in the discourse of the subject, and so also by the place to which the subject believes himself assigned by the other whom he thus imagines. . . . Which suggests that any description of the relationship in terms of an autonomous narrator and an autonomous narratee is at best an oversimplification, and at worse a falsification, of the necessarily complex rhetorical situation that holds.

But if such is the "normal" situation of any narrative, what of the *alienated* narrative, which can be defined by the fact that its subject is (believes him/herself to be) assigned the position of outsider, or stranger, and hence projects onto the other a degree of alterity amounting, at the furthest extreme, to unknowability? In "Aurélia," this alienated status of the subject is inscribed in the text as a "given" by medical diagnosis of "madness," and it informs the enunciatory situation as it is understood both by the subject and by the other he takes as addressee. The initial difficulty—the revolving door of the dialectic that "gives something like a definition of the vertigo of being human"—is here radically intensified. Indeed, the narrative is faced with an apparent impossibility, since the position assigned the narrator from the start, and acknowledged by him, is such that the other can only be conceived of as *a priori* incapable of taking, or at best unlikely to take an interest in the narrator's discourse, which he defines as alienated. Yet it is precisely in such circumstances that a narrator such as the narrator of "Aurélia" must operate, attempting to produce a "parole intermédiaire" in which the other can recognize sufficient of his own interests to give the subject's discourse his attention. How is such a narrator to speak the (radically alien) language of the other without simultaneously sacrificing his own dialectical opportunity of (re-)positioning himself in the other's eyes?

To succeed in such conditions would be a sign of "cure." To produce an acceptable narrative of madness in which the "mad" subject would nevertheless displace the alienating positioning of his madness in such a way as to be able to project his own experience of it, would be to give clear evidence, perhaps not of "sanity," but at least of *nonmadness* (a category which, while it may not be equated with rationality, corresponds to the category of the nonforbidden in which oppositionality thrives). An alienated subject will have demonstrated a right to acceptance and dignity by showing an ability, as Barthes puts it, to "speak the listening" he imagines, on the part of the other, to his own discourse, that is by demonstrating that necessary respect for the other without which there is, in the common understanding, no sanity. What is at stake in "Aurélia" is precisely this demonstration of narrative "cure," or this narrative demonstration of "cure," conceived as a means of reducing if not eliminating entirely the social alienation, with its attendant pain, of which the narrator is a victim.

Not surprisingly, then, the narrative is traversed by an anxiety, not of influence, but of reception, an anxiety that determines its different rhetorical and stylistic moves. And it is the tactics of writing within such a situation of anxiety that produce in the narrative the characteristics of textuality: in the first instance, those of a "collective enunciation." For there can be no question of abandoning the values of madness in favor of those that are imagined to be the values of the social "other," in the position of power and authority. In that case, there would be no disalienation but only another form of alienation, through self-censorship and repression. What Nerval's narrator has to do amounts to a discursive balancing act, in which the values of madness are *not denied*, while the interest, sympathy, understanding, and indeed "pardon" of a "sane" readership—the readership that holds the view of madness that produces the narrator as alienated—are nevertheless obtained. This will entail a symmetrical *recognition* of the values of such a readership *without affirming them*, that is, an appropriative adoption of the discourse of the other as a tactical move on behalf of the discourse it excludes or represses. . . . Oppositionality as the use of power against itself here takes the form of a strange ventriloquism, in which alienated values are "not denied" (and, to that extent, are affirmed) in writing that nevertheless avoids "affirming" the alienating values it must nevertheless (under pain of failure) acknowledge—values which, to that precise extent, it does not deny and even gives authority to, but which, at the same time, it *relativizes*, since the presence of the equally undenied countervalues makes them readable as alienating.

The values of madness are those of collective identity. As Nerval describes it, "madness" is a mode of initiatory access to the world of the Spirits and the universal community of souls, an experience that makes nonsense of any notion of individual identity. It is to this vision of all-encompassing harmony that the narrative wants to initiate, in turn, a readership presumed, by virtue of its ideology of the autonomous self and individual responsibility—the ideology by virtue of which the narrator is declared "mad"—to be hostile. This readership is represented, as I have said, by medical authority, which encloses (excludes, represses) the mad; but it is figured also, on the metaphysical plane of the "visions," by a jealous and disapproving, if not vengeful, God whose "pardon" is to be obtained. Two conceptions of identity—one all-encompassing but "minoritized," the other exclusionary but in the position of power—are to be reconciled; and the regaining of the lost figure of Aurélia depends on this reconciliation. There would clearly be no difficulty in including the "individual" identity in the "collective," if only the individual was not *in power* and, hence, in a position to reject and minoritize the collective by declaring it alien and mad, that is, by excluding it. The difficult but necessary process—the one that requires the full deployment of oppositional tactics—is the one that will lead the individual to accept, and include, the collective, adopting to that extent and with that result the values of the collective itself.

What tactics are available to a narrator so placed and with such a project, whose authority must be gained *against* the authority whose goodwill must nevertheless be earned and maintained? What discursive effects derive from the deployment of so radically divided a "parole intermédiaire," not denying madness—that is, speaking madness in a way that is inflected by a desire to make it accessible to the sane—without affirming the "reason" it must acknowledge—that is, speaking reason in a way that makes it convertible, and able to *comprehend* (etymologically to "take with," to take into partnership with itself) the mad; in a way, that is, that deflects or negates its alienating power? I will propose the same answer to both these questions: the "tactics" available are those of melancholy; the discursive characteristics that result from such tactics are those of the melancholy text.

Melancholy, as has already been suggested, cannot be an individual disease, to the extent that its *truth* (from the point of view of the melancholic) is that there is no individual ("I am the other"); its natural proclivity is to engulf individualities in its own sense of existence as shifting, plural, and collective. Indeed, as a matter of observation, the tendency of melancholy to occur in epidemic form—Western society has known a number of such outbreaks over its history—demonstrates that it is a *social* disease, one that is "catching" and can be passed from "individual" to "individual."[26] The melancholy text, as a site of collective enunciation, in which discourses meet and cross without underpinning in an individual subject, appears in this light as the channel, or the means, whereby the contagion of melancholy is passed on and picked up, through the phenomenon of *reading*—itself always describable, I would maintain, as an experience of "I am the other." "Aurélia" will be committed, as a consequence, to *speaking the truth of melancholy* in language that, perceiving it as a form of madness (or "melancholia"), describes its convictions as illusions—language which, thereby, *enacts itself as melancholic* because it speaks the "self" in the discourse of the "other." In the lexicon of the text, however, such a procedure, and such discourse, will come under the more traditional, and less "tainted," heading of the initiatory.

But the first dream in "Aurélia" is a mourning dream: it "confirms" the narrator in his interpretation of certain signs that tell of the death, either of Aurélia or of himself. It is a labyrinthine dream of wandering ("J'errais dans un vaste édifice . . .") in a space whose own identity shifts, from being a place of knowledge to being a "sort of hostelry." It culminates however in the vision of a strange figure:

Je me perdis plusieurs fois dans les longs corridors, et, en traversant une des galeries centrales, ju fus frappé d'un spectacle étrange. Un être d'une grandeur démesurée,—homme ou femme, je ne sais,—voltigeait péniblement au-dessus de l'espace et semblait se débattre parmi des nuages épais. Manquant d'haleine et de force, il tomba enfin au milieu de la cour obscure, accrochant et froissant ses ailes le long des toits et des balustres. Je pus le contempler un instant. Il était coloré de teintes vermeilles, et ses ailes brillaient de mille reflets changeants. Vêtu d'une robe longue à plis antiques, il ressemblait à l'Ange de la *Mélancolie,* d'Albrecht Dürer.—Je ne pus m'empêcher de pousser des cris d'effroi, qui me réveillèrent en sursaut. (P. 362.)

[I became lost several times in the long corridors, and, in crossing one of the central galleries, I was struck by a strange sight. A being of inordinate size—whether man or woman I do not know—was hovering laboriously above the space and seemed to be struggling in thick clouds. Short of breath and strength, it finally fell in the middle of the dark courtyard, catching its wings and rumpling them against the roofs and balustrades. I had a chance to gaze on it for a moment. It was colored in ruby hues, and its wings shimmered with a thousand shifting reflections. Clad in a long robe pleated in the ancient style, it resembled the Angel of *Melan-*

choly, by Albrecht Dürer.—I could not stifle cries of fright, which awakened me with a start.]

The whole narrative is thus placed under the sign of this sighting of the Angel of Melancholy, interpreted as signifying the narrator's death, a loss of selfhood for which the loss of Aurélia will also stand. "The next day I hastened to visit all my friends. I was mentally taking my leave of them. . . ." But this loss of (individual) self is simultaneously identified with an entry into the forbidden underworld of dreams, of which the narrator's first experience will be a kind of euphoria, a liberation resulting from his initiation into collective identity, the abolition of difference in the vast family of souls: "I thought I was an uninterrupted chain of men and women in whom I was and who were myself," etc. (368).

By the end of the narrative, however, another figure of melancholy, this time in the form of a sharing of identity with a personage—not an Angel but another patient in the clinic and the narrator's own double—significantly named Saturnin ("it seemed to me that our two minds were joined by a certain magnetism," 408) will function as a sign of cure and "pardon," cure of and pardon for the initial, guilty penetration into the melancholic world of dreams and collective identity. Or, at least (for the text produces two readings of Saturnin, as I will try to show), the encounter figures, if not cure and pardon, then a purgatorial expiation, something perhaps endless but hopeful, albeit still under the sign of the saturnine. "Aurélia" thus moves from an understanding of melancholia as loss (but also revolt and collective euphoria) to an understanding of it as a *communicative gain* (but also as an expiation with respect to the power of individuality), a thematic movement of the text that figures a rhetorical transformation *in* the text of its own status with respect to its readership.

For if, initially, there is a rupture of communication and understanding that the text attempts to compensate for by a writing of the language of the other that nevertheless attempts to draw the other into its own ambit, there is a compensatory and opposite movement in the latter part of the work, where its rhetoric espouses an outward movement towards the position of the other, whose "pardon" it seeks to obtain, a movement that mimes and is mimed by the narrator's move in "love," "sympathy," and "pity" (407) towards a sharing of self with Saturnin. This, then, is an expansive and almost enfolding movement of recognition of alterity—the alterity of God, the alterity of the reader—whose radical otherness is recognized as a possibility of failure (the narrator may not be pardoned, the text may not succeed in communicating its experience of madness to the sane reader), but must be *addressed*, as both the narrator, with respect to God, and the text, with respect to the reader, now know. Since the catatonic Saturnin, "placed between death and life, as a sublime interpreter" (408), is a figure both of God and of the reader, melancholy and the melancholic text are being described, here, as that whose "identity" is *dependent* on the other, but also as that which, as a consequence, can most effectively reach out to and embrace its own most radical other, the figures of individual, selfsame identity and of the father's law itself: Saturnin, the reader, God.

The way in which the text fails to *end* is consequently significant. Where the thematics of visitation and of pardon announce a successful conclusion of the melancholic outreach to the other, its attempt to embrace the other and enfold it in its own identityless textuality, the thematics of purgatorial expiation—of doubt and deferment, of the failure of closure ("I am in purgatory, I am accomplishing my expiation," says Saturnin, p. 413, when he is at last led to speak)—simultaneously affirm another (but related) melancholic truth, that of drift and uncertainty, of the always possible episodic "Et puis . . ." that can start things over afresh. It serves simultaneously then, to remind us of the oppositional truth that its very success is always a form of failure, or at least is subject to the possibility of failure, dependent as it is on forms of power that, in the last analysis, must by definition be intractably hostile to any attempt to convert them to ends other than their own.

At the outset, however, the narrative problem for "Aurélia" is clearly and relatively simply posed. It will be a matter of setting up, against medical discourse, which judges from outside and condemns the madman's experience as "aberration," a form of narrative able to communicate the internal logic of the latter's lived experience, the coherence of what, *for me* (as he says) was true and is here explicitly described as furnishing the *point* of the whole enterprise:

L'état cataleptique où je m'étais trouvé pendant plusieurs jours me fut expliqué scientifiquement, et les récits de ceux qui m'avaient vu ainsi me causaient une sorte d'irritation quand je voyais qu'on attribuait à l'aberration d'esprit les mouvements ou les paroles coïncidant avec les diverses phases de ce qui constituait *pour moi* une série d'événements logiques. (Pp. 371–72. My emphasis)

[The cataleptic state in which I found myself for several days was explained to me scientifically, and the narratives of those who had seen me in such a state caused me a kind of irritation when I realized that they attributed to mental aberration the movements or utterances that coincided with the different phases of what constituted, *for me*, a series of logical events.]

This project determines an investigative ambition that is of a hermeneutic and ontological nature: "I applied myself to seeking out the meaning of my dreams" (412), the meaning, that is, that will demonstrate the inner logic of the experience. This meaning, the narrator will conclude (413), resides in knowledge of a link ("lien") between the world of mortals (confusingly called *monde interne*) and the world of the Spirits (or *monde externe*) (413), a link that is, however, not clearly specified (we will see why). But the search for meaning is not in itself sufficient: it coexists with a rhetorical enterprise, the purpose of which is to make this concealed meaningfulness accessible to others (that is, to those who might tend to see its signs as symptoms of mental aberration).

The first tactical move of this rhetorical undertaking is, boldly, to adopt the alienating language of medical discourse itself; and this use of medical discourse will persist through the final sentences of the text:

Telles sont les idées bizarres que donnent ces sortes de maladies; je reconnus en moi-même que je n'avais pas été loin d'une si étrange persuasion. Les soins que j'avais reçus m'avaient déjà rendu a l'affection de ma famille et de mes amis, et je pouvais juger plus sainement le monde d'illusions où j'avais quelque temps vécu. (Pp. 413–14)

[Such are the bizarre notions these kinds of diseases produce; I acknowledged to myself that I had not been far from a similarly strange persuasion. The treatment that I had received had already restored me to the affection of my family and friends, and I was able to judge more sanely the world of illusion in which I had lived for a time.]

But the rhetorical trick consists of grafting onto this "scientific" discourse of illusion, treatment, sanity, etc., another language carrying its own form of authority and conveying a quite different and much more prestigious set of connotations, a language borrowed from the esoteric traditions of sacred initiation. Immediately after the above concession to medical authority, one reads, as the concluding sentence of "Aurélia":

Toutefois, je me sens heureux des convictions que j'ai acquises, et je compare cette série d'épreuves que j'ai traversées à ce qui, pour les anciens, représentait l'idée d'une descente aux enfers. (P. 414)

[Nevertheless, I feel happy with the convictions that I have acquired, and I compare the series of ordeals I traversed to that which, for the ancients, represented the idea of a descent into the underworld.]

Strangely, then, the narrator seems unaware of any contradiction between the two discourses about madness that he coolly maintains, either in a relationship of juxtaposition (as here) or (as elsewhere) even more closely intertwined, a practice unsettling to the reader and to the effect of which it will, of course, be necessary to return. But a mediating term exists between the two apparently hostile discourses in the idea of the "dream," and a clue to the maneuver being performed in the text is provided in the opening paragraph of the narrative, which exploits a certain implicit affinity between these two discourses in such a way as to permit the text to slide imperceptibly from diagnostic conceptions to views less alienating for the subject, and indeed to substitute the latter for the former. It is necessary to know that, in the psychiatry of Nerval's time, as represented for example by Moreau de Tours (whose relevance to "Aurélia" has been pointed out by Michel Jeanneret),[27] madness was conceived on the model of nocturnal dreams, but as *dreaming without being asleep*. For Moreau, "two lives have been accorded human beings as their lot," a waking life and a sleeping life, so that the only pathological aspect of madness lies in the fact that it is a dream in which the barrier of sleep that normally separates waking life from nocturnal life has been effaced, with the result that "these two lives tend to mingle." Nerval's famous opening formulation: "Dream is a second life" [*Le Rêve est une seconde vie*], and later the no less famous description of hallucination as the "overflow of dreaming into real life" [*l'épanchement du songe dans la vie réelle*] are consequently entirely compatible with the best scientific thinking of his period.

But the effect of the opening sentences is, subtly and gradually, to shift these notions from their medical connotations to an esoteric context. The word "dream" acquires a capital letter ["Rêve"]; the illusory quality of dreams is subtly put in doubt by means of a classical allusion ("the gates of ivory *or* of horn," my emphasis); sleep becomes "the image of death," and the distinction between sleeping and waking—psychiatrically crucial—is now blurred, for, as the text says, "we cannot determine the precise moment when the *self* [*moi*] continues the work of existence in another form." Very soon, from sleep as the image of death, the text will have slipped into a description of dreaming as a "limbic place" ["séjour des limbes"] and the "world of the Spirits." Without ever having been explicitly opposed, medical authority has by now been subverted, as it were, from within, and has been invested with, or replaced by, a type of authority that derives from another tradition, that of the descent into the underworld, with its esoterica and literary connotations, which are themselves now confirmed by a whole cascade of intertextual references (after Homer and Virgil, Apuleius, Dante, and Swedenborg). These function to strengthen, by the invocation of *precedent*, the narrative (re-)positioning that has shifted the frame of reference to one more apposite to the logic of the *for me*.

This quiet initial maneuver is accompanied, moreover, throughout the narrative, by a discursive tactic that might be more properly described as seductive, in that it addresses itself less to a (re-)positioning of the alienated subject than to an active recruitment of the textual other—its reader—into the narrative programme (the search for the "meaning of my dreams"). This recruitment is the function of the narrator's apparent gaucherie and of the generally disorderly state of his narrative, a first example of which we have already seen in his way of shifting, sometimes very abruptly, between medical discourse and an initiatory framework. For the principle of this (mimesis of) disorder is parataxis, the elision of connections and relations—in short of "links"—such that the reader is invited to supply the missing "logic": the logic, for example, that permits the text to speak, in two successive sentences, and as if there were no contradiction, of the "illusions" the narrator has been subject to and the "convictions" he is happy to have acquired.

But this technique of suppressed connectives is macrotextual as well as microtextual: it governs the narrative ordering of the text as a whole, whether it is describing dreams proper or—what follows from the "overflow of dreaming into real life"—the hallucinated experience of events in waking existence. Thus, the first dream of all—the one I have already cited for its thematization of melancholy—has also the melancholic syntax of a series of disconnected happenings:

J'errais dans un vaste édifice. . . . Je m'arrêtai avec intérêt. . . . Je passai dans une autre salle. . . . J'y pris part quelque temps, puis j'en sortis. . . . je me perdis plusieurs fois. . . . et je fus frappé d'un spectacle étrange. . . . Je ne pus m'empêcher de pousser des cris d'effroi, qui me réveillèrent en sursaut. (Pp. 361–62)

[I was wandering in a vast structure. . . . I stopped with interest. . . . I moved into another room. . . . I took part in this for a while, then I left. . . . I got lost several times. . . . and I was struck by a strange spectacle. . . . I could not stifle cries of fright, which awakened me with a start.]

But this is a nocturnal dream. Here, taken from Part II, is the exactly similar syntactic outline of a fragment relating to the events of real life:

Une nuit, j'allai souper dans un café. . . . J'allai ensuite à la halle. . . . A une certaine heure . . . je me pris à penser aux luttes des Bourguignons et des Armagnacs. . . . Je me pris de querelle avec un facteur. . . . je me sentis attendrir: et je le laissai passer. . . . Je me dirigeai vers les Tuileries . . . , etc. (pp. 398–399)

[One night, I went to supper in a café. . . . Then I went to the market. . . . At a certain o'clock . . . I fell to thinking about the struggles of the Burgundians and the Armagnacs. . . . I fell into a quarrel with a postman. . . . I felt myself relenting, and I let him pass. . . . I headed for the Tuileries . . . , etc.]

The narrative as a whole is similarly shot through with fissures and gaps, produced by abrupt transitions (for example from direct speech to reported style at the beginning of Part II), ellipses (cf. the sentence on p. 390 that tails off into suspension points) and omissions (notably the famously missing "lettres à Aurélia"). The circumstances of publication (Nerval died before being able to pull the text together on the proofs, as was standard practice in the period) are certainly partly to blame for this disorder, but perhaps do not fully account for it. The section entitled *Mémorables*, for example, is paradigmatic of the whole: it is a series of discrete dreams following an internal order of succession that is without apparent logic, while the series itself is inserted somewhat clumsily into the text, from which it is marked off at the beginning and end by rows of dots; but in this case there is no reason to think that this disorderly presentation would have been corrected had Nerval had the time. The English-speaking reader is irresistibly reminded by "Aurélia" of the chaotic composition of another work of melancholy, the *Confessions of an English Opium-Eater* by De Quincey.

What then is to be made of all this small-scale and large-scale parataxis? Can one assume that the textual disorder is the "natural" projection of a "madman"'s disordered mind? Or is it a "rhetorical" disorder, miming (with whatever degree of conscious or unconscious savoir-faire) that "aberration d'esprit" which the narrator knows was attributed to him by certain observers? In that case, it would be a miming of the effects of madness in the framework of a communicative project, a project that consequently would be relational and would produce the text as a "parole intermédiaire." And in this respect, we can note that the text certainly offers itself as evidence of "naïveté" and "sincerity" on the part of a narrator who declares himself persuaded that a writer "must sincerely analyse his experiences" (364) and who believes himself engaged in accomplishing "something good and worthwhile by naïvely putting forward the succession [of his] ideas" (394).

But a naïveté that *knows* it is naïve, a sincerity that *declares* its sincerity is always worth a second, and suspicious, look: these declarations certainly set out to reassure the reader, who is thus confirmed in his prejudices. (What should one expect of a madman except a text that naïvely reproduces the "disorder" of his mind, a text that has the sincerity of its own lack of control?) But what might be the purposes of such reassurance? It is important to realize that "mental disorder," in this text, is not simply a sign of madness, something like the "aberration" noted by the observers; it is also described by the narrator, and quite explicitly so, as that which makes it difficult to grasp the meaning of dreams (i.e., the famous "link" between the world of Spirits and that of mortals—but we should think also of the "link" that is missing in the text's own paratactic style).

Je crus comprendre qu'il existait entre le monde externe et le monde interne un lien: que l'inattention ou le désordre d'esprit en faussaient seuls les rapports apparents—et qu'ainsi s'expliquait la bizarrerie de certains tableaux . . . etc. (P. 413)

[I understood somehow that between the outer and the inner worlds there existed a link; and that only inattentiveness or mental disorder falsified their visible connections—and this accounted for the bizarreness of certain tableaux (. . .) etc.]

"Mental disorder" and "inattentiveness"—or more exactly the paratactic style that mimes them—can thus be seen in this context as what *mediates* between the "for me" of the text, the supposed underlying coherence or meaningful-ness of the dreams, and its "for you" aspect, its turn towards the other, to whom they signify aberration and illusion. It is in this respect like the rewrit-ing of "madness" as "initiation" by means of the common term that is the dream.

But if narrative disorder constitutes a kind of admission of incompetence on the narrator's part, the text works to suggest that such incompetence is not necessarily due exclusively to madness; it results also—and more especially, it seems—from a deficiency inherent in the disproportion between the grandeur and sublimity of the "meaning" to be grasped and the necessarily imperfect conceptual powers and means of expression that are available to a narrator whose mind is subject to human limitations. For other admissions of incom-petence of a more explicit and punctual kind dot the text:

Je ne puis espérer de faire comprendre cette réponse, qui pour moi-même est restée très obscure. (P. 369)

[I cannot hope to render this response comprehensible; for to myself it has re-mained very obscure.]

Je ne puis rendre le sentiment que j'éprouvais au milieu de ces êtres charmants. (P. 371)

[I cannot express the feeling I experienced among these charming beings.]

Je ne sais comment expliquer que, dans mes idées, les événements terrestres pou-vaient coïncider avec ceux du monde surnaturel, cela est plus facile à *sentir* qu'à énoncer clairement. (Pp. 380–81)

[I do not know how to explain that, as I saw it, terrestrial events were able to coincide with those of the supernatural world; such a thing is easier to *feel* than to say clearly.]

Comment peindre l'étrange désespoir où ces idées me réduisirent peu à peu? (P. 382)

[How to portray the strange despair to which these ideas gradually reduced me?]

C'est un de ces rapports étranges dont je ne me rends pas compte moi-même et qu'il est plus aisé d'indiquer que de définir.

[It is one of those strange connections that I cannot account for myself and which it is easier to point to than to define.]

The function of these recurrent phrases is fairly clearly to recruit the reader's cooperation in the narrator's own project: the reader is invited to compensate by an effort of empathy and imagination for the faults that are as much attributable to the specific character of what is being narrated—its momentous import, its elusive meaningfulness—as to weaknesses in the narrator. Similarly, it seems that the narrative disorder of the whole functions, not only as a mimesis of the mental disorder of madness but also, and perhaps primarily, as an invitation to the reader to enter into a collaborative effort with the narrator in the imposing task—on which the rhetorical success of the text must depend—of figuring out the meaning of the narrator's dreams.[28]

Not coincidentally, after speaking of the "irritation" caused him by those who saw only "aberration" in the movements and utterances of his cataleptic state, the narrator added:

J'aimais davantage ceux de mes amis qui, par une patiente complaisance ou par suite d'idées analogues aux miennes, me faisaient faire de long récits des choses que j'avais vues en esprit. (P. 372)

[I preferred those of my friends who, out of good-natured patience or because they held ideas analogous to my own, had me relate long narratives of the things I had seen in my mind's eye.]

The self-reflexive reference could not be clearer ("de longs récits des choses que j'avais vues en esprit" is an excellent description of the content of "Aurélia"). But its function is to designate the ideal reader of the text, either as an adept (sharing the narrator's "ideas") or simply as a person of goodwill, provided with virtues not dissimilar from those (of "patience" and "trust") traditionally demanded of the candidate for initiation, or *mystos*. It is important that the reader need not be *already* the holder of ideas "analogous to my own": patience and *complaisance*—a willingness to let the narrator have his say and to hear him out—will suffice.

For this is the crucial moment where the *alienating* "other"—one not necessarily predisposed to agree with the narrator's understanding of things—is being (re-)positioned as one disposed to pursue the task that the narrative itself, in its disorder, cannot carry out, the quest for the underlying logic, for the "mysterious formulations that establish the order of the worlds" (404), for the elusive "link," glimpsed by the narrator and imperfectly conveyed in his discourse, but too difficult to grasp for him to be able to comprehend and communicate it in its wholeness and perfection. Such a reader is one willing to listen, and hence to assume a task that implicitly integrates him/her into the constitutive structure of all initiatory communication. This is a matter of accepting the narrator in the role he assumes as initiatory guide (and so as himself a successor to a long line of initiatory ancestors, from Homer to Swedenborg), and thereby of accepting for oneself a function that consists of following in the guide's footsteps in his attempt to perceive the truth. But the initiatory assumption is always that the *mystos* has hope of going further than the guide and of reaching a point closer to the goal than the initiator/narrator has himself succeeded in attaining.

Such an "initiatory" reader will have responded to "seductive" tactics on the part of the text: the confidence inspired by narrative sincerity, as the textual mimesis of mental disorder, will have merged into active cooperation—inspired by textual disorder as the imperfect signs of important truths—with the initiatory project that is itself a rewriting of the "original" positioning of the discursive subject as medically insane. . . . The empirical reader, of course—as empirical readers always are—is free to accept, or not, this rhetorical positioning of the addressee; but what is striking in "Aurélia," and what even the rejecting empirical reader must read, is precisely its *acknowledgment* of this power, invested even in the "ideal" reader, to resist or reject the textual programme—an acknowledgment clearly symptomatic of the text's self-consciously oppositional status as a "minoritized" discourse, or "minor" literature.

For the problematics of the other is inscribed in the text, in clearly readable guise, in the form of a thematics of the double, or *Doppelgänger*. The whole narrative is traversed by a nostalgia for *communion* of the self and the other that is based on the similarity and reversibility of "I" and the "double," but which is readable as a nostalgia for perfect *communication*. Thus, the passage in which the "scientific" reception of the narrator's speech and gestures in catalepsy is unfavorably compared to the patience and indulgence of friends more attuned to his "ideas" or more willing to listen to them, concludes with an embrace presided over by a God whose existence is both affirmed by the "other" of this particular illocutionary situation and acknowledged by the subject:

L'un d'eux me dit en pleurant: "N'est-ce pas que c'est vrai qu'il y a un Dieu?"—"Oui!" lui dis-je avec enthousiasme. Et nous nous embrassâmes comme deux frères de cette patrie mystique que j'avais entrevue. (P.372)

[One of them said to me, weeping: "It is true, isn't it, that there is a God?"—"Yes," I replied with enthusiasm. And we embraced like two brothers of that mystical homeland of which I had caught a glimpse.]

The passage is crucial because it encapsulates, *en abyme*, what will be—after, one, the re-positioning of the narrator-subject as initiatory hero and, two, the (re-)positioning of the alienating reader as willing or would-be *mystos*—the third rhetorical shift of the text, in which the subject now moves "with enthusiasm" toward the Christian God to discover that God's existence is not incompatible with his own "patrie mystique" and that the values and identity of madness can join in an embrace with the values and identity of legitimacy, authority, and power.

For this foreshadowing of the reconciliations that will take place at the end of the text demonstrates the connection between the problematics of identity, in the text, and its communicational self-situation. The passage is one in a series concerning (in Part I) the guilty splitting-off from the "other" of the subject who chooses madness, and (in Part II) the difficult process by which he earns the other's pardon and achieves a reconciliation, the "other" being in both cases synonymous with a self that, in remaining sane and in maintaining contact with God, instead of entering the prohibited underworld of extended and plural identity, defines the split as one between a "good" and an "evil" self. This thematic, with its stress on the pain and guilt of the split-off subject, enables us to understand what is rhetorically at issue when, after its transformation of medical discourse into an initiatory register and its attempted recruitment of the reader, through narrative disorder, into cooperation with that initiatory programmme, the programme of "madness," the text attempts in its second half a new, parallel but inverse transformation. This time, it attempts—without abandoning initiatory discourse as that of the quest for meaning—to rewrite that discourse in a redemptory language derived from Christian doctrine, so that the initiatory quest for truth is transformed into a moral quest for pardon. The key mediating term here will be that of the "ordeal."

For such a reinterpretation of the situation in the very religious terms that earlier had appeared hostile to the initiatory programme (as descent into the infernal underworld of madness) signals a conversion of the concept of the "ordeal" (*épreuve*), such that the underworld of "madness" ceases now to be the abode of complicitous spirit-ancestors and becomes a purgatorial place of expiation. But this new shift in rhetorical practice, this new adjustment of the discursive register, amounts also to an acknowledgement on the text's part of the power of its addressee, in the position of legitimacy. In rewriting its initiatory discourse (itself a rewrite of medical discourse) in the language of the "other," the text operates now a new shift of the discursive subject, away from a self-positioning favorable to his narrative cause, and into a position closer to that in which he supposes the other will prefer to see him. In so doing, the text demonstrates clear "understanding" (if the word is appropriate) of itself as a place of dialectical adjustment and readjustment, of "room for maneuver," in conformity with that dynamics of the "revolving door" that defines the vertigo of being human. In short, it acknowledges its status as "parole intermédiaire." But in enabling us to read the evolution of the textual rhetoric as a function of the developing thematics of the double, it also demonstrates a sense of the duplicity of dialogic discourse as a matter of dual situational input, a sense that explains why it can plausibly expect a move from hostility to reconciliation to be effected by textual means.

In terms of the thematics of the double, "madness" is interpreted then as a breaking apart. Its first appearance coincides with the quarrel between the narrator and his friend, the latter taking on the "features of an apostle," the former remaining faithful to his star, and to the East. "No," said I, "I do not belong to your heaven" (363). The repudiated friend reappears, at the end of Part I, as the victorious *Doppelgänger* who now reduces the narrator to impotence and is about to marry Aurélia in his place.

Je croyais entendre parler d'une cérémonie qui se passait ailleurs et des apprêts d'un mariage mystique qui etait le mien, et où l'*autre* allait profiter de l'erreur de mes amis et d'Aurélia elle-même. (P. 381. My emphasis)

[I thought I heard talk of a ceremony that was going on elsewhere and of the preparations for a mystical wedding that was my own, and in which the *other* was about to take advantage of my friends' error, and of Aurélia herself.]

The division of identity between the mad self and the other does not only pose a moral problem ("'Am I the good one? Am I the evil one?' said I to myself. 'In either case, the *other* is hostile to me . . .'"), but also a problem of communication. For it is explained that "in every man there is an actor and a spectator, he who speaks and he who responds" (381); the implicit homology signifies that the actor-spectator relationship that governs madness (cf. "I judged myself to be a hero living under the eyes of the gods," p. 403—this is the madman as actor—and "those who saw me in that state," p. 372—these are the [medical] spectators) is analogous to the relationship between a narrative self (*celui qui parle*) and that "other" (self) who is his audience and from whom he expects, or hopes, for a response (*celui qui répond*). But precisely the victory of the other, who has retired to heaven with Aurélia, has now made the spectator-addressee, from whom response is desired, completely inaccessible, unreachable by discursive, or indeed by any other means. And the proximity of this victorious other to God can only nourish in the "mad" subject his growing awareness that, of the two, it is he who is the guilty party and who must, as a consequence, amend his behavior—even though it is, perhaps, too late.

Thus it is that the greater part of the second half of "Aurélia" is devoted to the narrator's anxious, and indeed anguished, return to God, culminating however, as has already been mentioned, in the reaching out to Saturnin, whose cure, effected by the narrator's care and concern, coincides with the return of Aurélia to the latter's visions and the pardon she pronounces. But the catatonic Saturnin, "placed between death and life as a supreme interpreter" (408) and exactly symmetrical, in his removal from contact, with the narrative subject's own state of catalepsy at the beginning, signifies not only the inaccessibility of the *Doppelgänger* in his proximity to God, but also the distance of the narrative addressee whose judgment as an "interpreter" of the text can determine its death or life as a communicative act—an adressee who, here, and at this stage, is presumed to be rhetorically beyond reach, to be radically *other* to the concerns of the text. The narrator will have to break out of the "circle" of his own obsessions and effect a movement of love toward the other before his own cure, as a communicative subject, can occur, a cure that will be signaled by the cure of the other, i.e., his emergence from the catatonia in which he lies and his eventual willingness to reply, with speech, to the narrator's discourse. Hence the narrator's initiative:

Abandonné jusque-là au cercle monotone de mes sensations ou de mes souffrances morales, je rencontrais un être indéfinissable, taciturne et patient, assis comme un sphinx aux portes suprêmes de l'existence. Je me pris à l'aimer. . . . (P. 407)

[Given over until then to the monotonous circle of my own sensations or my own moral sufferings, I was now encountering an indefinable being, taciturn and patient, seated like a sphinx at the supreme gates of existence. I began to love him. . . .]

This initiative produces as its reward an acknowledgment, on the part of the other, of his status as an *interlocutor*: "I felt delighted when for the first time a word fell from his lips" (408). In this way, *he who speaks* and *he who responds* are again joined, and the problem of communication appears solved.

The narrator's achievement of *altruism* functions, then, both as the means of "curing" the other of his alienating distance and, consequently, as the sign of his own cure, that is, of his success as a communicating subject. To the narrator's own outgoing rhetorical movement—his adoption of the language of Christianity—something responds: there is a participatory answering of his loving élan on the part of the other. Similarly, the oppositional success of the narrative will have been won, partly by its own discursive altruism but partly too by its having drawn from the other a responsive echo, a symmetrical return of the other toward the text and its anguished subject. But this is tantamount to recognition that narrative "cure" as a form of oppositional success is always ultimately dependent on a power it cannot control, on the good-will or the grace of a more powerful "other"—even though now, by contrast with the situation of power that prevails in La Fontaine, the other is *only another version of oneself*.

This modern version of the power situation is consequently one that generates considerably more uncertainty, doubt, and indeed anguish than is generated in the classical situation, where the position of power is fixed, clearly demarcated, visible, and verifiable; and it is for this reason that a new problem can spring, in "Aurélia," from the fusion and brotherhood of the doubles. For the alternating success of the pair throughout the text strongly suggests the likelihood of a new reversal. The narrator's loss of Aurélia was the double's gain: but his regaining of her and his reconciliation with the other will be marked by the moment when the double comes to speak—but speaks only to reveal himself to be engaged in his own purgatorial ordeal. *He* is now "dead" and accomplishing in his turn an "expiation." And the narrator's comment is significant: "je reconnus en moi-même que je n'avais pas été loin d'une si étrange persuasion" ["I acknowledged to myself that I had not been far from sharing his strange persuasion"] (413). The mirroring of self and other cannot produce a closure and a resolution; for although the narrator's ordeal has achieved a successful outcome, it has not brought about a final harmonization of identities, but rather a *turning of the tables* that continues the process. Seeing his own position mirrored in the situation and discourse of an *alter ego* now indistinguishable from the *ego*, the narrator is forced, on learning that the other is still undergoing an ordeal, to realize that his own ordeal can consequently not be over either.

In this way, and for this reason, "Aurélia" has two conclusions. After the triumphant conclusion brought about by the curing of Saturnin, a conclusion sealed by Aurélia's pardon and the subsequent dreams of the *Mémorables*, the narrative returns to a more uncertain note as it now raises explicitly—as it had done implicitly at the beginning—the question of its own status as narration. In so doing, it frames its narrative of the protagonist's now "completed" ordeals with reference to its own ongoing ordeal as a problematic discursive act. It is at this point that happiness in the (initiatory) convictions acquired is exactly balanced by a (medical) discourse of illusion reiterating the diagnosis of illness. And the passage that begins with the definition of the "audacious attempt" to "find out the secret" of dreams ends with an expression of the narrator's gratitude for having been brought back to the "shining paths of religion." These pages consequently repeat, in speeded up or even perhaps slightly caricatural, and at least schematic form, the complex rhetorical moves of the text as a whole, its dizzying vertigo, as if there had been no successful resolution and everything must continue as before.

The dialogue with Saturnin, so much desired, figures this rhetorical extension of the metaphysical ordeal. "And now, where do you think you are?" the narrator asks, and is told: "In purgatory, accomplishing my expiation." Thus are recalled and repeated the many pages of Part II devoted earlier to the narrator's own expiatory anguish of reception, as he desperately visited father and friends, prayed, followed unknown funeral processions, and plumbed the depths of apocalyptic terror in his attempt to *move* the other (God). It is not perhaps that nothing has been gained and nothing changed, but nothing—discursively speaking—is *over*; and it is not accidental that Barthes speaks of the "parole intermédiaire," our vertigo, as a dialectic and a revolving door. In it, the shifts and readjustments of discourse are necessarily *endless*, given that neither the subject nor the other correspond to a knowable essence but are condemned ceaselessly to produce themselves as images in the mirror of the unknown other. The process can go on forever; there is always—to borrow Aquin's title—a *prochain épisode*.

What I have called the "narrative programme" or the "project" of "Auré-lia"—the recruitment of the other to the task of discovering the "meaning of my dreams"—is consequently a mirage. Ultimately, it cannot unify the text, which explodes rather into a congeries of disparate discourses, each tending to a specific rhetorical end, but producing the whole as a singularly desperate gesticulation in a communicative vacuum, each discursive act—be it affirmation, repositioning, concession, or compromise—rewriting all the others in a multiplicitous dialogical *play* (take the word in all its meanings) that has no possible resolution. This is the *textual purgatory*, and it is perhaps to the element of hopefulness implied in the idea of purgatory that we owe the fact that "Aurélia" was written. But to the endless uncertainties inherent in the idea of an expiation we can ascribe the strangeness and incoherence—to what extent "apparent?" to what extent "real?"—of this writing, the undecidability of the enunciatory situation it constructs and in which it contextualizes itself.

So that, finally, we can say that it is not the success or the failure of its narrative programme, its search to give meaning to dreams, that fulfils (or not) the text's evident desire to *speak the truth*. The veridiction lies rather in the readability in the text of that desperate and pathological, endlessly unre-solvable enunciatory situation which itself accounts for the text's most promi-nent enunciatory features, as a "collective enunciation"—one in which the antagonistic discourses of a society meet and their harmonization is attempted. "If I did not think that the mission of a writer is to analyze sincerely what he experiences in the grave circumstances of life, and if I did not have a goal that I believe to be worthwhile," writes the narrator early in the text, "I would stop here and would not try to describe what I experienced next . . ." (364). But the mission he thus sets himself is, I would say, not so much accomplished by the descriptions of visions and dreams with which the pages are filled, as it is implied by the *attempt* to describe them under circumstances of communica-tion so evidently discouraging. For what it implies is that, in "the grave cir-cumstances of life," discourse tells its (oppositional) truth when it is enacted as a rhetorical "room for maneuver" out of which it is possible for some change to be produced in the reader. "Aurélia" stands at the center of this book not only because it transforms irony into the maneuverings of melancholic textual identity, but because it simultaneously produces change within the reader as the only possible sign of its oppositional success.

Let us note, then, the following key points:

1. Oppositional writing in the language of the other is a form of irony, and as such is subject to the ironies of irony (see chapter 2).

2. But it also appears as an appropriative gesture, best illustrated by Nerval's "recruitment" of medical discourse for "initiatory" purposes opposed to the implications of medical diagnosis.

3. Appropriation, in turn, can only succeed if there is a corresponding conversion of the reader, who must shift from the repressive position of power to one of "initiatory" patience and openness to textual "appeal".

4. This implies an abandonment of "self" on the part of the reader that is necessarily purchased at the price of a corresponding "self"-abandonment on the part of the text, best exemplified by the rewriting of the initiatory, in "Aurélia," in the language of Christianity and moral redemption—a new version of the language of the other.

Such maneuverings—clearly open-ended and potentially endless—constitute the melancholic text as a place where a sort of mutual "suicide" of the self (on the part of the narrative and on the part of its reader) can produce the ongoing "life" of the text as an always potential agent of change.

2. The Suicide Tactic

Aquin's writing has much in common with Nerval's. Doubles and doubling—not to say doubleplay and double-crossing—proliferate, and are expressive of the equivalence and hence reversibility of self and other, text and reader. As in the case of "Aurélia," *Prochain Épisode* presents itself as the writing of love, and indeed as a loveletter; but the love is much more strongly eroticized, and simultaneously the responsiveness of its addressee is more dubious. Indeed, if the love motif develops in later novels into a thematics of sadoeroticism,[29] it is perhaps because love is already presented here as betrayed (double-crossed) and the amorous writing as therefore both nostalgic and objectless. And for this reason, the writing finally "doubles" back on itself so that it becomes in a very explicit way, like "Aurélia," the writing out of its own lonesome situation of enunciation, a situation symbolically equivalent, as I will attempt to show, to that of a suicide note.

All the novels, in fact, emplot the writing situation as their own subject-matter, and become, in Flahault's terms, a positioning of the melancholic self as a plural textual subject: "the subject of enunciation as lack, as cleavage of the self and as an agent of repetition," to borrow Wladimir Krysinski's elegant summary.[30] Krysinski's impressive chapter on Aquin explores this writing subject as the place of passage for desire, governed as it is by the pleasure principle and "beyond" that, as Freud puts it, the death drive. But I want rather to explore some of the ways the doubling back of the text on itself—the narrator's production of a "hero" who in turn *becomes* the narrator—mimes the cleavage of the subject as a divided self but a shared identity, and simultaneously produces writing as the place of the self's suicide and—as such—an act of political opposition. In Aquin, the equivalence of self and other signifies the defeat of individuality and of revolution, but it is the condition of oppositional writing.

For the political connection is here explicit; and Krysinski himself, whose interest is largely psychoanalytic, takes as his epigraph a phrase from *Trou de mémoire*: "Cher pays déboussolé, comme je te ressemble . . . " ["Dear disoriented land, how I resemble you . . ."]. Perhaps the verb should be taken here as third-person ("comme 'je' te ressemble," "how 'I' resembles you"), so clear is it that the allegory of national subjection lies in the uncentered instability of a pseudo-subject invaded by and sharing identity with the other and drifting in language—in a watercourse of words which he does not control but which constitutes him: "pris dans un lit de glaise, je suis le cours et ne l'invente jamais" ["caught in a bed of clay, I follow the flow—or: I am the flow—and never invent it"] (90–91). But it is this thematics of drift, both personal and national, that the text converts into an oppositional gesture, both individual and political; it becomes a long suicide, episode by episode, a drowning in writing ("noyade écrite"). And in this way *Prochain Épisode* forms an exemplary manifestation of Deleuze and Guattari's "minor" literature, as a place of "deterritorialized" language and an "assemblage" of collective enunciation, in which the private and the political, the individual and the collective are always connected and are ultimately indistinguishable.

But Krysinski has some interesting and important reservations about the minority status of Québec literature. This literature arises, as he points out, in conditions considerably less uncomfortable than those of Kafka's Prague ghetto, and Québec intellectuals live in the first-world luxury of an "enfer confortablement organisé," a comfortably set up hell. "If Québec literature can be designated as 'minor,' in conformity with the characteristics cited by Gilles Deleuze and Félix Guattari, it is a literature naturally destined to undergo majoritization."[31] One cannot deny the pertinence of this assessment, and one must observe also that Québec writers have access also to a similarly international readership.

But what is at issue in Aquin's writing is something more fundamental than the degree of political power and/or cultural status enjoyed by Québec province or the material conditions in which its intelligentsia work. What we can read in Aquin is the problematics of oppositionality, as the (re-)minoritization of the language of the other, *when that other is oneself*—that is, when it has become difficult, if not strictly impossible, to distinguish the "minor" self from the "major" other, and hence to identify as other than oneself the site of power. In "Aurélia," the problematics of enunciation arises from the radical otherness of the alienating other; in Aquin, from the equally radical identity of the other and the self. When, however, the other is a version of self and *inhabits* the self, inextricably bound up with it, it is still possible to "oppose" that situation; it is just that the object of one's opposition will have become extraordinarily elusive, since it is identified with the very self on behalf of whose values the oppositionality is supposed to occur. . . . In terms of the political situation of Québec, such an analysis would suggest, for example, that the *pays* has already betrayed its "national" identity to an invasive power (let us say, capitalist, English-speaking North America), so that to oppose that power on behalf of Québec is simultaneously to oppose Québec itself. "Two centuries of conquest," Aquin wrote in an early essay, "have turned us into happy and grateful counterrevolutionaries."[32]

These are, indeed, the conditions of oppositionality (to oppose the other is to oppose oneself) that apply in the case of a "major" literature. And in such circumstances, where there is no distinctly identifiable seat of power as "other," the location of otherness and the site of power will tend to become symbolically situated in language itself, including one's "native" language, as that "flow" that one follows, or *is*, but does not invent. It is clear that a writing subject who is not socially minoritized, à la Kafka, and whose native language is culturally hegemonic, is still capable of experiencing such a "minoritized" relationship to language. And there is in any case a characteristic modern trend, in the major cultures of the West, towards a social marginalization of the arts and of artists (as the "anti-bourgeois bourgeois," etc.) which suggests that hegemonic societies in the present age produce their own artistic subculture as a specific—and specifically marginalized—as well as specialized, source of oppositionality. (This is the tradition of the poète maudit, for instance—one that is more than germane to Aquin.)

But the oppositional sense of *one's own* language as the site of *otherness* is obviously very much strengthened in circumstances of bi- or multi-lingualism (and/or culturalism), such as prevailed precisely in Kafka's Prague, or such as are experienced by writers in "exile" (Beckett, Nabokov . . .). And Aquin's French, as a dominant world-language, is singularly denaturalized by its being also, in Québec, the language of a colonial motherland that historically "abandoned" its North American progeny. It is strongly relativized furthermore, on the one hand by its relation to "joual" (the creolized *Umgangssprache*) and on the other, of course, by its relation to the ubiquitous and economically dominant presence of English. It is a native language that it must be strangely difficult to speak without self-consciousness.

My assertion, then, is that it is not necessarily possible—and it is certainly not necessary—to draw clear distinctions between "major" and "minor" literatures; and my reading of *Prochain Épisode* will attempt to illustrate that assertion. I will take the novel, on the one hand, as a paradigmatic case, after that of Nerval, of a "minor" literature in the Deleuze and Guattari sense; but

I will simultaneously aim—more clearly than is possible in the case of Nerval, where the issue is clouded by the author's "madness"—to study the way a "major" literature, which Québec literature (Krysinski is right) at least potentially is, can be *self-minoritizing*. One of the themes of this book is precisely the balance within literature of its relation to power and its relation to oppositionality, its "Court Poet" and its "Wild Child" aspects, and I will here take Aquin's divided and hostile attitude toward language as a sign of that balance, when it tilts toward the "Wild Child" side of the equation. In an essay of 1964, Aquin wrote: "I am a prey to destructive impulses against the tawdry French tongue [*cette méchante langue française*], majestic to be sure, but in second place." But as early as 1961, in the same essay in which the Québec people are described as "happy counterrevolutionaries," he had already formulated the need to cultivate what he called a *malheur d'expression*, that is, as a critic puts it, a "style which, in its very infelicity, would embody the profound unhappiness of a dispossessed and alienated people."[33] Of a people, that is, whose dispossession and unhappiness takes the form of being, as "happy counterrevolutionaries," their own double agents.

So it is on Aquin's practice in *Prochain Épisode* of a *malheur d'expression* that is an expression of "malheur" (of misery or woe) that I propose to focus, hoping in studying it as an exemplary performance of literary oppositionality to make some contribution to our understanding of an area extraordinarily difficult to theorize: the politics of style. What is *in common* between the miming of a certain discomfort in a language whose every resource one knows intimately and can take advantage of and the submission of a Québec that has "happily" sold out to its political "other" to such an extent that its own self is identical with that other? By what mediations can one get from the author's ubiquitous punning and play with *double meanings* ("malheur d'expression" is an example), and from modes of episodic writing described in *L'Antiphonaire* as an epileptic "spasmographie," to an understanding of the Aquin text as itself an oppositional enunciation of political significance?

It is perhaps already clear that, after La Fontaine and Nerval, Aquin's writing will again demonstrate that, in the oppositional politics of style, one succeeds by failing—but only by failing in a certain way. It is the successful performance of failure in expression—so different *intuitively* from a failure of expression *tout court*, but so difficult to distinguish analytically—that I will be studying again here. But in this case, it is the poetics and politics of suicide that explicitly provide the model of successful failure. If the act of suicide is frequently taken as a sign of defeat, the Aquin text (let alone the Aquin biography) produces it rather as an oppositional gesture, a failure that is, like melancholy, an accusatory message. Even more appositely, however, in contradistinction to the act of suicide itself, what the Aquin text demonstrates—

and enacts—is the possibility of *discursive suicide* as a tactic of *survival* and hence, as an undeniable oppositional success. For, as we shall see, "malheur d'expression"/"expression de malheur" here takes the form of the dissolution of the discursive subject, another version of the Mallarméan disappearing act we saw in Nerval; and, as such, it *takes advantage* of, or appropriates, the otherness of the self, which at its extreme would seem to inhibit and frustrate all oppositionality, in order to produce a poetic suicide that is precisely a discursive oppositional act of the utmost efficacy.

In Aquin, then, it is of the essence that the *same phenomenon*—the equivalence of self and other, the otherness of the self and the "selfness" of the other—has a double function: it signals the impossibility of political *resistance* (in a world where everyone has become "happy counterrevolutionaries"), but it furnishes the mode and means of discursive *oppositionality*. It destroys the possibility of an individual self and makes possible a suicide of self that produces "malheur d'expression." The whole economy of *Prochain Épisode* thus derives from the fact that its principal figuration of the language of the other (and so of alienating law) is simultaneously the means by which textual oppositionality is both thematized and achieved. This can be demonstrated in a number of ways and at many different levels of the text. Let us start with its intertextuality. John Frow has demonstrated how literature can enact its oppositional status through the complexities of generic belongingness (a text that is generically uncategorized or uncategorizable—as, say, "a novel," or "literature"—would be an unreadable text; but each text achieves a degree of individuality within its generic category or categories, and this deviation is the sign—in my vocabulary—of its "oppositionality"). More precisely, Frow has shown that oppositional social reference does not occur directly in text so much as it espouses the mode of intertextuality.[34] In *Prochain Épisode*, the relevant intertextual reference is to the spy novel, a rule- and convention-bound genre in which the narrator nevertheless proposes, as he says, to "faire original" (7).

That this oppositional gesture is simultaneously a self-defeating and self-contradictory stance (since the spy novel is *defined* by adherence to certain conventions), is something of which the narrator is, or becomes, fully aware. His would-be original *livre à venir*, as he says (with a sly intertextual reference to Blanchot)[35] has been always already "foreseen and marked off ahead of time, according to the Dewey decimal system, with the tiniest possible coefficient of individuation" (92). But the result is not a defeat, although there is a necessary failure of originality; for "it is no longer the operational originality of literature that I am defusing, but individual existence that suddenly explodes and disenchants me" (91). As in "Angélique" with respect to the Riancey amendment, forced conformity to the "rules and unwritten laws" (7) of a genre produces not submission, or rather not *only* submission, but also an *éclatement* of the individual self and a multiplication of the subject. For the equivalence and reversibility of the spies and counterspies which constitute the "law" of the spy genre, a law to which the narrator's story abundantly conforms, produce here a phenomenon of textuality that enacts the dispersal of individual existence as a self-disenchantment (it denies the possibility of "originality") that is simultaneously, with respect to the law of the genre, an oppositional success. . . . And although this deviation from convention can indeed be accommodated by the Dewey classificatory system, which has always already foreseen it (as it has foreseen all possible deviations), the system must accommodate it, precisely, *as* a deviation, and hence an appropriation, marking it with the "tiniest possible coefficient of individuation."[36] Thus the status of the oppositional, whose place is (ironically) foreseen in the system but which (no less ironically) uses that place against the system, is defined.

The narrative "folding over" of the text on itself, whereby the narrator produces a hero who becomes a narrator, is a second device of oppositionality, achieved with similar economy and pivoting on the selfsame mechanism. Once again, the identity of self and other implies defeat for certain aspirations (here, revolutionary ones) but becomes the modality of oppositionally successful writing and "malheur d'expression." If the narrator's revolutionary loyalty is inscribed diegetically in his production of the hero as an agent of the FLQ (the militantly separatist Québec Liberation Front) engaged in battling counter-revolutionaries, then the failure of that aspiration is marked, on the one hand, by the (apparent) double-cross of the heroine, K (who is associated by the narrator with Québec and its people but who seems at the end to "choose" the counterspy, H. de Heutz), but on the other hand by the fact that this counterspy turns out to be a *Doppelgänger* of the patriotic hero, an "other" who is the self. The disintegration of the hero's individual self in the confusion of double games and double-crossings and the proliferation of characters who appear as each other's alter ego is inseparable from his defeat as a revolutionary agent.

But this leads him to become the melancholic subject of the narration: he now produces writing that, in telling his own story, is the site of an explosion of that individual subject and the place of an oppositional discursive suicide. Moreover, the explosion of the subject is nowhere produced more notably than in the fact that the narrator and his hero consequently themselves share a divided identity. The hero is originally produced as a first-person protagonist in a fiction, but "becomes" the narrator through his defeat and arrest as a spy, with the result that we must either accept the hero as "real" to the extent that we accept the narrator as real, or we must acknowledge the narrator as a "fiction," to the extent that the hero has been produced as fictive. But both of these propositions are equally operative, so that what we have is a novel that produces itself as its own *Doppelgänger* because it is the site of a double writing—that of the hero's adventures and of the narrator's enunciation—in which self and other, although different, are also identical. Moreover, this is the case whether we adopt the point of view of the hero (who becomes the narrator who writes the hero) or that of the narrator (who writes the hero who becomes himself); so we can say that the text not only produces itself as its own *Doppelgänger*, but does so twice.

What then is being signaled here? In the diegesis, a revolutionary hero becomes, in defeat, a narrator-writer whose subject disappears, or tends to disappear into the selfsame doubling and double-crossing that produced the hero's defeat but now comes to signify writing itself as the "drowning" of the individual self and as oppositional textuality. In short, what *inhibits the revolution* is precisely what *enables the writing*: the dispersal of the self—the fact that the other is oneself and vice versa—is a negative feature of the revolutionary context but it is what positively constitutes writing as text. The text thus enacts itself as the oppositional alternative to a world of action and resistance, the world it represents diegetically. How, then, are we to understand these alternative options?

Revolution is imagined here, on a very simple model, as the *act of killing the other*. The hero is assigned the task of assassinating the counterrevolutionary counterspy, H. de Heutz. But when the other proves to be identical to oneself, that operation becomes impossible. Almost immediately, the hero experiences difficulty in identifying the polypseudonymous other, with his near-perfect cover identity or identities. When finally a confrontation does take place, the equivalence of the two characters becomes inescapable, in the symmetry of twin situations in which each has the other at his mercy, but each produces plausible and near-identical aliases and alibis. Just as the narrator is producing the hero as a fictional subject who tends to become real, so each character here produces himself as a fictional subject who might well be real; and their mirroring of each other flows over into a confusion of self and other, experienced by each on the plane of a fictionality common to both. . . . It will be necessary to return in more detail to these important scenes; but we can note for now that the result, with respect to the hero's revolutionary action, is a kind of paralysis:

Tout se ralentit. Mes pulsations mêmes semblent s'espacer. L'agilité supersonique de mon esprit s'affaisse soudainement sous le charme maléfique de H. de Heutz. Je m'immobilise, métamorphosé en statue de sel, et ne puis m'empêcher de me percevoir comme foudroyé. Un événement souverain est en train de se produire. . . . (P. 88)

[Everything slows. Even my pulse beat seems more widely spaced. The supersonic agility of my mind suddenly collapses under the evil spell of H. de Heutz. I stand stock-still, transformed into a pillar of salt, and cannot help perceiving myself as thunderstruck. A sovereign event is occurring. . . .]

It is this paralysis that marks the moment of transformation of the hero, from the active, agile, constantly moving protagonist he was (the revolutionary spy) into a figure who already foreshadows the immobility and confinement of the narrator, under house arrest in a psychiatric clinic. It is a "sovereign event" indeed. The following episode confirms this new similarity of hero and narrator, as the former awaits his victim (H. de Heutz) in the château, gradually becoming aware of the fact that he is not in control of the situation, as he thought, but is *caught*, much as he previously had been a prisoner there when held at gunpoint by H. de Heutz ("I am dying of inaction and impotence," he had then reported, p. 63). And simultaneously, this hero who thus resembles the narrator but who occupies H. de Heutz's château and has been driving his car, comes to doubt his own identity again. Not for nothing has he admired the taste of H. de Heutz, as evidenced in the decoration of the château; and not for nothing does he now wonder *who lives here*:

Mais si ce n'est pas H. de Heutz qui demeure ici (lui ou Carl von Ryndt ou même ce lamentable François-Marc de Saugy, qu'importe!) et qui couvre son espace vital de ces ornements, qui donc est l'autre? (P. 129)

[But if it's not H. de Heutz who lives here (he or Carl von Ryndt or even the lamentable François-Marc de Saugy, who cares?) and who covers his living space in all this ornamentation, who then is the other?]

An *espace vital* covered in ornamentation is one into which another can slip (as the hero has done) and occupy it, as if it were his own, the "other" thus becoming the "self." But it is simultaneously a figure for writing (what the narrator is doing), and the vehicle by means of which the slippage of identity between narrator and hero—another version of the equation of self and other—can take place. Under the inextricable scrawl—the "fouillis"—of the ex libris or the carved lid of the empty chest, whose initials are readable? To the reader it is already apparent that the hero and H. de Heutz, but also this hero as "I" and the narrator-"I," have a shared identity, that none of them is an autonomous self. But the hero knows only that he is waiting, as he puts it, for his man. "Tout cela porte une signature, celle de l'homme que j'attends" ["All this bears a signature, that of the man I am awaiting"]. His identity, like the narrator's book, is *à venir*: still to come, deferred.

So it is significant that the outcome of his wait will be the failure of his encounter with H. de Heutz (whom he wounds but does not kill, and who gets away) and a (narrowly) missed rendezvous with K, who seems to leave (but is it she?) with the other (but is it H. de Heutz?). . . . Shades of the marriage of Aurélia! Where the killing of the other and a successful meeting with K would have been the sign both of a successful revolutionary action and of the achievement of an autonomous identity, the missed date and the survival of the other mean failure and deferment, if not absolute defeat. The hero will now return to Montréal, where he will be arrested in a crackdown by the police; and he thus "becomes" the confined, if not strictly incarcerated, narrator. So the suggestion is, very strongly, that if revolutionary action on behalf of a Québec "nation" is condemned to failure, it is because *the counterrevolutionary is oneself*, so that the "other" can consequently not be killed without simultaneously destroying the self on whose behalf the revolution is undertaken. In short, the (apparent) betrayal of the hero, and hence of the Québec revolution, by K (if it is K) must be read as signifying the *same thing* as the hero's own failure to kill H. de Heutz: a deep complicity on the part of the Québec people with their own oppression. The betrayal of the revolution occurs because all these people—K, the people of Québec, but also the hero himself—are already identified with their own "other."

An other who perhaps speaks English. It is difficult to think of a French name of which "K" might be the initial (and we learn that K occupies an apartment in London, specifically on Tottenham Court Road). In *Trou de mémoire*, also, the relation of another Québec "patriot" (this term, in Québec usage, recalls the insurgents of 1837) to an Anglo Montrealer named Joan is central. And the toponymy of Québec itself bespeaks a certain investment of that land's identity by an alien presence—a presence that is nevertheless inseparable, as a consequence, from Québec itself. The narrator recalls an afternoon's drive in the Eastern Townships, along their "river of inspiration" (*fleuve*, so the St. Lawrence is intended), with "la femme que j'aime" (hence, perhaps, K):

Sur cette route solitaire qui va de Saint-Ciboire à Upton puis à Acton Vale, d'Acton Vale à Durham-sud, de Durham-sud à Melbourne, à Richmond, à Danville, à Chénier qui s'appelait jadis Tingwick, nous nous sommes parlé mon amour. (P. 10)

[On that lonely road that goes from Saint-Ciboire to Upton and on to Acton Vale, from Acton Vale to Durham South, from Durham South to Melbourne, Richmond, Danville, and Chénier which used to be called Tingwick, we talked together my love (*or*: we spoke my love together).]

To the "international" French ear, these English-sounding names in a French text are incontestably strange and alien—yet they are Québec place-names.

But there are, of course, French place-names in the province, and precisely, a significantly contrasting passage celebrates a road in the Ottawa valley that goes from Papineauville (Papineau: the leader of the abortive uprising of 1837) to a place not coincidentally called "La Nation" (which I have not been able to find in my atlas, although there is a La Patrie in the Eastern Townships).

C'est là que j'achèterai une maison. . . . Cette maison que je trouverai entre Portage-de-la-Nation et La Nation, ou bien entre La Nation et Ripon, ou entre La Nation et le lac Simon sur la route de Chénéville, je pleure de ne l'avoir pas trouvée plus tôt. (P. 78)

[That's where I'll buy a house. . . . I weep not to have found it earlier, that house I'll find between Portage-de-La-Nation and La Nation, or else between La Nation and Ripon, or between La Nation and Lake Simon on the road to Chénéville.]

But *this*, of course—as the obsessive scansion of "La Nation" makes clear— is an idealized, dreamed-of road. The problem is to realize, on the deterritorialized territory that is Québec, an itinerary of liberation—the road to nationhood—but to do it both *with* and *in spite of* "les noms impurs de nos villes" ["the impure names of our towns"] (143).

Sur cette route des Cantons de l'Est, entre Acton Vale et Richmond, tout près de Durham-sud, et partout où nous sommes allés [,] à Saint-Zotique-de-Kotska, aux Éboulements, à Rimouski, à Sherbrooke, à la Malbaie pendant trois jours et trois nuits, à Saint-Eustache et à Saint-Denis, nous n'avons jamais cessé de préparer la guerre de notre libération, mêlant notre intimité délivrée au secret terrible de la nation qui éclate, la violence armée à celle des heures que nous avons passées à nous aimer. (P. 143)

[On that Eastern Townships road, between Acton Vale and Richmond, very close to Durham South, and everywhere we went, in Saint-Zotique-de-Kotska, Les Éboulements, Rimouski, Sherbrooke, La Malbaie for three days and three nights, in Saint-Eustache and Saint-Denis, we never ceased preparing for the war of our liberation, mingling our own liberated intimacy with the terrible secret of the nation exploding, and armed violence with that of the hours we spent loving each other.]

The "terrible secret" of the revolution is therefore bound up, on the one hand, with remembered erotic intimacy with a woman thought or known to have betrayed her lover and the revolution, and on the other with a problem of onomastic "impurity," a "malheur d'expression" on the national scale, recalling a confused and unfortunate history, and expressive of a multiple and shared collective identity. This problem, as we know, means that the revolution cannot happen, it can only be dreamed of in the future, deferred to a *prochain épisode* that is referred to in the text as lying outside its own scope and of which the narrator claims to know "not the first thing" ["pas le premier mot"] (171). And yet this wonderful list of place-names, English, French, and also Indian, does not read like the expression of a sense of defeat: it seems rather to be a *celebration* of linguistic impurity, and an exploration (in the nomadic mode) of the strangeness and yet familiarity of an identity that is both other and one's own.

For instead of the revolutionary act, the killing of the other, there is writing—and there are the place-names of another territory, that of the Rhône Valley and Lake Geneva, an area which stands for the writing (the geological pun was inevitable and it is in the text) of depression:

C'est autour de ce lac invisible que je situe mon intrigue et dans l'eau même du Rhône agrandi que je plonge inlassablement à la recherche de mon cadavre. (P. 10)

[It's around that invisible lake that I'll situate my plot and into the very waters of the widened Rhone that I'll plunge tirelessly in search of my own corpse.]

The alternative to the failed act of revolution, as the killing of the other, is suicide—to kill oneself as a gesture of defeat, and indeed a symbolic murder (if one cannot kill the other, then the other must kill oneself):

Cet homme, H. de Heutz ou von Ryndt, je ne l'ai pas encore tué et cela me déprime. J'éprouve une grande lassitude: un vague désir de suicide me revient. (P. 67)

[I haven't killed my man yet, H. de Heutz or von Ryndt, and that depresses me. I feel a great weariness; a vague desire to commit suicide returns.]

But this is the hero speaking, not the narrator; and even he speaks rather of depression and the desire to commit suicide than of the act itself. Just as his "mission" as a spy is not resolved by the death of the other, it is not to be resolved either by his own death. Or one might say that the suicide he commits is rather the symbolic one of becoming a writer and merging his identity with the "other" who, for the hero, is the narrator.

For suicide as writing, writing as suicide, unlike the act of physically killing oneself, is not final: rather it is a prolongation—and for the hero, it is the prolongation of his defeat. Not immediate death, but the long-drawn-out practice of writing as an enactment of the abolition of the self, dissolved in the otherness of language, is what the hero inherits as his lot when he becomes the narrator. This is a version of Mallarmé's "disparition élocutoire," but a melancholic version, a long plunge into the depths, or "noyade écrite," that is simultaneously an endless playing out of the multiplicity of identity in the flow of words, the stringing together of "episodes" which have this in common that they are *neither* the originary episode (of lovemaking), now available only to memory, *nor* yet the resolving, closing episode that would be another explosion, that of the revolution itself. Between an explosion of love and the revolutionary explosion it foreshadowed and symbolized, another form of *éclatement*—the shattering of identity into multiplicity and the splintering of time into endless episodicity—is what constitutes the recourse to writing as suicide. A Werther without pistols, like the hero/narrator of "Sylvie," the writer is a suicide, then, but a *suicidé vivant*, a living suicide—and if this self-survival arises as a prolongation of the hero's defeat, the *éclatement* of identity, recalling an explosion of love and foreshadowing the revolutionary explosion, can have for the narrator a more positive value and the oppositional quality of an *alternative* to defeat.

How are we to understand this? As the hero waited for his man in the empty château, so the time of writing is also a time of waiting, its episodes "la ponctuation détaillée et quotidienne de mon immobilité interminable et de ma chute ralentie dans cette fosse liquide" ["the detailed and daily punctuation of my interminable immobility and of my slow-motion fall into this liquid pit"] (9). Its space is, in another sense, a between-space, shared between the space of confinement of the clinic, on one hand ("I am writing on a card table near a window through which I can see a park enclosed by a sharp iron fence which marks the border between the unforeseeable and the shut-in," p. 7), and, on the other, the space of the spy fiction, set in the French-speaking region of Switzerland. But this space is a space of depression, "la grande dépression au fond de laquelle j'apercevais la face lumineuse du lac Léman" ["the great depression at the bottom of which I could glimpse the shining face of Lake Geneva"] (66). And so, just as the narrator and his hero join in a single, divided but shared, identity, so too do the two spaces of writing join to form the single (but divided) space of an "I" whose cover story is the ornamentation of intricate writing into which he disappears.

This is the space—at once confined and sinking into the watery depths of depression—that he calls his "sous-marin clinique" (10), or clinical submarine.

D'ici là, je suis attablé au fond du lac Léman, plongé dans sa mouvance fluide qui me tient lieu de subconscient, mêlant ma dépression à la dépression alanguie du Rhône cimbrique, mon emprisonnement à l'élargissement de ses rives. J'assiste à ma solution. (P. 11)

[Meanwhile, I am seated at my writing table on the bottom of Lake Geneva, plunged into its fluid surge which serves me as a substitute subconscious, mingling my depression with the Cimbric Rhône's own lethargic depression, and my imprisonment with the widening [*or:* setting free] of its shores. I am witnessing [*or:* am present at, *or:* am helping] my own dissolution [*or:* solution].]

The lake as depression, and as the place of writing, is thus the place where individual identity is dissolved ("J'assiste à ma solution"), just as the landscape of the lake region is the fictive space in which doubling and duplicity figure the explosion of self—an explosion that the doubling of lake region and space of confinement, their mingling in the practice of writing itself, also effects. But consequently, the dissolution of identity is—just possibly—a "solution" ("J'assiste à ma solution"); and the confinement of writing a means of "élargissement": a widening that is also a setting free.

"D'ici-là . . ." ["Meanwhile . . ."]. As in space, so too in time, betweenness is what characterizes writing: but here too we can now acknowledge something positive. The love-bed has become the sticky "lit de glaise" (90–91) of the Rhône, and its waters are fed only in memory by the "river of inspiration that still flows in me this afternoon" (10). But that lost time is, consequently, still in a sense present; and it was itself a premonition of a future time that would repeat the originary moment of love and simultaneously put a stop to the time of melancholy.

Ce soir-là, je me souviens, quel triomphe en nous! Quelle violente et douce prémonition de la révolution nationale s'opérait sur cette étroite couche recouverte de couleurs et de nos deux corps nus, flambants, unis dans leur démence rythmée. (P. 72)

[That evening, I remember, what a triumph there was in us! What a violent and sweet premonition of the national revolution was brought about on the narrow couch strewn with colors and covered by our two naked bodies, aflame, united in their rhythmic frenzy.]

Meanwhile, the revolution itself, of course, does lie somewhere in the future:

Mais tout n'est pas dit. . . . Je me sens fini; mais tout ne finit pas en moi. Mon récit est interrompu parce que je ne connais pas le premier mot du prochain épisode. Mais tout se résoudra en beauté. . . . Après deux siècles d'agonie, nous ferons éclater la violence déréglée, série ininterrompue d'attentats et d'ondes de choc, noire épellation d'un projet d'amour total. . . . (Pp. 171–72)

[But all is not said and done. . . . I feel myself finished; but everything does not finish with me. My narrative is interrupted because I don't know the first thing about the next episode. But everything will turn out beautifully. . . . After two centuries of dying, we will unleash an explosion of uncontrolled violence, a series of attacks and shock waves, a dark spelling out of a project of total love. . . .]

Now, writing is an enactment of slow death, a continuation of Québec's two centuries of agonie, but then writing will no longer be needed or appropriate— "The pages will write themselves in machine-gun fire, the words will whistle over our heads, and sentences will fall to pieces in the air . . . "(173)—for it will be possible to kill H. de Heutz and to finish the book. But it is significant that the very description of the revolution as the end of discourse employs a metaphorics of language; and a certain continuity, on the level of discourse, between the period of writing and the time of revolution is implied by such turns of phrase as "Tout n'est pas *dit*," or "pas le premier *mot*." Just as the dissolution of identity in space may be an expansion and even a liberation, an *élargissement*, so too the splitting of time into a long series of episodes that "punctuate my immobility" allows the imagination to conceive of its "end" as being not discontinuous with the series, but a *prochain épisode*. In this context, the suicide of writing, as an *éclatement* of self akin both to the act of love and the act of revolution, has the sense of a *buying of time* for a revolution that is less defeated than it is deferred.

That is why a refrain of revolutionary dates scans the writing: especially June 24, the Québec national day and the date of the remembered afternoon of love; August 4 (1792), the famous "nuit d'août" when aristocratic privilege was abolished in France; and July 26 (1960), the date ascribed, in memory of the attack on the Moncada barracks, to Cuba's accession to revolutionary in- dependence. To these can be added, it seems, the unknown future date of the narrator's *élargissement*, his liberation from confinement in the *prochain épi- sode* of a Québec revolution. But it is *between* those dates that his writing situates itself: "Between the anniversary of the Cuban revolution and the date of my trial . . .", "Between Cuba's July 26 and the lyrical night of the 4th of August . . .", etc. Between those momentous dates, as he says, "J'ai le temps de divaguer en paix, de déplier avec minutie mon livre inédit et d'étaler sur le papier les mots-clés qui ne me libéreront pas" ["I have the time to ramble on in peace, to unfold in minute detail my yet-to-be-published book and to spread over the paper the key words that will not set me free"] (7). Writing in and of itself does not free one; its *mots-clés* do not open the locks of imprison- ment; it is neither the moment of love nor the revolutionary moment between which it unfolds its endless drivel (*divagations*). But it *is* a mode of survival, and just possibly something more.

And so, exiled between the dates of love and freedom in time, just as, in space, he is "exilé de La Nation et de ma vie" ["exiled from La Nation and my life"] (145), the narrator does know a "tristesse," a "spleen," an "ennoiement brumaire" (68) that is a personal version of the "catatonia" (58) affecting the nation itself. "After two centuries of slow death [*agonie*] (172), "After two centuries of conquest and 34 years of confused sadness [*tristesse confusion- nelle*]" (25), "After two centuries of melancholy and 34 years of impotence" (69), the slow suicide of writing, a suicide "qui n'en finit plus" (26) continues the agony of dying. It simultaneously prolongs the defeat of the revolutionary hero, as I have said. But it can also be seen, now, to prolong his efforts as well. "Me suicider partout et sans relâche, voilà ma mission," he says ["To commit suicide everywhere and without respite, that is my mission"] (25); and the word "mission" (curiously, it is in Nerval too) is significant. But so too are the words "partout" and "sans relâche," suggesting as they do that if the dissolu- tion of identity in space could be carried "everywhere," and if its fragmenta- tion into the episodicity of time could be carried out "without respite," then they might achieve a kind of absoluteness and so lead, without discontinuity, to the grand explosion that will be the *prochain épisode* of revolution itself.

So we can say, it seems, that writing as suicide serves simultaneously as a *means* of (symbolic) death—a sign of defeat—and as the equivalent of a *suicide note*, a genre in which discursive self-survival is attempted, and usually some settling of accounts. Like many suicide notes, including Werther's, the narrator's writing is a loveletter, addressed to the distant and beloved K, who is also the people of Québec—but to a beloved, therefore, whose betrayal is not only the occasion of the suicide itself, but has also made her remote, so remote, as an addressee, (she has joined the "other") as to be unreachable by the message. In turning in on itself, as it does, and in becoming therefore a self-enclosed message, the writing figures the confinement of depression and the loneliness of a discourse that seeks survival beyond death but without being able to count on finding a reader. So there is an irony, and indeed an absurdity, in its gesture. For whom is the dissolving of identity to be a "solution," and an *élargissement*? Who will benefit from the "prochain épisode" of revolution ("Je me sens fini, mais tout ne finit pas en moi")? And what is the purpose of a lucidity that finds discursive expression in the writing of melancholy, but from whom no one will benefit, it seems, except the *suicidé* himself, enclosed in his sinking submarine? For the final pun that catches the ambiguity of suicide as at once an admission of defeat and an oppositional "revanche" is the one that links depression as a sinking to the depths with lucidity and veridiction, as a getting to the bottom of things.

"Cuba coule en flammes au milieu du lac Léman pendant que je descends au fond des choses" ["Cuba sinks in flames in the middle of Lake Geneva while I descend—*or*: get—to the bottom of things"]—the opening sentence reads like a piece of surrealist automatic writing, a string of associations of ideas, and as such it enacts the practice of writing as drift, episode by episode, which is the hallmark of the text. Simultaneously it situates the subject and his writing in a context of revolutionary defeat (since Cuba stands in the text for revolutionary independence, and Lake Geneva for the place of depression). But it also identifies his sinking into melancholy as a gain in clear-sightedness: "je descends au fond des choses." The following sentence picks up these motifs and in addition explicitly thematizes the notion of drift; but most importantly, it situates the subject simultaneously as a cadaver, encoffined in words, and as one who survives, phantom-like, in the drift of those selfsame phrases: "Encaissé dans mes phrases, je glisse, fantôme, dans les eaux névrosées du fleuve et je découvre, dans ma dérive, le dessous des surfaces et l'image renversée des Alpes" ["Encased in my sentences, I slide, a phantom, in the neurotic waters of the river and, as I drift, I discover what lies beneath surfaces and the inverted image of the Alps"]. In this way, the two opening sentences function together as *mise en abyme* of the whole text: that is, they define it as being strictly *equivalent to its own enunciatory situation*, and they define that situation as one of depression: depression as sinking, depression as drift. But they also define depression as the site from which the truthful aspect of things becomes visible and a phantom-like subject survives his own death in order to speak it, and to do so with lucidity. But to speak it for whom?

The irony does not lie solely in the lonely position of truth telling without an audience, however. To tell the truth of melancholy is itself a contradictory operation, an attempt that plumbs depths that are unfathomable and closes off what is a potential for endlessness. To make melancholy the occasion of a veridiction is, in short, to systematize it (to make it classifiable in terms of the Dewey system, for instance), whereas its truth lies in its "ontological incoherence." "Condamné à une certaine incohérence ontologique. . . . J'en fais même un système dont je décrète l'application immédiate," says the narrator with obvious irony ["Condemned to a certain ontological incoherence. . . . I even make a system out of it and decree its immediate application"] (14). So the paradox of melancholic writing—and one can see the connection with the problematics of communication in "Aurélia"—lies on one hand in its loneliness as a veridiction without an audience, and on the other in its inability to *say the truth* of melancholy without simultaneously betraying it, as the otherness of language betrays the self or K the hero. Melancholy is a solution ("j'assiste à ma solution"), but this solution is a dissolution, a dissolving of the self in its own "ontological incoherence." How is its truth to be said, in language, without the otherness of language betraying that truth? Writing, even as the disorderly mimesis of that "ontological incoherence," must somehow succeed in solving the problem of dissolution without systematizing it; it must be, simultaneously, a solving and an unsolving of this dissolving of the self. . . .

Not surprisingly, then, in view both of the absence of appropriate addressee and of the communicative conundrum posed by the saying of the truth of melancholy, the narrator perceives his writing as an absurd activity, governed by a "je ne sais plus pourquoi" and a "plus rien à gagner":

Non, je ne sais plus pourquoi je suis en train de rédiger un casse-tête, alors que je souffre et que l'étau hydrique se resserre sur mes tempes jusqu'à broyer mon peu de souvenirs. . . . Je n'ai plus rien à gagner en continuant d'écrire, pourtant je continue quand-même, j'écris à perte. (P. 13)

[No, I have no idea why I am writing a *casse-tête*, when I'm suffering and the hydric clamp is squeezing my temples to the point of crushing my few memories. . . . I have nothing to gain now in continuing to write, yet I continue anyway, I write for the heck of it.]

But, if writing the truth of melancholy is impossibly bound up in the problematics of the betrayal of the self in the language of the other, then perhaps the truth of the message, its getting to the bottom of things, does not lie so much in saying something that the act of saying will betray, as in the very problem, or puzzle, that constitutes the enunciatory situation itself, as the struggle of the melancholy subject to say its truth in the language of otherness? The "message," in this case, would lie, not in any possible solution to the puzzle, but in the discursive puzzle itself. The "solution" is not a solution but a puzzle; and the puzzle "solves" both the problem of expression and—as I will show in due course—that of audience. A cryptogram (a jumble of letters that is both a message and an unsolved puzzle) plays an essential role in *Prochain Épisode*, as *mise en abyme* of the textual enunciation: it is handed to the hero as a message he cannot decipher, and only to betray him, later on, to the counterspies and so determine his becoming narrator. . . . The cryptogram figures the textual enunciation, then, as a *casse-tête*, a headache (or melancholic migraine) that is simultaneously a puzzle—*the* puzzle, in short, that *is* the headache of melancholy.

Furthermore, as commentary has frequently noted, the plot of *Prochain Épisode*—the spy story—poses questions that manifestly cannot be solved (this is Aquin's most obvious debt, and perhaps his only real one, to the French *nouveau roman*). There is no way of identifying the characters with certainty or of specifying what has actually happened. But this, we can now see, is not a matter of formalistic play: it figures the writing itself as a problem without a solution, or whose solution is dissolution (the writing itself as a laying out of a series of separate episodes, like the letters of a cryptogram). A truth *is* being said here, then, but a truth that is beyond the grasp of saying or conceptualizing, a truth that will not be pinned down because the very inability to be pinned down is its truth. This truth becomes synonymous, not with the resolution but with the enunciation of a puzzle, the enunciation that *is* the puzzle of melancholy. To pin melancholy down, to systematize it, is to destroy it, by translating it into the language of the other—yet melancholy *is* precisely that sense of the investment of self by the other. But simultaneously and consequently, there is no language of the self that is not the language of the other— and melancholy is *also* the sense that there is no self except insofar as the other constitutes it. So the puzzle of melancholy is the dilemmma that arises from the fact that between these alternatives there are no options.

If we view *Prochain Épisode* not as the saying of a message but as the enunciation of a puzzle, it becomes clear that the text's "doubling" on itself, the way it folds into a duplicitous but single writing, such that the narrator writes the fiction of a hero whose failure turns him into the narrator, is itself an enunciatory miming of the puzzle that results from the otherness of the self, the puzzle of melancholy. It is not strictly the enunciation of a puzzle, but the puzzle of the enunciation that counts; for the truth of melancholy lies, not in an unsayable "something," but in a certain *mode of saying*, a saying that needs to be strangely duplicitous in order to mime an existential duplicity: that incomprehensible *division* of a self that coincides with its other, such that its identity is simultaneously divided and yet a *shared* one. There is no self but the other, and so, as the narrator notes, "mon livre m'écrit" ["my book is writing me"] (94); and the result is that, "après deux siècles de mélancolie et trente-quatre ans d'impuissance, *je me dépersonnalise* ["after two centuries of melancholy and thirty-four years of impotence, *I am depersonalizing myself*, or: *I am being depersonalized*"] (69, my emphasis). This is the form the suicide of writing takes, it is a depersonalization of the self through its identification with the other. But the very form of this phrase—the conflict between its grammar ("je") and its semantic content (there is no "person" to say "je"), and the doubling of self implied by the reflexive verb ("je me . . .")—reproduces in little the puzzle of melancholic writing, mimes the duplicitousness of an enunciation that can say the self, affirm the subject as a site of oppositionality, only by denying it, dissolving it in words, suiciding it in otherness.

It is this same relationship of duplicity and shared identity ("depersonalization" for short) that governs the activity of the narrator and his hero. The curves and zigzags of writing are doubled by the hero's high-speed careening and skidding ("dérapage") on the twisting Alpine roads, each engaged in a chase—long drawn out in one case, rapid and exciting in the other—after the elusive "man," his identity. The two "I's frequently coexist in the same sentence (as they do in "je me dépersonnalise"):

Je dérape dans les lacets du souvenir, comme je n'ai pas cessé de déraper avec ma Volvo. . . . (P. 45)

[I skid on the hairpin bends of memory as I have never stopped skidding in my Volvo. . . .]

En deux jours d'une course lente de la place de la Riponne à l'Hôtel d'Angleterre, du Château d'Ouchy à la Tour de Peilz, de Clarens à Yvorne et à Aigle, d'Aigle à Château d'Oex en passant par le col des Mosses, de Château d'Oex à Carouge, puis d'Échandens à Genève et de Genève à Coppet, je n'ai fait que circonscrire la même voûte renversée, tournant autour du grand lit fluviatile qui me subjugue en ce moment même, alors que je m'abandonne à la course effusive des mots. . . . (P. 110)

[In two days of slow chase [*course*] from the place de la Riponne to the Hôtel d'Angleterre, from the château d'Ouchy to the Tour de Peilz, from Clarens to Yvorne and Aigle, from Aigle to Château d'Oex by the col des Mosses, from Château d'Oex to Carouge, then from Échandens to Geneva and from Geneva to Coppet, all I have done was to circumscribe the same inverted vault, turning in this way around the great river bed that subjugates me even now, as I give myself over to the effusive flow [*course*] of words. . . .]

The strange place-names of "Suisse romande," themselves dissimilar from but mirroring the "noms impurs" of Québec, function like clues to a huge territorial puzzle, which each self—narrator or hero—is trying to solve simultaneously, hoping that the curves of the road or the "courbes manuscrites" will generate (or in the case of the narrator, reinvent) a *story*, "mon récit" (120). But no clear story comes: just as, in "Angélique" and other nineteenth-century texts (*Lorenzaccio* or *La Chartreuse*), the difficulty was to produce history out of competing "stories," here the difficulty is to produce so much as a satisfactory "story" out of the skids and curves that form the puzzle of writing. One is left with the puzzle itself, the puzzle of "depersonalization."

As for the trick of writing—the "malheur d'expression"—that mimes the depersonalization of self by making it impossible to identify a single sentence-subject because successive "I"s refer to subjects that are different-but-the-same, it is so pervasive in Aquin's text that the careful reader soon begins to scrutinize every bipartite sentence in the growing suspicion that even when the reference is to an apparently unified and cohesive subject—either "hero" or "narrator"—there still lurks a duality, whether resulting from the *division* of identity (on the one hand the "hero," on the other the "narrator") or from their sharing of identity (both "hero" and "narrator"). I quote in illustration, and at random, a couple of episode beginnings:

Ce soir, pendant que je roule entre Échandens et le fond d'une vallée . . . , je me sens découragé. (P. 66)

[This evening, as I drive between Échandens and the floor of a valley . . . , I feel discouraged.]

(It is the "hero" who is driving, but it could be either the "hero" or the "narrator"—or both—who is discouraged, the one with driving, the other with writing.)

Cela me fait drôle de me trouver seul dans cette grande demeure. (P. 123)

[It gives me an odd feeling to find myself alone in this great dwelling.]

(Both the "hero" and the "narrator" are alone in a *grande demeure* and it could be either or both who feels odd about it.) Usually, the hesitation disappears within a sentence or two; but this constant unsettling of the reader's ability to distinguish between the two "I"s has the cumulative effect of establishing their joint identity, as one that is both clearly divided (between self and other) and no less evidently shared (the self is the other and vice versa). The rhetorical trick of the text, whereby the "hero," who has been produced as a fictional protagonist by the "narrator," becomes the subject of an autobiographical narrative that recounts the events resulting in the "narrator"'s enunciatory situation, reproduces macrostructurally this syntactic enactment of divided/shared identity.

So too, on the diegetic level, does the encounter with H. de Heutz, which functions as a major *mise en abyme* of the textual situation itself by figuring the production of self in language as an encounter with the other who proves, unsettlingly, to be the self. But it is here also that we find a figuration of the mode of reception the text foresees for the puzzle of its own enunciation. For under circumstances of arrest and confinement (just like the narrator) each character resorts (just like the narrator) to storytelling. Each storyteller produces a fictive version of himself as subject, a "cover"-story; but in each case (just as in the narrative proper) the apparently inventive cover story proves to have a strange plausibility: perhaps it is real? H. de Heutz cannot be sure the hero is not the depressed bank employee he claims to be, and the hero himself is close, not just to believing his own story, but to becoming the other that is the subject of his fiction:

A vouloir me faire passer pour un autre, je deviens cet autre; les deux enfants qu'il a abandonnés, ils sont à moi soudain et j'ai honte. (P. 62)

[By dint of passing myself off as another, I become that other; suddenly the two children he abandoned are mine, and I am ashamed of myself.]

(In exactly similar fashion, the narrator, recounting the adventures of his hero, becomes that hero, so that the hero in turn becomes the narrator.) And inversely, when H. de Heutz tells *his* story, the listening hero is strangely troubled by an effect of reality: perhaps this man *is* who he claims to be (one François-Marc de Saugy)? "H. de Heutz is really crying like a father who has troubles, like a man overwhelmed with grief and who has lost the strength to deal with life" (84). All the certainties crumble:

Cet homme qui pleure devant moi, qui est-ce enfin? Est-ce Carl von Ryndt, banquier pour la couverture mais surtout agent ennemi; ou bien H. de Heutz, spécialiste wallon de Scipion l'Africain et de la contre-révolution; ou encore, serait-il plus simplement le troisième homme, du nom de François-Marc de Saugy, en proie à une dépression nerveuse et à une crise suraiguë de dépossession? (P. 87)

[Who *is* this man, standing crying before me? Is he Carl von Ryndt, a banker for the sake of cover but mainly an enemy agent; or is he H. de Heutz, a Walloon specializing in Scipio Africanus and counterrevolution; or again, more simply, maybe he is the third man, named François-Marc de Saugy, a victim of nervous depression and a hyperacute attack of dispossession?]

But what intensifies the hero's bafflement and fascination in this situation is, of course, the fact that the cover story H. de Heutz produces is in all essentials the *same* cover story that he himself has produced an hour or two earlier at the Château. In other words, the two identities meet on the shared terrain of an identical "cover," on the common ground of fictivity. And what is essential from the point of view of the *mise en abyme* of the novel itself and its textual self-figuration is the fact that the shared cover story in which these two self-mirroring identities meet and merge creates a "psychiatric version" (62) of each narrative subject: each narrator claims to be clinically depressed to the point of suicide, a victim of nervous depression and "dispossession." Thus fictionality—a fictionality that becomes true, as the language of the other produces the self—is identified with suicidal melancholy, and vice versa. And so, the hero ends his tale: "Je veux en finir. Je ne veux plus vivre . . ." ["I wan to end it all. I want to stop living . . ."] (61); and H. de Heutz echoes him: "Tuez-moi! C'est encore ce qui peut arriver de mieux. Je vous en supplie. Tirez. De grâce . . ." ["Kill me! That's the best thing that could happen to me. I beg of you. Fire. *Please* . . ."] (86). The self-mirroring narratives thus themselves exactly mirror the suicidal writing that is *Prochain Épisode* ("me suicider partout et sans relâche, c'est là ma mission") while each listener figures the puzzlement with respect to identity that the textual enunciation, as *casse-tête*, itself produces. The reader's reception of the text is thus figured as a puzzlement that corresponds to the puzzle of the textual enunciation: a form of fascination, of bafflement, but also of involvement—on the common ground of fictivity, the shared terrain of "cover"—a recognition of oneself-as-other in the very otherness of this fiction, and hence an association of oneself, in complicity, with the discursive suicide that it is performing.

But these narratives demonstrate also that suicidal discourse—the expression of a desire to die that is at once the production of a fiction and the realization of a "depersonalized" subject—the type of self-doubling enunciation, then, in which all these subjects (the narrator and his fictional double, the hero; the fictionalizing hero and his own fictionalizing double, H. de Heutz) are involved, is an *oppositional tactic*. It is a *mode of survival* in which the threat of death is defused by a stated desire to die, and by the discourse of melancholy as a fiction that is real. Both the hero and H. de Heutz argue for their survival by suggesting that to kill them would be supererogatory, a realization of their own desire for death; and indeed, as a result, each in fact does manage to escape confinement and the threat of being killed by the other (their suicidal discourse and the puzzlement it induces having acted as a diversionary tactic). The textual narrator, on the other hand, is not so lucky, and there seems to be no escape for him from his "clinical submarine."

But the spinning out of his own discourse, its inability to end, as it moves from episode to episode, with always another episode in sight, the endlessness of its drift, as a mimesis of melancholy . . . all this does for him what their escape realizes for the hero and for H. de Heutz, it ensures a prolongation of existence. Consequently, it is suggestive of a certain strategy—albeit an involuntary one, perhaps—of *incompletion*, of suicide as the buying of time that I have already referred to.

J'ai perdu le fil de mon histoire, et me voici rendu au milieu d'un chapitre que je ne sais plus comment finir. (P. 142)

[I've lost the thread of my story, and here I am in the middle of a chapter I have no idea how to end.]

Cf. the "prochain épisode" of revolution, about which "I don't know the first thing" (171). Or again:

Je m'étends sur la page abrahame et je me couche à plat ventre pour agoniser dans le sang des mots. . . . A tous les événements qui se sont déroulés, je cherche une fin logique, sans la trouver. Je brûle d'en finir et d'apposer un point final à mon passé indéfini. (P. 167)

[I spread-eagle myself over my Abrahamian page and lie prone, slowly dying in the blood of words. . . . I seek, but without finding it, a logical end to all the events that have occurred. I burn with desire to end it all and to put a final period to my past indefinite (*or:* my indefinite past).]

The production of the text as puzzle, without a "logical end" even for the narrator himself, corresponds here to the enunciation—"Je brûle d'en finir"—that reproduces the suicidal claims of the hero and H. de Heutz: "Je veux en finir. Je ne veux plus vivre . . ."; "Tuez-moi! C'est encore ce qui peut m'arriver de mieux." . . . It is an updated and melancholic version of the Scheherazade tactic.

Survival through suicide, then; and through the association of the dangerous other with that suicide. How is this to be interpreted? In political terms, that is, to the extent that Aquin's narrator is, as he says, "the fractured symbol of the Québec revolution but also its disordered reflection and its suicidal incarnation" (25), the novel's meaning is perhaps readable as a judgment that the vocation of Québec is oppositional: it lies in survival, not revolution, but in a form of survival that consists, Scheherazade-like, of a slow suicide, episode by episode, as a means of deferment of what would be the *worst* possible outcome: absolute defeat by the other, total loss of "national" identity. The revolutionary alternative is indeed "fractured" in circumstances where the other is a version of oneself, or is indeed identical with oneself; but the opposite threat, that of being eliminated by the other (who is oneself in the position of power) can be averted, and the outcome of defeat at least delayed—in hopes of the revolution's nevertheless eventually becoming possible—by the suicide tactic. Papineau, we learn (the defeated patriot of 1837–38, who went into exile) "would have done better to commmit suicide" (161).

It is as if collective survival depends on the spread of melancholy as the contagious effect of a series of individual suicides, something like the epidemic of suicide that swept Europe in the wake of *Werther*. But suicide here means symbolic suicide, that is, the renunciation of the individual subject, an act of "depersonalization" that produces a collectivization of the self. Such a suicide realizes the narrator's conviction: "je me sens fini, mais tout ne finit pas en moi. . . ." For, in this text, individual suicide, as the renunciation of a self that is damagingly identical to its own counterrevolutionary other, is not an end but a continuation, a means of survival and a buying of time; and it is also an *élargissement* of self that is a possible "solution" because it makes possible the constitution, through self-dissolution, of a collectivity of shared identities. A solution through dissolution, then, and through the conversion of a people of "happy counterrevolutionaries" to an identity of melancholy. But how is this spread of melancholy to occur?

To put the mode of survival that is suicide in discursive terms, one can say that in "collective enunciation," a phantom-subject survives the self's "disparition élocutoire" into the puzzle of writing, but that this phantom can be an effective oppositional agent only if the gesture of disappearing does not pass unnoticed: it must be read. For in the writing of melancholy as a "noyade écrite," the narrator becomes the revolution's "fractured symbol" and signifies defeat. "The wages of the undone warrior are depression. The wages of national depression are my failure" (261). But simultaneously, he regards himself as the revolution's "suicidal incarnation," by which one should understand an oppositional figure capable of *saving* the revolution from ultimate defeat by the employment of suicide as a *tactic*. This he does not only by his simple survival but also by means of the lucidity he has achieved in defeat.

Condamné à la noirceur, je me frappe aux parois d'un cachot qu'enfin, après 34 ans de mensonges, j'habite pleinement et en toute humiliation. Je suis emprisonné dans ma folie, emmuré dans mon impuissance surveillée, accroupi sans élan sur un papier blanc comme le drap avec lequel on se pend. (P. 27)

[Condemned to blackness, I hurl myself against the walls of a dungeon that at last, after 34 years of lies, I inhabit fully and in all humiliation. I am imprisoned in my madness, walled up in my impotence under guard, crouching listlessly over paper as white as the sheet with which one hangs oneself.]

It is the lucidity of his vision, substituting itself for thirty-four years of lying, that constitutes its revolutionary potential: the veridiction of melancholy, the puzzle of depersonalization, ultimately form a discourse of protest, inscribed on paper as white as the sheet with which the prisoner hangs himself. They fulfill the Freudian dictum that the lamentations of melancholics are accusations. But they do so only on the condition of finding a reader who can be *converted* to the lucidity of a "suicidal" view of the world.

Then the text as suicidal discourse would be not only an act of symbolic suicide (an enactment of "elocutionary disappearance"), and not simply a tactic of survival (through the puzzle of the "depersonalized" self), but finally too—as a puzzle that produces puzzlement in a reader, who thereby becomes "involved" in its discourse—a *positively* oppositional form of discourse, mediating the spread of melancholy and symbolic suicide pending the revolution proper. . . . Such a text, as an enunciatory staging of the conditions of existence that make for melancholy but against which melancholy is itself a form of protest, would function as an instrument of lucidity, not only for its narrator, but for readers as well. Between the "fractured symbol" of a defeated revolution and the "suicidal incarnation" that looks forward to the explosion of its future success, it would function, as it says, as a "disordered reflection"—the enunciatory puzzle in which it is, precisely, the survival of the "fractured symbol" *as* a "suicidal incarnation" that can be read.

But the trick, then, is to make suicide a tactic in an ongoing struggle, and not—as it would be were H. de Heutz, for example, to take the hero *at his word* and kill him—a mode of defeat and the equivalent of a murder. The trick, in short, is to keep on talking: to *talk* one's death, not live it.[37] (That is perhaps the most radical definition one can give of oppositional discourse.) But to talk one's death, as it happens, means to produce a *text*, that is, a discourse that becomes meaningful only through being read, in the strong sense of the term. Even in "everyday" life, to say one is suicidal and to wish openly for death is not necessarily to wish to be *taken at one's word*. It is rather to produce a form of discourse that asks to be *interpreted*, as a cry for help or an oppositional protest—and that seeks, therefore, to produce for itself, in its addressee, an understanding and participatory "reader." What we have seen in *Prochain Épisode* is a talking of the death of self—a symbolic suicide through "elocutionary disappearance"—that itself functions to produce a text capable of surviving, phantom-like, through its readability. But in the absence of K, the narrator's explicit addressee (i.e., the textual "narratee"), we have yet to understand the nature of the *textual addressee* such readability presupposes, and seeks.

The name of that readability is the text-as-puzzle, the puzzle of the melancholic enunciation that has no solution that is not identical with the puzzle (a dissolution, not a solution): what opens the discourse up to the act of reading is the "fold" in the text that produces the "narrator" and the "hero" as a single, exploded (divided but shared) identity. But what can be read is only the puzzle itself of a divided identity, in which the self is the other, and vice versa, *unless* one simultaneously reads the enunciation of the puzzle as the puzzle of the enunciation. At that point, the reader has no option but to identify with the (suicidal) subject ("subject?") of that enunciatory puzzle; and two consequences follow. One is that one shares the gain in lucidity of that subject, and understands his suicide as the protest, the accusation that it is. The other is that one enacts a symbolic suicide of one's own, in permitting oneself to undergo the puzzlement that is reading, in becoming oneself the subject of a discursive puzzle. Like the hero discovering his identity with H. de Heutz, his alter ego, through the similarity of the latter's cover story with his own, one yields in this way to one's own otherness, and one performs that act of reading as a form of suicide that corresponds exactly with, and so responds to, the symbolic suicide that is the narration. No less surely than the text of "Aurélia" depends, for the realization of its narrative programme (the "meaning of my dreams"), on an agency which it knows it cannot control, that of *Prochain Épisode* relies, for the spread of its revolutionary depersonalization, on readers willing to be seduced into a type of "noyade lue"—into reading as drowning— a drowning whose subject follows, and is, the flow of the textual waters, and does not invent or control them.

So it is not simply that, from being the place of a symbolic suicide, the text becomes the functional equivalent of a suicide note, in which the phantom of the dead self survives—or, in more technical terms, a plural *sujet de l'énonciation* supersedes an autonomous *sujet de l'énoncé*—with the express purpose of affecting a reader. It is that such a suicide note seeks to convert its reader to its own suicidal values and to spread the contagion of its discursive melancholy. It seeks to change the world of "happy counterrevolutionaries" by changing its reader(s) into melancholic subjects of puzzlement. It seeks to be the functional equivalent of a suicide pact.

I have not counted the number of times characters in Aquin threaten suicide, nor the number of accidents in his text that might be suicides (or vice versa), nor that of the suicides that might be murder (or vice versa). Nor have I calculated the correlation of rape with these other violences, although it is high. But it seems logical, in the light of *Prochain Épisode* alone, that the fragment we have of a fifth novel, which was to be entitled *Obombre*—an earlier title, *L'art de la fugue*, is also significant—should have the discursive structure of a suicide note. "I shall be dead when you read this. . . ."

Quand tu liras ces lignes, je serai déjà absent. . . . Si ce livre me représente, c'est uniquement dans la mesure où tu le fais accéder, par la photogénie des cadratins de cette page, à la vie de ta pensée. C'est toi qui vis, lecteur, et non pas moi, non plus moi! Rien de moins métaphorique que cette dernière phrase.[38]

[When you read these lines, I will already be gone. . . . If this book represents me, it is exclusively to the extent that, thanks to the photogenic quality of the em quads of this page, you bring it to life in your own mind. It is you who are alive, reader, and not me, no longer me! Nothing could be less metaphoric than this last sentence.]

A "quad" [*cadratin*] is a printer's term, and reference is being made to the intervention of publication between the writing of this message and its reading: more specifically, it is being ironically implied that the reader will have to read the *blanks* (the absences) in the text in order to bring it to life. So what will intervene here, between the writing of the "note" and its reading, will be the death of the subject, the blanking out of him who says "I". . . . But this death is to be superseded by a form of survival, that of the text ("le livre"), by means of which an act of reading can accord the now absent self, "represented" by the book, the "life of [the reader's] thought," "la vie de ta pensée." In this sense, the text is *haunted*: "L'auteur est absent; mais son ombre encre chaque caractère" ["The author is absent; but each printer's character is inked by his shadow/shade"].[39] And the verb *obombrer*, from which the title derives, implies something like a complete coverage by shadow, a saturation of the text, if one will, by the "shade" of the (absent) writing subject.

    It would be difficult to imagine a more suggestive way of underlining the similarity between what, in contemporary culture, we understand to be "literature" and the rhetorical structure of the suicide note: an announcement of death intended to be read, after the fact, as a surviving trace of the self, and as a denunciation, in the manner of the ghost of Hamlet's father, of the circumstances of that death. What we call "text" is both the place of death or the means of suicide (in which the "subject" becomes dissolved in writing) and the suicide note itself, whose continued readability, after the event, ensures a form of self-survival of that subject. The "shade" inking each letter of the text and obumbrating the whole invites the reader to construct—it is what we call interpretation—the story of that elocutionary disappearance, which is identical with the becoming of the text. Such a story is the one told, precisely, by the narrator of *Prochain Épisode*. But without reading, there is no survival of the writerly shade, which can live only in "la vie de ta pensée . . . lecteur," and hence no effective denunciation of the circumstances of death. And we must ask also what it is to be a reader, and to give life to another in one's "own" thought, as such a text demands.

    It is because of the crucial importance of reading that we have seen, first in Nerval and now in Aquin, what I called an anxiety of reception, that is, an anxiety about readership that takes the form of an attempt to discriminate the "bad", or persecuting, reader (the "other" who is the cause of death) from a "good" reader, whose function is to give life to the text, to understand it, to realize it as the obumbrated shade of the disappeared self. For "c'est toi qui

vis, lecteur, et non pas moi, non plus moi". . . . That suicide notes are so
often addressed precisely to the "other" who is regarded as the persecutory,
alienating cause of death, in the way that the text of *Prochain Épisode* is
addressed to K, is not at all contradictory if one considers that (a) no other
reader may be conceivable, and more particularly, (b) that the function of the
note is precisely to effect a postmortem *conversion* of that persecuting other
into an understanding reader. The suicide dies in order to live in text; but
this sacrificial passion is simultaneously intended as redemptory with respect
to the other. It seeks to "save" the reader in a kind of double enactment of
the profoundest of Romantic myths—the myth that love is stronger than
death—since the renunciation of self on the part of the textual subject implies
and attempts to bring about a renunciation of self on the part of the reader.
Thus Werther can embrace the cup of death as a protest against the circumstances of his death—"Du reichtest mir ihn"—that remains an act of love.

It is this same attempted *shift in the nature of their readership* that can be
seen to motivate the textual "work" in the writing of Nerval and Aquin: in
the technical terms I am using in this book, the attempt is to convert the
narrative addressee into a reader of *text*. Thus "Angélique" designates the
persecutory reader as the paternal figure of law and authority (represented by
the *amendement Riancey*, Angélique's father, the police, etc.) and seeks out
by preference a community of complicitous readers attuned to the community
of voices that speaks dialogically in the text, and hence apt to join that community. "Aurélia" pursues the implications of this operation by attempting to
convert the "bad" reader—here designated as those who interpret the signs
of madness as symptoms of mental aberration—into a figure more like the
friendly and brotherly others (the alter egos, in short) who listen indulgently
to the narrator's long stories, or to whom he in turn reaches out with love.
This attempted conversion of the reader is a conversion to the values of madness, which are simultaneously those of writing as the disappearance of the
individual self into an *agencement collectif*. Or, in Aquin's terms, a conversion
to textual suicide: the suicidal text implies reading as a symmetrical act of
symbolic suicide.

But in Aquin, whereas the "bad" reader is clearly figured as the "other"
who responds to love by an act of betrayal (K, but also the Québec people),
the alternative, understanding reader of the textual discourse is a much vaguer,
more "open" and indeed *shadowy* entity. The only clear figuration of the
"good" reader in *Prochain Épisode*, as we have seen, lies in those moments of
perplexity and hesitation that beset both H. de Heutz and the "hero" when
they are confronted with the puzzle of identity in the form of a "cover" story
that is fictional but might also be real. But in *Trou de mémoire* and *L'Antiphonaire*, the eighteenth-century device of the "MS found in a bottle" is in-

terestingly modernized, and characters take turns at finding texts written by other characters and reading them, sometimes editing them, and more frequently adding further text—another "episode"—to them. One sees that, just as the characters are involved, as lovers and/or alter egos of each other, in each other's lives, so too readership is being figured as a matter of involvement in the (complex and elusive, not to say puzzling) events themselves: it is in fact almost a literalization of the idea of *lecture-écriture.*

As it happens, *L'Antiphonaire* ends with two suicide notes in quick succession (Christine's and Dr. Franconi's), notes that are left, so to speak, to be read by *whoever finds them.*[40] But one is found by a character named Suzanne and the other is actually addressed to Suzanne and presumably intended to be found by her (although, since it furnishes the last words of the text, we cannot know for sure that that happens). Suzanne, however, is a character of whom one has heard for most of the novel, almost anonymously, as being *outside* of its main characters' concerns; and it is only now, in a surprise twist, that we learn of her own deep involvement in them. . . . In these various ways, then, the text is figured as a suicide note, but as complementary in its modes of address to the suicide notes of "everyday life," which tend to be addressed to a specific person but must constitutively be left (or entrusted to the mails, etc.) to be read by whoever finds or receives them. The act of suicide is a *renunciation of control with respect to address.* The literary text, however, in Aquin, is figured, inversely, as a suicide note *without specific addressee,* but whose reader will turn out to be *caught up in its writing,* as an alter ego of its characters (who are, as we know, alter egos of each other). A "No One, in particular," then—*tiers exclu* and *tertius gaudens,* like Suzanne—but caught up in the explosion of self that is discursive suicide; involved in a *lecture-écriture.*

"Ma course involvée," says the narrator/hero of *Prochain Épisode* (59) of the complicated chase through the Swiss landscape that is simultaneously the hero's manhunt (or pursuit of identity) and a metaphor for (or diegetic double of) the narrator's more writerly chase (or flow). The word "involvée" jumps from the page, in the first instance because of the "horrible" pun (the speaker drives a Volvo)—and puns, as we have seen through this study, are a privileged means by which the text enacts the otherness of language, its power to say "other" than what is meant (or to mean "other" than what is said). But simultaneously, the word "involvée" is a *stranger* in the French text, like the place-names of Québec and Switzerland ("involvé" is not cited in standard French dictionaries, nor in the dictionaries of Canadianisms I have consulted). Is it a Latinism, like so many of the learned words (we just met "photogénie des cadratins") that stud Aquin's writing and give it a carefully calculated air of pedantic ungainliness? Or is it rather an Anglicism, reflecting the ease with which the French of Québec incorporates lexical items and semantic features derived from English usage? In either case, the phrase is as important for what it is enacting—the strangeness of language in general and the investment of the narrator's native French by linguistic otherness—as for what it says. It is an emblematic "malheur d'expression."

But, if it is a Latinism, the word refers, of course, to the involuted twisting and turning of the *course*, whether the hero's zigzag itinerary or the "courbes manuscrites" of the narrator's (dis-)course (120). Turned in on itself in this sense, or folded over on itself, the text is "involved" also in the English sense, of complicated, intricate, tangled: it is a puzzle. But both the hero's chase and the narrator's are involved, finally, in that the characters themselves are, in another English sense, deeply "involved" in their twisting and turning: I mean that momentous issues, both political and personal, are at stake in what are for them critical moments of their existence. In a quite similar sense, of course, one might say that the act of suicide and the discursive act of writing a suicide note are deeply "involved" actions. They are *turned in on themselves* (it is oneself one kills; one writes in one's own "clinical submarine"), but also they are of *momentous importance to the subject*. However, "involved" as they are in these ways, they seek also to be *involving*, that is to involve an addressee in their own involvements, for without that involvement of an other they are, themselves, strictly meaningless, and governed by the "je ne sais plus pourquoi" and the "plus rien à gagner" we found under the narrator's pen. Without such readerly involvement, there is no survival of the subject as "phantom" (since he must live in the reader's mind); nor can there be any redemptory conversion of the addressee from mere "narratee" to the status of textual reader (as one who shares, and enacts, the text's own "suicidal" values).

Thus it is, certainly, with respect to readership in the Aquin text. It relies on its own (self-)involvement—its own structure as an unsolvable puzzle—in order to be involving, that is to draw into the volutes of its writing a reader who, as a consequence, will prove to be, like the other characters, an alter ego or a double of those "involved" in the textual action. But unlike them, such a reader would be a sympathetic and understanding, not a hostile and double-crossing, "other," that is, an alter ego of the text(ual subject) in the best possible sense, one who can give its (obumbrated) subject life in his or her own mind, "la vie de [s]a pensée."

Such a reader would not *solve* the textual puzzle, but become *involved* in it, and experience as a subject the perplexity of depersonalization that it expresses, a perplexity modeled, in the text, by the reactions of puzzlement that characters like H. de Heutz and especially the hero display at key moments of confrontation with the otherness of identity. Like "Aurélia," *Prochain Épisode* is relying, then, on the "catchingness" of melancholy: if it *is* catching—that is, if the intuitions of melancholy are not, as Nerval would say, "illusions" but are expressive of a lucidly grasped truth—then it offers an alternative theory and mode of "communication," in which it is not the transmission of a message that constitutes communication, but the mediated *sharing of an identity*. The commmon ground of "fictionality," that is discourse, in which the self-as-other can encounter the other-as-self is what founds such an enterprise. But it does so, obviously, in a deeply hazardous and aleatory way: control is what is sacrificed when the autonomous, or "narrative" subject dies and is superseded by an obumbrated textual phantom. And, precisely, the oppositionality of such a gesture lies in its abandonment of the mechanisms of authority in favor of the contagiousness it seeks to impart to the *agencement* it substitutes for discursive authority, defining reading as a suicidal act that mirrors and reproduces the suicide that is writing, and defining itself, in consequence, as a suicide note that functions as an invitation to suicide.[41]

Such a "MS in a bottle" may obviously, first not find its reader, and second not convert the reader from the otherness of betrayal to an involvement that is a joining with the textual subject as a *suicidé vivant*. That is the risk that has to be taken. The enterprise, in short, is a matter of *confidence*—of a confidence that is exactly homologous with the narrator's blind confidence in the coming of the revolution, of which he knows "not the first thing." At a deep level, the two hopes are the same hope:

J'ai confiance aveuglément, même si je ne connais rien du chapitre suivant, mais rien, *sinon qu'il m'attend et qu'il m'emportera dans un tourbillon*. (Pp. 171–72. My emphasis)

[I am blindly confident, even though I know nothing of the next chapter, nothing whatsoever, *except that it awaits me and will whirl me away*.]

Just as the hero in the castle *awaits his man* ("l'homme que j'attends"), so the narrator is confident, and perhaps equally unwisely, that *another awaits him*: another chapter, *the* next episode. And he expects that the twists and turns of his *involvement*, the puzzle of his suicidal discourse, will permit the other to carry him off in an all-encompassing *tourbillon*, a whirlwind. To await (expect) the other is foolhardy; it leads to defeat, as the hero learns. But one can hope that another waits ("il m'attend"), symmetrically to one's own awaiting of the other, and that, by the involvement that is reading, that other will join in the twists and turns of an involved and involving puzzle that, suiciding "everywhere" and "without respite"—spreading its contagion suicide by suicide—will lead to the revolution. That is the text's hope.

But a suicide note, in this strange sense, is *always* a hopeful document. It is *posited* on there being, beyond the death of the subject, a *prochain épisode* that will be the scene of reading of the posthumous text, the *livre à venir*—a text which, *by virtue of the death of the subject*, will have acquired a certain power that it would not otherwise have had. This is the power to *change* the reader, to convert that reader from oppressive and death-dealing other to an oppositional alter ego of the disappeared self. And it is that posited reading, as an act of conversion—a reading that *Prochain Épisode* so curiously links with the expectation of revolution itself—that makes such a document, whether suicide note or novel, an exemplary model of discursive oppositionality.

Je suis l'autre, I am the other. Only a formulation such as Nerval's, which responds to the new diffuseness of power with a similarly diffuse sense of identity, can give an account of the conversion of the reader anticipated in texts like "Aurélia" or *Prochain Épisode*. For the tautological formula of "autonomous" identity ("I am I, you are you") accounts neither for the ("external") interrelation of subjects in mutual communication nor for the ("internally") split subjectivities which are the two necessary preconditions for the phenomenon of influence understood as an "internal" subjective change wrought through "external" contact with a text; for precisely that formula assumes identities that are both all of a piece and without *means* of contact. An identity constructed through the mediation of alterity is however, on the one hand, subject to mutual interaction with other subjects of the kind posited in Flahaut's concept of "parole intermédiaire," an interaction enacted—as a space for maneuver—by the endless discursive shifts and adjustments I drew attention to in "Aurélia," and on the other a site of endless "internal" splitting, since each of these shifts and readjustments defines and redefines "I" as a difference from the "me" produced in discourse that reflects, not "I," but only the "me" I am for the other. And it is in the light of such a conception of identity as mediated by alterity that it becomes possible to understand reading as the "room for maneuver" in which a double, or rather a joint, mediation of identity is produced. Through the mediation of reading (as its "other"), the *text* is produced as ironic, duplicitous, split—as endlessly other than itself, as the "textual function" is the other of the "narrative function" (and, of course, vice versa). Simultaneously, however, the text so read mediates in turn a change within the *reading instance*, from "narratee" to understanding, interpreting subject (the internal "other" of the narratee-subject, but produced as a "self" corresponding to the external alterity of textual "meaning"). This change could itself not have occurred, however, unless it was always already *potentiated* by a latent split within the reading subject, a split in the absence of which that subject could not have read the text as "meaning" other than it, in its address to the narratee, "says." The reader, in short, must have been capable of producing the text as capable of mediating the "conversion" of the reader. Such a conversion is therefore quite naturally experienced as a *conver-*

sio ad se: what one is converted to is one's "true" self, the self that can be defined only as the other of one's constructed "me."

Reading is thus the form of communication in which an irony—the irony of textual duplicity—works a conversion. It will be recalled, however, that my prefatory formulation spoke rather of an irony that works (as) a *seduction*. In a mediated world, the structure of power—as a shared phenomenon of inter-relation, a matter of more or less, of minorities and majorities but not of absolute "power" versus absolute "powerlessness"—proves to be homologous with the diffuseness of identity, in such a way that the alienation of the subject, as a manifestation of the power of the other, turns out to be able, and available, to function simultaneously as an oppositional principle, that of the always-already-otherness of the subject from the "me" produced, alienatingly, as its identity. But the thematics of love in the texts of Nerval and Aquin—the text as suicide note but the suicide note as loveletter—requires us to turn now to the question of desire and to ask whether the transformation of alienation into the oppositional self-education that is *conversio ad se* does not presuppose an agency that would be identical with the phenomenon of mediation itself. For, as we shall see, it is as an agent of mediation that the figure of the oppositional seducer is best understood, whereas the seductions of power seek rather to suppress the effects of mediation through denial, and to produce communica-tion, instead, as the absolutely alienating act I shall call "dictation."

4 Graffiti on the Prison Wall: Writing Under Dictation

Las palabras no caen en el vacío (Zohar)

[Words do not fall into the void (Zohar)]

—Epigraph of *El siglo de las luces*

Although graffiti occur in many circumstances, they are archetypically the writing of prisoners and lovers—and it is the lover as prisoner I am interested in in this chapter. Having explored with La Fontaine the question of power (and the power to oppose) and examined with Nerval and Aquin the problematics of oppositional identity (in a world in which power itself has become diffuse), it is time to consider—through a reading of three novels of "dictation"—the question of desire, and more particularly the conditions of possibility of oppositional desire when one writes under circumstances of metaphorical imprisonment. The problem I am concerned with arises from the perception that it is through our desires that we are "imprisoned" within a universe of ideological representation, the dominance of which functions as a principal means of social control. What and how we desire—the "desirable" in short—is socially mediated; but desirability simultaneously strengthens the grip of dominant representations of the real by making them the objects of libidinal attraction. The "charismatic" figure of authority that is the modern dictator thus emblematizes—but does not exhaust—this phenomenon of power through the control of desire; and the masculinist ideology within which the dictator's attractiveness as object of desire is constructed (and which it thereby simultaneously strengthens) can alert us to the fact that the ideology of gender exercises a dictation of its own.

If our desires are constructed, however, as instruments of social control, some questions arise that I will explore in what follows. What does it mean—and how is it possible—to "fall out of love" with a figure of power? How can one bear witness to the alienations produced by a system of power—how represent it?—without simultaneously reproducing the desirability on which it flourishes, acknowledging and transmitting its power? Are there forms of desire that arise within ideological systems, like "noise" in systems of information, as by-products of the system that are not, however, fully controlled by it? And if "reality" is a function of the control of desire, can the oppositional emergence of such "parasitic" desires function as a principle of historical change? These are not questions that have simple or easy answers, and they arise in most anguished and dubious form in Miguel Angel Asturias's *El Señor Presidente*,[1] a novel which analyzes the production of social control as a function, precisely, of epistemic darkness, a "murk" that precludes any certainty either about the status of discourse—oppositional or complicitous— or about the nature of the desire for freedom that arises in prison (and so is perhaps only prison's cruellest torment). . . . The complexities of this novel are such that I make no apology for the labyrinthine twists and turns into which it will lead my own reading, and although I frame it between an analysis of the problematics of "witnessing" as a manifestation of opposition in Carpentier's *El siglo de las luces* [*Explosion in a Cathedral*][2] and a reading of Puig's *El beso de la mujer araña* [*Kiss of the Spider Woman*][3] in which the character Molina emerges as a figure for "seduction" as the mode of oppositional appropriation of the structures of desire, and hence of the possibility of change, it is in honor of Asturias's disturbing text that I situate the whole chapter in terms of a thematics of prison and assign to the writing of oppositional desire the problematic status of graffiti on the prison wall.[4]

What, indeed, are we to make of the jumble of graffiti on the walls of a prison cell? What does it mean to read them, as Niña Fedina does in the terrible Casa Nueva?

Cruces, frases santas, nombres de hombres, fechas, números cabalisticos, enlazábanse con sexos de todos tamaños. Y se veían: la palabra Dios junto a un falo, un número 13 sobre un testículo monstruoso . . . y guitarras con alas, y flechas. . . . (P. 113)

[Crosses, holy texts, men's names, dates, cabalistic figures, were jumbled up among sexual organs of all sizes. There was the word God beside a phallus, the number thirteen atop an enormous testicle . . . guitars with wings, arrows. . . . (P. 109).]

What does it mean to write them, as Cara de Angel does in his dungeon-tomb?

Con un pedacito de latón que arrancó a una de las correas de sus zapatos, único utensilio de metal de que disponía, grabó en la pared el nombre de Camila y el suyo entrelazados, y, aprovechando la luz, de veintidós en veintidós horas, añadió un corazón, un puñal, una corona de espinas, un áncora, una cruz, un barquito de vela, una estrella, tres golondrinas como tildes de eñe y un ferrocaril, el humo en espiral. . . . (P. 292)

[With the only metal utensil at his disposal, a little piece of brass torn from one of his shoe-laces, he engraved Camila's name and his own intertwined on the wall, and making use of the light which came every twenty-two hours, he added a heart, a dagger, a crown of thorns, an anchor, a cross, a little sailing-boat, two swallows like the tilde on an ñ, and a little railway-train with a spiral of smoke. . . . (P. 281)]

Should we interpret this prison writing as a sign of hope, some sort of resistance to the tomb-like world of death in which prisoners are incarcerated? In the jumble, it is easy to pick out signs (crosses, hearts, intertwined names, caricatures of magistrates) that are interpretable as oppositional. But others—sexual organs, suns with policeman's moustaches, anchors—are more like evidence of submission, just ways of passing the time. Do boats, trains, sea- and landscapes bespeak a desire to escape (the central oppositional desire of carceral existence)? Or are they simply part of the childish iconography of doodlers? Do the devils and daggers speak of some hankering after revenge, or are they "just" devils and daggers?

It is perhaps the very interpretability of graffiti, combined with the absence of certainty as to their meaning, that gives them their point, the only point they can have in a prison world in which they will be read exclusively by other prisoners and perhaps their guards (who are prisoners themselves). The question I ask of my texts concerns the status and powers of literature in such a society—not so much what literature *is* as what it can do, and what are the conditions of its action. Can writing under dictation ever be anything other than a way of transmitting the fascinating power, the so-called "charisma" of the dictator? Or can it acquire meanings that oppose dictatorial power? I will propose that such texts understand writing under dictation as being, like graffiti, a jumble—an *interpretable* jumble (and because interpretable able in that degree to elude the control of "dictation"), but also a jumble of *interpretability* (and for that reason forced to recognize that it can always be interpreted as a transmission of the dictator's will). In a prison society, where there is no "freedom of speech," it is the incarcerated prisoner who paradoxically becomes free, albeit free only to inscribe graffiti on a cell wall; so the graffiti that are the signs of freedom are simultaneously the signs of an imprisoned consciousness. At the same time as it opposes the violence of dictation, writing necessarily submits to its rule—that, as we know already, is the very condition of oppositionality, a condition that is manifested here in the most extreme terms.

I know of no more striking encapsulation of the problematics of writing under dictation than the opening page of Augusto Roa Bastos's extraordinary novel—if that is what it is—*Yo el Supremo* [*I the Supreme*],[5] a text too complex to be usefully discussed within the confines of this chapter but too important and too relevant to the paradigm of dictation (revolving as it does very largely around the relation of the dictator to his private secretary) not to be mentioned in this context. We are given to read, in rounded cursive handwriting that suggests both (in the context of print) personal penmanship and (in the nineteenth century historical context) bureaucratic officialdom, a document (but is it a pamphlet imitating an official document? or an official decree that reads like a lampoon?) in which El Supremo orders the humiliating disposal of his body after death and the hanging of his henchmen. On the face of it, it is not implausible that, in a mood of guilt, the Supreme should himself have dictatorially decreed the summary disposal of his body and the execution of his officers. After all, the Supreme's death itself is foreseen here as a natural event, not as the result of an uprising or counter-coup; and there have been many cultures in which the servants and/or wives follow their Master into the grave. Besides, under dictatorship—as Gabriel García Márquez's El otoño del patriarca [The Autumn of the Patriarch] makes clear—nothing is ever implausible (and that is certainly one of the implications of what is called "magical realism"). But it is equally probable that the document is the scurrilous oppositional pamphlet the Supreme treats it as—an oppositional document, that is, but one that bears all the trademarks of dictatorial authorship (notably the violence of what it proposes). Who is the author of the pamphlet? This question traverses the book, but it is always something of a rhetorical question, and its point is clear from the start: dictation and opposition are so closely bound up with each other that the distinction between the two can become badly blurred, and indeed disappear altogether. It is as if dictation necessarily engenders opposition, while the oppositional cannot itself escape the dictator's signature. Thus, Roa Bastos's "dictator" is himself an oddly oppositional figure, while the novels I focus on here concern themselves rather with opposition's strange complicity with, or dependency on power.

How these things can be is what we will need to try to understand; but we can arm ourselves at the outset with an anxious discovery the Supreme makes: "Cuando te dicto, las palabras tienen un sentido; otro, cuando las escribes. . . . El Yo sólo se manifiesta a través del Él" (65) ["When I dictate to you, the words have a meaning; when you write them another. . . . The I manifests itself only through the He" (67)]. And a little later: "Escribir es despegar la palabra de uno mismo" (67) ["To write is to disconnect the power of words from oneself" (59)]. This observation is crucial because it situates the potential for opposition in the phenomenon of mediation, that is, in the fact that the dictator must inevitably employ discursive means ("las palabras") that prevent his dictation from being the direct expression of a (first person) identity or will, and introduce instead a distance that makes the (now third-person) identity and will subject to reading or interpretation ("Yo no me hablo a mí. Me escucho a través de Él" (65) ["I do not speak to myself. I listen to myself through Him" (57)]. This distance simultaneously produces in the system of dictation a gap in which the "sentido" can become a "contrasentido," "meaning" a misreading/countermeaning. Thus a measure of play—if not freedom—is inserted in the system, since the addressee of the dictation must necessarily produce its subject, the dictator, not as directly present in his discourse but as an object of interpretation. He thus ceases to be a dictating subject, and becomes a readable object, whose power to "dictate" is in that degree diminished. I will try to show precisely that oppositionality is dependent on the phenomenon of mediation and caught up in its problematics (which is the problematics of interpretability); for mediation is both that which obliges dictation to engender opposition, and that which links opposition inescapably to dictation.

But let us note for now that, in discursive terms, it is opposition's kinship with mediation that distinguishes it from what I have called "resistance." Where the former opposes the dictator's would-be direct first person expression by some degree of consciousness of mediation, the latter is an attempt to replace the dictator's first person by a (would-be direct) first person expression of its own, that is one form of discursive violence by another, but similar, discursive violence. Viewers of the film of *El beso de la mujer araña* will recall the moment when the wily Molina, having succeeded (by oppositional means) in turning the tables on the Director of the prison, proceeds to *dictate to the "dictator"* his shopping list of nutritious groceries for Valentín (cf. in the novel pp. 153–54 [156–57]). The delight of the audience at this ironic reversal of power relations, its savoring of Molina's victory, is palpable; and the moment is indeed a liberating one. But it is liberating, I think, only because it *is* momentary. A reversal of power relations of this (dictatorial) kind would, if it were permanent, only be a perpetuation of the relation of dictation: the alienating relation would remain, and only the individuals occupying its subject positions would change. The audience's pleasure demonstrates the degree to which our desires are mediated by—that is constructed in conformity with—a system that identifies freedom and identity with dominance and control, that is, the power to dictate. But the novel is itself not much concerned with the Pyrrhic victories that result from reversal within the power relation of dictation. It is rather an exploration of the never fully victorious and always already half-defeated circumstances that attend the practice of opposition—a practice fully bound up with the nondictatorial relation of love that arises through the mediation of Molina's storytelling between the two powerless and, at the end, still hapless (but strengthened and dignified) prisoners.

For *El beso* is a love story; so too are *El siglo de las luces* and *El Señor Presidente*. All three novels have recourse to a pathos that derives from one of the oldest of Western *topoi*: the balancing of love, as a manifestation of oppositionality, against death—the death brought by dictation. But where Puig's novel is concerned with the growth of a mediated love between prisoners, the two earlier novels work with a contrast between two kinds of love, the "love" of the acolyte for the dictator who fascinates (Esteban's fondness for Victor Hugues, Cara de Angel's submission to the President and his whims), and a love that is identified with the discovery of "humanity," in oneself and in the object of love. This is Esteban's self-sacrificing love for "the secret reserves of potent humanity" (286) [279] that he discovers in the symbolically named Sofía; and it is Miguel Cara de Angel's love for Camila—a love that has its origin in the henchman's presidentially inspired plan to kidnap and rape the girl but which finally lands him in prison, as a figure of oppositionality more dangerous to the President, it seems, than the revolutionary General Canales himself. That both Esteban and Cara de Angel are figures for the writer under dictation—the one by his employment as translator and clerk in the offices of Hugues, the other by virtue of the striking similarity of his name (Miguel) and nickname (Cara de Angel) with the name of the author (Miguel Angel Asturias) on the volume's cover—needs no demonstration. It is rather the linkage of writing to the phenomenon of love—a homosocial[6] albeit seemingly nonsexual love of the acolyte for the dictator, and the heterosexual and sexual love of a man for a woman (and more ambiguously of the woman for the man)—that calls for some reflection and commentary.

A point of departure is furnished by Freud's 1921 study of what in English is called group psychology but goes by the more suggestive names in German and French of "Massenpsychologie" and "psychologie des foules."[7] Freud focuses on the role of the leader in the formation of "groups," positing that the power of what I have called "charismatic" leadership lies in a certain ability, related to that of the hypnotist, to "divert" the conscious mind so that, as in dreams, the unconscious is freed of the ego's control. The fascination of each member of the crowd for the leader is then none other than a form of narcissistic love, an introjection of the object (the leader figure) as a substitute for the "ego ideal," elsewhere called the superego. The unanimity of the crowd, the fraternity that binds it into one unit and makes it into a collectivity, derives from its collective narcissistic focus on the leader onto whom each individual projects a self-image. It follows that the leader's control of the crowd, or charisma, results from a protean ability to serve as an object of projection to each member of the group—to be, so to speak, "all things to all men," or as it is said of Robespierre in El siglo de las luces, "algo así como un Don Juan para machos" (107) ["a sort of Don Juan for men" (105)]—let us just note for the moment the masculinist overtones. Like the archetypal seducer, the leader who caters to so many individuals' sense of selfhood must be himself identity-less, if by identity one understands a self-identity that is independent of the mediation out of which desiring relationships are produced. Freud says that the leader must be loved by all without loving in return; I would say that he must be capable of *becoming* Someone by *being* "nobody," for the leader is fantasized as the center and foundation of all identity—the very epitome of self-identity—to the precise extent that he (more rarely she) succeeds in allowing that identity to be constructed by the desires of others. Paradoxically, then, the subject of dictation is nothing if not a product of mediation.

This is a suggestive analysis. Some difficulty arises, however, from the contrast between narcissistic love and nonnarcissistic ("altruistic") love, since for Freud there is a strong component of narcissism in all love. We tend to choose as partners substitutes for the very parent who, through identification, furnished our narcissistic sense of self-identity. For this reason, and particularly in view of the equivalence the novels construct between love and writing under dictation, the Lacanian categories of the Imaginary and the Symbolic are more cogent. The Imaginary corresponds to the illusory sense of self-identity formed at the mirror-stage and to which we cling all our lives; the Symbolic to the constitution of the *subject* (as "split") at the moment of entry into discourse. As a construct of the Symbolic, and consequently a product of alterity, such a subject can have no self-identity that is not an illusion of the Imaginary; inhabited by the Other—that discourse that simultaneously constructs the ego and constitutes the unconscious—the split subject of the Symbolic can have no unity, nor can it have autonomy.[8]

If Freudian narcissism can be identified with the illusory identity of the Imaginary, we can say quite economically that the subject in the Symbolic is a product of mediation and that, as a consequence, what it is subject(ed) to is a regime not of dictation but of *interpretability*. Such a subject cannot know itself or control its meanings because, being discursively constructed, it is constituted as split: its "I" manifests itself only as a "He," as El Supremo says, or, in the language I used in chapter 3, it can only say "I am the other." Since in addition all subjects are so constituted, no subject is knowable either to itself or to others; and the subject who becomes an object of love, for example, is of necessity a manifestation of otherness, a metonym, as Lacan proposes, of that Other that is the whole, ungraspable and unattainable system of discourse, discursivity itself. The relation of two such subjects is of necessity a relation of mutual interpretability: *not* the transparent presence, one to the other, of identities that can be known to themselves and others, but an uncertain relation in which subjectivity appears as the product of a discursivity that constitutes it and depends, therefore, on the particular discursive framework in which one subject may opt to "read" another.

The category of the Symbolic permits us to understand what "altruistic" love, as a manifestation of mediation, has in common with writing, when writing is conceived, not as the direct transmission of a message (its Imaginary function as writing under dictation) but a phenomenon "subject" to reading and interpretation (its Symbolic function). To the interpretability of discourse corresponds the unknowable alterity of the beloved other, a status referred to in the texts as the beloved's "humanity" and consistently figured by a thematics of unavailability (that of Sofía to Esteban, of Camila to Cara de Angel, and when at last we move out of the masculinist identification of the desiring subject as male and the desired object as female, the mutual difference of Molina to Valentín and Valentín to Molina). But the novels add an insight of the greatest importance: "altruistic" love is mediated desire, but the sign of its mediated character (that is, the unavailability of the other) is in each case a manifestation of the power of dictation. It is Hugues, not Esteban, whom Sofía desires; and although Esteban and Sofía are officially cousins they are like brother and sister, so that their relation has overtones of incest and is governed by the Law of the Father. Cara de Angel's love for Camila is mediated by the figure of her father, General Canales, and even more so by that of the President, who initially "inspires" it and in due course becomes its public "sponsor," before forcing Cara de Angel into exile and eventually prison and death, so that the lovers are eternally separated. The homosexual love of Valentín and Molina has the status within the culture of *machismo* of an infringement, of that which escapes control; but the two are both brought together and separated by relations of difference that are constructed by a society that imprisons them. It is the gender roles of masculine virility and feminine silliness and the ideological divisions between the political prisoner and the civil offender, brought together in the same cell as a ruse of the controlling power, that constitute their prison even as they overcome them by incorporating them in their love.

It becomes evident, then, that if desire is a phenomenon of mediation (and so, oppositional with respect to the regime of dictation), what mediates desire in such a regime is the culture of dictation itself. The figures constructed as the objects of desire are figures that manifest the liberating power of the symbolic only as a simultaneous manifestation of the Father's powerful Law, the law of dictation. On the one hand, "altruistic" love as a phenomenon of mediation represents—in a prison society under the control of dictation and "narcissistic" love—a dangerous form of opposition: Asturias's President recognizes it as such and ruthlessly suppresses it. But on the other, in such a society, where there is no other framework available for the construction of desire than that of dictation, the oppositional itself necessarily comes under the control of that law. (Our desires are mediated; but what we desire is power, self-identity, mutual transparency, knowable essences and firm categories that "hold still" and do not deconstruct; our desire is mediated as a desire for the unmediated. The lesson is valid for societies other than those of Latin America.) Mutatis mutandis, writing is open to the same analysis. The graffiti on the prison wall are oppositional, not only because some of them (hearts transfixed by arrows, intertwined names) are signs of love, but more generally because they are all *signs* (provided only that one understand the sign as a mediation and as necessarily subject to interpretation). As such, the signs of graffiti stand for the always potential oppositionality of writing. But the readability of such signs makes them always open to interpretation, also, as signs of the power of the prison; and all the more so when the signs are unlikely to be read by any except prisoners, whose whole universe is constituted by the prison. The reading of the signs, like the love between the prisoners, is always mediated, in other words, by that which the signs oppose; and signs *in* prison are always susceptible of being read as signs *of* prison.

So oppositional novels such as the three I want now to turn to can only be oppositional, by their own estimation, on the condition of courting the dangers that accompany their oppositional status as readable (not dictated) messages— and the dangers are those of encountering a reading mediated by the kind of desires that arise within a framework of dictation: the desire for the dictator, for instance, or some equivalent thereof (such as the search for a "clear message"). Such a reading would indeed separate the reading from the writing, as Esteban and Sofía, Camila and Cara de Angel, and in the end Valentín and Molina are separated, by the very mediation that produces their relation as a relation of love. Such, it seems, is the problem of "humanity," the problem of being human—and it is easy to calculate therefore that the risk such texts run is great. Mediation makes oppositionality possible, but mediation implies (mis)reading, and the misreading of mediation is called dictation. (The readings that follow do not, of course, escape that problematic set of conditions.)

On a memorable occasion, Roland Barthes referred to language as fascistic,[9] and Lacan consistently identifies the Symbolic with the Law of the Father. We can see, from the vantage point of the problematics of opposition under dictation, why that might be the case. The question, however, is whether it is *necessarily* the case, or whether it is only locally (historically and/or culturally) so. Can there be a culture of mediation that would be free of dictation and the desire for dictation? A culture whose desire would take the form of respect for the other, acknowledgment of the other's otherness, as opposed to the cult of the selfsame? I want to leave the question open, for it may be that, unthinkable as such a concept might be to us now, it is our most urgent need to think it. The *desire* for it is certainly making itself increasingly felt—a desire that must be being somehow mediated; and the first step ought perhaps to be, therefore, to cultivate that desire. That is what this chapter, and indeed this book, attempt to do.

1. Falling Out of Love

Traditions of authoritarianism and violence are so deeply rooted in most parts of Latin America that they seem originless. Carpentier's brilliance is to have seen that, because it was a crisis of legitimacy, the French Revolution offers an ideal case study in which to observe the conditions of emergence of political violence in its modern form, that of the charismatic (or would-be charismatic) dictatorship founded on terror—the reign of death. His novel accordingly opens, famously, with a description of the bringing of the guillotine to the "New World," its frame set in the ship's bows like a gateway to the beyond. Columbus brought the cross, and with it terror and servitude (128) [125]; the Revolution opens a new era in which it is Liberty (the decree abolishing slavery) that arrives on the same ship as Death.

Unlike ancien régime monarchies and ancient tyrannies, the new dictatorships are paradoxical phenomena, in that the imposition of terror and the establishment of a régime of dictation have their raison d'être in the new ideas, the "enlightened" and supposedly emancipatory values of freedom, justice, and fraternity, the abolition of social hierarchies and privileged authority; ideas to which they may be genuinely committed or to which they may only pay the merest lip service, but which in either case make of them startlingly contradictory social formations. Such contradictions, taken as the very sign of modernity, are the stuff of Carpentier's novel: and they obviously pose the question of their alternative—how can society be changed *without* recourse to the guillotine, to violence, to "dictation?"

If, as proposed in chapter 3, the Revolution quickly found itself faced with a problematics of representation, it is the emergence of a politics of Terror that Carpentier therefore invites us to consider. With the execution of the King and the disappearance of monarchical authority as the "natural" (read: unquestioned) guarantor of legitimacy, the Revolution was plunged into a confusion of competing forces, each of which claimed the legitimacy of "representing" the People, itself an unknowable concept. The Terror is interpretable as a reaction to those early years of confusion and an attempt to restore something equivalent to the absolute power that had been destroyed, a power that would be "above" the arena of political conflict and untouched by it. My guide is again Marie-Hélène Huet, who shows that in its management of festivities as well as of executions the Terror sought to produce an effect of pure *sublimity*, deliberately avoiding the "theatricality" that had attended such events in the earlier stages of the Revolution.

Thus the Festival of the Supreme Being was conceived in terms of "mâle sublimité," that is as a deliberately purified ceremonial that would blot out the memory of the feminized Festivals of Reason, with the erotic appeal of their allegorized representations embodied in actresses and attractive young women. Meanwhile, the guillotine suddenly and quietly disappeared from center stage, at the heart of Paris, and was removed towards the periphery, where its operations were pursued less spectacularly. The attempt was to remove Power to a position of absence—the absent "presence" of God or an absolute mon-arch—with respect to mundane affairs, and thus to produce for it a position of permanence that would contrast tellingly with the procession of ideologies that had marked the history of the Revolution since 1789.

The desire to attain the sublime and the concern with putting a stop to the chain of spectacles that parodied death or the sacred, would have made it possible, also, it seems, to arrest the palimpsestic effect of revolutionary ideology which endlessly blotted out its own representations by means of new images, new laws, new cults.[10]

Unfortunately, absolute authority is like innocence: if there is ever such a thing, once it is lost it cannot be regained; and restorations not only necessar-ily stand in contrast with the upheavals that preceded them, a semiotic relation that alters the meaning of their absolutism, but they are also always tinged with mimicry, that is, they stand as the relation of a copy to a model. Revo-lutionary Terror is not an escape from the Revolution's ideological palimpsest, but part of it, one more addition to the ideological layers, one more item in the political parade. Recourse to sublimity is not an escape from representation and rhetoric but itself a rhetorical device, another form of representation. The years of the "teflon presidency" in the United States or the De Gaulle years in France gave the world an intimation of the contradictions that are entailed when a politician adopts a stance of being "above politics" (and they can serve as a reminder, if one is necessary, that the forms of authoritarianism current in the Terror and known to Latin America are not irrelevant to Western democracies).

The effect of sublimity sought by the concentration of power in one indi-vidual thus inevitably leads, on the one hand, to the falsifications, illusory gestures, and "poudre aux yeux" of the conjurer (or of Freud's hypnotist), and on the other, and in due course, to an awareness on the part of the public of the gap between the god-like status claimed for the individual in power and the political shifts and rhetorical devices by which that power is maintained. There is no escape from mediation because there is no communication that is not mediated; and the denial of mediation is itself a mediated communication, not "sublimity" but a representation of the sublime. That is why such power inevitably becomes embroiled in the problematics of discursivity—that is, of "dictation"; and that too is why it is equally inevitably led to enforce its in-adequate representations by a régime of repression, terror, and death. (It does not belittle the suffering of so many people under imprisonment, torture, and summary execution to point out that these means are "rhetorical"; rather it makes the fear and suffering all the more painful and absurd.)

But the contradiction already noted as characteristic of modern dictatorships (between "enlightened" social ideals and the violence by which the régime maintains itself in power) is therefore subtended and engendered by a second contradiction between the desire for absolute authority and the necessity—from which neither divine-right kings nor the divinity were ever themselves exempt—of *producing authority* by the deployment of certain "means": the means of rhetoric, theatricality, and illusion, in conjunction with those of violence and terror. This underlying contradiction is between the illusion of the *direct* (unmediated) exercise of power and the inevitable acknowledgement that there is no power without authority and no authority that is not an authorization and so obtained through mediations, dependent as it is on the concurrence and perhaps the complicity of others. Because the allegedly "direct" power of "dictation" cannot function except as a mediated representation of power, the facts of mediation become the deepest secret and most buried scandal of authoritarian régimes, so that "dictation" can be defined most precisely as the (mediated) attempt to suppress the consciousness of the mediations on which power rests.

In the novelistic literature, this contradiction is often analyzed in terms of the contrast between a dictator's vulgar humanity and low-class origins and his (always his) grandiloquent posturings and god-like "presence" as an elusive absence at the heart of things. It is figured in *El siglo de las luces*, for instance, by the contrast in Victor Hugues's two names, the Latinate first name with its connotations of supremacy, and the common last name, which Sofía makes fun of early in the novel: "she took a malicious delight in distorting it a little more each time" (36) [35]. Hugues is an ex-baker turned slightly shady businessman, who becomes the (mini-)Robespierre of the (micro-)cosmic Caribbean. His carefully cultivated solitude, more a matter of aloofness than of loneliness, and his cruel implacability—that is, his "inhumanity"—conflict with everything that shows him to be "human": his womanizing, his mercantile instincts, and especially his intermittent need for the companionship of Esteban. For it is, of course, the stress in dictator-novels on the figure of the acolyte that most prominently thematizes the inability of the dictator to *be* sublime and his dependency, for the representation of sublimity, on *agency*. But, since these figures tend always to be writer figures, the theme also signals literature's fear that it might itself be cast precisely, and however involuntarily, in the role of agent of dictation.

The theme goes back, in modern literature, at least to Musset's *Lorenzaccio* (1834). But Cara de Angel, the President's henchman, and Esteban, clerk to the Revolution and only confidant of Victor Hugues, do not only signify the dictator's "human" side and his inability to practice dictation without there being a means of dictating. They are also the dictation's first addressees, and the victims of its violence. In dictator-novels, clerks and secretaries are always being viciously maltreated; and the sadomasochism of the relation between

Asturias's President and Cara de Angel—mirrored in the case of the secretary who makes a blot[11] and is flogged to death—is paradigmatic, not only for the relation of, say, the Supreme and the Secretary in *Yo el supremo*, but also for the less luridly delineated relation of Esteban to Hugues, who on occasion enjoys playing cat and mouse with the life and liberty of his young friend. Literature is thus figured, in these characters, as being simultaneously the agency on which dictation necessarily relies, and as dictation's exemplary victim, the butt of its violence; and it is in its status as victim, in the distancing from the subject of dictation that is implied by its role as object of violence, that the potential lies for a *falling out*, for the disaffection to arise that marks a transition from freely accorded to enforced agency, and the emergence of oppositionality. Mediation in short is both the indispensable agency and the Achilles's heel of dictatorial power; and it is that realization that underlies and gives point to the narratives in which both Asturias and Carpentier portray the dictator's acolyte falling out of love with the dictator.

But when one falls "out" of love, one always falls out of love "with" the object of that love: the process of disaffection and distancing never attains complete emancipation from the other's sway. To be "out" of love is not the same as having never been "in" love. This difficulty, indeed impossibility, of attaining complete and genuine detachment finds expression, as far as literature goes, in the theme of surviving to tell the story. The oppositional function of literature and the sign of its disaffected, distanced status from the power of dictation lies in its potential as "witness"—a role that would ideally produce the text as neither acolyte to nor victim of the dictator's power, but as a *detached* observer of its conditions and functioning, as if there could be an "outside" of power. The historicization in *El siglo*, the epilogue in *El Señor Presidente* (discussed below), are distancing devices that function in this direction. But one who has survived a terror, like one who has fallen out of love, cannot be an "independent" or "dispassionate" witness: the story so told is necessarily tinged with involvement. Indeed, in extreme regimes, the fact of having survived—the necessary condition of being able to tell the tale—is itself suspect, readable as it is as a sign of oppositional collaboration, as opposed to both victimage and resistance. As a result, any tale of (would-be detached) witness—for example Esteban's "Vengo de vivir entre los bárbaros" (254) ["I have been living among the barbarians" (248)] as Sofía opens the door of the old house back in Havana to him—must always communicate simultaneously something of the fascination with "dictation" that it seeks to denounce or deny. This is suggested precisely by the excess and emotion in Esteban's exclamation here, the theatricality of its rhetoric. There is no "outside" of power.

Such discursive *uncontrollability* is the inescapable condition of mediated communication: just as it is impossible for the dictator to dictate without employing means that have the potential to produce disaffection, so, quite symmetrically, it is impossible for the survivor to relate without, at the same time, running a risk of communicating fascination for the dictator, of relating *that* relation. In short, there is always something "telltale" in the telling of a tale. We can say that, where Cara de Angel's defeat and death in prison figures literature as the object and victim of dictatorial power, Esteban's survival and witnessing—for he never in fact becomes the dictator's victim and escapes the prison of Guadeloupe under the latter's protection (the very oppositional act in which Cara de Angel fails)—stand for its ability to function as observer and analyst of the conditions of dictatorship. But not only will I need to modify both of these characterizations in due course as a result of closer analysis, but also, taken together, they can be seen already to define dictatorship as that which takes its own means as its object (its agent as its victim) but conversely, its own object as its means (its victim as its agent). By extrapolation, this means that the whole society that undergoes the terror of dictatorship is *also* its instrument. But it also signifies that mediation, as the agency of dictation, is that which it most violently suppresses; while, as that which betrays dictation, it most manifestly bears dictation's mark and transmits its power. Without escaping these ironic conditions, only *El beso de la mujer araña*, in proposing a form of oppositionality that does not rely on witnessing or "telling the tale," will show how such conditions nevertheless allow room for *something*, within the system, to change.

But in general terms, then, the oppositionality of the characters, and the oppositionality of literature that they figure, derive from the simultaneity and mutual entailment of the two roles: betrayal of dictation, and transmission— that is mediation—of its power. The oppositional signals deep alienation from power and its depredations, combined with a continued availability to serve as its agent, and in that sense continued allegiance, however involuntary, to it. It is the process of falling out of love, with its attendant failure to achieve detachment, that most aptly figures, therefore, the emergence of oppositionality. But in *El siglo de las luces*, this process occurs twice: where the bulk of the narrative relates Esteban's gradual falling out of love with Victor Hugues, a significant section is devoted to the repetition of the same process in the case of Sofía, who thus commits the same error, with the same consequences, as her cousin. One must ask therefore why this repetition is structurally necessary. I will try to show that it is essentially bound up with the novel's exploration of the problematics of mediation, and hence of oppositionality.

But in order to fall *out* of love, one must first fall *in* love; and the novel accordingly presents also a compelling portrayal of the charismatic figure of Victor Hugues,the object of both Esteban's and Sofía's desire and fascination. Announced by a dreadful Beethovenian knocking, he appears in the house of

Sofía, Carlos, and Esteban at the very moment of their father's death, quickly becoming a substitute "paterfamilias" (35) [35]—albeit a comradely, egalitarian one—and gradually bringing some order to the self-indulgent chaos in which the orphans live, seeing in particular to the cure of Esteban's asthma and attempting to dislodge the profiteering business agent. That all this constitutes a politico-historical allegory of the coming of the Revolution to late ancien régime society needs no demonstration.

But whence comes Hugues's prestige in the eyes of the children? From his tale telling, his histrionic ability—he is already rehearsing the revolutionaries' ability to play Roman roles—his initiation into Masonic secrets, which gives him an aura of mystery, remoteness, and unknowability. In short, it comes from a mastery of means that is already a means of mastery, the combination of "sublimity" and removal from the mundane with the deployment of discursive and mediating skills that will account later for his ascendancy as the future "Robespierre of the Caribbean." The key moment is therefore the one in which, dismissing the abusive business partner (a figure for the Revolution's attempt to sweep away social abuses), Hugues deploys the full range of effects of rhetoric, "liberando una garganta de cuerdas tensas, toda entregada al esfuerzo final de una estentória peroración" (63–64) ["exposing a throat taut in every fibre with the final efforts of his stentorian peroration" (63)], and thereby inspiring in Sofía the first stirrings of desire. The gaping waistcoat "liberating" the taut throat conveys with wonderful economy the combination of the erotic and the rhetorical in the politics of revolutionary "dictation." "For the first time Sofía found him handsome as he stood there like a tribune, his fist falling on the table to mark the culmination of a period" (64) [63].

Esteban's desire for Hugues will be no less troubling but it is more intellectually mediated (there is to be no hint of homosexuality but many suggestions of the Revolution as a moment of intense homosociality). He is stirred by the idea of Revolution as Apocalypse, "un Apocalipsis que estaba anhelante de presenciar cuanto antes, para iniciar su vida de hombre en un mondo nuevo" (71) ["an Apocalyse that he longed to witness as soon as possible, so that he might start his life as a man in a new world" (70)]. There is evident irony here, not only in the hint that Esteban's revolutionary fervor is grounded in adolescent and masculinist desire for a *firm* identity—the identity of the "Imaginary"—but also in the coincidence of the emergence of this fervor with the first clear manifestation of ideological discord between the two revolutionary initiates, Victor and Ogé, the white rationalist and the black mystic. For the moment foreshadows the ideological confrontations, confusions and contradictions which will be at the origin of Esteban's eventual disaffection, contradictions, confusions, and confrontations of which the novel treats the Revolution's (Victor Hugues's) attitude to slaves and slavery (Ogé) as the most significant and the most telling. . . . This, then, is the second key moment, in which, repeating Sofía's experience (as she will later repeat his), Esteban's desire is aroused in the very moment that predicts the inevitability of his falling out of love. What predominates for now, however, is the young man's narcissistic identity-formation through identification with Hugues. "Esteban . . . se sentía más sólido, más hecho, más levantado en estatura masculina, junto a Víctor Hugues" (90) ["Esteban . . . felt more solid, more mature, more of a man, when he was with Victor Hugues" (89)].

What is ideologically at stake, then, as the novel develops, is the conflict between the "virility" of a certain phallogocentric conception of power (the sublimity of an absolute) and the inevitable "fall" into mediation, represented by the Revolution's palimpsest of policy swings, from representative government to autocracy and the cult of personality, and from there to directories and consulates; from festivals of reason and the cult of the Great Architect to festivals of the Supreme Being, with returns both to the previously vilified Freemasonry and finally—at the Concordat—to Catholicism itself; from the Jacobin emancipation of slaves to the Consulate's restoration of the institution of slavery. Such swings are evidence that power cannot be divorced from questions of policy, that is, from the tractations and negotiations that characterize a political world of representation, where no one has access to unmediated truth. And that is why each swing is enforced with unmitigated ferocity and bloodshed, the secret of Victor Hugues's rise to power being precisely the imperturbability with which he accepts and the implacability with which he administers the political doctrine of the moment. To Esteban, however, these large deviations in policy—enforced as they necessarily are in such a way as to produce the largest contradiction of them all, that between Liberty and the Guillotine—bring increasing intellectual and emotional confusion, and in due course alienation and disaffection. The Revolution which, in the person of Hugues, had seemed to promise identity and the possibility of becoming a "man" in a "new world," has become for him only a dangerous maze of political zigzags through which he must pick his way with utmost care if he is to survive even physically.

His distancing from Victor Hugues consequently goes hand in hand with increasing oppositionality with respect to the Revolution which he nevertheless continues to serve and the revolutionary society of which he is willy-nilly a member. The two men are perhaps never closer than in the early days of their stay in Paris, when the Revolution has an appearance of carnival and homosociality can be enjoyed in evenings of drinking and whoring, and (for Esteban, at least) of indulgence in the excesses of revolutionary rhetoric. But already Hugues's involvement in power separates him from Esteban, who is so uninformed that he undergoes Masonic initiation at the very moment when the Jacobin reaction against Freemasonry sets in. Sent as a translator and propagandist to Bayonne, where the peasantry remain recalcitrant to the Revolution, Esteban shows his own first oppositional traits, clinging (internally) to the old calendar, and disturbed by the Jacobin intransigence that refuses to modify its stances (to mediate its revolutionary message) for Spanish sensibilities. When the opportunity arises to accompany Hugues to Guadeloupe, it looks to Esteban like escape—the possibility of evading the alienations of the Revolution and returning home, without breaking either with revolutionary ideals or revolutionary power. Such an escape would obviously be the ideal oppositional response, and a solution to the young man's conflicting emotions and loyalties.

What he does not know is that Hugues has already been the scourge of Rochefort, and that he will be escaping the prison of France only to find himself in a smaller, closer, and vastly more dangerous one on the island of Guadeloupe, where the war with the British (and counterrevolutionary French whites) is waged with maximum brutality, and where the guillotine functions both to impose the reign of "liberty" and to ensure Hugues's personal domination. Already on the ship, discovering Hugues's new aloofness and faced with the horrible surprise that it is transporting the guillotine, Esteban has begun to feel a new desire that would compensate for the disappointment of the desire that led him to follow Hugues. He again wants to "do something that would give meaning to his life" (130) [127]; but he now thinks that this might take the form of writing—of writing something oppositional, "something perhaps which would greatly displease Victor Hugues." It might be a work of social theory or perhaps "a study of the errors of the Revolution."

Such a work, the idea of which Esteban immediately abandons, because it sounds too much like something a hated émigré might write, is obviously comparable to *El siglo de las luces* itself ("Algo importante . . . ; algo necesitado por la época" (130) ["Something important . . . ; something which the age needed" (127)]; so that the novel designates itself in this way as having overcome the fear of comforting the reaction that inhibits Esteban. But by Thermidor, when Hugues confidently decides to ignore Paris and to continue playing Robespierre in Pointe-à-Pitre, Esteban is totally confused, having not ceased to believe in, and to hope for Liberty, Equality, and Fraternity, but noting guiltily his feeling of relief (159) at the idea of the possible restoration of a monarchy he continues to execrate.

His world is now absurd, his sense of unreality the measure of his alienation. The Revolution proclaims the Rights of Man only to violate them incessantly; it takes the Bastille only to found Cayenne, "which is far worse" (114) [111]. "Todo, aquí, se está volviendo un contrasentido" (113) ["Everything here is coming to mean its own opposite" (111)—but "contrasentido,"

implying misreading or an error in translation, insists on the failure of meaning as an effect of mediation]. Indeed, Esteban is himself a living "contrasentido" as he continues to work for a Revolution he no longer believes in while
nevertheless subscribing to its official principles and yet feeling that he is not
by current definitions a "good citizen" ("lo que hoy se entiende por un buen
ciudadano" (242) [236]). So he participates in Hugues's money-making priva-
teering "war" as clerk and accountant in exchange for the opportunity to escape from Guadeloupe; and when at last he is able to make good a final escape,
travelling to Surinam and from there back to Havana, it is still in an official
role as an agent of the Revolution, charged with fomenting slave uprisings and
spreading the Revolution according to Jacobin principles. He plans, of course,
to dump his pamphlets into the nearest river—until he witnesses slaves
undergoing cruel punishment, whereupon he reverses himself and makes a
last minute attempt, as his ship starts downstream, to distribute his copies
of the Decree of Pluviose of Year Two. The irony is, of course, that this decree
is itself soon to be revoked, a turn of policy which Hugues (whose pride it
was to have brought the original decree of freedom to the New World) will
enforce in Cayenne, this time to Sofía's disgust, with the utmost rigor and
implacability.

For, if Esteban has now fallen out of love (which does not mean that his
fascination with the figure of Hugues has ceased), it remains, as I have mentioned, for Sofía to repeat his experience. The repetition functions to confirm
a thematic equivalence in the novel between political allegiance to the dictator
and an erotic relation to the charismatic figure he presents; but it is necessary
also in terms of the novel's figuration of itself as an oppositional discursive act,
and hence as mediated discourse—a discourse that is not in a position to "dictate" its meanings. On his return to Havana, Esteban, without having lost his
faith in the ideals of the Revolution, must needs tell his own story, which is
that of a stay among barbarians and a descent into hell. "Y concluía el narra-
dor, amargo . . . : 'Esta vez la revolución ha fracasado. Acaso la próxima sea
la buena'" (267) ["And the narrator concluded bitterly . . . : 'This time the
Revolution has failed. Perhaps the next will be the real one'" (261)]. But his
negative account of the Revolution ("fracasado" implies disintegration as well
as failure) cannot displace in the minds of his hearers (those he calls the Jacobin
Club of Havana) the influence of those other writings of his, his writings
"under dictation": "his own translations, made at Victor Hugues's direction in
Pointe-à-Pitre and set by the Loeuillets" (269) [263]. Poor Esteban is forced to
acknowledge the provenance of this influence by the most particular evidence,
the specific signs of any careful writer's craft: "por la personalidad de ciertos
giros, el acierto de ciertas transposiciones, la presencia de un adjetivo cuya
equivalencia castellana le había costado trabajo hallar" (269) ["from the idio-

syncracy of certain turns of phrase, the dexterity of certain transpositions, the presence of an adjective whose Castilian equivalent had cost him a lot of trouble" (163)]. Small wonder he lets out an angry oath: *Vous m'emmerdez!*

The irony of this moment, so intense for Esteban, applies equally to the text of *El siglo de las luces*, which as a study of "los errores de la revolución" displaying great stylistic precision is simultaneously a narration of Esteban's stay among the barbarians and descent into hell, and which, like Esteban, never ceases to present the *idea* of the Revolution as emancipatory (cf. the thematic insistence on the freeing of the slaves) and life giving (cf. the symbolic significance of episodes like the cure of Esteban's asthma). The novel must simultaneously, therefore, share with Esteban's story the responsibility for transmitting (mediating) the power of Hugues's "dictation" and the fascination he exerts, even as it analyzes the means by which this effect is produced. For, in his conversations with Sofía about Hugues, Esteban stresses the mimicry and theatricality of Hugues's career as a worshipper and imitator of Robespierre, and so the humanity of this would-be god-like figure, and his dependency on *means* to produce the effect of absolute power. "Aspiraba a héroe de tragedia y se quedó en comparsa. Además, sus escenarios eran malos. Rochefort, la Guadalupe . . . Escaleras de servicio!" (273) ["He aspired to being a tragic hero, and he never got beyond a minor part. Moreover he played in the wrong theatres. Rochefort, Guadeloupe. . . . The back stairs!" (267)]. (We can note parenthetically that this analysis redounds equally on Robespierre himself; the "tragedian" Hugues aspires to be is himself a theatrical figure.) But the effect on Sofía, as we will soon learn, turns out to be the opposite of the one intended. Esteban's portrayal of Hugues has not communicated his disillusionment with the "monster" but fed her love.

Admitía hipocríticamente que era un monstruo, un ser abominable, una bestia política, para saber más y más, a retazos, a tirones, a trancos, acerca de los gestos, apetencias y acciones del Investido de Poderes caído y rehabilitado. Y tenazmente había seguido trabajando la voluntad reprimida, silenciada, hasta desatarse en apetencias que ni siquiera hubiesen sido refrenadas por la presencia de un moribundo. (Pp. 294–95)

[She had agreed hypocritically that he was a monster, an abominable person, brutalized by politics, so that, bit by bit, with little quick tugs, she could extract more and more about the gestures, desires, and actions of this disgraced and reinstated Plenipotentiary. And this silent, repressed longing had continued to work industriously away, until it broke out into a hunger which not even the presence of a dying man had been able to restrain. (P. 287)]

Here the novel acknowledges the possibility, or the probability, that something equally "hypocritical" and "tenacious" may "work away" in its own readership, since the love of power and the desire for identity—Sofía "iba hacia quién le había dado una conciencia de sí misma" (296) ["was going to the man who had made her conscious of her own being" (289)]—can feed on the most disabused and negative of representations. Sofía must undergo her own disillusionment by rejoining the "extraordinary character" (283) [277] in Cayenne, where she too will be disgusted in due course by his political versatility. But the novel has demonstrated that, since reading is mediated by desire and desire is mediated by power, no oppositional narrative can hope to control its own reception: not being able to "dictate" its meanings, it is always subject to being an agent of "dictation."

But while his stories of Hugues nourish Sofía's love for the "monster," Esteban is discovering his love for *her*, with her "poderoso estilo humano" (286) ["potent humanity" (279)]. Whereas his love for Hugues, as we have seen, was a form of self-love, this new love is a "self"-sacrificing one: in order to allow Sofía to escape to Cayenne, Esteban will deliberately delay the police who have come to arrest her as a revolutionary sympathizer by confessing (he whom we know to be so out of sympathy with the Revolution) to revolutionary activities of his own. Having thus escaped the prison society of the Revolution, he ends up, as a result, in the prisons of the reaction. The moment is crucial because, even more than the scene of Esteban's telling his story to the "Jacobin Club," it signals the high degree of complexity and interpretability that characterizes mediated discourse. What to the inquisitors is a truth they have uncovered is a kind of lie (Esteban is no longer a revolutionary and his confession is a shield for Sofía's escape); yet it is simultaneously no more than (a version of?) the truth, since his confession is another, admittedly selective, telling of his actual story. Moreover, the pseudo-confession, deceptive in this way towards the police, is simultaneously, as the reader knows, a genuine act of love, an *indirect* expression of Esteban's love for Sofía (one that has to be "read" out of the situation).

All this, needless to say, adds a further degree of complexity to the self-figuration by means of which *El siglo de las luces* represents itself as mediated discourse, for like his previous narration to the Havana Jacobins, Esteban's confession is a summary of the events recounted in the novel itself, of which it is therefore a *mise en abyme*.

Esteban, entonces, lo largó todo de un solo y pormenorizado tirón: Se remontó a la llegada de Víctor Hugues a la Habana. . . . Habló de sus contactos personales con Brissot y Dalbarade; de sus trabajos de propaganda . . . ; de su amistad con los abominables personajes que habían sido los traidores Marchena y Martínez de Ballesteros. Luego, la ida a Guadalupe; la imprenta de los Loeuillet; el episodio de Cayena. . . . "Apunte, escribano; apunte", decía el Importante, colmado por tales revelaciones. (Pp. 301–02)

So then Esteban let them have the whole story in detail: he went back to Victor Hugues's arrival in Havana. . . . He talked about his personal contacts with Brissot and Dalbarade. About his propaganda activities. . . . About his friendship with those abominable men—the traitors Marchena and Martínez de Ballesteros. Next, his journey to Guadeloupe. The Loeuillets's printing press. The events in Cayenne. . . .

"Make a note of it, make a note of it," said the Important Man, who was quite overcome by such revelations. (P. 295)

This, then, is Esteban's own moment to "dictate": cf. "el relato que el escribano iba pasando al papel con desacompasada caligrafía" (301) ["the story which the clerk was feverishly scribbling down" (295)].[12] But to understand his dictation, or that of the novel, as a simple transmission of Revolutionary fervor and allegiance to Hugues is to understand it only as the police do, and so *not* to understand it at all. Where Esteban's first telling (to the "Club") shows that oppositional discourse runs the risk of confirming the power it opposes, this new telling demonstrates with perfect symmetry that even such confirmatory discourse has itself the power to subserve a deeply oppositional function, as an act of love and a gesture of liberation (Esteban's sacrifice of "self" permits the freedom of Sofía, who still believes in Liberty). If oppositional storytelling can always be a vehicle of dictation, dictation itself can—conversely—become an expression of oppositional love. In this episode, the reader of *El siglo* is consequently invited not to adopt the position of being the addressee of a dictation, and of hearing therefore, as Sofía did in the case of the first narration, and as the police do here, only what he or she *wants* to hear. Instead of succumbing to the *desire for dictation* (which will always be satisfied), the reader is encouraged to understand the possibility of making oppositional meanings from discourse that will always have that potential because it is an act of mediation. It is a condition of Esteban's story, as an act of love, that he dictate; but to reduce it to dictation is to misread the narration grievously.

Mediation, then, can subvert dictation—but only at the risk of being (mis)taken for dictation, depending on the nature of the reader's desire; for it seems that mediation and dictation are in a relation of mutual entailment. We can see more clearly why this is so if we look a little more closely at the mediated character of Esteban's love for Sofía. René Girard would have no difficulty in pointing to the triangularity of a relation that first has the configuration of an adultery (while Sofía's husband is alive) and then becomes a matter of rivalry between Esteban and Victor Hugues, he who has given Sofía—after Esteban himself—a sense of identity, "una conciencia de sí misma" (296). What is remarkable is, therefore, not so much that a mediated love is contrasted with a form of love that associates the sense of identity with the illusion of an unmediated relation, but the fact that this mediated love, as a manifestation of oppositionality, is mediated by the very power—the power of the Father, whether represented by the husband or by Hugues himself, the substitute "paterfamilias"—the power of dictation, then, that oppositionality as mediation opposed.[13]

It is very striking that the culture of *machismo*, as it is represented here, imagines homosocial relations (between men) as "direct," "natural," and unmediated—a matter of dictation—whereas it represents heterosexual love as simultaneously oppositional and complex (a complexification of the homosocial relation, turning men into rivals through the phenomenon of mediation). *El Señor Presidente* is in perfect agreement with *El siglo de las luces* on this point, including the perception that it is the Father (General Canales or the President himself) who mediates this "human" love. Heterosexual love, in other words, is controlled by the same power that is vested in homosocial relations, which are therefore implicitly primary; so that the mediated relations of heterosexuality can appear as oppositional—they involve respect for the other as opposed to affirmation of self, they institute a kind of equality instead of the relation of domination and submission—without challenging the system that in fact governs them.

So it is finally the culture of *machismo*, present in the revolutionary world as much as it is in patriarchal, colonial Havana, that constitutes a prison society, and the sign of this is the carryover of the power relations of male to male into heterosexual gender relations, controlled by the Father. As a result, the options between dictation and oppositionality, homosocial relations and heterosexual love, amount to a choice of prisons (thus Esteban eludes the prison of Guadeloupe in order to end up imprisoned in Havana). That is why the depiction in *El beso de la mujer araña* of a homosocial relation (defined by the gender roles of *machismo*) that becomes *homosexual* (a relation of equality) acquires radical significance, proposing a way out, or an apparent way out, of the impasse. For that reason we shall need to look carefully at the way this novel shows homosexual desire to be mediated and see to what degree and in what sense it is itself generated by the conditions of prison and the ideology of dictation.

My point for the moment, however, concerns the demonstration in *El siglo de las luces* of the mutual dependency of "dictation" and "mediation," power and oppositionality. The dictator cannot dictate, cannot produce the awe-inspiring effect of sublimity, without the means of dictation that necessarily flaw the effect of fascination and thus make oppositionality—as a falling out of love—possible (indeed inevitable); but oppositionality cannot itself arise, as a manifestation of mediation and of mediated love, without being mediated—and thus controlled—by the power it opposes. What the oppositional is "against," in the adversative sense, is simultaneously that "against" which, in the anaclitic sense, it leans; and its desire for liberty is oddly compromised, therefore, with a desire for power. Indeed, power itself, in the end, is definable, precisely as the power to determine the nature of desire, and thus the forms of desire taken by the opposition to power itself. One corollary of this, in political terms, is that "liberation" movements will tend always to be drawn into the conventional power struggles of everyday politics, and are thus vulnerable to recuperation by the system they oppose, as we have seen in this century; Carpentier, in effect, analyzes the Revolution itself as a liberation movement, originally oppositional, but co-opted by the desire for power. That is why Liberty comes accompanied by Death. Siempre sucede.[14]

No wonder *El siglo* ends on a note of deep ambivalence as Esteban and Sofía disappear together in the Madrid uprisings of the *dos de mayo*. They are together again—but with what degree of intimacy? The suggestion persists of Sofía's continued unavailability to Esteban, the unavailability of "Wisdom," "Liberty," or "Truth" in a world of necessary mediation, necessarily mediated by Power. And how should we understand the *dos de mayo* itself as an event? The Madrileños's revolt against French occupation looks both revolutionary (a manifestation in favor of liberty) and counterrevolutionary (a manifestation of the desire to return to the monarchy). Like Esteban and Sofía, similarly caught between repression, a repression at home that fires their revolutionary spirit, and a Revolution that turns out to be a hell of terror, the insurgents of Madrid have only a choice of prisons. So it is their failure that is perhaps most exemplary, signifying that oppositionality can succeed, as a revolt against power, only by simultaneously failing, only by confirming power, as the *power to mediate*, in its position of power. . . . Unless desire itself can be changed (but that is precisely the concern of *El beso de la mujer araña*), Love cannot be as strong as Death—it can only be more human.[15]

2. Voices in the Dark

Accordingly, *El Señor Presidente* tells the story of a falling out of love (with the President) that is conjointly a falling in love (with the human)—but whose oppositionality, after a brief moment of hope, is ruthlessly crushed, confirming the power of Death over Love. Whereas Esteban does escape from Guadeloupe and is in turn released from his Cuban prison (albeit only to die in the Madrid uprisings), there is *no* escape for Cara de Angel. The implication for oppositionality, and hence for the novel's own discursive status, is correspondingly dark: under the régime of dictation, oppositionality is possible but it is always already defeated. There is no choice but to stay under dictation, "escuchando," as one character remarks, "la voz del amo" (270) ["listening to my master's voice" (260)].

The joking reference to the famous gramophone company's logo is a bitter one, and not only because it reflects the impossibility of escape or even because it implies that under dictation the master's servants are reduced to a state of animality. *El Señor Presidente* decisively shifts the problematics of dictatorship to a question of discursivity—a matter of "dictation"—and poses it, more explicitly than *El siglo*'s eighteenth-century reference perhaps allows, as a problem in information control. More specifically still, it asks who controls in information control: can information be controlled or does it control us? The dog in the logo is disturbed and fascinated because the voice of authority is a disembodied one, it issues from a machine. The gramophone, as one of the earliest "media" (the novel is set in 1917), figures a new form of inhumanity, standing as it does for the *machine* of presidential government, a machine which largely depersonalizes even the President himself, who harnesses for the purposes of dictation the phenomena of mediated communication, thereby creating a universe of gossip, rumor, and misinformation in which "truth" has become inaccessible, even perhaps to the manipulator himself.

Certainly his subjects live in a world of discursive uncontrollability, where no information can be reliably verified and misinformation increases exponentially; and the epistemological uncertainty that results—what the anthropologist Michael Taussig calls the "murk"[16]—is the source of their fear—the fear of death—while it constitutes the immaterial walls of the prison that holds them. The President controls, in short, because the citizens have lost control of their discursive universe; so that—to the extent that the President is himself a disembodied presence, "la voz del amo"—it is to them as if they were controlled by the uncontrollable information machine itself. But in this system the President, in turn, into whose mind no one penetrates, is something like a "black box," comparable to the body of the gramophone through whose horn information pours. His mind is a simple switching mechanism towards which all information gravitates (the exclusivity of his knowledge making it unverifiable to everyone else) and out of which it emerges again, having undergone a process of selection and/or modification (that is, after becoming "misinformation" or "disinformation") for the purposes of power. So the President serves the system of information, as its key component, more than the system serves him.

What dictates, in short, is less a "dictator" than the machine of dictation, and once again the reliance of dictation on mediation is evident. The citizens inhabit a discursive universe that is *fully* mediated (there is no access to an independent "truth") and is mediated by *power in an almost pure state* (the president has no interest in using power for specific purposes, but only in maintaining it). For them, it is simultaneously equivalent to the uncontrollable Lacanian *ça parle* (talk is going on in epistemological darkness) and to the

Barthesian language that is fascist. Their prison is a discursive one, in which no one can take "responsibility" for the discourse that traverses them in its circulation, endlessly moving towards the President and emerging again from his office, and in which the prisoners themselves consequently become mere voices talking in the dark. This place is therefore a site of living death, a tomb for the living, because personal identity is necessarily deeply impaired by such a machine of disembodied information that controls all. People dance, in short, to the tune of the God Tohil, in Cara de Angel's vision: "No habrá ni verdadera muerte ni verdadera vida. Que se me baile la jícara!" (270) ["There will be neither true death nor true life. So dance the jícara in my honor!" (260)]. Chapter heads like "Habla en la sombra" ["Voices in the Dark"] (chapter 38) and "La tumba viva" ["The Living Tomb"] (chapter 22) are thus, ultimately, rigorously equivalent in their designation of a society under dictation as a prison and a hell—but a prison of discursive uncontrollability, a hell of epistemological darkness, resulting from the strict monopolization of the control of information in the presidential "black box."

It follows from this analysis that we would *all* experience the terror of discursivity as a mediated phenomenon—the unreliability of all information, the impairment of identity, the sense of being controlled by that which itself cannot be controlled—were it not that the availability of alternative sources of "information" in liberal societies fosters illusions of verifiability and control, and hence of personal agency and identity. But what Asturias's President has learned is that one cannot dictate (in the sense of imposing one's discourse) unless, as a prior condition, one eliminates all possibility of rival discourses, and with it those necessary accommodations of policy that were so damaging to Victor Hugues's prestige, as we saw, in *El siglo*. The world of *El Señor Presidente* is certainly subject to presidential caprice, but it does not know the zigzags of policy because the machine of power is, in political terms, an "empty" one, functioning for no purpose other than to maintain power. That is why its citizens are so anxiously aware of power as the universal signified of discourse—a discourse that controls them utterly because they cannot control it.

In that sense, the reclusiveness of the President, near-identical as he is with the system of information control and discursive uncontrollability in which he functions as the "black box," makes him also a figure of the unknowability, the unverifiability that characterizes the world of the novel. At the heart of things there is a central darkness, an impenetrable void, knowable only by the *signs* of its presence, which are also the signs of its elusiveness. Mail reaches the President, he receives verbal and bureaucratic reports, even the leaves of his park transmit messages to him, but he remains concealed in the recesses of his various residences, where his presence is signaled only by his guards.

No one knows what he thinks, even his closest confidants; no one knows where or how he sleeps—"se contaba que al lado de un teléfono con un látigo en la mano" ["some said beside the telephone with a whip in his hand"]—or even whether he sleeps—"sus amigos aseguraban que no dormía nunca" (13) ["his friends declared that he never slept at all" (10)]. More effectively than Hugues, whose aloofness is intermittent, the President wraps himself, therefore, in the trappings of the terrorist sublime; and more than Hugues's, consequently, his power rests on visible signs (such as the sentries) and on a mediated discursivity—the "se contaba que . . .", the "sus amigos aseguraban que . . ." of rumor and gossip—which is now subject to the greatest unreliability.

As a consequence, his people greet him as God, on the rare occasions when he emerges from concealment: "Lord! Lord! heaven and earth are full of your glory!" (100) [96], their endless circulation around the park serving as yet one more *sign* of his invisible power, while it functions as a figure for their imprisonment. But he himself will later describe himself, more accurately, not as God, but as playing the role of a divinity, and of a divinity more threatening than the God of Justice because functioning in a universe that is absurd: "hasta de diosa ciega tengo que hacer en la lotería . . ."(267) ["I have even to take the part of the blind goddess in the lottery . . ."(257)]. This confirms a view the novel has already put in the mouth of a toothless old lottery seller and soothsayer: "Amigo, amigo, la única ley en egta tierra eg la lotería: pog lotería cae ugté en la cagcel, pog lotería lo fugilan, pog lotería lo hagen diputado . . . (etc.)!" ["The lottery ith the only law on thith earth, my friend! The Lottery can thend you to prithon, have you shot, make you a deputy . . . (etc.)!" (102)]. The President is not God, then, but a man playing at being a god in a world that is in fact governed by chance. His game is the fly-game, in which he vents—but on people, not insects—the bitter resentment he has retained from his humble and poverty-stricken childhood; but his own role as "pregidente de la Gepublica" is itself on the list of things that can happen "pog lotería."

If the President is himself dependent, therefore, as a man, on the chance he pretends ("tengo que hacer") to administer, so that he is subject to his own machine—the machine of contingency—it is appropriate that we should know with much greater certainty and precision this "God"'s messenger, the *means* of his government, his *angelos* Miguel Cara de Angel. But the "angel," too— insistently described in a textual refrain as "bello y malo como Satán"—is at best a fallen one, and in fact a human substitute for the fallen angel ("*como* Satán"), just as the President is a stand-in for the blind goddess of chance. The angel is just an errand boy and toady, who is *nick*named Cara de Angel because his name is Miguel and his face has the beauty of the devil. And where gods and angels are only common human beings transcendentalized by power, it follows that their subjects must slip, correspondingly, one further rung in the hierarchy of being. As power becomes superhuman, its subjects become sub-human, and the counterpart of the usurped transcendancy of the terrorist sublime is the animalization of the terrorized general population.

So "el Pelele," the Zany, ends up on the trash heap; Niña Fedina is inhu-manly tortured and sold like chattel, with her dead baby, to a brothel-keeper. Of her, the Judge Advocate is reported to have remarked that "if a cow dies after it's been bought it's not the seller's but the buyer's loss" (172) [166]. A staff officer, as we have seen, can compare himself implicitly to a dog. And in a world where the streets themselves are animate and subject to panic after a gunshot (55) [51], events in the animal world have the same status as events in the human world: the General's canary, scheming for birdseed, is a kind of politician (97) [92]; and a hen pursued by servants with an ax comes to figure the whole culture of terror that prevails in the President's country. "El pollo se les iba de las manos palpitante, acoquinado, con los ojos fuera, el pico abierto, medio en cruz las alas y la respiración en largo hilván" (273) ["Palpitating and terrified, the hen escaped from their hands, its eyes starting from its head, its beak wide open, its wings spread out like a cross, its breathing reduced to a thread" (263)].

What is evacuated by the joint process of transcendentalizing power and animalizing its subjects is obviously humanity itself; and the President's fly-game is therefore vulnerable to any realization on the part of the "flies" that they are human. The sublime is never far removed from the grotesque (as the ceremonies of the national day demonstrate), and it is the absurdity of the whole bloodthirsty charade of terror that becomes evident when a character, such as Señora Carvajal, contemplating the prospect of her husband's execu-tion, suddenly realizes, in a flash of momentary insight, that all involved are just "men": "hombres como él, con ojos, con boca, con manos, con pelo en la cabeza, con uñas en los dedos, con dientes en la boca, con lengua, con gali-llo . . . (etc.)" (227) ["men like him, people like him with eyes, mouth, hands, hair on their heads, nails on their fingers, teeth in their mouth, with a tongue, with a throat . . ." (219)]. How can "people" so brutalize other "people?" Such a demystifying shattering of illusion, were it to become general, would have devastating effects for the President.

That is why Cara de Angel's falling in love, and the awareness of humanity that results from it, is such a threat. To his own great surprise, the toady is led to discover, not only human emotions in himself—"a new humanity shining in his eyes" (228) [220]—but also the humanity of the girl whom originally he had kidnapped and planned to rape—whom he had treated, that is, as an object, simply a means to the end of covering the General's presidentially inspired escape. Another soothsayer, significantly called "El Tícher" ["the Teacher"] makes the point clear: "A la muerte únicamente se le puede oponer el amor, porque ambos son igualmente fuertes, como dice *el Cantar de los Cantares* . . ." (220–21) ["The only thing that can oppose death is love, because they are equally strong, as the Song of Songs tells us . . ." (213)]. And the Teacher, in his role as Jesus-figure, had sent Cara de Angel on his way with the message (in English): "¡ *Make thee another self, for love of me* . . .!" (221) [213].

Miguel's making of another self through love forms a parallel, but also a contrast, with the General's political development from "Prince of the Army" to resistance fighter and leader of the rebellion (or revolution? both terms are used) on the frontier. The General fights force with force and he does it in the name of a coherent set of principles, a reformist program (not essentially different from that of the French Revolution). Cara de Angel's opposition has no political program; he acts blindly and seeks only to escape personally, with his wife, from the area of the President's control; moreover he seeks to do it, like Esteban in *El siglo*, without overt revolt and armed with the President's *laissez-passer*. His "new self," in short, continues to coincide with that of the trained dog, submissive to his master's authority: "Seguía siendo el perro educado, intelectual, contento de su ración de mugre, del instinto que le conservaba la vida" (23) ["He went on behaving like a well-trained, intelligent dog, content with its portion of filth and its instinct for self-preservation" (222)].

By contrast with the General's overt resistance, Cara de Angel's behavior is, in short, paradigmatically oppositional; and so it is crushed. It is crushed because the presidential machine for collecting information is absolute and permits no secrets: Miguel's marriage—the very symbol of his new-found devotion to another person—becomes known to the President who, significantly, becomes its "sponsor," just as his good deed towards Major Farfán (warning him that he is in the presidential bad books and advising him to worm his way back into favor, preferaby by committing a crime) turns against him. It will be Farfán, whom Cara de Angel had warned as a token of his love, who arrests the former favorite at the frontier; and everything suggests that, denounced to the President by a prostitute, Farfán has prostituted himself in turn, regaining favor by denouncing Cara de Angel. Oppositionality is dangerous to the system of dictation, but it cannot escape that system's *universal* control.

But we should not too quickly conclude that the path of resistance, represented by the General, is preferable to Miguel's oppositionality. The takeover of Cara de Angel's marriage, which foreshadows the latter's arrest, imprisonment, and death, also destroys the General, whose "revolution" has thus been both instigated and crushed by presidential maneuvering—it too, in short, is part of the fly-game. Moreover, although the General has a social program, as mentioned, he is in many ways a mere alter ego and rival of the President: as "Prince of the Army" an ambitious rival, whom the president replaces, however, in the role of father of the bride, and whose revolutionary methods and expeditive justice (he shoots an abusive doctor in cold blood) are finally no less violent than the President's own. It is hard to escape the conclusion that revolution and dictation, dictation and revolution are, as in the Carpentier novel by that title, part of the same *recurso del método*; and we encounter again here the *siempre sucede* of *El siglo de las luces*.

The President's rage at Cara de Angel's "betrayal" of him suggests, however—especially by contrast with the cool way he goes about setting up the General as a revolutionary and then destroying him—that the oppositional, as the discovery of human values, is actually more dangerous to the presidential "method" of government than overt, armed resistance. This seems to be because, where "resistance" takes the form of *open* rivalry (the General quits the country and returns with an army), "opposition" is a kind of resistance *from within*, and so more insidious—more difficult to identify, more difficult to stamp out. For in Cara de Angel, it is of course the President's own means of government that demonstrates an oppositional potential of its own. Oppositionality, in short, appears here as the mode of resistance that is characteristic, not of the dictator's rivals for power, but of the system's own prisoners; and that is why the novel so firmly identifies opposition with prison, both to indicate the form of "freedom" it represents under a system of dictation, and to show that such freedom is itself conditional on the carceral situation that constrains it. It is in the confined space of the cell that one finds the dubious forms of resistance that are represented by graffiti on the wall or voices speaking in the dark. But since, metaphorically, the *whole* of the President's country is such a prison, "cuyos muros de niebla a más correr, más se alejan" (21) ["a prison with walls of mist so that the more one runs the more they recede" (19)], we need now to go back and look more closely at the mist of words that forms the President's prison, so as to identify and question the discursive forms of oppositionality that arise there.

By the same token, we will be examining and questioning the novel's own oppositionality and the conditions of its practice; for I want to suggest that its status is necessarily bound up with that of the gossip and rumor that surround the President. Like Cara de Angel's love, these can be viewed as a form of oppositionality—they arise because of presidential control of information, and as an alternative to it. But they are also either always already part of the system or easily brought under its control, in which they are again like Cara de Angel's love. They are, in short, a means of government that can turn against the president, but which continue to serve presidential purposes as they do so. One might say that the President's monopolization of information produces gossip in two ways, as a "practical" consequence and as a "theoretical" necessity. It is as a practical consequence that it has oppositional value: where information is unavailable, people interpret signs as best they may (and there are always signs, since there can be no "sublimity" without the signs of sublimity). They thus invent for themselves an alternative knowledge to substitute for the information that is unavailable; and they do so—in full or partial awareness of the unreliability of such knowledge—because of their sense that their very survival, in both a physical and an ontological sense, depends on "knowing" (and particularly on knowing the President). Speculation, in short, is preferable to no knowledge at all, and Niña Fedina is one, for example, who pays the price for being insufficiently informed.

But the unreliability of gossip is not accidental, it is structural; it is the theoretical necessity I just mentioned, and it makes gossip, not oppositional now, but the President's ally. For, where "truth" has become inaccessible, *all* information without exception becomes *mis*information, there being no guaranteed criterion against which to measure its veracity and/or accuracy. This is the case even for the information that reaches the President via his mailbag since it is collected by people (spies, informers, the *Auditor* or "Judge Advocate" himself), none of whom are in a position to know false information from true. But, as a result, for people to whom knowledge is essential to survival, the only unchallenged knowledge they do therefore have, which is the knowledge that they do not and cannot *know*, necessarily produces anxiety and fear. This is the terrible uncertainty that tracks all the characters—from Dr. Barreño to Cara de Angel himself—when they are in a position to have any insight at all into the workings of the system. And its function, clearly, is to reinforce the President's power. Epistemic "murk" is the theoretical entailment of the monopolization of knowledge; and it turns gossip, in spite of any oppositional status it may have as an alternative source of information, into an agency of fear and an instrument of power.

Furthermore, the necessarily unreliable information that filters back to the President through the channel of bureaucratic report, police spying and citizen informing, makes a further contribution to the system in spite of its unreliability, since his exclusive access to all such information means that it can be used in the interests of maintaining power, quite independently of its truthfulness or accuracy. For one thing, it serves, at the very least, as a report to the President on the state of his country (in the sense of what people know or think they know). For another, there is no essential difference in this context between any misinformation the President may make use of, on occasion, and the disinformation he similarly spreads, since we are in a system where information is always already, and by definition, *false*. The ease with which the system thus recuperates gossip, regardless of any oppositional function it may (also) have, is a sign of the fact that gossip is not a mere accidental by-product of the system, but its essential component: *gossip is the system* because its unreliability produces epistemic "murk" and the atmosphere of terror that accompanies it, without in any way impeding the President's operations, which have no need of or use for "truth." Indeed, gossip *is* the President's operations.

Itself a rival source of information about the President and the presidential régime, the novel,then, can claim no more reliability than the gossip and rumor, the "se contaba que . . . " that circulates endlessly around the President's mainly absent person, like the crowds circumambulating the park on the feast day. Since *no one* can know the President, *all* information about him has the status of gossip. As a consequence, the novel cannot claim any more independence from the working of the machine than the gossip whose effects it examines: its "witnessing" function is impaired by the unreliability that affects all information; it consequently contributes to epistemic "murk" while seeking to dispel it, and so enters actively into presidential purposes; and finally, it too can end up as "El parte al Señor Presidente" ["The President's Mail-Bag"] (title of chapter 23), part of the information that is tirelessly channeled back to him to serve as a report on the state of his country. It too is the President's portion.

Both the voices in the novel and the voice of the novel itself are therefore "in the dark," in the sense that they cannot have knowledge of the truth, knowing only that they do not know, and in the sense that there is no way to calculate the degree to which they function oppositionally or as part of the presidential system. Certain characters do not even know that they do not know (Niña Fedina is one such character); others know too much and consequently must be destroyed (such is the case of Lucio Vásquez, and by implication Cara de Angel himself). Others (such as the two toughs at the start) are in confident possession of entirely fictitious information; others again know something of the truth, albeit uncertainly (Dr. Barreño knows his father was probably assassinated, probably by Sonrientes). But all are to some degree excluded from reliable knowledge. In such circumstances, access to the truth would change everything, for a rival source of information would be set up to the President's office and the whole system of misinformation would consequently be destroyed. But truthful witness can itself be manipulated, as is demonstrated early in the novel, when the beggars who saw Sonrientes killed by el Pelele are tortured into testifying, instead, to the *official* truth, that the deed was done by Carvajal and General Canales.

Meanwhile, the false information that emanates from the office of the President and circulates in the society produces perfectly real events, while totally distorting others. Sonrientes's death at the hands of "some blind force"

(13) [11], of which the "Zany" is the instrument and the symbol, becomes a political crime for which Carvajal is executed while the General in his turn is manipulated into flight, and thus into revolution. But the real events that result from the falsification of other real events are themselves subject to falsification: Cara de Angel's love for Camila, a by-product of the politicization of Sonrientes's chance death, is used first to destroy the General (who is made to believe that Camila has betrayed her filial duty) and finally to destroy the ex-favorite himself (who is made to believe she has betrayed their love). The whole system is self-generating (the political interpretation of Sonrientes's death is automatic), self-reproducing (fact becomes falsity which produces fact which becomes falsity), and capable of limitless proliferation.

In such circumstances, storytelling has an understandably low status. On learning that in North America "everyone says exactly what they feel" (263) [253], a local citizen draws the conclusion: "Entonces allá, con ustedes, no se conocen los cuentos . . ." ["So, in your country, stories are unknown . . ."], and the gringo concurs, so clear is it that in the President's country, stories are the vehicle for the spread of misinformation, itself the agent of terror. And yet, there *are* circumstances in the novel where narrative does serve a positive function, witnessing the truth rather than serving as a vehicle for falsehood, and it is these cases that offer a first possible model for the novel's own truth-telling ambitions. It is an anonymous letter that partly enlightens Barreño as to his father's fate; and another anonymous letter—giving Señora Carvajal an eyewitness account of her husband's last moments—is directly relevant as a figure of the novel's own discursive status since, like the novel, it is a testimonial to the conditions that prevail in prison, coming from one who has witnessed those conditions and survived them. Although in each case the information is incomplete and perhaps dubious, a survivor of the system has nevertheless taken upon himself (or conceivably herself) the responsibility of making a truthful report, and one that is not directed to the President—an act that is subversive not only because it attests to the inhuman conditions of the régime but also, and more fundamentally, because, in short-circuiting the system and putting the truth into circulation, it challenges the very structures and mechanisms of the culture of terror. One may reflect moreover that, if the President does have a rival for the possession of knowledge, it is the novel itself which—less incomplete than these fragmentary notes—seems to know everything that the President himself knows, with one crucial exception, however, to which it will be necessary to return. The novel does not have access, any more than any of the characters, to what goes on in the President's mind as he "treats" the information that reaches him.

But in the fog of misinformation, fragments of truth do seem to surface; and they owe their appearance to the survival of eyewitnesses capable of giving testimony. The problem here, however, is that, in order to survive the system and make a report on it, one must pay a price, and the novel explores these conditions of survival with some interest. Part of the price to be paid is the probable unreliability of one's information (even if it is not misinformed it will be partial, like the tattered letters, with missing pages). But the other price of survival is consequently that one's serving of the truth still ends up being part of the general system of misinformation, disinformation, rumor, and gossip. . . . It is complicitous, in spite of itself, with the régime. The example of Genaro Rodas is eloquent. Where his luckless friend Vásquez dies for knowing too much, Rodas survives, as he puts it, to tell the tale: "Yo siquiera puedo contar el cuento . . ." (241)—but the tale he is telling goes into the ears of *el Auditor*, the President's inquisitor; and the price of his survival is one that he concedes both voluntarily and involuntarily. He is the Judge Advocate's dupe (ignorantly signing a document that disculpates the official from his dealings with the madam and thus becoming a party to the affair); and he also willingly agrees to become a spy for the President, making reports on Cara de Angel that correspond, tellingly, with the "report" the novel is itself making as it follows (or "tails") the favorite through his various activities.

So one can know too much (like Vásquez and Cara de Angel), in which case one is brutally suppressed. But to survive to tell the tale therefore means—if it is true that nothing escapes presidential knowledge—that one's tale is so mystified as either to be harmless to the President, or what is worse, as to play into his hands (since his system depends on storytelling). Worse still, since we know that unreliable gossip can become useful information when it reaches the President, a survivor's story, however suspect it may be as oppositional testimonial, may yet serve, like Rodas's spying, as a report to the President, "el parte al Señor Presidente." Storytelling can always be tale telling—that is the telltale sign of its complicity, however involuntary, with the system. It is necessarily part of the system of "dictation" even as it opposes it, and this conclusion applies to the novel as a narrative of witness as much as it does to the characters themselves.

If witnessing is suspect, we may still look, however, among the voices in the dark, to another category of truth-tellers in the novel, its prophetic sooth-sayers: figures such as the lottery-seller and "el Tícher"—their discourse marked as it is by the signs of its mediated and therefore opaque status (the lottery-seller's speech impediment, the Teacher's use of English)—may serve as a model for the novel (itself a visionary and indeed denunciatory text) that is less compromised with the power of dictation. That is why the self-reflexive chapter entitled "Habla en la sombra" is crucial, establishing the paradox that, within the general prison of epistemic murk, the voices that rise in the dark of an actual prison cell enjoy more freedom—freedom of witness, freedom of denunciation—than those on the outside, whose oppositionality is inextricably compromised with the working of the system.

It is not that the prisoners are free of the all-pervading fear; but in the "tomb of the living" they are so close to the reality of death that talk (which on the outside signals the uncontrollability of discourse and the impairment of individual identity that results) now seems more like a sign of life. "El silencio me da miedo," as Carvajal obsessively repeats ["Silence scares me to death"]; and so the three talkers tell their stories, as prisoners do, to pass the time, to give each other the comfort of company, and also to bear witness to the sort of society in which they live (the sacristan, the revolutionary student, and the jailed liberal are clearly emblematic figures). But suddenly they become aware that there is a fourth person among them:

—Entonces es . . . Entre nosotros hay un muerto!
—No, no es un muerto, soy yo . . .
—¿Pero, quién es usted . . . ? atajó el estudiante.—¡Está usted muy helado!
Una voz muy débil:
    —Otro de ustedes . . . (P. 208)

["Then . . . Is there a dead man among us?"
"No, it's not a dead man. It's me. . . ."
"But who are you?" put in the student. "You seem very cold."
An extremely weak voice replied:
    "I'm one of you. . . ." (P. 199)]

Otro de ustedes. . . . This anonymous voice in the dark, rising faintly from the body of a survivor (so close to death, yet alive), is one we will not hear again; nor will the character ever be identified. But *this* voice in the dark gives expression to a despairing picture of the state of society, in prophetic, denunciatory, and quasi-apocalyptic terms:

Las voces del cielo nos gritan cuando truena: "¡Viles! ¡Inmundos! ¡Complices de iniquidad!" En los muros de las cárceles, cientos de hombres han dejado los sesos estampados al golpe de las balas asesinas. Los mármoles de palacio están húmedos de sangre de inocentes. ¿Adónde volver los ojos en busca de libertad? (P. 210)

["When it thunders, it is a voice from heaven saying: 'You are evil, and corrupt, you are accomplices in wickedness!' Hundreds of men have their brains blown out against prison walls by murderous bullets. Our marble palaces are wet with innocent blood. Where can one turn one's eyes in search of freedom?" (P. 201)]

Like the other soothsayers—and like the vision of Tohil—with whose vision its own vision is entirely consonant, this voice suggests that the President's real rival, in terms of access to the truth, lies in religious inspiration: the voice of

God speaking through (mediated by) man. The conflict of mediation and dictation here takes the form of a rivalry between God and the man-god produced by the terroristic sublime.

But if this is the voice of truth, its denunciatory message is far from comforting, because the truth it tells is the truth of complicity in the system—it confirms and underscores what we have already learned, that there is no escape from involvement in the presidential régime. Knowing the value of freedom, it acknowledges its own status as accomplice; it is simultaneously an expression of truth and just another voice in the dark; its privileged vision does not prevent it from being "otro de ustedes. . . ." Where, then—if the truth is that of universal complicity in the oppressive system (the truth that there can be no truth)—to look for freedom? When the student in the group answers the question by speaking of the revolution, he feels himself embraced, presumably by the owner of the mysterious fourth voice. But the embrace does not authorize revolutionary action—one needs only to think of General Canales and his status as presidential alter ego, but also of the simple implausibility of the student's desire to break down the prison door. What is being embraced is the accent of hope. "Muere tranquilo, que no todo se ha perdido en un país donde la juventud habla así" (210) ["Die in peace; all is not lost in a country where youth can talk like that" (202)].

Is this anonymous prisoner also the author of the anonymous note to Señora Carvajal? His role in the text is in any case to signify the novel's own narrative function. In a country where "the President's rule of conduct is never to give grounds for hope" (242) [243], words of hope are ipso facto oppositional, even when they arise in the dark of prison. But so too are words of despair, when they bear the accent of truth; and the reason is not simply that truth is in itself oppositional (for no one can guarantee its truth) but also that despair, like hope, is a manifestation of the *desire* for freedom, a desire the presidential system cannot control or stamp out since it is precisely in prison —under oppression—that such a desire necessarily arises. As a lucid analysis of an oppressive system of dictation that functions *perfectly*, the novel is itself an expression of despair; but simultaneously, as a voice rising in the dark of prison, that despair is itself an expression of "hope"—the prisoners' *last* hope—because it demonstrates that the desire for change is still alive.

But the question is still, obviously, how to weigh the hope and the despair produced by the underlying desire for freedom. For despair is precisely what the system seeks to produce (which is why a despairing voice can also act as a truthful "witness" to the nature of the system), whereas hope is oppositional to the system, but delusive, unrealistic and untruthful. Just as the President's means of government can always turn against him, so the presidential system has an uncanny power of turning its rivals into accomplices and making them part of the system. This is true whether the rival is (delusive) hope or (lucid) despair, whether it takes the form of an attack from outside, like the General's revolution, or arises insidiously within the prison itself, like the voices in the dark. But in the long run the novel, I think, favors denunciatory despair as an expression of the oppositional desire for freedom; and it does so because despair has the power of truth, albeit of the truth that all are complicitous—"¡Viles! ¡Inmundos! ¡Cómplices de iniquidad!" (210)—in the presidential system. I say this because the novel itself works through its own techniques of narration to bring home to its reader this truth of universal complicity—a complicity from which neither the reader nor the novel itself are exempt.

An insistently mentioned intertext of *El Señor Presidente* is the Bible, with its message of love but also its model of apocalyptic and denunciative discourse. If the struggle is between the man-god of the terroristic sublime playing the role of blind goddess in the lottery, and a God of Justice whose voice addresses itself to humans in human language that expresses their own desire for freedom, the Bible becomes the necessary model of oppositional discourse. Thus, the gringo specifically exempts the Bible from the general devaluation of storytelling (263) [253]. But should one think of the Bible as a message of hope? So the explicit references would suggest. The Teacher proclaims the message: "Make thee another self . . . " and declares love to be as strong as death, "como dice *El Cantar de los Cantares*" (220–21); and when Farfán mentions the word "esposa," the Song of Songs is again evoked. "The sweetest word in the Song of Songs floated for a moment, like some charming embroidery, among trees full of cherubs and orange blossom" (182) [176]. But at the President's reception, it is a recitation of the Song of Songs that the President demands of the sycophantic Poet in attendance, who of course hastens to oblige. The moment is ambiguous, for the President reacts balefully to the recitation and stalks away, as if momentarily defeated by the power of this text, leaving the Poet and the audience stunned and uneasy. Yet the song was ordered by the President, and offered to him—a declaration of love, so to speak—by the Poet.

Although it is a love story, *El Señor Presidente* is not a version of the Song of Songs, precisely because it demonstrates, here and elsewhere, that "under dictation" love is *not* equal to death: Cara de Angel's love for Camila is first co-opted for presidential purposes (their secret marriage is announced as a brilliant society affair, sponsored by the President himself, a piece of disinformation that effectively breaks the revolution by killing the General), and Cara de Angel is then destroyed for the crime of having loved another than the President himself. The novel *is* biblical, however, in the prophetic, illuminary and apocalyptic quality of its vision—and the truth of this vision, like that of the anonymous voice in the cell, lies less in its witnessing function, as a depiction of the President's society, than in its denunciative force, as a condemnation of universal complicity in the presidential system. As witness, the novel is flawed, in spite of its access to so much knowledge, by its failure to know what goes on in the President's mind, a failure that puts it back among the voices in the dark, as part of the network of gossip and stories that surround the President. In this respect, the text can only be a kind of General Canales (to the extent that its rivalry with presidential knowledge makes it an alter ego of the President) or a sort of Cara de Angel (demonstrating that to oppose the system with insufficient knowledge is either to be complicitous with the system or to be destroyed by it).

But the novel's dubious status as witnessing discourse has an important effect on the reader, and it is here that its denunciative capacity makes itself felt. Because of the novel's failure of knowledge, and notably its inability to know what the President is thinking, the reader is led to attempt to *make good the deficiency* by supplying speculations as to the President's thoughts and motivations. To the extent that these speculations are necessarily unreliable, the reader is put into the position of the President's subjects; but to the extent that the reader is led to identify with "el Señor Presidente" himself—as the black box in the system where information is converted into power—the reader is led to enact a certain involvement with the machine of power itself. To be *part* of the system is to *be* the system: the reader is drawn into the system of fascination and fear and simultaneously occupies, by identification, the seat of power—while the novel consequently enacts the truth of universal complicity itself, because its very effort at truth-telling has made it, in this way, a mediator of presidential power.

This double effect is never clearer than in the chapter devoted to the President's mail. It is impossible not to read the information here with the President's eyes, and to draw the conclusions the President might draw. But simultaneously, the reader is forced to equate the novel he is reading with the information supplied to the President—to read it, too, with presidential eyes and to imagine the presidential uses to which it might be put—as if it, too, were simultaneously part of the President's mail. The narrative that transmits fascination with the President, as part of the system of unreliable, uncontrollable discourse that presidential unknowability generates, thus comes to function also, in the eyes of the "reader-as-President," as part of the information on which the President relies, like the gossip that is recycled into his mailbag.

Were it not for the epilogue, indeed, the whole novel would be retrospectively converted into a report to the President by the fact that its final pages conflate the novel's account of Cara de Angel's imprisonment with the report made to the President by the Chief of Secret Police on the final trick played on the favorite, and his death. The two documents merge, and the final words of the final chapter are: "Es cuanto tengo el honor de informar al Señor Presidente" (293) ["This is all I have the honor to impart to the President" (283)]. *El Señor Presidente* is information addressed to el Señor Presidente; but el Señor Presidente, in *this* case, is identical with the novel's reader, whose complicity in the presidential system is thus inescapably enacted. Thus, the novel's attempt at witnessing resolves into an enactment of universal complicity, making inescapable the denunciatory realization that both it and its reader are ineluctably part of the presidential system.

It is a moot point, I think, whether the epilogue can be said to change this reading situation, or whether it merely refigures it. Carvajal is dead, but his two cell-companions, the student and the sacristan of the night of speech in the dark, have been released. They watch as a string of prisoners goes by: one of the turns of the blind goddess's wheel has made it a crime to demolish the cathedral porch, an action originally undertaken as a gesture of support for the President. . . . Relieved as they are to be "free" (cf. "libres," 295 [285]— the word comes as a surprise in the context of this novel), their fascinated sympathy nevertheless relates them to the prisoners, and one—the student—cannot help speculating about the story behind the demolition of the porch. "¡Cállese, por Dios!" warns the other. "Eso no es cierto . . ." (294) ["Be quiet for God's sake. It's not certain" (285)]. There is an echo of Carvajal's obsessive words in the cell: "Pero no se callen; el silencio me da miedo" (205) ["But don't stop talking. I'm terrified of the silence" (197)]. It seems that the voices of those who are "free" are no less in the dark ("eso no es cierto") than those that arise in the cells; while the fear that *hushes* them on the outside is not discontinuous with the fear that causes them to *speak* on the inside.

Like the novel, in short, these voices cannot *not* speak, for they too are survivors and witnesses, but neither can they *speak* freely, since all speech is subject to the régime of dictation. Like the reader, their interest in the prisoners makes them prisoners too, and part of the system, even though they are "free": the distinction between outside and inside prison does not hold. And meanwhile, the "life" of the city goes absurdly on, as the symbolic figure of Don Benjamín, the crazy puppeteer, spews out senseless words, the shop and office workers emerge into the streets on their way home, and, while the student returns to his praying mother, the procession of prisoners continues. "Ser ellos y no ser los que a su paso se alegraban en el fondo de no ser ellos . . ." (297–98). The sentence is accurately translated: "What must it be like to be them instead of the lookers-on who are so deeply thankful not to be them" (286). But the clarity of the translation, filling in the ellipsis, misses an important ambiguity of the syntax, suggesting as it does an equivalence between "ser ellos" and "no ser ellos," between being them and not being them:

being a prisoner and being a looker-on are not fundamentally different states. For the novel has taught us, precisely, what it is like to "ser ellos," that has been its truth as a novel of witness. But the truth of being them is to know that it is impossible not to be part of the régime of dictation, the prison of discursivity that it produces. The lookers-on are prisoners too: that is the truth the novel enacts and forces the reader to enact, in its function as a voice in the dark that denounces complicity. [17]

El beso de la mujer araña, to which I now turn, does not denounce: the mode of its alliance with mediation is seduction, and its "voices in the dark" are those of the movie house as well as those that arise in prison. But, like *El Señor Presidente*, it sees that the prison is a prison of information control, to which it associates, moreover, the control of desire that we saw in *El siglo de las luces* as a function of the culture of *machismo*, regulated by the Law of the Father. As a result the oppositionality which, as a last resort, *El Señor Presidente* situates in a somewhat mythic "desire for freedom" that is readable in expressions of deluded hope or lucid despair becomes for Puig's novel a matter of central concern. But it cannot posit a (God-given?) desire for freedom that somehow escapes the system of control; rather, in a way that is crucial for the overall argument of this book, it understands freedom—such freedom as the system allows—as the possibility of changing desire within the overall constraints of the prison that seeks to control it. If there is room to maneuver even within prison, it is because seduction can operate there as the deflection of desire.

3. An Enigmatic Ending: Opposition by Appropriation

The involvement of the reader as spectator in the world of prison is enacted in *El beso de la mujer araña* even more inescapably than in *El Señor Presidente*. For where Molina tells the stories of his movies to his cellmate Valentín as an act of opposition to the conditions of prison, creating an island of "strange love" (137) [133] within the harsh carceral context, and doing it through devices of narrative seduction he has learned from the "trucos del cine" (80) ["movie tricks" (73)], the novel in turn works seductively on its reader, as the narration of a movie similar to those Molina recounts. This movie might be called "El misterio de la celda siete" ["The Mystery of Cell Seven"], as the two prisoners joke (49) [43]. But the movement between cell and cinema, mediated by storytelling, works in reverse for the novel's reader, who is introduced "por trucos del cine" *into* the world of prison and confronted with its mystery—a mystery that is first of all that of the power of love in the world of death and of the paradoxical "inner" freedom enjoyed by the prisoners within their cell. But it is also one that questions, as I will argue, the innocence of looking (what

the reader-as-movie-goer does) when prison is itself defined as a place of surveillance. Like the last of Molina's own movies, a story of star-crossed lovers,
the novel *El beso*, doubling as the movie "El misterio . . ." we are watching,
has a "final . . . enigmático" (263) ["enigmatic ending" (259)] (cf. again 284
[281]); but it is doubly enigmatic. Thematically, the "external" victory of carceral horror, in the death of Molina and the cruel torture of Valentín, is balanced by the strength each has learned from the example of the other; while
rhetorically, the act of reading is situated in terms of loving sympathy with
the characters, but of complicity with the structures of oppression.

The hero of Molina's movie mingles the words of a bittersweet bolero with
the graffiti on a barroom table, "llena de inscripciones de corazones, nombres
y también groserías" (234) ["full of carved hearts, names, dirty words too"
(231)]; and the novel, at the end, has the same sweet sadness as the bolero
and the movie, the same openness to interpretation as the graffiti. What we,
as readers, cannot do is dismiss its love plot as sentimental manipulation and
clichéd pathos, for what Molina has taught Valentín and the novel its readers
is, precisely, that kitschy popular culture (B-grade movies, boleros and tangos)
has its value. In prison, it is an aid to survival "because . . . locked in this cell,
what else can I do than think of nice things, so as not to go nuts, right?" (85)
[78], as Molina puts it and as Valentín rapidly comes to acknowledge. But
also, schmaltziness is not incompatible with powerful verities: "es que los
boleros dicen montones de verdades" (143) ["it's that boleros contain tremen-
dous truths" (139)], as the reader in particular, following the characters, is led
to see.

On the other hand, however, Valentín's early point—that too much reliance
on glamorous illusion is itself a form of madness—retains all its validity:
"te podés volver loco no sólo desesperándote . . . sino también alienándote
(. . .)" (85) ["you can go crazy not just out of despair . . . but also from
alienating yourself" (79)]; and the novel also allies itself with Valentín's more
analytic mode of vision—glib as his own (Marxist and Freudian) clichés are—
in such a way as to maintain a distance of its own from the kitschy material it
simultaneously incorporates and whose truths it exploits. As a result, popular
culture is being assumed by the novel, but not mindlessly so, since we are
simultaneously instructed not to despise its exploitive kitsch and to acknowledge its function as an ideological opiate. In other words, it is being *appropriated*, and turned to purposes that are demystifying. There can be no
temptation, for example, for any reader to conclude smugly that Molina's and
Valentín's love redeems the dire reality of state terrorism and a society under
dictation, or that a few remembered movies from the forties can counter-
balance the realities of carceral existence. But the same reader is invited to see
that such love can have an oppositional value that is real, just as exploitive
movies and sentimental love songs can be strengthening and instructive.

In short, we are invited as readers to concur in an ironic view of things that is however not a negation but a lucid acknowledgment of losses and gains, pluses and minuses, strengths and limitations, possibilities and constraints. This irony, if one will, is the "graffiti" aspect of the writing that it mingles with its strong deployment of "bolero" pathos. But its central metaphor for such a matching of differences and such an acknowledgment of incompatibilities is love itself, for the coming together of Molina and Valentín does not involve the submerging of one personality or identity in the other, but a mutual and equal recognition of each other's integrity and difference. Such a recognition does not require of either partner anything comparable to Esteban's heroic self-*sacrifice* (his denial of everything he knows about the Revolution so as to permit Sofía's pursuit of ideals he knows to be deluded), but rather a mutual self-*effacement*—an ability to change by learning from the other— that does not preclude the other's recognition of one's own truth and identity. Esteban's self-sacrifice can be read, in the end, as an act of paradoxical self-affirmation; Valentín and Molina, learning to recognize the other without denying themselves, achieve a mediated identity, through recognizing the other who simultaneously validates themselves. In this, they provide a model of the text-reader relation, and of the mutual interaction it entails, as I understand it in this book.

If this relation is a representation of love as a positive—because mutually— ironic practice, it is also significant that love in this case is not heterosexual— as is the love of Esteban and Sofía or Cara de Angel and Camila—but homosexual. As two men, the prisoners are in a position, it seems, to overcome the implications of power and submission—or "dictation"—inherent in the gender-roles characteristic of an intensely homosocial and patriarchal social formation; so that, although they embody those roles, the *macho* Valentín and the *loca* Molina—the young man imbued with the values of "virility" and the silly queen in love with glamor—succeed in achieving a relation of genuine equality, based on mutual acceptance, affection, and respect.[18] They do not transcend the roles, but they make them work *for* them—in short, they *appropriate* them into their love.

An emblem of this is that, although each of them has a full name—"Luis Alberto Molina" and "Valentín Arregui Paz"—the novel adopts what is at first sight the peculiar usage of referring to the queen by his (patriarchal) last name and to the tough young resistance-fighter by his (affectionate) first name. Each is named, in other words, as the other would name him, so that the reader who accepts this odd usage (which becomes the novel's norm), simultaneously adopts Valentín's way of viewing Molina, according to the style of male equality, and Molina's way of viewing Valentín, in the more feminine mode of intimacy. . . . This reader is thus put in the position of experiencing the exchange of identity that comes of the two prisoners' love; but what goes with that double view of the characters is necessarily an ironic point of view, since it implies simultaneous acceptance on the reader's part of Molina's "uncritical," "irresponsible"—but not unconscious or mystified—enthusiasm for everything he finds "divine" (which includes a Nazi propaganda movie), and of Valentín's much colder, "objective" and "realistic" habits of clear-eyed social analysis.

As a conquest of equality not constrained by the gender roles that enact relations of power and submission, the "extraño amor" of the two surely functions as an allegory of gay liberation, in the terms suggested by the novel's long, didactic footnotes which, in their latter part, survey the emergence of an understanding of homosexual desire as capable of opposing the power relations characteristic of patriarchal society because it no longer imitates them.[19] We can note straightaway that this result presupposes an evolution both on the part of the "gay" partner (Molina in his feminine role must learn to expect and require social respect) and on the part of the heterosexual partner (Valentín must break free of the inhibitions and repressions of *machismo*, and in the first instance of his homophobia). There can, in short, be no gay liberation without a concurrent liberation of heterosexual men. Thus Molina learns from Valentín's obdurate male pride a pride of his own, a new dignity; but Valentín learns from Molina's enthusiasms that it is possible and necessary to "let go," and to accept emotional realities.

That this can be done without revolution—that the constrictive gender roles do not have to be left behind, or sublated in a dialectical *Aufhebung*, but can instead be appropriated into a love that realizes an ironic coexistence—is a major part of the novel's oppositional point. Thus, when Molina speaks Valentín's language towards the end (quoting Pascal) to *instruct* him that there are reasons of the heart that reason cannot know, he adds immediately in his own self-mocking, gender-marked dialect: "¡Chupate esa mandarina!" (263) ["What a little pedant this queen is!" (259)]. A moment later, Valentín gruffly spells out for Molina, in his own didactic and sloganeering style, the recipe for Molina's new dignity: "Y prometeme otra cosa . . . que vas a hacer que te respeten. . . . Porque nadie tiene derecho a explotar a nadie." (265) ["And promise me something else . . . that you're going to make them respect you. . . . Because no one has the right to exploit anyone." (261)]. These ironies mean that the characters have not escaped from the prison of gender identity, that homosexual love and gay liberation cannot revolutionize the conditions in which homosexual love and gay liberation appear, because those conditions have made them what they are; they can be oppositional phenomena only. Something has changed (for Valentín and Molina); but that does not, in itself, change the social structures themselves in which the change appears. It means only that there is room for maneuver within them. An enigmatic ending, therefore—"Que final más enigmático, ¿verdad?" (263) ["Such an enigmatic ending, isn't it?" (259)]—but enigmatic because ironic.

Because each is an appropriative achievement, of which irony is the sign, we can say that the relation of Molina and Valentín is comparable to the novel's own appropriation of mystified and mystifying popular culture for demystifying purposes. Within the prison, from which there is no escape, this much can be achieved, that the law can sometimes be turned against itself. The phenomenon of homosexual desire in patriarchal culture is precisely a case in point. Homosociality, as Eve Sedgwick (see note 6) describes it, involves male bonding whose power rests on the exclusion of women but the enforcement of heterosexuality: homophobia, in such a system, is of a piece with misogyny. That an unwanted form of desire should emerge "between men," and as a consequence of the exclusion of women which is the centerpiece of the apparatus of control destined to regulate heterosexual desire in patriarchal interests, is profoundly ironic. It is also an appropriative phenomenon, insofar as an appropriation by definition makes use of a power structure, taking it over for "other" purposes, a structure from which, as a consequence, it cannot "free" itself. Male homosexual desire is mediated by the patriarchal system as heterosexual desire is, but its emergence is an outcome of the system's own mediations that the system fears and represses, classifying it as a deviation because it eludes the system's control.

Puig's novel carefully traces the complex mediations that produce desire "between men," showing in particular that if the homosexual is a "deviation" from heterosexual desire—Valentín's case—it is nevertheless mediated by the exclusion of women from power (an exclusion figured by the all-male environment that constitutes the prison) on which that patriarchal system of heterosexuality is grounded. Molina, as male "queen," stands for the odd *presence* of the feminine "between men," that results from the mediation of male-to-male relationships by an "excluded" feminine: for Valentín he becomes "she" who substitutes for the absent women in his life. He is of the people, like Inés, and "feminine" in tastes and behavior, like Marta (although he is neither "liberated," like Marta, nor political like Inés). But it is Valentín's curiosity about Molina's love for another absent figure, his (heterosexual) waiter-friend Gabriel, that shows the reader an initial stirring in him of sexual interest for his cellmate. If the latter's "seduction" works through his recounting movies, it also takes the form of the narrative of his friendship with Gabriel. "Mirá lo que es la vida," comments Valentín in some surprise, "voy a estár desvelado y pensando en tu novio" (78) ["See how life is, I'm going to be kept awake thinking about your boyfriend" (71)]. The all male triangularity of Molina-Gabriel-Valentín is thus superimposed on the gender-differentiated triangularity of Valentín-Marta/Inés-Molina, in which the absent mediator, furnishing in each case the indispensable middle term, suggests a relation of mutual entailment between male rivalry and the exclusion of women from power.

Mediated as it is, then, by the very arrangements that constitute the homosocial system of society—the exclusion of women and the rivalry of men "imprisoned" in a gender-identity that cuts them off from the feminine—male homosexual desire is unwelcome proof that the system that controls women by regulating heterosexual desire is vulnerable *from within*, vulnerable, that is, to homosexuality arising—*un*controllably—within the "prison" of homosociality. If one reflects that the exclusion of women from power is simultaneously the exclusion of that which *mediates* the heterosexual system (marriage is the exchange of females between males), then the emergence of a homosexual desire that is mediated by such a (mediated) system of exclusion comes to look very much like the revenge of mediation itself—the return of the repressed—on a system of "dictation" that seeks to omit it from the system even though it is essential to it.

El beso, then, is not simply reflecting the commonplace observation that homosexuality flourishes under conditions of sexual segregation. It is using prison as a metaphor for the "carceral" arrangements of homosociality, in which both men and women are damaged by the alienating gender constructions and gender relations that we see embodied, at the beginning, in the *macho* Valentín and the "feminine" Molina. But it is also suggesting, I think, that such arrangements are more vulnerable to appropriative opposition— understood as the deflection of desire within the system of power—than to forms of opposition that are less frankly allied with the realities of mediation. It is striking that both *El siglo de las luces* and *El Señor Presidente* figure oppositionality in terms of heterosexual love, the love that is *regulated* (but not repressed) in patriarchal society, as opposed to the love that is *repressed* (but not regulated) in that system. Simultaneously these two novels conceive discursive opposition either wholly or largely as a matter of witnessing: like Esteban's account of his sojourn among the barbarians, or the anonymous letters that circulate in the President's country, the novels produce themselves figuratively as eyewitness accounts. As a result, they find themselves enmeshed in the difficulties that arise from the mediated status of their discourse, and notably in that of not being able to guarantee that their witnessing will not serve the dictatorial power it seeks to oppose. But we can now note that the concept of witnessing, implying as it does the possibility of a "true," that is direct, unmediated representation of its object, shares its understanding of the function and role of discourse with dictation itself: where dictation seeks discursive fidelity as a matter of conformity to the subject, witnessing seeks it as a matter of conformity to the object of discourse. Mediated by the law of the father, heterosexual desire is an easily recuperable form of oppositionality: so, too, is testimonial discourse, itself traversed by a dream of "dictation."[20]

But mediation is the necessary precondition and ally of appropriative practices. Unmediated discourse, if such a thing could exist, would be perfectly literal and so absolutely dictatorial; it is the fact of mediation that introduces into any discursive situation the element of distance and otherness that splits what is said into "what is said" and "what is understood," and it is this possibility of understanding *otherwise* that makes appropriative (re-)interpretations possible. What systems of control consider a deviation is actually a deflection—a *clinamen*—that is inherent in the system itself. So, just as *El beso de la mujer araña* takes the discourse of the movies and deflects it towards other (novelistic) purposes, and just as Molina and Valentín take a prison cell and make it a place for love, any would-be discourse of dictation, because of its reliance on means, can be turned from itself and used in some other way. There is thus always an element of *wit* in the appropriator, whose "practical intelligence"—what the Greeks called *metis*—can see *other* possibilities in a given situation; and appropriation, as the revelation of those other, unexpected possibilities, always works—as we have seen—an irony.

Appropriative practices, with their ironic effects, are available, of course, both to the "right" and to the "left" of the political spectrum; and to the powerful as well as to the less strongly empowered. A group in Sydney can take over a billboard and, with a few strokes of a paintbrush, transform the advertizing slogan: NEW. MILD. AND MARLBORO into NEW. VILE. AND A BORE.[21] But anti-abortion groups in the United States have borrowed the political rhetoric of the civil rights movement to the advantage of (patriarchal) "family values," so that in 1989 the folk one sees on the TV screen going limp and being dragged off to police vans are mainly white and middle class. Appropriation can occur, also, with varying degrees of conscious "intent" or spontaneous "reflex"—it does not necessarily imply active individual agency. According to a fascinating study by Sander Gilman—who does not use the word "appropriation," however—psychoanalysis at its inception was, among other things, an appropriation (by generalization) of certain anti-Semitic myths current in German-speaking Europe in Freud's time[22]—surely an unconscious move on the latter's part! But when, later, psychoanalysis itself produced misogynistic discourse of its own about the "enigma" of woman, it was open to Sarah Kofman to appropriate the methods of psychoanalytic interpretation quite deliberately, and to demonstrate that the real enigma in the lectures on femininity is the psyche of Sigmund Freud himself.[23]

That "enigma" is a term used, to oppressive effect, of that which one does not understand is however a fact relevant to appropriative practices themselves, since *El beso* itself, with its "enigmatic ending," produces its appropriative figure, Molina—whose action is responsible for the enigmatic ending—as something of an "enigma" in himself. He is enigmatic, precisely, because of the difficulty for the reader of judging the degree of spontaneity and calculation that enters into his appropriative, seductive behavior: it is not possible, at any given moment, to be sure whether he *knows what he is doing*, or not; and in this respect he is a kind of "black box" in the system, or if one will, an "anti-black box" corresponding to the presidential, dictatorial "black-box" in *El Señor Presidente*. But if appropriative behavior is enigmatic at its "source," it is equally enigmatic in its outcome. For if there is irony in its revelation of unexpected "other" possibilities in a given situation, the irony of the irony is that any appropriation is itself always available to further appropriations of an undeterminable kind, to further revelations of "other" possibilities, so that any outcome is always provisional, unstable, and open. The appropriation of TV by the civil rights movement was vulnerable to reappropriation by the anti-abortionists, which in turn . . . etc. In such circumstances, there can be no "last word": the ending is always "enigmatic." The openness of Puig's novel—its "graffiti" quality—lies, then, in its acknowledgment that the changes produced at the end by Molina's appropriative behavior are themselves subject to further change. What does it mean to have achieved, briefly, one genuine relationship in a lifetime subject to temporality and death? Ironically enough, it will be Valentín who repeats: "nothing is forever" (263) [259], and Molina the appropriationist who wants to believe in permanence: "Yes, it's easy to say. But feeling it is something else" (263) [259]. But the very possibility of appropriation is evidence that *no* meaning can be "dictated" permanently and that change is therefore always possible.

It is for that reason that appropriation looks "irresponsible" to those who seek stability and definitive meanings. Valentín voices disapproval one evening of a book he is reading, according to which honesty is out of place in political action because the honest man's conception of responsibility is a constraint on him ("su concepto de responsabilidad lo impide" 104). But he goes on to point out that it was precisely *his* concept of responsibility that led him into the struggle, leaving the reader to reflect that the "dishonesty" of appropriative means is not necessarily incompatible with honesty of purpose. Valentín's own group, for instance, does not hesitate to appropriate the mails so as to send coded messages in apparently personal letters; and they do this because the authorities of the prison and the state use "means" of their own—what is delicately referred to by the Director of the prison as "los técnicos necesarios" (154) ["the necessary experts" (151)]—in order to gain their ends. The Director is hinting delicately at torture, of course—but Molina's presence in Valentín's cell is itself one of the "technical" agents employed by the system of power, since he has been planted there as an informer to try to worm out of Valentín some details about the structure and operations of his group.

Here the thematics of information control, so carefully explored in *El Señor Presidente*, joins with the thematics of sexual politics. For against the techniques of information control, there are not only the appropriative counter-techniques of Valentín and his group, but also the tactics of Molina, who does not only appropriate the movies but also deflects the techniques of information gathering, which he uses to obtain food and comfort for Valentín and thus to further his own work of seduction. Power *always* needs an agent (the group needs means of communication, the authorities need informers); but *any* agent can become a *double agent* (Valentín thoughtlessly reveals the code to Molina, the informer—but Molina the informer is using the system of information control for Valentín's comfort and protection). Further ironies accumulate, since the "agent" of information control will become, precisely, a "messenger" for the group; but the group's "messenger" remains a (now involuntary) agent of information control, since he is placed under surveillance and his message carrying may well, in the end, betray the group he thinks he is working for (even though, in the upshot, it doesn't quite do so). Both sides of the political struggle, in other words, are *taking a risk* in employing means that can be appropriated; and the novel demonstrates that the "irresponsibility" inherent in such means is an inevitable given of political activity. The appropriator's "irresponsibility," in other words, is only a realization of the uncontrollability that is the necessary corollary of all discursive relations, including the discourse of power, and including also the discourse of literature, for which Molina—as acolyte to power and double agent of resistance—is a figure.

Molina himself, however, is neither in power nor a resister, and his "irresponsibility" is that of one who has no other means of survival than those of appropriation. He is not politically unaware (he is perfectly conscious of the ideological implications of the Nazi movie he so loves, for instance); but he is politically disempowered, notably by his working-class origins and lack of education and by his marginalization as a homosexual and, worse, as a homosexual identified as a "woman." He has no option but to be opportunistic and to live by his wits, using the means provided by the power situation in which he finds himself, that is of the "prison" that is constituted, on the one hand, by the gender relations of *machismo* and on the other, by the system of information control. Part of the intertext of *El beso* is Sartre's play, *Huis Clos* [*No Exit*]; and one can see that Sartre would have treated the situation of the *macho*-stud-cum-political-activist cast into the same cell as the compliant-informer-cum-nellie-queen as an inescapable hell, as a place without room to maneuver. With his phenomenological focus on the "subject," Sartre necessarily views the "other" as the torturer of the self. But the appropriator's alliance with mediation implies the self-effacement that goes along with a recognition that there is no identity that is not other-constructed (i.e., mediated)—and the Supreme's insight in Roa Bastos that "I" is always a "He" (or a "She") is one that comes especially easily to marginalized people whose identities are so visibly constructed for them by the discourse of power.

One such as Molina, however, who is simultaneously able to efface the self and to take advantage of the mediated character of desire so as to deflect another's desire from the object decreed by the system of power, is ordinarily called a seducer. "Seduction," in other words, is the manipulation of desire when it is carried out, not to the benefit of power, but appropriatively— "playfully" or "irresponsibly"—that is, by an individual who is not strongly empowered but is making use of the means furnished by the structures of power and deflecting them to "other" purposes (purposes normally more advantageous, at least in the immediate, to that individual). Molina is a seducer in that sense. He appropriates the discourse of power (whether gender identities or the movies) in such a way as to deflect the forms of desire they construct (in this case Valentín's *macho* heterosexuality) in ways that the systems of social control necessarily define as *deviant*—deviant because their significance is oppositional.

I hope it is clear that I am not suggesting that power does not itself employ seductive techniques. In that case, however, they are less frequently called seductive, or the word "seductive" is used with less pejorative connotations. Power seduces exploitively, the disempowered seduce opportunistically and oppositionally; and the ambiguity of the traditional Don Juan figure—not the "Don Juan para machos" that is Robespierre—is that he combines the dazzling brilliance of the exploitive aristocrat with the ready wit of the marginalized outsider who survives by his wits, defining the aristocracy in consequence as a social parasite. For the appropriator as seducer is also the seducer as parasite: the deflection of desire that defines seduction is simultaneously a parasitic "taking" from the system, and one the system cannot control. Because it is uncontrollable, it is "parasitic" in the sense in which "noise" in information theory is parasitic—it is the element of disturbance that scrambles the messages and makes them "other." But, as Michel Serres has pointed out,[24] there can be no system without parasites, and parasites (the incarnations of mediation) are therefore fundamental to any system: it follows, as Serres also points out, that in any system the position of parasite is also a position of power. Serres refers in this connection to the Lion in La Fontaine, a figure of absolute monarchy; and elsewhere to politicians and theorists. We might think also of "el Señor Presidente" as the parasite of the presidential machine of information control, and by extension of Victor Hugues as the parasite of the French Revolution. But Don Juan is the best instance because his ambiguous social status demonstrates the equally ambiguous relation of seductive parasitism to power: those who exert power are parasitic, but appropriative seduction—as a taking from the system that the system cannot control—is the form of empowerment that is available to the marginalized and the disempowered, to the Molinas of this world.

To the system of control, with its own parasitic figures of power (such as el Señor Presidente) seeking to "dictate" appropriate meanings, the marginalized parasite—the appropriative, seductive "troublemaker"—is consequently the greatest enemy. Male homosexuality has that inimical status in the homosocial formation: it is the unwanted "deviation" from the forms of desire fostered by homosociality, and it is not surprising, therefore, that gay men are so frequently classified (more accurately, stigmatized) as "seducers" and their employment (when they are "out") so typically restricted to modes of information—entertainment, glamor, or (Molina's avocation) window dressing—regarded as inessential and/or parasitic. In this light, we can begin to see the underlying coherence of the double thematics of gender and of information that is deployed in *El beso*, where Molina the homosexual appropriates the system of information control at the same time that he appropriates the system of gender control. The "parasite" in the information system is the "seducer" in the gender system. But "gender" is consequently only another name for, or the other face of, information control; and indeed, information and its control—that is, ideological mystification—is exactly what gender is all about.

The prison in which Molina operates is therefore, to summarize, the prison of ideology. That is why, although all the movies recounted in the novel figure aspects of the two prisoners' situation, the crucial film in the series is the zombie movie. The living dead are workers who, having once revolted against their condition, are now condemned to hopeless pain and endless labor, under a system of absolute control in which Valentín recognizes a figure of ideological alienation, and in the first instance, of the alienation under which he himself suffers. He catches the essence of the problem in a reflective comment on the movie: "everything that's wrong with the world and that I want to change . . . is it possible that all that won't allow me to . . . behave . . . even for a single moment, like a decent human being?" (206) [202]. The problem of the zombie, then, is to change the world when it is the world that has made one what one is.

But what one *is*, in Valentín's case, is the site of a contradiction ("contradiction" being another name for "alienation")—the contradiction that arises from ideological repression. And it is in such contradiction that room for maneuver arises within the strict system of control that is the ideological prison. If Valentín feels like a zombie—"me siento como muerto" (280) ["I feel like I'm dead" (176)]—it is because he is torn between his politically correct attachment to Inés, his guerilla companion, and the desire, for which he is ashamed but which he comes to recognize as too strong to be denied, for Marta, the beautiful bourgeoise with whom he cannot share his political secrets. What will revive the zombie is therefore an acknowledgment of the love he seeks to repress: "Tengo la impresión que nada más que [Marta] me podrá revivir" (180) ["I have this notion that nothing except [Marta] could ever revive me again" (176)]. This acknowledgment of "private" emotions separate from political convictions is of a piece with Valentín's belief that the cell itself offers an area of privacy, a "desert island" that protects him from the oppressors outside:

En cierto modo estamos perfectamente libres de actuar como queremos el uno respecto al otro, ¿me explico? Es como si estuviéramos en una isla desierta. . . . Porque, sí, fuera de la celda están nuestros opresores, pero adentro no. Aquí nadie oprime a nadie. . . . (P. 206)

[In a sense we're perfectly free to behave however we choose with respect to one another, am I making myself clear? It's as if we were on some desert island. . . . Because, well, outside of this cell we may have our oppressors, yes, but not inside. . . . (P. 202)]

This version of the paradox of the prisoners' freedom is, of course, an ideological contradiction indeed: the Marxist analyst believes, like the bourgeois intellectual he also is, in a realm of privacy that escapes political control. But this contradiction is also what makes possible for Valentín the move that will "save" him from his ideological zombiehood. Molina knows, because he is its agent, the extent to which the system of information control penetrates the cell; but Valentín's deluded and contradictory belief in privacy is the alibi, or at least the rationalization, that enables him to divert his love for Marta—the desire that he is ideologically repressing—into homosexual love for Molina. Ideological contradiction, in short, has an enabling role to play.

But the other enabling factor in bringing Valentín to this point has been Molina's own deployment of "womanish wiles" as a seducer. Molina, too, is an ideological zombie, locked into a gender role—he is, precisely, the "zombie woman" of the movie, as in other cases he is the panther woman or the spider woman. But he is simultaneously—as always—the movie's heroine, who in this case is the male lead's second wife, a living person who introduces the disturbing element of love into the oppressed island of the zombies and in due course frees it from thralldom. The motif of the two wives, as alter egos of each other, thus signifies, not ideological contradiction in Molina's case, but the alternative ways that one may view the ideological construction of his identity: as zombie and as liberator. Molina does not need to distance himself from the alienating gender identity that is his—that of the queen—because it is precisely this womanish identity that makes him so adept at appropriation, and hence the seductive disturber of the whole system. He is not divided by ideological contradiction, like the *macho* Valentín; rather he is the product of the system's own contradictions, and indeed their embodiment. As the mediator the system needs to deny, he is produced *by* the system *as that which disturbs it.* And so, if he can substitute so effectively, in Valentín's psyche, for Marta, it is because he is not really a dangerous panther woman who destroys men but, as Valentín assures him, the seductive spider woman, "la mujer araña, que atrapa a los hombres en su tela" (265) ["the spider woman, who traps men in her web" (260)]. In saying this, Valentín is thinking of Molina as the spinner of glamorous tales, the appropriator of the charm of the movies; he cannot know how apt the image is for Molina's *other* seductive activity, weaving the net of duplicity that deceives the Director into providing the food and comforts that will then, in turn, seduce Valentín's hunger for maternal affection. The deflection of desire Molina works per medium of the movies, making himself the spider woman who can replace Marta in Valentín's affections, has as its counterpart the deflection of desire that turns the Director's desperate hunger for information into the means of deviating Valentín's no less desperate hunger for emotional satisfaction—figured, of course, by his appetite for food—from Marta to himself.

The implication is that Molina's seductiveness—his own rival deployment of necessary "techniques"—works for two reasons. The first is that it is able, as I have said, to appropriate the system of power (information control and gender identity) to purposes the system knows not of. But the second is that the system itself produces a *need for the seducer* at the same time that it produces the seducer—a need figured by Valentín's unsatisfied hunger for affection, his alienating contradictions, the prison of his self-oppressing personality. Without these, Molina's wiles would be without effect. But *given* these conditions, they function better than the "techniques" of the authorities. For Valentín is able to resist torture, and he reveals nothing of note, *through* Molina, to the authorities; but *to* Molina he makes a full confession, not so much of his revolutionary activities, but of the prison like world in which he lives because it is that of his own oppressed identity. In other words, he has a need to *talk* that is of a piece with his need for *love*; and like his need for love, it works against repression: in the end, Molina's "seductive" role consists only of offering occasions, and some encouragement, for such a confession.

The movie narratives are one such occasion, since they foster identification with the characters and their situations and, through identification, reflective commentary on their meaning: what the prisoners refer to as their *cocheca*, or needlework—their mutual "embroiderings" on the subject matter of the film (29) [23]. Another occasion of outlet is the symbolic episode of Valentín's dysentery (induced, ironically enough, by the prison apparatus, in *its* effort to soften him up and extract information). Molina is content to offer care and motherly support, along with the advice to *let it all out*. "Estoy largando todo líquido," as Valentín says; and Molina urges him: "Aflójate bien, largá todo que después yo lavo la sabana" (144) ["Relax and let it all come out, and afterwards I'll wash the sheet" (140)].

But the moment of greatest figurative importance, since it pinpoints Valentín's abandonment of the *macho* desire to control, is the deflection of his decision to *dictate* a letter for Marta, for the letter dictated to Molina turns into a confession addressed to him, a confession of Valentín's divided emotions and confused identity, his loneliness and fear: "debajo de la yema de los dedos lo que siento es el frío del miedo a la muerte, en los huesos ya siento ese frío . . ." (184) ["beneath the tips of my fingers what I feel is the chill of the fear of death, and in my marrow I feel it . . . " (179)]. This is exactly the "me siento muerto" of the zombie, as the prisoner of an alienating, ideologically constructed and oppressive identity; and Molina's response will be a symbolic washing, some sort of absolution perhaps, or the laving of a newborn child. For his alleged "seduction" has been in fact a maieutic operation: appropriative certainly, but not exploitive, it has had the force of an education. And this is the model to recall when we consider the novel's own appropriative practices, and its own seductions of the reader.

But meanwhile, the sign that the "extraño amor" of the two prisoners is not so much founded on an exploitation (a "seduction" in the pejorative sense) but arises rather out of the oppressions of gender identity and information control as their own inevitably oppositional product, is what has already been described as the ironic crisscross of identities the two lovers achieve, such that no identity dominates while neither is sacrificed. Its limitations, however, have also been already mentioned: the strength each derives from the memory of the other's love serves them in good stead, as Valentín takes refuge in comforting but morphine-induced dreams after undergoing terrible torture, and as Molina emerges into the world to command a new respect but also to die in a failed attempt to contact Valentín's group. The novel's final image—that of morphine administered to a suffering prisoner—expresses powerfully both how appreciable is the comfort the two achieve, and how illusory the hope that it can abolish the carceral conditions in which they exist. The imagery of desert islands and private cells can perhaps be read as figuring the "distance" that mediation introduces into all discursive situations and hence the measure of freedom to maneuver that results; it corresponds, in that sense, to something that is real and positive. But there is so much irony in Valentín's mistaking of a prison cell for a private place that the thrust of the novel's comment is unmistakable: as in *El Señor Presidente* the theme of the paradoxical freedom enjoyed by prisoners is in coexistence with that of prison as the tomb of the living dead, "la tumba viva," and the relation of the two can only be the "enigmatic" one of ironic coexistence.

But the difference between the novel's maieutic operation and that performed by Molina lies precisely in this ironic and enigmatic vision. The characters achieve their love through Valentín's stark and terrifying comprehension of what constitutes the prison of his identity; but the reader takes cognizance of a love story that is set in prison—one that necessarily, therefore, has a "final . . . enigmático." Where love is what the prisoners achieve, out of the circumstances of imprisonment, the reader is led from their love to an understanding of the nature of the imprisonment in which it occurs. The reader's education is, however, like Valentín's in one key respect: it is an education in *seeing*, since readerly desire is deflected from the "scopophilia" of movie viewing (the movie in this case being "El misterio de la celda siete") to a vision of prison. But this "vision" is in turn the "liberating" realization that in a society under surveillance "looking" is not an innocent activity and is itself constitutive of the prison. Where Valentín realizes that his prison is that of his own self-oppressive gender identity, the reader comes to see something similar, which is the inseparability of the reading "gaze" from the systems of information "control" that make us all prisoners. It is just that, where in a sense the characters invent the space of the movies within the space of their prison, the reader discovers the space of prison through the experience the novel gives of the space of the movies. But the reader is no less seduced into becoming educated (into a self-education) than Valentín; and the methods employed by the novel are no less appropriative than the practices of Molina. In both cases, it is our love of the movies that is put to "other" uses. Puig's postmodernism, indeed, resides in his implicit definition of art as an appropriative practice; and in *El beso de la mujer araña* there is—with the exception of paratextual features—no part of the text that is not "citational." Molina, of course, is cited retelling movies and quoting boleros; the two prisoners are cited in their conversations—whether discussing practical matters, commenting on movies, discussing how things are, or making love—but so too, on the one hand, are (some of) their inner thoughts and private fantasies, and on the other, the conversations and official reports of prison officers and surveillance agents in the carceral context. Where the novel thus appropriates the resources of mass culture and the documents of political control ("imitating" Molina's own double appropriation of movies and the system of information control), it also taps an extremely rich literary intertext, including the subgenre of the epistolary novel (for the example of its appropriative techniques and of its ironic deployment of multiple perspectives), the collage techniques invented by literary and artistic modernism, and of course the long tradition of modern carceral writing, from Silvio Pellico through Byron and Stendhal, Wilde and

Gramsci, to Sartre and Jacobo Timerman.[25] In this tradition, *El Señor Presidente* occupies a particularly seminal position by virtue of the narrative techniques it explores in its "Voices in the Dark" and "Presidential Mailbag" chapters ["Habla en la sombra" and "El parte al Señor Presidente"].

But the bulk of the novel is occupied, on the one hand, by the movie narratives told by Molina and on the other by an "objective," "scholarly" voice that takes over in the lengthy footnotes which appropriate the discourse of knowledge and which, with one exception, are concerned with sociological and psychoanalytic and, in due course, liberationist theories of homosexuality. In particular, a view—attributed to one Anneli Taube, presumably a fictive reference[26]—is presented of male and female homosexuality as a would-be "revolutionary" nonconformity (a rejection of the male gender role by men, and of the female role by women) that, however, has no option in patriarchy but to "imitate" what it is rejecting (the homosexual man has no model other than female submissiveness, the lesbian "imitates" male aggressiveness); and the feminist critique of such gender roles in the sixties is therefore presented as the point of departure for a more genuine social revolution in which the new "frentes de liberación homosexual" (211) [214] would have their place. This final footnote thus brings us, in an important sense, to the point at which the "movie" of Valentín's and Molina's relation itself begins, since it will be Valentín's role to introduce Molina to the feminist critique of gender roles (which he appears to have learned from Marta), while Molina will carry out in Valentín the feminist liberation that the notes refer to as being the most urgent, that of "la 'mujer' que cada hombre lleva encerrada en los calabozos de su propia psiquis" (200) ["the 'woman' every man keeps locked inside the dungeons of his own psyche" (196)]. Footnotes and movie, in this way, work thematically in harmony one with the other.

But, like the difference between the two prisoners—a difference of class, style, culture and gender identification—the stylistic contrast between the two blocks of prose is extreme. And since Molina is identified with the "trashy" but seductive movies, the style of the footnotes—the "neutral" style current in the social sciences—identifies them with Valentín, the former political science student with his knowledge of psychoanalysis and his habits of "serious" reading. Although some of the notes are placed, it seems, at random, it cannot be coincidental in this respect that the first of them responds (66) [59] to Valentín's own first stirring of human interest in Molina and the "gente de [s]us inclinaciones" ["people of (his) inclination"]. They thus represent the contributions of knowledge and analysis—Valentín's intellectual strengths—as opposed to the survival skills, the seductive techniques and the "montones de verdades" demonstrated by Molina and his movies. As a result, they have the oppressive and alienating quality—like others of Valentín's heavy-handed analyses—of that which objectifies human experience (the implied definition of homosexuality as gender "confusion" is particularly egregious); alongside of Molina's courage and wit, his wisdom and caring, his ability to conjure a form of happiness out of the most adverse conditions, their contribution seems dry, pedantic, alienating, and negligible—almost irrelevant.

But in a text that situates homosexuality itself as the return of the social repressed and identifies it with the appropriations and seductions of the parasite, we do well not to undervalue the role of footnotes—that is, the place in the text that is itself conventionally classified as marginal and parasitic but in which, precisely, the text's own repressions can return—and in particular the role of footnotes about homosexuality. Indeed, just as the analytic, self-oppressing and oppressive *macho* comes together with the intuitive, spontaneous (and also self-oppressing) seducer in an unlikely love (is not the "strangeness" of this "extraño amor" precisely the uncanniness that marks the return of the repressed?), so the novel's own juxtaposition of seductive storytelling and oppressive scholarly prose can be seen as working an ironic strangeness of its own, and one whose connotations are not at all negative. The reader who is slightly repelled by this dull prose is certainly led to realize that the scientific discourse on homosexuality could do with a lot of what Valentín finally gains, something like a loving understanding and appreciation of Molina's humanity. But it is also clear that Molina needs something that Valentín finally teaches him, the ability to analyze his social situation and the empowerment that the discourse of knowledge—as embodied in the notes—can give.

Reading *El beso*—its "movie" and its footnotes combined—is thus something like living both sides of the love affair that constitutes "El misterio de la celda siete." In the novel, each of the characters tends to identify only with one character or group in the movies Molina recounts, Molina always with the heroine, Valentín with the psychoanalyst in the panther-woman movie, the son in the motor-racing movie, the zombies, etc. Even in the final movie, with its enigmatic ending, and in which the two principals act in ways that are deeply and mutually empathetic, the identities and the identifications (Molina and the singer, Valentín and the journalist) remain separate. But the reader of the novel itself, who may initially favor one or another of the characters, is rapidly forced into a double identification, if only because identification with the one—Molina or Valentín—means discovery of the validity, integrity, and humanity of the other's style, point of view, and way of being, with all their deficiencies and limitations. This miming of the growing sympathy and mutual understanding between the two prisoners themselves is one way in which the education of the reader is effected; and it implies that, in reading the novel, one can afford neither to skip the dull footnotes (so as to wallow in the glam-

orous movies) nor to despise the trashy movies (and over-value the intellec-
tualism of the notes).

But the reader who gives due weight to the footnotes and to the story of
Molina's seduction is also necessarily led to make the connection between the
novel as love story and the novel as an account of metaphoric imprisonment,
that is, between the image in the footnotes of the woman imprisoned in the
dungeons of the male psyche and the imprisonment of the female-identified
male, Molina, and the self-imprisoning *macho*(>masculus), Valentín, in the
cells of a dictatorial social system which their love opposes. Such a reader
cannot be content with reading only "El misterio de la celda siete" (with viewing the "movie" about Valentín and Molina), but must also read *El beso de la
mujer araña* as a whole (movie and footnotes), and in doing so go beyond the
movie the characters live out to an understanding of the carceral society that
is its context. The scenes that move out of the cell to the Director's office, to
the streets in which Molina's every movement is followed, and the infirmary
in which the tortured Valentín lies, all have the function of making it impossible for the reader to swallow Valentín's convenient belief in the privacy of
the cell, of the isolation of "la celda siete" from the oppression "outside."

But in this respect the reader's education is completed in a particularly
significant way by the all but final chapter, in which, after Molina's release,
the novel specifically transforms the metaphor of reading as movie viewing
into the metaphor of reading as social surveillance. Reading (of) Molina's
movements around Buenos Aires through the eyes of the surveillance team,
one is led first of all to reflect on the extraordinary power and extension of a
system that penetrates the private lives of each and any citizen (not only
Molina but everyone he comes in contact with, his mother and relations, his
friends Lolo and Gabriel, his own or Gabriel's employers, etc.). But reading
through the eyes of the spies, one is also led to read *with* those eyes, and to
see Molina as they must see him: without sympathy (as perhaps Valentín
may initially have viewed him), rather scornfully (we are reminded that he is
"just" a little gay window dresser who goes to the movies a lot and is devoted
to his mother), but above all as an *enigma*.

To the spies, anything Molina says may be a code, anything he does may
be part of his mission to contact the guerilla group. As readers, we know that
most of what he says and does is entirely innocent behavior, and we are in a
position to interpret and understand much that remains mysterious to the
police (his standing at the window looking in the direction of the prison, for
instance). But as readers with the eyes of police spies, we are forced to reflect
also that, throughout the novel, Molina has been an enigma to us also. There
has been, for instance, the difficulty I have referred to of making sense of his
seductive behavior: to what extent is it voluntary and calculated? And how

much is spontaneous and instinctive in his practices, techniques or tactics? But more generally also, to the probably educated and middle-class reader of a high-cultural book such as *El beso*, to a reader who has nine chances in ten, statistically speaking, of being straight, the character of Molina is enigma itself because he is the reader's other. We cannot and do not get "inside" him, a fact that is underlined rather than contradicted by the one episode in which we are admitted into the self-pitying film he fantasizes to himself. Molina's enigma is the enigma of the homosexual, the enigma of the working class, the enigma of "practical intelligence" and *metis*. His is the enigma of seduction, of appropriation, of opposition—that is, of everything we cannot *theorize* (etymologically, everything that resists our *look*). For what we call enigmatic is what we do not understand; what we do not understand, however—as the novel teaches us—is that with which we cannot produce an exchange of identity, that which we cannot love—as Molina and Valentín love each other—and from which we are *distanced*. We thus reproduce with respect to Molina the gesture of Freud defining (objectifying) "woman" as enigma; but the novel turns the tables on this gesture, as Sarah Kofman does Freud's, by making the conclusion inescapable that what produces the enigma that is Molina is our own lack of love and the distance produced by our gaze. In the (movie) theater of theory, he is a prisoner of our looking as surely as he is the object of the police surveillance through whose eyes, in chapter 15, we are forced to *see* him.

The seductions of *El beso de la mujer araña*—the textual webspinning that justifies the title as much as Molina's own—thus work in two ways. Through the seduction of identification, the reader is drawn into the mystery and strangeness of love; through the education in spectatorhood the novel gives us, we are obliged to face the implication that as readers we are part of the prison. We are, in short, simultaneously prisoners with Molina and Valentín, enjoying the comforts of love and the empowerment of understanding, and officials in the jail, like the Director and the surveillance team. If the "mystery" of cell seven ends enigmatically, it is finally because each of these roles is inseparable from the other: if we need love it is because we imprison ourselves and one another; but our love entails an education in (not an escape from) what imprisons us, including our self-imprisonment. "¿Qué final más enigmático?"

That, I think is the final(?) irony of this intricately ironic novel. It works to make the oppositional gesture of *El beso* significantly different from the witnessing ambitions of *El siglo de las luces* and *El Señor Presidente*, in spite of evident similarities with the latter novel particularly. Puig's novel, as a maieutic text, does not tell "how it is," does not dictate its vision, and does not adopt a denunciative tone. It leads us, like Valentín, to an act of self-recognition, a recognition of *what we knew* but could not acknowledge. In that recognition we see that we are ourselves—again like Valentín—*both* victims of the carceral system *and* its administrators. As prisoners we are in desperate need of comfort and empowerment; but there can be no ultimate liberation unless and until we cease to be ourselves agents of oppression and sites of self-oppression. The content of this recognition is not essentially different from the lesson of *El Señor Presidente;* but here there are no condemnatory soothsayers, because what we have learned is what we already knew but needed to be *seduced* into discovering. And the implication of that knowledge is that, like Valentín, we must change the nature of our alienating and self-alienating desire. But to acknowledge *that* is already to have changed our desire.[27]

Two further comments need to be made. First, these lessons have particular relevance to, and make a particularly chastening comment on, a scholarly book that seeks to understand, through critical analysis, the phenomenon of oppositionality—defined from the start as that which resists and escapes definition, a form of know-how that eludes theorization—in short, an "enigma." How is this book's project to be understood, in the light of what we have learned? Is it a function of *surveillance*, part of the attempt on the part of the prison administrators that we are, to control the prisoners that we also are, by converting their (our) spontaneous oppositionality into "information?" Or is it rather to be understood as an *irony*, something similar to the juxtaposition in the novel of Molina's brilliant storytelling and the plodding analyses of the footnotes, or even to the kind of strange love the two prisoners achieve? To the extent that my enterprise *does* qualify as the latter—but I fear it is clearly both an ironic and an oppressive move, and that that is the deepest irony—I hope that my reader will give some credit to the idea, prompted by *El beso,* that such an irony can be a product of love, and indeed its sign.

Second, however little we may be able to understand the practice of oppositionality, what can be learned from *El beso de la mujer araña* is important. It tells us that the world can be changed—not revolutionized, not even changed dramatically, but changed a little, changed locally, and perhaps changed more globally by an accumulation of small changes—and that it can be changed, not by dictation, but by changing our desires. Desires can be changed because they are mediated by power: being mediated, they are subject to the operations of appropriation and seduction—operations that are not exploitive or violent when their effect is maieutic, and when the deflection of desire results from a self-education, an awareness of the damage done, to ourselves and to others, by the desires that are controlled by power. I do not mean by this that the lesson of *El beso* is that all heterosexual males should become homosexuals; but that desire is the area of control in which there is enough "give," enough "play," enough room for maneuver, for change to occur.

Emerging, then, from a reading of situational self-figuration in oppositional texts that has extended over three lengthy chapters, it is time to attempt a summary and a conclusion. The key words might be irony, conversion, and, as we have just seen, desire. My study of La Fontaine demonstrated that textual oppositionality resides in the form of readability that is irony, a readability that has its own irony in the fact that its power to oppose turns out to be a manifestation of the power it seeks to oppose. In the melancholic texts of Nerval and Aquin, irony is "converted," however, as a result of the "disappearance" of self consonant with the insight that *I am the other*, into an appropriative practice that functions as an appeal for the conversion of the reader—a conversion from the position of alienating other to that of an understanding, cooperative, complicitous, and therefore symmetrically "self"-effacing other capable of mediating the text's oppositional identity. The focus in writing "under dictation"—not only in Puig, but also in Carpentier and Asturias—is on love as a metaphor of oppositionality and, hence, as a manifestation of the mediated relationship that is exemplified in reading. Here, then, the problematics of desire is to the fore: desire's complicities with the structures of power are acknowledged; but the very acknowledgment of those alienating complicities is understood, already clearly in Asturias but in a more developed thematic form in Puig, as itself the sign of the emergence of an "other" desire. It constitutes a change in the reader, in response to a seductive appropriation of the discourse of power on the part of the text; but it is itself a desire for change. A theory of oppositional reading that attempts, however loosely, to formalize the knowledge gleaned from these texts must therefore find the syntax that converts (the reader's production of) textual irony into an appeal for readerly "conversion" and identifies that conversion as a seductive deflection of desire capable of producing change.

Conclusion: Room for Maneuver

It is possible now to affirm the idea I foreshadowed at the start, that oppositionality in literary narrative can be described as the "place" where an irony works (as) a seduction. Textual irony is the trope of opposition because it is one of the major tropes of reading, and as such an enactment of the implications for the production of meaning of discursive mediation—without "reading" there can be no ironic implication, just literal discourse. But reading brings about change because, again as a function of mediation, it produces the text as the seductive occasion for a deflection of desire, a *clinamen* resulting from what is on the reader's part an act of self-recognition, involving the emergence of a desire repressed by the codes of control. The text thus mediates a shift in the forms of desire mediated by the structures of power.

So, if there is room for maneuver in the universe of discourse—the world that constitutes human "reality"—it arises because of the essentially ironic fact that no discourse can "dictate" its meanings absolutely. From that fact, two shifts arise, each the product of reading: discourse always has the potential, realized by reading, to mean other than it says (it is always open to interpretation); but also, the act of reading that produces discourse, in this sense, as ironic, has the power similarly to produce, within the socially constructed identity of the reader, an equivalent *emergence of otherness* that shifts the nature of readerly desire. As Lyotard puts it,[1] there is always "moyen de moyenner," a way to mediate; and reading, understood as that which operates this double shift, is consequently that which mediates change. But *how* does it mediate between the ironic production of meaning that is one aspect of oppositionality and the shift in desire occasioned by the seductive text that is the other?

In literary theory, the term traditionally used to designate the kind of change that is brought about by reading is *influence*. But oddly, "influence" has largely been conceived as a relation between authors and/or between texts. Influence as the kind of change that cultural texts of all sorts (not just literary ones) can bring about in desire is a topic that has been left to moralists, who have of course understood the deflection of desire as a deviation from legitimacy, and so have fulminated (in former times) against the pernicious influence of the theater or of novels, or (in our own times) against the supposed depredations of TV or pornography. Because of the negative implications "influence" has in moralistic discourse, the usual gesture is to attribute its effects to populations other than those to which the moralist belongs, and described as weak and vulnerable: the class of servant girls, or adolescents, or whatever. And not surprisingly, where literary theories of influence now tend—under the "influence" of the work of Harold Bloom[2]—to employ a vocabulary of "misreading" and "swerves" that acknowledges the effect of mediation (its joint effect as a misreading that shifts desire), the moral condemnation of influence relies heavily on a theory of "dictation." Moralists, who want their own words to be "respected," conceive of people being affected by their reading or viewing matter through the kind of direct action of the one on the other that was once attributed to the "influence" of the constellations on human affairs. Indeed, it is from astrology that the term "influence" itself derives.

My argument is that there is no relation that is not mediated, and that influence should be defined as the effect of a (mediated) misreading that itself mediates a deflection of desire. What I am influenced by does not change "me" (for what is "me?"); but it changes "my" sense of the desirable, and to that extent—as Deleuze and Guattari rightly insist[3]—my "production" of the real. But this will happen in a way that depends in the first instance on the overall "landscape" of desire—that is, the economy of repression—in which I undertake my reading and the influence occurs; with the result that the effects of influence cannot be predicted from knowledge of the "influencing" text, as they would be in a "dictation" theory. This is the case not only because there can be no unmediated knowledge of the influencing text in the first place, on which to base such a prediction, but also because the effects of influence arise from the context of reading in which the "influencing" writing finds itself. A simple example will make this clear. Any reader of this book who also knows *Story and Situation* will see that there has been a "swerve" in my sense of what constitutes critical desirability, that which it is desirable for a critic to do. That swerve can be attributed in part to my reading, in or around 1982, of Michel de Certeau's *Arts de faire* (since translated as *The Practice of Everyday Life*).[4] But *Room for Maneuver* is unlike *Arts de faire* in a number of significant ways: it represents a "misreading" of the de Certeau volume, and that is because the "swerve" my (mis)reading of de Certeau mediated began in a different place: something like the "formalism" I still largely subscribed to (even while criticizing it) in *Story and Situation*. That formalism represented the "landscape" of desirability in which the "influence" of de Certeau occurred, as could be deduced from the fact that my readings in *Room for Maneuver* continue in some degree to rely on the "models" of reading that were theorized in the earlier volume.

Similarly, all teachers know that the "influence" attributed to them by students (who will sometimes say, dramatically, that such and such a course "changed their life") tends to be something they themselves scarcely recognize, or do not recognize at all, as corresponding to their own pedagogical "project." The change reported by the student is a result not of the teacher's "dictation," but of the student's own *self*-education. But that self-education finds its necessary occasion in the *readability* of the teacher's discourse, a readability that (ironically) produces education itself as a *misreading* of pedagogical discourse—a misreading that in turn mediates a change in the student's desiring "landscape" and so constitutes the teacherly discourse as seductive.

In chapter 1, I proposed a distinction between the "narrative function" and the "textual function" of discourse (specifically, but certainly not exclusively, literary discourse). The narrator-narratee relation *simulated* by a text (by discourse), and the referentiality that is articulated through deixis on that relation, coincide with a "textual" relation—the relation of a reading to a writing—that is effected through *figuration*. This relation of "narrative function" to "textual function," as a *clinamen* brought about by reading, can now be seen as a manifestation of the inevitable "difference from itself"—the difference between a discourse of control, for instance, and its inescapable misreading—that characterizes discourse as a result of its mediated character, that is, of the fact that it is inevitably *read*. And reading can be described both as that which produces the textual "difference from itself," and—as I shall shortly try to suggest—as a complex and protracted negotiation, a "to and fro" shuttling between the two functions that it thus produces. Reading works, in other words, within the room for maneuver produced by the difference that reading produces.

But both textual "irony" and textual "seduction" can be described as consequences of the discursive split between "narrative" and "textual" functions. Irony is the reading of that split as a disjunction between *what is said* and *what is meant* (and vice versa); seduction names the way a reader is led to make the shift from reading in the "narrative function" to reading in the "textual function," with the attendant exploration of *otherness* (of textual otherness with respect to "itself" but also of the reader's own difference from "self") and the shift in readerly desire that can result. The mediation of textual irony and textual seduction may well be a function, therefore, of the room for maneuver that is opened up by the interplay of the two functions in what I shall call a site of conversion.

1. Modes of Irony

There can, of course, be no particular trope of reading because all tropes imply reading as their condition of existence. Figuration is distinguished from the "literal" as precisely that mode of discourse that requires to be *read*: its meaning is not "given" (or "dictated"), but must be produced as a difference from *what it says* (a difference that makes the literal itself, like the "narrative function," an object of reading; it has the status of difference from the figurative, as the figurative has that of a difference from the literal, so that each acts as the negative determinant of the other's identity. This is a point I shall return to in due course.)

But, in the way that metaphor and metonymy are frequently taken to be the key tropes of discursive *genre* (in Jakobson, for example, they are the trope of the poetic and the trope of the prosaic respectively)[5], so irony and allegory, which are just as frequently paired—that is associated and distinguished (for example, and most influentially, in Paul de Man's seminal essay on "The Rhetoric of Temporality")[6]—can be understood as the key tropes of discursive *authority*. Each produces the authority of a given piece of discourse as dependent on reading (there can be no allegory and no irony except "as read"), and so they manifest "authority" as a consequence of *authorization*, and therefore as a product of mediation. In both irony and allegory, the text is dependent on its "other" (on reading) for an authority that derives from something "other" than *what it says*.

As tropes of authority, however, allegory and irony are symmetrical and complementary, since allegory produces the textual meaning on which its authority depends as "other" than but *continuous* with (analogous to, or even better, structurally homologous with) what is said. The relation of discourse and meaning, of "narrative function" and "textual function," is produced in allegory as a matter of coherence, and reading thus has the effect of confirming and reinforcing textual authority (depite the phenomenon demonstrated by de Man, that the allegorical "other" that is meaning must itself have an "other," produced by further reading, and so on). Allegory is thus the trope of "authoritarian fictions" of all kinds, not just of the *roman à thèse* described by Susan Suleiman,[7] but of all ideological discourse whose authority is accepted, that is, is perceived as structuring reality in a way that is confirmed by experience. Ideology maintains its authority to the extent that it functions as an unrecognized allegory, that is a (mediated) figuration of the real that passes for literal, so that the unacknowledged authorization on which such authority rests is a manifestation of ideological complicity and the "literal" can be described as a result of the "forgetting" of discourse's allegorical structure.

Irony too can only work as a matter of ideological complicity, but it is the trope of opposition because in irony the reader's complicity produces the relation of the "narrative" to the "textual" function as a split between the two, even though there is necessarily a relation—and hence a continuity of some kind—without which the "split" could not itself be conceived. *What is meant* is defined, in other words, as a negative relation to *what is said* (and, of course, vice versa), so that a discontinuity is produced between the two. But this recognition of split must itself be an ideological one (the ideology that recognizes another discourse as "ideological"), and furthermore there must also be a (usually unrecognized) relation between the ironizing ideology and the ironized ideology to mediate the "split." As a result there is a dependency of the ironizing on the ironized that enacts the general law of oppositionality, the law that it depends on the power that it opposes. As Barthes pointed out in *S/Z*, Flaubertian irony that takes bourgeois "bêtise" [stupidity] as its target necessarily assumes a complicity of the "intelligent"—"comment épingler la bêtise sans se déclarer intelligent?" ["how can stupidity be pinned down without declaring oneself intelligent?"]. But this complicity qualifies, consequently, as another form of "bêtise": the *other* of "bêtise" is necessarily linked to that from which it differs (even as it defines "bêtise" by producing its own "intelligence" as different from it).[8]

But from the split that irony introduces between *what is said* and *what is meant*, a double source of oppositionality arises, as an "anamnestic" realization of discursive mediation, according as irony works as a "negation" of the ideological discourse it cites and ironizes, or as an "appropriation" of that discourse. In the first instance, the ironic meaning is inferred simply as being "not" the meaning specified in the discourse that is ironically "mentioned."[9] The negation does not necessarily imply a relation of "oppositeness" (as in the classic definition of irony as "saying one thing and meaning the opposite"), but it does imply a relation of *otherness* in which ironic *oppositionality* arises. Thus, in La Fontaine, the power of fable may be described, in the narrative function, as that enjoyed by the Orator of Athens, while in the "textual function," *another* understanding of that power is implied, having to do with "plaisir extrême" and the "amusement"—both the entertainment and the gulling—of the world. Or, in "Les femmes et le secret," what seems a misogynistic "histoire gauloise" becomes readable as an ironic comment on the ideological and political functions of male secrecy as an instrument of control. A fable that presents itself as an epithalamium and a theory of kingship ("Le milan, le roi et le chasseur") manages, in the "textual function," to "tweak the king's nose," as a theory of oppositionality—a theory of how to tweak a royal nose and get away with it (see chapter 2).

Needless to say, the irony of all these ironies of negation is that of oppositionality in general. "Amusing" the world is as much what the Orator does as what the fable does, and the fable's use of narrative pleasure is "political" just as the Orator's is. The secrets of male ideological control are available, and can be divulged, only by one who shares in male power, so that the ironic fable is part of the sexual rivalry it ironizes—it is on the side of "couvade," the husband's side, with respect to the fertility of women. And of course, the power to tweak the royal nose necessarily depends on kingly clemency—that is, on the very theory of kingship the fable ironically commends. There is no break with power, but only a deviation from, or a split within, the structures of power that makes the irony possible. The irony of negation thus shares with grammatical negation an inescapable feature that has already been commented on: negation necessarily "mentions" and therefore acknowledges the power of what it negates (whereas an affirmation does not have to acknowledge that which it is negating).

But the second oppositional resource of irony depends on the fact that irony, as a relation of "disjunction" between *what is said* and *what is meant*, characterizes the discourses of power themselves, which are vulnerable—in spite of their effort to maintain the literality of "dictation"—to what I just called "deviation" and so to ironic appropriation, that is to being used "otherwise." Opposition here takes the form of turning a discourse of control to "other" purposes, or making use of it in "other" interests, as Molina does in *El beso de la mujer araña* with the discourse of the movies and the structures of information control. The oppositionality of the irony, in this case, lies less in the readability of a negation (which necessarily affirms what it negates) than in the demonstration that control cannot be absolute, the potential for its being turned to "other" purposes lying in the very means that serve to exercize control. If La Fontaine's irony is generally of the negating type, as the studies in chapter 2 suggested, a fable such as "Le Loup et l'agneau" can nevertheless be seen without difficulty, as I pointed out in chapter 1, to work as appropriative irony. It takes the discourse of power—here the "ethics" of wolfishness—which its "narrative function" simulates, and turns it, in its "textual function," into a readable demonstration of the power of the oppositional irony. Its own discursive "muddiness" both opposes the opacity of wolfish discourse and, contrasting with the mendaciousness of the pedagogical project enacted in the "narrative function," constitutes a form of readerly education.

This fable thus simultaneously negates the discourse of power it cites in its "narrative function" and appropriates it for the purposes of an educational demonstration (that of the oppositional role of irony). It consequently illustrates the (doubtless obvious) fact that the irony of negation and the irony of appropriation cannot be distinguished from each other in any absolute sense because each entails the other. An appropriation will always function as a negation of that which it appropriates, under pain of being a *simple* "use"—not an appropriative one—of the discourse it mentions. And equally, a negation necessarily appropriates the affirmation that it mentions, in order to turn it to an "other" purpose. What I have wanted to suggest, however, is that the (inevitably blurred) distinction between these two modes of irony—always a matter of emphasis rather than a distinction of kind—can be used to historicize the practices of oppositionality in terms of an evolution in the "nature" of power (that is, in the practices that produce power as their effect). It can be hazarded that the irony of negation is characteristic of discursive situations in which power occupies a position of visible centrality and legitimacy, such that opposition can *know what it is opposing* (without necessarily knowing in the name of what it is opposing it). Such, in general terms, would have been the position in ancien régime France.

The irony of appropriation, however, is more likely to flourish where power is more diffuse or more difficult to recognize—that is, where it has become ideological control—and/or where its legitimacy (as in the case of modern dictatorships) is dubious. Power, here, is "up for grabs," and it is in this modern situation that the irony of appropriation, as precisely a "grabbing" of power—a grabbing always subject (as was noted in chapter 4) to further appropriation, or to reappropriation by the system of power—might be expected to flourish. It is not coincidental, therefore, that La Fontaine's appropriative irony appears in a fable that specifically refers to a situation of absent legitimacy and usurped power, that is, a situation of social violence from which guaranteed sources of "justice" have disappeared. But if "Le loup et l'agneau" is truly exemplary, as specifically modern writing, it is perhaps also because its appropriative irony puts the discourse of power (its "narrative function") at the service of an educational project, the conversion of the reader('s desire) from the ethos of wolfishness to something "other." In that sense, it ironically puts the discourse of power, by appropriation, at the service of an (educational) "seduction" that subverts power, and specifically power as the (pedagogical) control of desire.

2. Melancholy and the Site of Conversion

If there has been some sort of historical shift between the irony of negation and the irony of appropriation, modes that are nevertheless in a relation of mutual dependency, something similar can be suggested with respect to the relation of textual irony and readerly seduction. I mean first that what these terms name are in a relation of mutual dependency: it is not simply that an irony can subserve a seduction and that the seductive text is consequently an appropriation of the ironic structure of that text's reading, but also and more generally that any seduction necessarily works an irony because of the shift it produces from the discourse of control(led desire) to its "other," while an irony is inevitably seductive to the degree that it implies a shift in the reader's (desiring) complicity, from the discourse that is ironized to the ironizing discourse. (In both cases, of course, the irony/seduction can only work if the reader is "predisposed" to it, as Valentín is predisposed to Molina's ironically seductive practices, which is why the ironic/seductive shift amounts to a self-education—an "acknowledgment" of what was already *known*.) But also the fading of the sense of centralized power that brought about the shift of emphasis between ironic negation and ironic appropriation seems simultaneously to have been accompanied by a related shift in the understanding of the relation of reading to writing: a shift that favors a "seductive" understanding of that relation over the "ironic."

One might capture the "nature" of this shift by suggesting that textuality has become less a matter of "address" and more the site of an "appeal." And to the (considerable) extent that textual address can be associated with "narrative function" as a way of defining the narratee, while textual "appeal" results from the "textual function" as a call for reading, one can point to the blurring of those two functions, with the consequent emergence of the textual that occurs in the suicidal texts of melancholy (those I examined in chapter 3), as both the sign of the interrelation and indeed the intrication of "address" and "appeal," and the moment of a historical conversion from one textual mode in the direction of the other. For, as I attempted to show in chapter 3, there is in the melancholic text a new degree of openness to readability, an openness signaled by the "suicidal" fading of the narrator's role as the site and subject of discursive control over meaning. This "elocutionary disappearing act" of the controlling subject in textuality has its historical counterpart—and (in this book) its major symbol—in the involuntary disappearing act of the guillotined Louis XVI in 1793 and the crisis of political legitimacy that ensued, both in revolutionary France and in the postrevolutionary Western world.

I want, then, to describe the melancholic text as the site of a "conversion" between textual "address" and textual "appeal"; but it is necessary also for each of these three terms to be understood in a double sense. For it is "skill" (the sense of *adresse* in French) in the handling of "address"—the skill that characterizes oppositional irony—that becomes, with the fading sense of who the addressee is and where, consequently, the site of power lies, more like an "appeal" to reading that requires of the text that it become more "appealing" in a seductive sense. And "conversion," too, as I have already suggested, should be understood not only in the sense of a linear conversion (from "address" to "appeal"), but also in the sense of a "to and fro" between the textual modes, a "to and fro" that corresponds to the interdependency of ironic negation and ironic appropriation, of irony and seduction, "address" and "appeal," this interdependency being itself reflected in the blurring of the "narrative" and "textual" functions. For if the melancholic text can function as a moment of conversion in the historical sense, it is because it models text itself as a site of conversion in the sense that it is subject to the "to and fro" of reading; and my text theory consequently implies a history of what has made that theory possible. My theory of text as the site of conversion presupposes a conversion of the historical "nature" of text.

The conversions mediated by the melancholic text can be described, then, in a number of ways, although each is a different version of the shift between "address" and "appeal" and each is mutually interdependent. An irony of negation moves towards an irony of appropriation, while irony itself, as a mode of production of textual meaning, shifts towards a text-reader relation modeled on the seductive relations of desire, a shift that implies an "appeal" to the possibility of a conversion in the reader from a form of desire assumed to be consonant with the structures of power to an "other" form, more congenial to textual oppositionality and simultaneously constituting the shift that is a *conversio ad se.* There is finally no need, therefore, to exclude from the various connotations of the word "conversion" as I am using it, the religious sense of the term, if we understand it—as the conversion of Augustine, for instance, might suggest, famously mediated as it was by the reading of texts—as a deflection of desire, mediated by reading, from alienating secular patterns to spiritually liberating ones. Such an understanding of conversion is relevant, for instance, to the initiatory appeal to the reader that is made in Nerval's "Aurélia."

Indeed, the late writing of Nerval manifests all these textual and readerly conversions with quite exemplary clarity. The discourse of "history," at first negatively ironized in "Angélique," can be seen in due course to be, rather, ironically appropriated to textual purposes, as the narrator, in the role of controlling subject of the discourse, begins to merge into the textual "symphony" of dialogic voices, a dialogism that simultaneously implies—already in "Angélique" but more urgently in "Aurélia"—an appeal to (and for) complicitous reading, as a kind of compensation for the narrative "failures" enacted in the text. In Aquin's *Prochain Épisode*, it is, quite similarly, "story" (the narrator's project of writing a spy novel) that "sinks" and merges into a mode of writing that constitutes an extended "malheur d'expression," an infelicity of expression that enacts the inevitable otherness of identity, its necessary "difference from itself." The appeal to the reader (as the textual "other" on which the text's identity depends) is thus an appeal for a conversion from "autonomous" identity to the type of suicidal personality represented by the narrator/subject of writing, so that reading becomes something like the enactment of a joint suicide in which the reader is given over to the flow of textuality as the text is given over to reading.

But in neither case is it implied that reading, however complicitous, can bring a final solution to the enigmas of narrative "madness" (Nerval) or to the textual "puzzle" (Aquin). Rather there is something of a relay effect, a shift in the responsibility for textual "meaning"—for making the project of writing a meaningful exercise—such that the abandonment of "narrative" control (with its attendant well-directed "address"), an abandonment mimed in the disorderliness of the writing, implies the intervention of a reader who is "appealed" to without its being assumed that readerly intervention can *save* the text, in the sense of closing its meaning. For the underlying irony in melancholic writing is the irony of the suicide note, which is that any putative "last word" always implies a "prochain épisode"—the episode of its reading—so that there can never be such a thing as a "last word." Reading itself cannot be assumed, therefore, to be capable of providing the last word the text is itself incapable of; it cannot *restore* the text's lost order or *complete* its project. The appeal is rather to a conversion of the reader—a conversion *away* from the understandings and desires that encourage conceptions like the idea of a "last word"—such that the textual "influence" is shifted endlessly onward, making of it an agent, not of closure but of change. The possibility of change can only imply further change; so that any change produced in the reader cannot close the process, it merely opens a prospect of yet more change.

In this way, the melancholic text models the way any oppositional text is constituted, through reading, as a place where the production of meaning, as an ironic operation, doubles with (and doubles as) an "education" in readerly desire. But it also enacts reading, now, as a manifestation of discursive modernity in the sense that—the "King" being dead—there can be no "last word," so that the textual appeal to (and for) reading simultaneously situates the text (and its reading) as an agent of history, that is, a site where change can, and indeed must, occur and go on occurring. Furthermore, occurring as it does through the agency of textual "influence" thus manifested as a mediated seduction, the direction of that change can no longer be "dictated" by means of something like "skill" in "address." In ancien régime France, La Fontaine's irony of negation corresponded to a certain centrality and legitimacy of power; but to the more diffuse and difficult situation I am now describing, only appropriative and seductive modes of oppositionality are germane.

They are germane because, paradoxical as it may seem, the new diffuseness of power has made its exercise "dictatorial" in the sense I described in chapter 4. The lesson of that chapter was indeed that, whether "dictation" is understood as the violent and abusive "usurpation" of god-like powers by ordinary humans, or rather as a figure for the depersonalized and dehumanizing power that is ideological control, there is—as both *El Señor Presidente* and *El beso de la mujer araña* made clear—no real discontinuity between the two. But the further lesson of the chapter was that, "under dictation," the more appropriate oppositional response is not a stance of "witness," itself bound up with the ideology of discursive control, but the production of textuality as a discursive act of appropriative seduction. Molina, more than Esteban, is the model of modern oppositionality because his alliance with the powers of mediation enables him to convert the discourse of power that imprisons us into a means of changing, that is, of deflecting desire.

In *Mélancolie et Opposition*,[10] I attempted a more specific reading of the historical emergence of textual melancholy as an "appeal" to reading in Second Empire France. But here, producing it more broadly as a characteristically modern phenomenon, I seek partly, as mentioned earlier, to historicize my own theory of reading, but also to suggest that melancholic writing has *symptomatic* status. Not all such writing is necessarily melancholic (as my chapter 4 attests), but modernity tends to produce oppositional textuality as a cultural "place"—a site of conversion—where there is the kind of room for maneuver that is capable of producing change out of the discourse of power through the deflection of desire, without its being possible to identify any agency of control over this process.

3. Seduction and the Space of Reading: Court Poet/Wild Child

If reading produces text which in turn changes the reader, the condition of its power is, then, that discourse be split, and that it be split in two ways: between power and its oppositional "other," and between desire, as it is mediated by the discourse of power, and an "other" desire. Reading, as a manifestation of mediation, is that which produces these splits; but it is also the means that mediates between the split discourse of power, producing textual irony, and the changes of desire that result from textual seduction. Thus, the site of conversion that is the space of reading tends to be described either as a landscape of power or as a landscape of desire, or as both; but it tends also to be a somewhat indeterminate place, a "room for maneuver" that results, on one hand, from the inextricable interdependence of the discourses of power and desire with their oppositional "other," and, on the other, from the to-and-fro transformability of power into desire and desire into power. Nerval names this place of reading the "Valois," in Aquin it is the jagged, "writerly" landscape of the Rhone Valley near Lake Geneva, superimposed on the river valleys of Québec—a deterritorialized place where the agents of power and the agents of opposition turn out, disquietingly, to be each others' doubles, while writing functions as the ultimate appeal for love that is the suicide note.

But another such place, as we have seen, is *gularabulu*, the coast where the sun sets in the sea and water and land meet and mingle. To this in-between place comes Stephen, armed with powerful Western knowledge (and indeed Parisian theory), where he meets, at the campfire, Paddy who enchants him with stories and, seducing his desire, teaches him wisdom. One such story, the tale of "Mirdinan," concerns precisely the "power in the belly" that enables the wise man, the "maban" ("he very clever man"), to turn the forces of an oppressive white culture to his own advantage, absorbing oppositional strength with his prison food. But the story has an even stronger "power in the belly," part of which lies in its appropriation of the modes of Western storytelling as a means of seducing Stephen, and through him Stephen's people, into a certain self-knowledge—the knowledge of the violence their culture visits on Paddy's—and hence into a shift of desire that initiates a change. A little of what Mirdinan lost, in terms of power, is thus gained back, seductively, by Paddy.

For one of the issues here, and it is more urgent than Paddy's deceptively "off-hand" translations indicate, is precisely the name of the space and, with it, the relation of power that goes into the naming of the landscape:

> Fisherman Bend in Broome, *karnun* -
> we call-im *karnun* -
>
> . . . .
> a place called *kibilarid* -
> that's where their camping ground is *kibilarid* -
> that's in Thangoo country -.

The issue of "land rights"—the historical dispossession by the European invasion of land that had been occupied for 40,000 years by Aboriginal people and in relation to which their cultural identity was defined—has been at the heart of the story of imperialist and colonialist oppression in Australia.[11] It would be a fair adjudication, therefore, to say, not that *karnun* and *kibilarid* win the day in Paddy's storytelling—for clearly this "camping ground" space of storytelling, whether *kibilarid* or Thangoo, is no longer the site of *that kind* of struggle (one in which there might be a "last word"). Thangoo Station and Fisherman's Bend cannot be eliminated from the scene because they have become, precisely, a necessary part of Paddy's armory, without which his seduction would have no "hook" and could not happen. *Karnun* and *kibilarid* do not win the day, then; but as a result of the storytelling their claim escapes its repression and comes to be recognized. In that sense, a shift in the desire that is productive of the real has occurred, on the part of Stephen and of Stephen's people, and a historical effect has been achieved in which narrative's seductive ability to deflect desire has produced some modification in long-standing relations of power.

Yet another name for the place of reading is Scythia, on the very outskirts of the Roman Empire, whence the boundless steppes stretch endlessly northward, beyond what we know as the Black Sea. To Scythia, in David Malouf's

An Imaginary Life,[12] the last text I will discuss in this book, comes the Roman poet Ovid, at once an exile and an emissary from the sophisticated culture of Rome and the power of the Imperial Court; and there he encounters a Wild Boy, a human child from out of the wilderness, who has been somehow drawn to this boundary space among the Getae. Relations both of power and of desire are implied by this meeting of Court Poet and Wild Child, for in teaching the boy the ways of his civilization, the urbane Poet is seduced by the Child (my capitals imitate the text's capitalization of the word "Child," as an indicator of allegory)—seduced into a revelation of his "true" place in the universe, of his position in the landscape. His culture has defined itself *against* the wilderness, but now, he writes, "I must drive out my old self and let the universe in" (96).

Like Paddy, the Child makes his accommodation to civilization (learning to speak, playing at writing), but it is the poet of the *Metamorphoses* who, like Stephen, undergoes the more important conversion, a *conversio ad se*. For this is a Child who has been in the Poet's memory since his own childhood; and the knowledge he brings is not really new, for it is knowledge the Roman once had, but in turning toward Augustan Rome, had lost, or forgotten. And so "the land I am about to enter is not entirely unfamiliar," he muses (137), as the two depart together, across the boundary river Ister, into the steppes where "the immensity, the emptiness feeds the spirit" (141)—a landscape into whose immensity the poet from Rome will soon himself be swallowed up. "I am turning into the landscape. I feel myself sway and ripple. I feel myself expand upwards towards the blue roundness of the sky. Is that where we are going?" (145–46).

It would do a profound disservice to Malouf's deeply romantic and richly polyphonic allegory to read it as "merely" an allegory of reading. But *as such* an allegory, its importance lies in its suggestion that what is at issue in reading is the nature of the human "landscape" and the potential for its limitless transformation through desire. For Ovid's self-education is a transformation of his desire in the sense of a discovery of the nature of his own most authentic longing, a revelation of what has been lost but can be regained through the Child. "How strange to find myself back there for odd moments, knowing that I have made nothing of whatever it was that was being revealed to me then—that I went some other way, into a man's world, the city, into the state. . . . But stranger still is that all this time it has remained there, untouched, unrecalled, but still brightly new—and so real that I smell the raw cleanness of it still" (85–86). But this individual recognition of desire that transforms the Poet is of a piece with Ovid's knowledge that what changes humanity itself is the force of desire, so that the steppes into which he disappears with the Child, in response to his own desire, represent the boundless future of a human history that must leave Rome, its power and its glory, behind—"I shall not go back to Rome" (94)—so that, in Nietzschean fashion, humankind can become what it is.

So the voyage into the future of Poet and Child on the thematic level coincides with the way Ovid's writing rhetorically turns its back on Rome in order to apostrophize its own future reader, as the distant and unimaginable outcome, somewhere at the other side of the steppes, of the Poet's own new desire: a desire for change that results from the change in his desire.

We have some power in us that knows its own ends. . . . This is the true meaning of transformation. This is the real metamorphosis. Our further selves are contained within us, as the leaves and blossoms are in the tree. We have only to find the spring and release it. Such changes are slow beyond imagination. They take gen- erations. But it works, this process. We are already the product of generation after generation of wishing to be thus. And what you are, reader, is what *we* have wished. Are you gods already? Have you found wings? (P. 64)

The empirical reader who knows that we are not yet gods and have not found wings is forced to reflect that the process is not completed, and invited to seek his or her own authentic desire—the Child within—a desire that may have nothing to do with gods and wings, and in pursuing it to imitate the Poet's own transformation, and his voyage into the steppes of the future. In this way, the text works a seduction comparable to that worked by the Child on the Poet, and one that implies its own agency in the endless transformation of humanity through desire.

But the Poet would not have discovered his desire for the Child if the Wild Boy, simultaneously, was not the site of a symmetrical longing—a desire for what is represented in this text by Rome. "He has begun to look for us, I know that, as we look for him. He feels some yearning towards us (. . .). Has he begun to ask of what kind he is?" the Poet asks quite early (60); and soon imagines himself guiding the Child out of an exile of his own "into his inheritance, into the society of his own kind" (81). There is some irony here, since the Poet is unaware that it is he who is to be the most powerfully transformed of the two; but it is indeed necessary for the Wild Child to come within the ambience of civilization *as it is*—itself the product of human desire—in order for the desire of the civilized Poet to be changed, and to turn away from civilization as it is towards the uncharted steppes of the future, with their limitless potential for change.

A text, then, to specify the allegory, must accommodate to the discourse of power before its seduction, as a turning towards the "other" of that discourse, can work. For there is, as Ovid recognizes, a "force (. . .) that makes things what they are and changes them into what they would be" (65); and it is the same force—the force of desire. The space of reading is that place where the desire that has made things what they *are* (represented by the Child's coming to the Poet) undergoes the deflection (represented by the Poet's turning to the Child) that moves the landscape towards what it can *become*. Thus Ovid, writing in Latin, knows that his own text must be "translated" into the language of his distant future reader, as the Child must undergo the effects of civilization, for that reader to be seduced in turn into an education in desire. Without accommodation to the status quo of power and to "things as they are"—without textual "address," that is—there can be no "appeal," and no deflection from that status quo, no emergent desire making things "what they would be."

I am tempted to abandon *Room for Maneuver* to its own reader here. David Malouf's allegory figures reading as I have begun to understand it in writing this book, as a self-education responding to a seductive appeal, an appeal, I would add, that itself depends on the fissuring of discourse—into its "Court Poet" and "Wild Child" sides—that is in turn an effect of reading. The system seems self-enclosed, but it generates change. *An Imaginary Life*, however, also suggests further questions I have not begun to investigate here, although they arise inevitably and consequently have their appropriate place in a Conclusion. These are the questions of the extension of the system, and in particular the two presumably interrelated questions of how *one* case of readerly change (say Ovid's) implies the necessity of a *history* of change, and of how an *individual* case of change is subsumed into the *collective* changes of "humanity," or at least of human social groups. What both these questions imply is a reading theory that does not tie the act of reading to an individual subject conceived as an autonomous self, but perceives it as an activity of mediation that is itself a mediated activity. As an activity of mediation, reading—as the production of a text-reader relation in which each component functions as the other's other—demonstrates that the production of identity is relational and systemic and that, as a consequence of this systematicity, its outcome is change. One need "only" extend the system, then, to show how the production of a given text-reader relation is in turn mediated to have access to a theory that would begin to account for the *spread* of influence, both through a collectivity and in history. But that is beyond my present range.

The reason I do not abandon the "last word" to David Malouf—the "last word" of a Conclusion that knows there is no last word, but always necessarily a "prochain épisode"—is however that in the figure of the Wild Child—as indeed in the allegorization I have imposed on Paddy Roe's storytelling—there is a certain primitivism that needs to be tempered by a return to the cooler climes of theory. For, if it is for theory to acknowledge that there is in oppositional behavior in general, and in narrative in particular, an element of *techné* or "know-how" that theory cannot master, try as it may, and that reading opens up a cultural space for maneuver that remains an "enigma," it does not do, for political reasons I need not specify, to identify this "enigma" with culturally marginalized figures. Reading as *techné* is manifestly, in the terms I foreshadowed in the Preface, a "technology of the self," an oppositional one to be sure, but one that nonetheless has the status of an acquired discipline with a function in the social order that has nothing to do with encounters with the "natural" or the "primitive" in the form of Wild Boys, and everything to do with the ways a society such as ours seeks to control even the uncontrollability of change by producing its own technologies of change. Let us rewrite, then, the allegory of Court Poet and Wild Child in my lexicon of "address" and "appeal," of "narrative function" and "textual function," so as to examine a little more closely the issue of the mutual entailments of power and opposition that they imply. It is because reading is fundamental to the production of their relation of interdependence, I will argue, that it is a skill or a technology that the social formation must foster through teaching.

If textual "address"—corresponding to the "narrative function" of discourse—is the seductive "hook" that engages the reader's interest and without which the reader quite simply could not read, we must define it as that which the text *gives to power*, the "portion" of power (or "el parte al Señor Presidente") that represents literature's inescapable "Court Poet" side. But, just as—because of the inevitability of mediation—there can be no "dictation" that does not produce an oppositional (mis-)reading, so there can be no "address," in the code of control, that does not inevitably slip into an "appeal" because it is necessarily subject to the effects of (mis-)reading associated with the "textual function." This "appeal" is the text's "Wild Child" side; and it is between "address" and "appeal" that there is a space for the deflection of readerly desire, and so for change.

But, just as "address" cannot not produce "appeal," because there is no communication that is not mediated, so too textual "appeal" cannot occur except as a deflection—sometimes viewed as a deviation—from "address." Each in this sense entails the other, as power implies opposition and opposition power; each can exist only as a difference from the other. I have defined reading, first, as that which produces the slippage, or deflection, between "address" and "appeal," and second as the complex and potentially endless negotiation, the shifting "to and fro" between the two positions out of which that deflection can emerge. But it is now necessary to notice the implications of the fact that reading is also, and indeed primarily, *that which produces the difference*, within discourse, between whose poles the room for maneuver exists that can produce change. This means that the discourse of power—"narrative function" as "address," manifesting the code of control that can appear as the literal—is itself as much a function of reading—dependent on being read as the discourse of power—as is the shift that I have referred to in terms of "textual function," "appeal" and the oppositional. There is, as Malouf's Ovid noted, a single force that produces things "as they are" and things "as they would be"; the whole forms a single system.

If reading, therefore, is a technology of the self that is fostered in social formations such as ours, we can understand that fact in terms of an apparent paradox. Power depends on that which simultaneously opposes it, that is, on "reading" as a manifestation of mediation. If we need to *learn* to read—learn, that is, to oppose power in acquiring the techniques of interpretive reading (an activity for which in our own society expensive educational institutions are maintained)—it is because reading is *also*, and primarily, a condition of the production of authority, and "power" is a product of the same system as "opposition." Power is not a given but a (produced) "effect of power," an allegory read as literal; and it depends therefore on being read, a by-product of that fact being that it is simultaneously vulnerable to oppositional (mis-)reading. And so the "effect of power," when it succeeds, is itself the product of a repression, since it is the inhibition of oppositional (mis-)reading through the ability to "forget" and to cause to "forget" the role of mediation. It is only as a result of that inhibition that the discourse of power comes to seem (to be read as) literal.

It follows, then, that oppositionality is the condition of power in two important senses. In the way that there can be no communication without "noise," so that noise becomes the condition of communication (which is consequently by definition [mis-]communication), so too oppositionality arises within the system of power as the manifestation of mediation without which there can be no system, and no power. But also, in the way that "repression" is a negative and negatively defined phenomenon, constituted as a relation to that which it represses and visible only through the "return of the repressed," so too power finally appears as the *product*, by negation, of the potential oppositionality that it represses in repressing mediation.

So, if oppositionality is a "deviation" from the discourse of power ("noise" in the system of power and so an inevitable component of that system), power in turn can be seen to exist only as a difference—produced by repression—from that which is its "other": the manifestations of mediation that constitute oppositionality. In an exactly similar way, the literal exists only as the other of the figurative (of that which requires to be read): where the figurative is a deviation from the literal, the literal can itself be defined only as the non-figurative. These differences, like the difference between "narrative function" and "textual function" or between textual "address" and textual "appeal"

certainly define reading as that which produces them—but they can themselves only be produced as a function of reading. The literal, then, the discourse of power, is that which is so read, by contradistinction from that which
is produced through reading as the "other" of the literal or of the discourse
of power.

If reading is produced as a discipline to be learned and a technology of the
self, it is therefore not because reading has the oppositional power to produce
deflections of desire and hence changes in the production of the real; it is
because there is a total system that must include reading, and its consequences,
as a condition of the production of power. One corollary of this, however, is
that, as a technology of the "self," it produces the self, not as coherent and
unified, but as the site of a split: the reading subject undergoes a shift, a
deflection of desire, that corresponds to the split in textual discourse between
the discourse of power, or the "narrative function," and its emergent "other,"
the "textual function." Reading is a technology of the self that *denies* the self,
then, if the self is understood as an autonomous entity, independent of the
whole relational system that produces change; that is why the melancholic
text, in which the "suicide" of the controlling subject is staged, is the exemplary text of reading. And Ovid, the poet of the *Metamorphoses*, is also the
poet of the *Tristia*, the song of exile of the "Court Poet" whose involvement
in the adventure of change implies the abandonment of his "old self," the
Roman self, the self of power.

A second corollary concerns the relation of change to power. In such a
system there can be no change that manifests a clear disjunction from the
"way things are," since change itself is systemic. There can only be a continuity of things that derives from the nature of mediation itself: its power
to produce power *and* its power to produce disturbance in the system of
power—a disturbance that is, however, part of the system that produces
power. It is only under these conditions that there *can* be change, even though
under such conditions, there cannot *not* be change. But I do not think it
possible, therefore, to say that a *dialectic* of "power" and "opposition" is at
work in the production of change; it is rather that change is the function of
an endless irony—an irony of negation and an irony of appropriation—that
does not achieve or even seek sublation. Nor is a Great Narrative at work
producing a *telos* of history, a destination for the human journey: "the notion
of destination no longer seems necessary to me," as Malouf's Ovid says (144).
But there is, instead, what Ovid calls a "fullness," at the moment when the
Child leaves him behind to merge in individual death with the vastness of the
landscape of humanity.

The fullness is in the Child's walking away from me, in his stepping so lightly, so
joyfully, naked, into his own distance at last as he fades in and out of the dazzle of
light in the water and stops to gather—what? Pebbles? (P. 152)

It *could* be pebbles. Pebbles might *well* be "what his eye is attracted by now" (152). The point is more in the Child's "walking away" than in what he gathers as he goes; it is, more precisely, and to introduce the emphasis the text implies, it is in his walking away from *me*, as the subject constructed in the discourse of power. It is in the "Wild Child"'s walking away from the "Court Poet."

For if desire—which is what the Child figures here—is the force that can change things, it is precisely because, as a mediated phenomenon, desire is not anchored in the "self" but instead produces subjects. In producing them as desiring subjects—products of mediation—it simultaneously makes them agents of change, but not agents who "produce" change by willing it. They are agents *through whom* change occurs, the sites of its occurrence. As reading subjects, we are thus the site of an endless *clinamen* of desire—a *clinamen*, however, in which each deflection produces a new state of affairs and a new situation of power, from which what can be predicted with confidence is only that it contains within it the potential—and indeed the inevitability—of new changes, further shifts.

So shall we become gods, reader? Shall we find wings? Is that our desire? And if it is, and supposing it might be realized, should we, *would* we not then immediately desire *otherwise*? Perhaps, after all, it is better to be humans and to recognise that, unless or until we destroy ourselves utterly, there will be no "last words." Our "last words" do not last because there is always a way to find a way, "toujours moyen de moyenner." If we could acknowledge that, the violence we visit on one another and on ourselves in the name of our "last words" might be considerably abated.

Appendix: Paddy Roe, "Mirdinan"

Edited by Stephen Muecke

Yeah ———
well these people bin camping in Fisherman Bend him and his missus
    you know —
Fisherman Bend in Broome, *karnun*[1] —
we call-im *karnun* ———
soo, the man used to go fishing all time —
get food for them, you know, food, lookin' for tucker —
an' his, his missus know some Malay bloke was in the creek,
    Broome Creek[2] —
boat used to lay up there[3] —
so this, his missus used to go there with this Malay bloke —
one Malay bloke, oh he's bin doin' this for —
over month —

so this old fella —
come back with fish one day he can't find his missus —
he waited there till late —
so he said "What happened to my missus? —
must be gone fishing ah that's all right" he said -
so he waited and he comeback he got nothing[4] —
"Where you bin?" he said, bloke said to him -
"Ah I jus' bin walkin' round" -
"Aah" -
soo all right next morning he start off again —
"Mus' be something wrong" this oldfella said —
oh he wasn't old but he was young —
said "'e must be something wrong" -
so he went fishing —
he come back from fishing —
got all the fish comeback —

From *gularabulu: Stories from the West Kimberly* (Fremantle: Fremantle Arts
Centre Press, 1983). For notes by Stephen Muecke, see pp. 283–84.

so he comeback on the other road —
near the creek, Broome Creek, you know —
comeback round that way —
when he comeback "Hello" he seen this man and woman in the mangroves,
    sitting down —
oh he come right alongside —
he seen everything what they doin' (Laughs) you know —
they sitting down —

so, he seen everything —
so he wen' back —
he wen' back home firs' —
he still waitin' for his missus -
his missus come up oooh —
prob'ly half an hour's time —
the woman must have give him time you know -
"Oh mus' be nearly time for my oldfella to comeback" -
but he was about half an hour late might be, his man was there already with
    the fish he was -
the oldfella was cooking —
fish, aaah they had a talk there —
that was about, dinner time —
now he said er —
"Where you bin?" -
"I wen' fishing —
err not fishing walkin' round —
I jus' lookin round for shells you know" he said aaah —
ah —
"You can tell lie all right" he said —
"What for" he —
"Oh I seen you —
you and that Malay man" he said (Chuckle) "Yeah" -
"No no no no I dunno nothing about these Malay p -"
"Oh yes, I was there standing up right alongside" he said
"I know what's goin' on —
so never mind" he said "Tha's all right —
never worry" —
say "Come on yunmi better go[5] —
see if we can get some —
we go this way bush" —
they wen' bush —
oh 'long the beach you know very close to beach ———

"You bin goin' round with that Malay bloke tha's right?"
he tell-im —
that man —
"Yes" he tell-im —
aah —
he had tommyhawk in his belt —
aah —
well, yeah —
"You see that one he say"[6] —
yeah that woman look -
he get the to(haha)mmy hawk cut his neck right off -
with the to(haha)mmyhawk, finish —
head fall down -
then he start to chop him up then finish -
(Soft) in little pieces —
chuck 'em in the sea —
tha's the finish -

soo —
that fella wen' back -
to his camp -
pick up all his things what he had there —
pack up all his things -
an' he went straight to Thangoo Station —
Thangoo Station, there is a big camping ground there belongs to people too -
"Aah" —
"Aah" —
"Where you come from?" these people ask-im you know -
"I come from Broome" -
"Aah what about you missus where you missus?" -
"Oh I left-im in Broome" say -
"Oh, oh yeah —
what time you goin' to go back?" -
"Oh I go back in couple days time" but coupla days time police already there
    (Laughs) -
lookin' for him —
police picked him up —
he had brother there too -
belongs to that woman, dead woman[7] -
"Tha's the man we gotta get" he said "tha's the bloke tha's him there sitting
    down" -
aah they come up police come up picked him up —

put a chain round his neck —
chain round his legs —
hand —
finish —

"All right" he say "We gotta take you back to Broome —
better come with us" -
"All right" he said "you bin kill your missus?" -
"Yes" he tell-im -
"Aha" —
now they took-im back -
they comeback —
they camp in —
no they got early there —
they comeback for dinner -
half way -
the one governmen' well -
tha's Cockle Well —
Roebuck Plain —
so policeman and policeboy was very tired you know —
they dragged that bloke all the way -
like a dog you know with a chain[8] —(Laugh)
walking -
footwalk -
and two bloke policeboy and policeman riding 'orse —
"All right we let the horses go -
let the horses have a —
rest (Exhales) you know -
let-im have a feed -
while we have our rest" -
so they let the horses go —
to take all the pack horses everything out packs —
they have their rest -
ooh till about -
three o'clock I think —
all right -
p'liceman tell his boy "You better get the horses I think now -
nearly time" -
all right -
policeboy go and get the horses -
bring all the horses back -

policeboy comeback -
policeman was packin' up all the gear -
plate an' billy-can an' everything puttin' them all in the pack
    you know ready -
tighten everything up —
policeboy come straight up "Hey" he said "Where's that man?" -
policeboy sing out to police -
"He's under that tree" -
"Where?" -
they look round -
"Oh Chris' he's gone!" -
so they walked up there an' had a look -
the chain -
from his neck -
still got lock -
from his leg -
still got lock —(laugh)
"Hullo" now they start thinking "What's wrong?" -
"Ooooh" the p'lice boy say "Might be tha's -
that man must be *maban* man[9] -
he very clever man" -
"Yeah?" -
"Yeah" —

so they went back to Broome -
they couldn't find him -
no track -
where he come out -
his track where he was layin' down there -
but after that no track -
nothing -
so they came back -
Sergeant asked them blokes -
"Oh, you find the man?" -
"Yeah we found-im" —(Laugh) —
"Where is he?" -
"Oh we lost him again —
here's the chain" -
they show that Sergeant (Laugh) —
"He come out of the chain jus' disappeared" —
(Gravel Voice)[10] "Aaaah doooon't -

Sergeant never believe —
(Laugh) he couldn' believe —

so next time they went back again -
lookin' for 'im -
they hear that man is back again in the same place -
"Oooh he's back there" -
so somebody grab-im over there too —
that sister er brother belong to that sister -
you know dead, dead woman -
he grabbed (Laugh) that man -
and send somebody -
from there on foot right up to police -
"We got that man here we holding him" -
so police must come and pick-im-up -
they pick-im-up —
they went out for him pick-im-up again from same place -
he come with them right up to police station this time -
right up to police station —
right up -
right up to police station -
yeah -
"Here's the bloke -
tha's the murderer -
we got him now" -
"Oh good" -
"All right" he say -
Sergeant -
oh they got a few statement off him -
when they got the statement and everything off him they put-im in the
    lock-up, room -
oooh cemen' wall too -
old lock-up -
police station -
lock-up room —
put the key everything in -
all right —

soo —
ooooh bat —
five o'clock I think in the afternoon -

they want to give him supper -
Sergeant went there himself with the -
with the supper you know he bring supper for him -
tea -
go in there open the put the plates down and everything tea -
open the -
door -
he went inside —
have a look in the (Laugh) lockup room -
he's not there -
he went all the place -
lockup you know, rooms -
nothing —
nothing -
couldn't find im -
"Aaah", *meow* -
meow -
one pussycat on top you know walkin' round -
(Growl)[10] "Aaah" Sergeant grab stick "Shhh! go on! get out!" -
(Laugh) OUT he go through the door -
gone -
soon as he went other side er police station he's a man walking in the
     footpath (Laugh) -
he go 'cross the creek -
Broome Creek -
oh everybody seen 'im —
all the people seen 'im -

so police went round now look -
"We lost one bloke from —
from the police station -
you people seen-im?" -
"Yes!" they say -
"Where?" -
"He was walkin' along the footpath here -
he gone -
to Fisherman Bend same place again that way" -
but that was him -
he turn himself into cat —(Laugh)
an' Sergeant himself hunt him out from (Laugh) lock-up room (Laugh) -
so he went -

finish -
(Stephen: True Story?) Eh? (Stephen: True Story?)[11] -
yeah, he gone -
finish -

sooo, when he wen' back they grab him again -
the same people —
same people -
oooh well he was thinkin' this time -
"I think no good" he say -
"My people don't like me" -
so they send one more man -
footwalk -
they grab that bloke they hold-im there —
a place called *kibilarid* —
that's where their camping ground is *kibilarid* -
that's in Thangoo country -
all right they come back —
policeman come again -
pick-im-up -
they bring-im right up to Broome —
this time they put 'im on the boat -
straight away -
boat was there too waiting -
they send him to Fremantle —
Fremantle —
they took him right up to Fremantle on -
the boat -
he was all right -
he was still in boat -
(Softer) he was on the boat -
he wanted to go too -
have a look at the country I s'pose (Laughs) he went right up to
    Fremantle —
they going to hang 'im —
hang 'im straight away -
'cos those days they hang people you know -

all right they took-im right up -
must be hangin' place there too eh in Fremantle big place is it? (Stephen:
    Yeah) yeah well tha's right -

so they took-im there —
all right —
they gave-im last supper -
ooh feed anyway —
tucker you know -
after that they put-im on ah -
I dunno what -
mighta been some sorta flatform?[12] -
they put the rope round his neck —
they put-im on that one —
it's ready —
(Soft) straight away before he get out you know -
they had to do everything quick -
while he was there -
you know —
(Soft) all right —
(Breathy) they musta count —
from ten backward I s'pose (Laugh) you know —
they count -
he know too he, he know all that counting -
he was, he had the rope round his neck -
the LAST number —
the, that flatform musta go down eh or something -
I, I dunno how they do that but (Stephen: Yeah, goes down) there's
    something, yeah -
right! GO! finish -
he fly out he's eaglehawk -
the loop was there (Laughter) the hang rope you know -
an' he's gone he's eaglehawk (Laugh) -
he fly away riiight back to his country (Laugh) -
(Stephen: Good one!) (Laugh) -
(Aside to Nangan) eaglehawk *iyena* —*ginyargu* -
(Nangan: Em[13]) -
waragan[14] you know, eaglehawk (Soft) he fly away —
(Softer) he was a eaglehawk then -

all right -
so when he land in his place -
he made a song -
for that one -
Fremantle -

you know —
he made a song now I gonna sing this song —
djabi, djabi song[15] —
I'll sing -
(Stephen: Mm) -

>(Start high)
>*ah brimanta la la la wiriri*
>*brimanta mudjaring ngalea*
>*brimanta la la la wiriri*
>*brimanta mudjaring ngalea*
>*brimanta la la la wiriri* (Growl)
>*brimanat mudjaring* (Out of breath)
>(Takes breath)
>*brimanta la la la wiriri*
>*brimanta mudjaring ngale*
>tali minma walburu ridjanala
>tali minma
>*tali minma walbur* — walburu ridjanala
>tali minma — *li minma walburu ridjanala*
>*tali minma*
>*brimanta* la la la wiriri
>brimanta mudjaring ngalea
>*brimanta la la la wiriri brimanta* mabu[16]

soo that's im —
so I'll tell you what the meaning on that one -
(Stephen: Oh yeah, yes please) on the song (Stephen: Yeah) -
brimanta means Fremantle (Nangan: Fremantle, Stephen: Oh yeah) —
(Laughs) you known but he never call-im proper, well that's Fremantle
     Fremantle *briiiimanta* -
la la la wiriri 'cos this man wanted to hang him had red clothes[17] —
(Stephen: Wiriri) *wiriri* -
wiriri means red -
you know (Stephen: La la la just tune) yeah *la la la* just tune *la la laaa*
     wiririii -
(Sings) *briiimantaaa la la laaa wiririii brimanta* you see he had red clothes -
that man wanted to hang this bloke (Laughs) —
and *mudjaring ngalea* -
mudjaring ngalea he bin run away *mudjari* -
mudjara means run away (Stephen: Yeah) -

run away -
mudjari -
mudjaraaa mudjariii ngalea that's his -
ngalea means that's his —
he had power in his -
in him you know -
in his belly[18] -
maban maban (Stephen: *Ngalea* belly) yeah —
(Sings) *mudjariii ngaleaaa* (Stephen: Why, why belly?) yeah -
an' *tali minma, walbaru ridjanala tali minma* that's telephone everybody bin
    ringin' up to hang this man (Laughs) (Stephen: *Minma*) on the
    telephone (Stephen: *Minma*, man?) eh? -
(Stephen: *Minma* is man) yeah — (Stephen: Is it?) -

> (Sings)
> *tali minma walbaru ridjanala*
> *tali minma andjirili irbina*
> *njirili ibina njirili ibina*

means the telephone -
njirili you know -
telephone -
poles -
(Stephen: Ya) that's, everybody bin ringin' up -
this man gotta get hanged today -
telephone -
taliii minma means he tell-im everybody you know -
just like he talk little bit in English too -
telephone you know (Stephen: Yeah *minma*) mm -

> (sings)
> *tali minmaa walburuu ridjanala*
> *tali minma andjiliri irbina*
> *tali minma walburu ridjanala*

yeah —
they didn' know I -
they didn' know me he say I gonta fly -
gonta (Laughs) turn into eaglehawk -
that's when he kept that inside here -
in his, *maban* in his belly you know -

(Stephen: Mm) so that's all (Stephen: That's a beauty that one) and that man
    name is[19] —
(Stephen: I got 'im — Mirdinan) ahh Mirdinan (Stephen: Yeah Mirdinan)
    Mirdinan yeah -
huncle too -
my uncle I call-im uncle (Stephen: Oh!) (Nangan: Mirdinaan *ngadja*)
    mirdinan ngadja his name -
mirdinan ngadja -
this one[20] call him *djambardu*, grandfather (Nangan: Mm *djambardu*)
    djambardu yeah grandfather -
call-im huncle -
(Stephen: That story's in your family!) (Laughs) yeah yeah -
oh yes he's a family -
he belong to this country too (to Nangan) *ginja marda?* he belong to this
    country (Nangan: Yeah yeah) yeah he's our people -
seaside -
yeah -
he mix with (Nangan: Aaaall what Nyigina) -
Nyigina Yaour Garadjeri everything he's -
we all one -
so he's one of our people too that fella -
you know this country people seaside —
ooh yeah[21] -
that's not the finish yet -
of the story —
that one (Stephen: Mm) -
but then people still -
when he come back -
now these people ask him -
"How did you come back? Where you come back from?" -
"I come back from Fremantle" say -
"Fremantle?" -
"Yes" -
"How you come back from Fremantle?" they said -
"I fly -
I bin turn meself into eaglehawk —
I fly from there right back to my country" (Laughs) -

and -
he come back from his country, that's from bush -
to these people where policeman used to pick him up all the time you know -

but these people didn't like him -
they still want the -
gibim to the police[22] -
if the police can' do anything well they ought to kill that old fella too you
    know his own people -
(Stephen: Yeah) they ought to kill him -
same way like how this woman but they gave him -
they didn't want to get trouble -
from the police, they had to give-im back to police -

so they gave him back to police one more time -
and everybody gave him a drink, policeman gave him a drink -
made him drunk — (Laugh)
and they put-im on the boat and nail-im up in the box -
you know they made a box for him nail him up inside -
chuck-im on the boat -
when they got halfway -
this bloke was drunk -
inside -
so he lost himself -
(Stephen: Mm) -
and they chuckled that -
they chuck-im overboard -
in the middle of the sea (Stephen: Oh) -
with the anchor -
or some sorta weight anyway (Stephen: Mm) -
so the box won't float -
so that's the finish of him (Stephen: Mm) -
he's dead -
that way -
they had to make-im drunk (Laughs) -
and the poor bloke -
they bin make-im drunk eh (Nangan: Yeah) -
yeah, an' he lose himself -
but he coulda come out of that box too if they didn' -
give-im drink -
(Nangan: Take-im outside Broome) -
yeah outside Broome, oh the middle of the sea -
(Nangan: That deep hole there) -
in er steamer passage you know -
in the middle of the sea -

but they put weight too so the box won't float -
so they got him that way -
but they had to give-im drink before they can (Laugh) -
before they can beat-im you know -
that's the only way they can beat-im the some other
     ways they couldn' beat-im -
he was a very clever man -
this fella -
oh everybody know this story you know[23]

Notes

Preface

1. Jean-François Lyotard, *La Condition postmoderne: rapport sur le savoir* (Paris: Éd. de Minuit, 1979); translated as *The Postmodern Condition: A Report on Knowledge* (Minneapolis: University of Minnesota Press, 1984). Hereafter titles of translations will be presented in brackets.

2. *L'Invention du quotidien* 1: Michel de Certeau, *Arts de faire* (Paris: 10/18, 1980); [*The Practice of Everyday Life* (Berkeley: University of California Press, 1984); and "On the Oppositional Practices of Everyday Life," *Social Text*, 3 (Fall, 1980), 3–43].

3. "Sur la force des faibles," *L'Arc*, 64 (1976), 4–12; "On the Strength of the Weak," *Sémiotexte*, III, 2 (1978), 204–12. I am grateful to John Erickson for drawing my attention to this important essay.

4. Lyotard is turning on its head the now usually truncated familiar expression: "(il n'y a) pas moyen (de moyenner)," in which "moyenner" survives from an obsolete verb meaning to mediate, to function as an intermediary, of which the preposition "moyennant" (by means of, by dint of) is another survival.

5. See Jean-François Lyotard, *Le Différend* (Paris: Ed. de Minuit, 1983) [*The Differend: Phrases in Dispute* (Minneapolis: University of Minnesota Press, 1988)].

6. Gilles Deleuze and Felix Guattari, *L'Anti-Oedipe* (Paris: Éd. de Minuit, 1972) [*Anti-Oedipus. Capitalism and Schizophrenia* (Minneapolis: University of Minnesota Press, 1983)].

7. Michel Foucault, *Surveiller et punir: Naissance de la Prison* (Paris: Gallimard, 1975) [*Discipline and Punish: The Birth of the Prison* (New York: Random House, 1978)]; and *Histoire de la Sexualité, I* (Paris: Gallimard, 1976) [*History of Sexuality*, vol. 1 (New York: Random House, 1978)]. See especially pp. 126–27 of *Histoire de la Sexualité* (pp. 96–97 of the translation).

8. See initially Jacques Lacan, "Subversion du sujet et dialectique du désir dans l'inconscient freudien," in *Écrits* (Paris: Éd. du Seuil, 1966), 793–827 ["The subversion of the subject and the dialectic of desire in the Freudian unconscious," in *Écrits: A Selection* (New York: Norton, 1977), 292–375].

9. Toward the end of his life, Michel Foucault had embarked on a new project that he described as a hermeneutics of the technologies of the self. These are not so much a matter of self-knowledge as of "care of the self," a concern which, according to Foucault, only gradually coalesced among the Greeks with the precept to know oneself. "'Know thyself' has obscured 'Take care of yourself' because our morality,

a morality of asceticism, insists that the self is that which one can reject." See Luther H. Martin, Huck Gutman, Patrick H. Hutton, eds., *Technologies of the Self: A Seminar with Michel Foucault* (Amherst: University of Massachusetts Press, 1988), quotation p. 22. See also Michel Foucault, *Histoire de la Sexualité, III. Le souci de soi* (Paris: Gallimard, 1984), esp. pp. 53–85 ("La culture de soi"), and for self-culture as a conversion (*conversio ad se*) pp. 81–84 [*The Care of the Self* (New York: Vintage, 1988), 39–68 (64–67)].

10. Ross Chambers, *Story and Situation: Narrative Seduction and the Power of Fiction* (Minneapolis: University of Minnesota Press, 1984).

11. Ross Chambers, *Mélancolie et Opposition: Les débuts du modernisme en France* (Paris: Corti, 1987).

Introduction

1. Richard Terdiman, *Discourse / Counter-Discourse* (Ithaca: Cornell University Press, 1985).

2. See Dolf Oehler, *Pariser Bilder, I. Anti-bourgeoise Esthetik bei Baudelaire, Daumier und Heine* (Frankfurt: Suhrkamp, 1979).

3. See Pierre Bourdieu, *Les Héritiers* (Paris: Éd. de Minuit, 1979) [*The Inheritors. French Students and their Relations to Culture* (Chicago: University of Chicago Press, 1979)].

4. See Michel de Certeau, *L'Invention du quotidien, 1. Arts de faire* (Paris: 10/18, 1980) [*The Practice of Everyday Life* (Berkeley: University of California Press, 1984); and "On the Oppositional Practices of Everyday Life," in *Social Text*, 3 (Fall 1980), 3–43].

5. De Certeau, "On the Oppositional Practices of Everyday Life," 3–4.

6. Ross Chambers, *Story and Situation. Narrative Seduction and the Power of Fiction* (Minneapolis: University of Minnesota Press, 1984).

7. I take the word "narrative" in broad definition to be synonymous with discursive, whereas in narrower definition (in the sense of "storytelling") it is a major subcategory of the discursive. But who can say where exactly to draw the line between storytelling and other modes of discourse?

8. Susan Suleiman, *Authoritarian Fictions. The Ideological Novel as a Literary Genre* (New York: Columbia University Press, 1983). See especially chapter 5, "Subversions, or the Play of Writing," 199–238.

9. See my essay "Violence du récit: Boccace, Mérimée, Cortázar," *Canadian Journal of Comparative Literature/Revue Canadienne de Littérature Comparée*, XIII, 2 (June 1986), 159–86.

Chapter 1

1. Paddy Roe, *gularabulu: Stories from the West Kimberley*, edited by Stephen Muecke (Fremantle: Fremantle Arts Centre Press, 1983). "Mirdinan," pp. 3–17.

2. Roe, *gularabulu*, "Introduction" by Stephen Muecke, p. iv.

3. Stephen Muecke, "Australian Aboriginal Narratives in English: A Study in Discourse Analysis." Ph.D. diss., University of Western Australia (Perth), 1981, 150–51.

4. Muecke, "Australian Aboriginal Narratives in English," p. 150: "It is the only case in the group of stories of a climactic repetitive structure."

5. There has been some discussion of the possibility of the narrative's ending twice, once with Mirdinan's victory, once with his defeat. See Enid Neal, "Oral Narrative and Audience Response," in Sneja Gunew and Ian Reid, *Not the Whole Story* (Sydney: Local Consumption Publications, 1984), 25–40, and discussion p. 41.

6. Strictly speaking, Mirdinan is not nourished on the second occasion; but it is in bringing him his supper that the Sergeant, by opening the lockup door, allows Mirdinan to escape in the guise of a cat.

7. On the relation of Aboriginal narrative to "country" see Stephen Muecke, "Ideology Revisited. The Uses of Aboriginal Narrative," *Southern Review*, 16, 1 (March 1983), 86–108, especially 91–92.

8. The most radical derivations from the notion of *sujet de l'énonciation*, which has its source in the linguistics of Émile Benveniste, are in the work of Julia Kristeva, and notably in her distinction between the *symbolic* and the *semiotic*. See in the first instance the opening section of *La révolution du langage poétique* (Paris: Éd. du Seuil, 1974) [*Revolution in Poetic Language* (New York: Columbia University Press, 1984)]. See also *Séméiotikè: Recherches pour une sémanalyse* (Paris: Éd. du Seuil, 1979); "D'une identité l'autre," in *Polylogue* (Paris: Éd. du Seuil, 1977), 149–72 ["From One Identity to an Other," in *Desire in Language* (New York: Columbia University Press, 1980), 124–47].

9. See in this connection my essay "Gossip and the Novel: Knowing Narrative and Narrative Knowing," *Australian Journal of French Studies*, XXIII, 2 (1986), 212–33.

10. Mireille Rosello, in "L'embonpoint du baron de Charlus," *French Forum*, 10, 2 (May 1985), 189–200, demonstrates that homosexual communication and desire is paradigmatic in *A la Recherche du Temps perdu* of the reading situation.

11. Julio Cortázar, "Continuidad de los parquos," in *Final del juego* (Buenos Aires: Editorial Sudamericana, 1978), 9–10, quotation p. 10 ["Continuity of Parks," in *Blow-Up and Other Stories* (New York: Random House, 1967), 63–65, quotation p. 64].

12. In Lucien Dällenbach and Jean Ricardou, eds., *Problèmes actuels de la lecture* (Paris: Clancier-Guénaud, 1982), 193–202. This chapter was already written when Vincent Kaufmann's important book on literary address appeared. See his *Le livre et ses adresses: Mallarmé, Ponge, Valéry, Blanchot* (Paris: Klincksieck, 1986).

13. Stéphane Mallarmé, *Oeuvres complètes* (Paris: Bibliothèque de la Pléiade, 1945), p. 106. For a more developed commentary on this quatrain, see my "An Address in the Country: Mallarmé and the Kinds of Literary Context," *French Forum*, 11, 2 (May 1986), 199–215.

14. Michel Serres, "Platonic Dialogue," in *Hermes. Literature, Science, Philosophy* (Baltimore: Johns Hopkins University Press, 1982), 65–70, quotation p. 67.

15. See Michel Serres, *Le Parasite* (Paris: Grasset, 1980) [*The Parasite* (Baltimore: Johns Hopkins University Press, 1982)].

16. See primarily René Girard, *Mensonge romantique et vérité romanesque* (Paris: Grasset, 1966) [*Deceit, Desire and the Novel* (Baltimore: Johns Hopkins University Press, 1969)].

17. For an important development of the narratological implications of the theatrical metaphor, see Marie Maclean, *Narrative as Performance. The Baudelairean Experiment* (London: Routledge, 1988).

18. Barbara Herrnstein Smith, *On the Margins of Discourse, The Relation of Literature to Language* (Chicago: University of Chicago Press, 1978), 8.

19. The only textual site in which "textual function" seems to be clearly separate from "narrative function" is the area of paratext, or "discours d'escorte": titles (and title pages), epigraphs, sometimes "editorial" footnotes, etc. On paratext, see Gérard Genette, *Seuils* (Paris: Éd. du Seuil, 1987).

20. Roman Jakobson, "Linguistics and Poetics," in *Style in Language*, ed. T. A. Sebeok (Cambridge: Technology Press, 1960), 350–77.

21. The demonstration is in Ross Chambers, *Story and Situation: Narrative Seduction and the Power of Fiction* (Minneapolis: University of Minnnesota Press, 1984).

22. See Jonathan Culler, *Structuralist Poetics: Structuralism, Linguistics and the Study of Literature* (London: Routledge and Kegan Paul, 1975), chapter 3 ("Jakobson's Poetic Analyses"), 55–74 and chapter 8 ("Poetics of the Lyric"), 161–88; and Barbara Herrnstein Smith, *On the Margins of Discourse.*

23. My model is superficially similar to that of Timothy Reiss who, in *The Discourse of Modernism* (Ithaca: Cornell University Press, 1982), describes the historically shifting dominance of "discursive classes" in terms of the gradual emergence of a previously "occulted" class of discourse. But I am describing a shift in the nature of (our reading of) texts within our current discursive class, rather than a shift in discursive class proper. "Text," as Reiss reminds us (p. 102, n. 83), is "something whose existence and production one interprets," whereas "*discourse* is something one inhabits and is inhabited by."

Since this chapter was written, I have devoted a book, *Mélancolie et Opposition* (Paris: Corti, 1987) to the oppositional moment that is represented by the emergence of French modernism as a "reversal" of the relation of "narrative" and "textual" functions. But in retrospect it is evident that my choice of nineteenth-century texts in *Story and Situation* was already a strategic one, since the prominence of the "textual function" in such texts made them convenient exemplifications of the phenomena of situational self-figuration in which I was centrally interested in that volume.

24. I cite here, in general terms, the conclusion of Michel Serres's influential essay, with which I agree, although I diverge radically from him in identifying the site of wolfishness as it is exposed in the fable. For Serres, wolfishness is "la raison," and "Western man is the wolf of science," whereas the fable, in my view, is about

wolfishness as it is manifested in the duplicities of discourse. See "Le jeu du loup," in *Hermès, IV. La Distribution* (Paris: Éd. de Minuit, 1977) ["Knowledge in the Classical Age: La Fontaine and Descartes," in *Hermes: Literature, Science, Philosophy* (Baltimore: Johns Hopkins University Press, 1982), 15–28, quotation p. 28].

25. See Michael Riffaterre, *Semiotics of Poetry* (Bloomington: Indiana University Press, 1978), 12–13 and passim.

26. See Dan Sperber and Deirdre Wilson, "Les ironies comme mentions," *Poétique*, 38 (nov. 1978), 399–412. In addition to Paul de Man's "The Rhetoric of Temporality," now in *Blindness and Insight*, 2nd edition (Minneapolis: University of Minnesota Press, 1983), 187–228, some major references on irony are: Douglas C. Muecke, *The Compass of Irony* (London: Methuen, 1969); Wayne C. Booth, *A Rhetoric of Irony* (Chicago: University of Chicago Press, 1971); Gary Handwerk, *Irony and Ethics in Narrative. From Schlegel to Lacan* (New Haven: Yale University Press, 1985); and Candace Lang, *Irony / Humor: Critical Paradigms* (Baltimore: Johns Hopkins University Press, 1988). For a critique of Booth's desire to stabilize irony, especially by grounding it in the intention of an authorial subject, see Jefferson Humphries, "Flaubert and the Fable of Stable Irony," in *Losing the Text. Readings in Literary Desire* (Athens: University of Georgia Press, 1986), 57–82. For a survey of the extensive critical literature on irony in La Fontaine, see Richard Danner, *Patterns of Irony in the "Fables" of La Fontaine* (Athens: Ohio University Press, 1985), 1–30.

27. My translation.

Chapter 2

1. Paul Willis and Phillip Corrigan, "Orders of Experience: the Differences of Working Class Cultural Forms," *Social Text*, 7 (1983), 85–103, quotations on p. 95 and p. 100. Paul Willis's *Learning to Labour, How Working Class Kids Get Working Class Jobs* (New York: Columbia University Press, 1981) is an exemplary demonstration of the interaction of working-class opposition and capitalist control.

2. Most recently, Susan Suleiman has read La Fontaine as an authoritarian writer, notably on the basis of an analysis of "Le bassa et le marchand" (VIII, xviii) that uses a method close to my own. "By a process of internal reduplication or mise en abyme . . . the fable of the bassa and the merchant points a finger at its own genre." *Authoritarian Fictions* (New York: Columbia University Press, 1983), 51. But a closer reading of this particular fable would show that the discrepancies between the embedded story told by the pasha and the embedding fable function to designate the pasha himself as the "wolf" from whom the merchant needs protection, and hence to discriminate the embedded tale from the embedding fable as an act of intimidation is opposed to the display of that act.

3. See Louis Marin, *Le récit est un piège* (Paris: Éd. de Minuit, 1978). The discussion of the La Fontaine text forms Part I, "Le pouvoir du récit," 15–34.

4. All translations from La Fontaine are my own.

5. See Michel de Certeau, "On the Oppositional Practices of Everyday Life," *Social Text*, 3 (Fall 1980), 3–43.

6. I have discussed the theoretical status of dedications at some length in "Baudelaire's Dedicatory Practice," in *Sub-Stance*, 56 (1988), 5–17.

7. See Charles Perrault, *Contes de Ma Mère l'Oye* (Paris: Ed. de Cluny, 1948), 77–98 (in verse) and 99–113 (in prose); and Bonaventure Des Périers, *Contes ou Nouvelles: Récréations et Joyeux Devis suivis du Cymbalum Mundi*, éd. P. L. Jacob (Paris: Garnier Frères, 1872), 294–96. (One is forced to go to old editions of Des Périers because "Peau d'Ane" is excluded from modern ones as apocryphal.)

8. René Girard, *Le bouc émissaire* (Paris: Grasset, 1982), p. 270.

9. It is symptomatic, as Anne Freadman has pointed out to me, that the Athenian's story provokes a question ("Et Cérès, que fit-elle?") which he does not answer, while the fabulist plants a question in his dedication ("Son sujet vous convient; je n'en dirai pas plus") to which his tale forms a response. What the fabulist and the Orator do have in common is their use of rhetorical questions, those which imply silence and manipulability on the part of their hearer(s) (compare the many self-answering questions in the dedication with the Orator's "Que ne demandez-vous ce que Philippe fait?"). Rhetoricity, in sum, is their shared domain; but the difference between them is pointed up sharply by the parallel between the question about Ceres that the Athenians ask and the Orator does not answer, and the structurally similar question ("Que fit le harangueur?") raised by the fabulist *in order to answer it.*

10. See Robert Jaulin, *La mort sara* (Paris: Plon, 1967).

11. See in particular René Girard, *Violence and the Sacred* (Baltimore: Johns Hopkins University Press, 1974). I have expanded my analysis of gossip in "Gossip and the Novel," *Australian Journal of French Studies*, XXIII, 2 (1986), 212–33. See also Patricia Meyer Spacks, *Gossip* (New York: Knapp, 1985).

12. Marin, *Le récit est un piège*.

13. Cf. Barbara Herrnstein Smith, "Narrative Versions, Narrative Theories," *Critical Inquiry*, 7.1 (Autumn 1980), 213–36, where narrative is defined (p. 232) as "someone telling someone that something happened."

14. See Lucien Dällenbach, *Le récit spéculaire* (Paris: Éd. du Seuil, 1977) [*The Mirror in the Text* (Chicago: University of Chicago Press, 1989)].

15. William Labov, *Language in the Inner City: Studies in the Black English Vernacular* (Philadelphia: University of Pennsylvania Press, 1972), p. 366: "one important aspect of narrative . . . is what we term the *evaluation* of the narrative: the means used by the narrator to indicate the point of the narrative, its raison d'être (. . . etc.)"; see also, of course, Ross Chambers, *Story and Situation*, (Minneapolis: University of Minnesota Press, 1984).

16. Cf. Sneja Gunew, "Feminist Criticism: Positions and Questions," Part II of Meaghan Morris, Sneja Gunew, and Anne Freadman, "Forum: Feminism and Interpretation Theory," *Southern Review*, 16 (March 1983), 139–73.

17. In *The Puritan and the Cynic* (New York: Oxford University Press, 1987), p. 78, Jefferson Humphries takes issue with my distinction between "secrets" and "secrecy," and more fundamentally with my view that what he calls "ironic paradox" can constitute a fable's pedagogical point. I hope that, appearing now in the

context of *Room for Maneuver*, the sense in which I make this assertion will be more evident than it was when my reading of "Les femmes et le secret" appeared as an isolated journal article (*Sub-Stance*, 32 [1981], 65–74).

18. One can read the story of Conti's disgrace (for unauthorized travel and indiscreet warfare on behalf of the Holy Roman Emperor; and especially, it seems, for incautious letter writing), of his "exile" (at Chantilly) and of Louis XIV's eventual "pardon" (in response to a death-bed appeal by le Grand Condé) in Duc de la Force, *Le Grand Conti* (Paris: Amiot-Dumont, 1948), chapters 3–4, and Jacques Roujon, *Conti: l'Ennemi de Louis XIV* (Paris: Fayard, 1941), chapter 3. In spite of his "pardon," Conti was still clearly under a cloud at the time of his marriage. Mme de Sévigné's opinion (quoted by Roujon, pp. 83–84) is significant: "Je ne comprends pas qu'on puisse être insensé et enragé dans une Cour si sage et sous un tel maître" ["I do not understand how one can be so senseless and crazy in such a decorous Court and under such a master"].

19. Unfortunately the term *savoir faire*—especially in English—has connotations of *sophisticated* skill. I mean to suggest rather that human beings can *do* things that imply a certain "know-how" but that they cannot necessarily theorize or, consequently, execute as a conscious "performance" (i.e., application of theory). Cf. Pierre Bourdieu's concepts of "habitus" and "strategy" notably in *Esquisse d'une théorie du la pratique* (Geneva: Droz, 1972), but used throughout his work.

20. My reference is the *Iliad*, translated by E. V. Rieu (London: Penguin Books, 1950), 36–39.

21. The literature on the buffoon includes Enid Welsford, *The Fool: His Social and Literary History* (London: Faber, 1968; first publ. 1935); William Willeford, *The Fool and His Scepter: A Study in Clowns and Jesters and Their Audience* (Evanston, Ill.: Northwestern University Press, 1969); Paul V. A. Williams, ed., *The Fool and the Trickster: Studies in Honor of Enid Welsford* (Cambridge: Brewer, 1979).

22. My understanding of the "wild man" owes much to Michael Taussig, *Shamanism, Colonialism and the Wild Man: A Study in Terror and Healing* (Chicago: University of Chicago Press, 1987). See also Richard Bernheimer, *The Wild Man in the Middle Ages: A Study in Art, Sentiment and Demonology* (Cambridge: Harvard University Press, 1952).

23. Active in the fable, albeit playfully treated, is the doctrine of divine right, founded on the notion of the "king's two bodies." It is the Kite's attack on the King's physical body that manifests the latter's superhuman qualities (of heroism and clemency), whereas inversely, in version two, the bird's attack on the Huntsman is the occasion for the King to manifest his humanity in laughter.

24. *S/Z* (Paris: Éd. du Seuil, 1970), sections XXI, LIX, LXXXVII [*S/Z* (New York: Hill and Wang, 1974)]. Barthes's point is that, because it is citational without quotation marks, the recognition of irony depends on the recognition of the cultural "code" that is being cited. But this recognition itself depends on there being operative, in the text-reader relationship, another cultural code—he calls it the code of "intelligence"—so that this new code needs to be ironized in turn, and so on. To

reformulate this in terms of power: irony as an oppositional response to dominant codes depends in turn on the ability of the reader-text relation to situate the discourse being ironized, and hence to adopt with respect to it a position of mastery.

Chapter 3

1. See especially Michel Foucault, *Surveiller et punir: Naissance de la prison* (Paris: Gallimard, 1975) [*Discipline and Punish: The Birth of the Prison* (New York: Random House, 1978)]; and *Histoire de la Sexualité, I. La volonté de savoir* (Paris: Gallimard, 1976) [*The History of Sexuality*, vol. I. *An Introduction* (New York: Vintage Books, 1980).

2. See Marie-Hélène Huet, *Rehearsing the Revolution: The Staging of Marat's Death 1793–1797* (Berkeley: University of California Press, 1982).

3. Gérard de Nerval, *Oeuvres*, I (Paris: Bibliothèque de la Pléiade, 1966), 273. All future page references to Nerval in parentheses are to this edition.

4. Gilles Deleuze and Félix Guattari, *L'Anti-Oedipe* (Paris: Éd. de Minuit, 1972) [*Anti-Oedipus: Capitalism and Schizophrenia* (Minneapolis: University of Minnesota Press, 1983)]; and especially *Kafka: Pour une littérature mineure* (Paris: Éd. de Minuit, 1975) [*Kafka: Toward a Minor Literature* (Minneapolis: University of Minnesota Press, 1986)].

5. Both Nerval and Aquin use foreign languages in their writing: English figures in the Aquin text as the dominant other of Québec French, and is so thematized, most particularly in *Trou de mémoire* (on English place names in Québec, see below). Nerval uses Germany and Germanic languages (the irretrievable book sighted in Frankfurt, "ville libre," and one of its variants in Dutch) in explicit opposition to the laws that govern writing in Paris.

6. Deleuze and Guattari, *Kafka*, 18. All page references are to the English translation.

7. My understanding of allegorization is, of course, indebted to the seminal essay of Paul de Man, "The Rhetoric of Temporality," in *Blindness and Insight: Essays in the Rhetoric of Contemporary Criticism*, 2nd ed., (Minneapolis: University of Minnesota Press, 1983), 187–228.

8. See Walter Benjamin, *Ursprung des deutschen Trauerspiels* (Frankfurt: Suhrkamp, 1963)[*The Origin of German Tragic Drama* (London: New Left Books, 1977)].

9. Hubert Aquin, *Prochain Épisode* (Montréal: Tisseyre, 1965). All future page references to Aquin in parentheses are to this edition. All translations of Aquin are my own. There is a commercial translation of the novel, *Prochain Épisode* (Toronto: McLelland and Stuart, 1967), but it is out of print and difficult to find and my commentary, for reasons that will become apparent, is "close to the text" and so benefits from *ad hoc* translations.

10. Sigmund Freud, "Trauer und Melancholie," in *Gesammelte Werke, B. 10 (Werke aus den Jahren 1913–1917)* (London: Imago, 1946), 428–46 ["Mourning and Melancholia," in *The Standard Edition of the Complete Psychological Works of Sigmund Freud* (London: Hogarth Press, from 1953), vol. 14, 239–60].

11. I have attempted to relate the "new writing" of early French modernism to post-1848 "historical melancholy" in a book that grew out of an early attempt to write the present chapter and now constitutes a framework for it: *Mélancolie et opposition. Les débuts du modernisme en France* (Paris: Corti, 1987).

The reading of "Angélique" given in *Mélancolie et opposition* is considerably more detailed than the one given here. That of "Aurélia" is substantially translated here, with modifications, from the study in the book, which itself derives from two previous articles, "Récits d'aliénés, récits aliénés," *Poétique*, 53 (février 1983), 72–90, and "Narrative as Oppositional Practice: Nerval's *Aurélia*," *Stanford French Review*, VIII, 1 (Spring 1984), 55–73. My thanks to Paul Erb for help with translation.

12. Criticism tends to distinguish *Neige noire* because—like Manuel Puig's *El beso de la mujer araña*—it is a novel in the form of a film scenario, and the sadoeroticism of the later novels does not appear in *Prochain Épisode*. But self-situation in terms of melancholy is common to them all. (An early novel of Aquin's, entitled *L'invention de la mort*, remains unpublished.)

13. See Jean-Pierre Richard, *Poésie et Profondeur* (Paris: Éd. du Seuil, 1955), and Ross Chambers, *Gérard de Nerval et la poétique du voyage* (Paris: Corti, 1969) for early studies of the thematization of movement in Nerval.

14. In "Sylvie," however, the progressive *embourgeoisement* of the Valois is specifically thematized as an aspect of the text's nostalgia for a lost past.

15. Gérard de Nerval, *Voyage en Orient*, *Oeuvres*, II (Paris: Bibliothèque de la Pléiade, 1961), 90. All translations from Nerval are my own.

16. See Stephane Mallarmé, "Crise de vers," in *Variations sur un sujet, Oeuvres Complètes* (Paris: Bibliothèque de la Pléiade, 1945), 360–68, quotation p. 366. See also Leo Bersani, *The Death of Stéphane Mallarmé* (Cambridge: Cambridge University Press, 1982).

17. Kurt Schärer, "Nerval et l'ironie lyrique," in *Nerval: une poétique du rêve*, ed. Jacques Huré (Paris: Champion, 1989), 153–64.

18. The difficulty of making history ("histoire") in a world characterized by the production of stories ("histoires") is a recurrent theme in the literature of the July Monarchy in France, e.g., Musset's *Lorenzaccio*, Stendhal's *La Chartreuse de Parme*, or Nerval's own play, *Léo Burckart*.

19. This terminology is of course that of Mikhail Bakhtin. See especially his *The Dialogic Imagination* (Austin: University of Texas Press, 1981).

20. See Dolf Oehler, *Ein Höllensturz der alten Welt* (Frankfurt: Suhrkamp, 1988).

21. See especially Michel Foucault, *Histoire de la folie à l'époque classique* (Paris: Gallimard, 1972) [*Madness and Civilization: A History of Insanity in the Age of Reason* (New York: Random House, 1973)]; and *Surveiller et punir* [*Discipline and Punish*].

22. François Flahault, *La parole intermédiaire*, (Paris: Éd. du Seuil, 1978).

23. In French, *jeu* means "play" as in children's play and "play" as in scope or freedom for movement or maneuver; but also playacting and gambling.

24. Flahault, *La parole intermédiaire*, 10. My translation.

25. This is a restatement, in Flahault's perspective, of the position I take in the conclusion of *Story and Situation*.

26. Cf. W. Lepenies, *Melancholie und Gesellschaft* (Frankfurt: Suhrkamp, 1969); and see the conclusion ("Brouillards, brouillages") of my *Mélancolie et opposition*.

27. See Michel Jeanneret, "La folie est un rêve: Nerval et le docteur Moreau de Tours," *Romantisme*, 27 (1980), 59–75.

28. It follows that readings that tend to produce "Aurélia" as a coherent text are responding, in some sense and to some degree, to the text's own attempt to recruit its addressee into the project of determining "the meaning of my dreams." For a recent example of such a reading, see Frank Paul Bowman, "'Mémorables' d'*Aurélia*: signification et situation générique," *French Forum*, 11, 2 (May 1986), 169–181, which specifically situates itself as a refutation of Michel Jeanneret's characterization of the text as a "discours incertain."

29. See Patricia Merivale, "Hubert Aquin and Highbrow Pornography," *Essays on Canadian Writing* (Summer, 1983), 1–12.

30. Wladimir Krysinski, *Carrefours de signes: Essais sur le roman moderne* (La Haye: Mouton, 1981), chapter 12: "Destins des pulsions, destins des narrations: Hubert Aquin," 345–75, quotation p. 368. My translation.

31. Krysinski, *Carrefours de signes*, 345. My translation.

32. Hubert Aquin, "Le bonheur d'expression," *Liberté*, 3, 18 (déc. 1961), 741–43; reprinted in *Blocs erratiques* (Montréal: Les Quinze, 1982), 47–50.

33. Anthony Purdy, "Form and (Dis-)Content: the Writer, Language and Society in the Essays of Hubert Aquin," *French Review*, 59, 6 (May 1986), 885–93, quotation p. 891. The references are to Hubert Aquin, "Profession: écrivain," *Parti Pris*, 1, 4 (janvier 1964), 23–31, reprinted in *Point de fuite* (Montréal: Cercle du Livre de France, 1971), 47–59; and to "Le bonheur d'expression."

34. John Frow, *Marxism and Literary History* (Cambridge: Harvard University Press, 1986), chapter 6 ("Intertextuality"), 125–69.

35. Cf. Maurice Blanchot, *Le livre à venir* (Paris: Gallimard, 1959), 243: "Seul importe le livre, tel qu'il est, loin des genres" ["All that matters is the book, the book as it is, far removed from genres"].

36. Similar conclusions would emerge from a more general and detailed study of intertext in *Prochain Épisode* (novels like Graham Greene's *Our Man in Havana* or Balzac's *Histoire des Treize*, films like *Orfeu negro* and *The Third Man*, poems like Byron's "The Prisoner of Chillon," etc.). The intertext functions simultaneously as a manifestation of the textual other and as a confirmation of oppositionality.

37. For a powerful articulation of the view that literature, in pitting writing against death, splits self-reflexively and thematizes that split as the double, thereby (re-)introducing death into its own discourse, see an early essay by Michel Foucault, "Le langage à l'infini," *Tel Quel*, 15 (1963), 44–53 ["Language to Infinity" in Donald F. Bouchard, ed., *Language, Counter-Memory, Practice. Selected Essays and Interviews by Michel Foucault* (Ithaca: Cornell University Press, 1977),

53–67]. I am grateful to Alina Clej and James Porter for drawing my attention to this essay.

38. Hubert Aquin, "Obombre, roman," *Liberté*, 135 (mai-juin 1981), 15–24, quotation p. 16.

39. Aquin, "Obombre," 18.

40. The homology is not accidental with Barbara Johnson's famous summing up of what emerges from the confrontation of Lacan and Derrida on "The purloined Letter": "The letter's destination is . . . wherever *it is read.*" See her "The Frame of Reference: Poe, Lacan, Derrida," in *The Critical Difference: Essays in the Contemporary Rhetoric of Reading* (Baltimore: Johns Hopkins University Press, 1980), 110–46, quotation p. 144.

41. Cf. Aquin's 1974 essay which takes Mallarmé's "disparition élocutoire du poète" for its title and speaks of the textual "omission of self" in terms of producing a symmetry of writer and reader, such that reading is "inverse writing" and vice versa. Having castigated unnamed Québec writers for their "*surprésence*" in their texts, Aquin concludes suggestively: "It is possible that because I have taken issue with [*je me suis insurgé contre*] the hyperpresence of writers, I will be considered a specter. How can one answer that charge? It is very difficult to disappear, and the fact that it is only an elocutionary disappearance, I know. . . . To disappear is to die a little. But dying a little is not what suits me. [*Disparaître, c'est mourir un peu. Mais il ne me sied pas de mourir un peu. . . . .*] *Cul-Q*, 4–5 (été-automne 1974); *Blocs erratiques*, 263–67.

Chapter 4

1. Miguel Angel Asturias, *El Señor Presidente* (Buenos Aires: Losada/Madrid: Alianza, 1981). Page numbers in parentheses refer to this edition. Translations, occasionally modified, are taken from *El Señor Presidente* (New York: Atheneum, 1980).

2. Alejo Carpentier, *El siglo de las luces* (Barcelona: Formentor, 1980) [*Explosion in a Cathedral* (New York: Harper and Row, 1979)].

3. Manuel Puig, *El beso de la mujer araña* (Barcelona: Seix-Barral, 1981) [*Kiss of the Spider Woman* (New York: Knopf, 1979)].

4. My study is not a reading of the Latin American "dictator novel" per se, and it is centered on the imagery of prison as much as on the figure of dictation because it is the dynamic of control and oppositionality that forms my main concern. I arrived independently at views and interpretations that can be taken in part as expansions of, extrapolations from, or glosses on a number of acute insights—on the dictator/macho relation, the dictator as Don Juan, and especially the relation of writing to dictating—to be found in Roberto González Echevarría's stimulating chapter, "The Dictatorship of Rhetoric," in *The Voice of the Masters: Writing and Authority in Modern Latin American Literature* (Austin: University of Texas Press, 1985), 64–85. On dictator novels, see also Wladimir Krysinski, *Carrefours de signes: Essais sur le roman moderne* (La Haye: Mouton, 1981), chapter 13, "Un

référent complexe," 377–444. For a brief but interesting history of oppositional graffiti in Hispano-America, see Angel Rama, *La ciudad letrada* (Hanover, N.H.: Ediciones del Norte, 1984), 52–55.

5. Augusto Roa Bastos, *Yo el Supremo* (Mexico: Siglo Veintiuno, 1974) [*I the Supreme* (New York: Knopf, 1986].

6. The term "homosocial" is taken from Eve Kosofsky Sedgwick's seminal essay, *Between Men: English Literature and Male Homosocial Desire* (New York: Columbia University Press, 1985), whose project is described as follows: "To draw the 'homosocial' back into the orbit of 'desire,' of the potentially erotic, . . . is to hypothesize the unbrokenness of a continuum between homosocial and homosexual— a continuum whose visibility, for men, in our society, is radically disrupted" (1–2).

7. Sigmund Freud, *Group Psychology and the Analysis of the Ego* (New York: Norton, 1959) ["Massenpsychologie und Ich-Analyse," 1921]. Freud builds on the work of Gustave Le Bon in his *Psychologie des foules* (1895).

8. My reference to the Imaginary/Symbolic distinction, like that of the narcissism/altruism distinction, is heuristic: I am not fully convinced that the Imaginary should be viewed as other than a Symbolic construct (in the way that "dictation" will be shown in this essay to be a *mediated* phenomenon).

9. Roland Barthes, *Leçon* (Paris: Éd. du Seuil, 1978), 14: "[La langue] est, tout simplement, fasciste; car le fascisme, ce n'est pas d'empêcher de dire, c'est d'obliger à dire" ["Language is quite simply fascist; for fascism is not in preventing from saying, but in obliging to say"].

10. Marie-Hélène Huet, "Le Sacre du Printemps: Essai sur le sublime et la Terreur," *MLN*, 103, 4 (September 1988), 782–99, quotation p. 797, my translation.

11. An accidental blot in calligraphy is a manifestation of "noise," and so of the mediated and uncontrollable character of dictation: whence the symbolic significance of the president's rage.

12. The clerk's difficulty with spelling—"¿'Biyo' es con 'y griega'?" ["Has 'Biyo' got a 'y'?"]—corresponds to the blot on the text of the presidential document (cf. n. 11) as an indication that the "dictation" is mediated.

13. This point was clarified for me by Ali Behdad's elegant demonstration, in a chapter of his University of Michigan Ph.D. dissertation "Split Orientalism" (1990), that Gérard de Nerval's Orientalist discourse is the site of an (oppositional) "desire for the Orient" that is mediated by the (dominant) "Orientalist desire."

14. "It always happens" (or: "The one always follows the other"). This is the epigraph from Goya to the fourth sequence of chapter 1—the arrival of Victor Hugues, with loud knocking, in the children's Havana house. But in Goya it is the title of the eighth in the "Disasters of War" series, representing a charge of dragoons that is emblematic of the brutal invasion of Spain by Napoleon's troops.

15. My study of *El siglo de las luces* has benefited particularly from Roberto González Echevarría, *Alejo Carpentier: The Pilgrim at Home* (Ithaca: Cornell University Press, 1977); and from a number of studies in Daniel-Henri Pageaux, ed., *Quinze Études autour de "El Siglo de la Luces" de Alejo Carpentier* (Paris: L'Harmattan, 1983).

16. Michael Taussig, *Shamanism, Colonialism and the Wild Man: A Study in Terror and Healing* (Chicago: University of Chicago Press, 1987), 121: "All societies live by fictions taken as real. What distinguishes cultures of terror is that the epistemological, ontological and otherwise philosophical problem of representation—reality and illusion, certainty and doubt—becomes infinitely more than a 'merely' philosophical problem. . . . It becomes a high-powered medium of domination, and during the Putumayo rubber boom this medium of epistemic and ontological murk was most keenly figured and thrust into consciousness as the space of death." On *El Señor Presidente*, see 5–7. Taussig very significantly relates what is called "magical realism" to the "murk" of the culture of terror.

17. Standard accounts of *El Señor Presidente* tend to stress the novel's oneiric writing and its allegiance to an aesthetic of "magical realism" as an expression of the "nightmare" of dictatorship. See Jean Franco, *An Introduction to Spanish American Literature* (Cambridge: Cambridge University Press, 1969), 311–13; and George R. McMurray, *Spanish American Writing Since 1941: A Critical Survey* (New York: Ungar, 1987), 20–21, which closely follows Franco's account of eighteen years earlier. I have attempted to shift the emphasis away from this effect to the analysis of discursive control that is its cause. But I have not been able to consult the following, perhaps relevant, articles: C. Teixera, *"El Señor Presidente" Texto Crítico*, 14 (1979), 132–42 (a sociological study); and C. Urza, "Metáfora y deshumanización en *El Señor Presidente*," *Explicación de Textos Literarios*, 14, 1 (1986), 79–83.

18. *El beso*, as a novel, is so homosocially focused that women characters play an extremely limited "off-stage" role in it, while "woman" as a gender category is, very significantly, *represented* by men. Its interest for feminism lies in its implication that everyone—women, gay men such as Molina, and straight men such as Valentín—stands to benefit from the critique of gender categories launched by feminism. But there is a further implication that, precisely because of the way these categories have produced differences between "men" and "women," men are currently able to subvert them more easily or effectively than women. The general picture that emerges is one of a solidarity of interests between women and, especially, homosexual men, but one that cannot under the conditions of homosociality be realized as an actual partnership. (I do not think the novel has any particular implications for lesbians.)

19. "Homosexuality" has been produced, and continues to be produced, in differing social formations, with a bewildering range of meanings: see for example David Greenberg, *The Construction of Homosexuality* (Chicago: University of Chicago Press, 1988). My purpose is of course not to say what "homosexuality" *is*, but to describe how this novel's production of homosexuality can be understood as a model of oppositionality in homosocially controlled societies.

20. In a characteristically subtle and resourceful article, Shoshana Felman, meditating on Camus's *La Peste* [*The Plague*], argues that the testimonial function of modern (i.e., post-Holocaust) literature lies, precisely, in its failure as literal or referential testimony, its "referential debt." In this understanding, testimony—like *La Peste* with respect to the Holocaust—is necessarily oblique, fictional, literary—

mediated—because, there being no one who is not implicated, no "onlooker" who is not simultaneously survivor and witness, there can be no language of testimony that is not involved with, and part of, what it is testifying to. See "Narrative as Testimony: Camus's *The Plague*," in J. Phelan, ed., *Reading Narrative: Form, Ethics, Ideology* (Columbus: Ohio State University Press, 1989), 250–71.

21. See Robert Hodge and Gunther Kress, *Social Semiotics* (Ithaca: Cornell University Press, 1988), 8–12. The group has an acronym that wittily bespeaks its socially disruptive role: BUGAUP (Billboard Using Graffitists Against Unhealthy Promotions).

22. See Sander Gilman, *Disease and Representation: Images of Illness from Madness to AIDS* (Ithaca: Cornell University Press, 1988), 185–91.

23. See Sarah Kofman, *L'Énigme de la femme: La femme dans les textes de Freud* (Paris: Galilée, 1980) [*The Enigma of Woman: Woman in Freud's Writings* (Ithaca: Cornell University Press, 1985)].

24. See Michel Serres, *Le Parasite* (Paris: Grasset, 1980) [*The Parasite* (Baltimore: Johns Hopkins University Press, 1982)]

25. *El beso* conflates and transforms, that is appropriates and thereby comments ironically on, a number of Romantic prison clichés (the taming of a "spider" or other insect or small animal, itself a version of the "strange cellmates" theme, the theme of falling in love with the jailer's daughter . . .), along with the leftist theme of prison as the "night school of revolution."

26. See Lucille Kerr, *Suspended Fictions: Reading Novels by Manuel Puig* (Urbana and Chicago: University of Illinois Press, 1987), 224–26. Kerr sees this fictional reference as a "quasi- borgesian maneuver" that "keeps under cover the work of an author whose position it also reveals" while simultaneously benefiting from the authority of the real research previously summarized.

27. My reading of *El beso de la mujer araña* has benefited especially from Lucille Kerr, *Suspended Fictions*; and also from Roberto Echevarren, "*El beso de la mujer araña* y las metáforas del sujeto," *Revista Iberoamericana*, 44 (1978), 65–75; Frances Wyers, "Manuel Puig at the Movies," *Hispanic Review*, 49 (1981), 163–81; Yves Macchi, "Fonctions narratives des notes infrapaginales dans *El beso de la mujer araña* de Manuel Puig," *Les Langues Néo-Latines*, 76 (1982), 67–81; Gustavo Pellón, "Manuel Puig's Contradictory Strategy: Kitsch Paradigms versus Paradigmatic Structure, "*Symposium*, 37 (Fall 1983), 186–201.

Conclusion

1. Jean-Francois Lyotard, "Sur la force des faibles," *L'Arc*, 64 (1976), 11.

2. See especially Harold Bloom, *The Anxiety of Influence* (Oxford: Oxford University Press, 1973); and *A Map of Misreading* (Oxford: Oxford University Press, 1975).

3. Gilles Deleuze and Félix Guattari, *L'Anti-Oedipe* (Paris: Éd. de Minuit, 1972) [*Anti-Oedipus: Capitalism and Schizophrenia* (Minneapolis: University of Minnesota Press, 1983)].

4. *L'Invention du Quotidien*, I: Michel de Certeau, *Arts de faire* (Paris: 10/18, 1980) [*The Practice of Everyday Life* (Berkeley: University of California Press, 1984)].

5. See Roman Jakobson, "Two Aspects of Language and Two Types of Aphasic Disturbances," in *Fundamentals of Language* (with Morris Halle) (The Hague: Mouton, 1956); now collected in *Language in Literature* (Cambridge: Belknap Press of Harvard University Press, 1987), 95–114.

6. Paul de Man, "The Rhetoric of Temporality," now in *Blindness and Insight*, 2nd edition (Minneapolis: University of Minnesota Press, 1983), 187–228.

7. Susan Suleiman, *Authoritarian Fictions: The Ideological Novel as a Literary Genre* (New York: Columbia University Press, 1983).

8. Roland Barthes, *S/Z* (Paris: Éd. du Seuil, 1970), 212 [*S/Z* (New York: Hill and Wang, 1974), 206]. "Épingler" would be more accurately translated as: "make a butt of," "show up."

9. See Dan Sperber and Deirdre Wilson, "Les ironies comme mentions," *Poétique*, 38 (nov. 1978), 399–412.

10. Ross Chambers, *Mélancolie et Opposition* (Paris: Corti, 1987).

11. On this story, see Henry Reynolds, *The Other Side of the Frontier: Aboriginal Resistance to the European Invasion of Australia* (Melbourne: Penguin Books, 1982); *Frontier* (Sydney: Allen and Unwin, 1987); and especially *The Law of the Land* (Melbourne: Penguin Books, 1987). On the significance of naming, see Paul Carter, *The Road to Botany Bay: An Exploration of Landscape and History* (New York: Knopf, 1988), a book I had not yet read when this paragraph was written.

12. David Malouf, *An Imaginary Life* (New York: George Braziller, 1978). Page references in parentheses are to this edition.

Appendix

1. *Karnun* is the local Aboriginal name for Fisherman's Bend.

2. This could be translated as "his wife knew a Malay man who was on a boat in the creek." The story refers to events which probably occurred in the early 1920s when many Malays, Japanese and Chinese were working in the booming pearling industry.

3. The pearling luggers were flat-bottomed and would be left dry in the creeks at low tide.

4. "Coming back with nothing" is a motif in these stories which indicates that something has gone wrong.

5. *yunmi* means "you and me."

6. Mirdinan points to something to avert her gaze.

7. "belongs to" means they were in a certain relationship, brother and sister in this case.

8. Many Aboriginal prisoners were brought into town in this way.

9. A *maban* is an Aboriginal "doctor." These are men or women who are well-trained in Aboriginal law and have special perceptive skills or fighting skills.

10. A "growling" voice used in disbelief, or to admonish someone, disperse dogs, etc.

11. A "true story" is like a legend. It is about identifiable people and events in the not-too-distant past. This classification is opposed to *bugaregara* stories (stories of the "dreaming"). The interruption also occurs at a structural break in the story.

12. "Flatform" is a linguistic hypercorrection. Since Aboriginal languages lack "f" sounds, these are mostly pronounced like "p." Somebody over-correcting their "p's" will therefore produce words such as this.

13. Butcher Joe Nangan.

14. *Waragan* is the word for eaglehawk in Nyigina.

15. *Djabi* is a type of "popular" Aboriginal song, found also throughout the Pilbara. See: C. G. von Brandenstein and A. P. Thomas, *Tarura—Aboriginal Song Poetry from the Pilbara*, Adelaide, Rigby, 1974.

16. *mabu* (Nyigina) means "good," "finished." This song was sung in unison by Paddy Roe and Butcher Joe Nangan. The words in bold lettering indicates their singing together, while the single underlining indicates Butcher Joe alone.

17. The judge.

18. The "belly" is seen as the location of personal power and personal feelings.

19. The listener is being tested to see if he remembers the name.

20. He is meaning Butcher Joe.

21. A certain amount of text, concerning the kinship of Mirdinan to Broome people was edited at this point.

22. "gibim" is "give him."

23. The narrator is pointing out that this is a public rather than a secret story.

Index